T0313962

AS GODS AMONG MEN

As Gods Among Men

A HISTORY OF THE RICH
IN THE WEST

GUIDO ALFANI

PRINCETON UNIVERSITY PRESS

PRINCETON & OXFORD

Published by Princeton University Press
41 William Street, Princeton, New Jersey 08540
99 Banbury Road, Oxford OX2 6JX

press.princeton.edu

All Rights Reserved

Library of Congress Cataloging-in-Publication Data
Names: Alfani, Guido, 1976– author.
Title: As gods among men : a history of the rich in the West / Guido Alfani.
Description: Princeton : Princeton University Press, [2023] |
    Includes bibliographical references and index.
Identifiers: LCCN 2023005736 (print) | LCCN 2023005737 (ebook) |
    ISBN 9780691215730 (hardback) | ISBN 9780691227122 (ebook)
Subjects: LCSH: Rich people—Europe—History. | Rich people—North
    America—History. | BISAC: BUSINESS & ECONOMICS / Economic History |
    SOCIAL SCIENCE / Demography
Classification: LCC HT635 .A54 2023 (print) | LCC HT635 (ebook) |
    DDC 305.5/234094—dc23/eng/20230518
LC record available at https://lccn.loc.gov/2023005736
LC ebook record available at https://lccn.loc.gov/2023005737

British Library Cataloging-in-Publication Data is available

Editorial: Hannah Paul and Josh Drake
Production Editorial: Kathleen Cioffi
Jacket Design: Haley Chung
Production: Erin Suydam
Publicity: Kate Hensley and Kathryn Stevens

Jacket image: *A Polish Nobleman* by Rembrandt (Rembrandt van Rijn).
    Oil on panel. 1637. Courtesy of Bridgeman Images

This book has been composed in Arno

Printed on acid-free paper. ∞

Printed in the United States of America

10 9 8 7 6 5 4 3

CONTENTS

v

ILLUSTRATIONS

Figures

Tables

ACKNOWLEDGEMENTS

IN THE LONG YEARS that it took me to complete this book, I have accumulated a vast debt of gratitude towards many colleagues who have kindly provided advice and support.

First of all, I would like to express my sincere thanks to Francesco Ammannati, Gabriele Ballarino, Samuel K. Cohn, Andrea Colli, Mattia Fochesato, Roberta Frigeni, Giacomo Gabbuti, Alexander Kentikelenis, Peter Lindert, Luciano Maffi, Donato Masciandaro, Maarten Prak, Simon Szreter, Giacomo Todeschini and Jenny Trinitapoli, who have generously read and commented on portions of the manuscript. Beyond their intellectual support, I am grateful for their friendship, which made it a real pleasure to discuss my work with them (convivially, whenever circumstances allowed). Peter Lindert deserves a special mention here, not only because he is partly responsible for putting me on this path of enquiry and went to great lengths to help me improve the literary, as well as the scientific, quality of my arguments, but also because he showed me a model of intellectual and scientific generosity. Thilo Albers, Dan Bogart, Neil Cummins, Jonathan Levy, Giuseppe De Luca, Marcelo Medeiros, William D. Rubinstein and Simona Feci were also generous with their data and/or with their advice about useful literature.

I am grateful to Felix Schaff and Sonia Schifano, who have helped me from the very first steps of this book to its completion, first as students, then as research assistants and finally, as fellow researchers and co-authors. They allowed me to fully experience the greatest of academic pleasures: learning from one's former pupils.

A number of research assistants, many now scholars in their own right or in the course of becoming one, have also helped me with different tasks during this years-long project: Vincenzo Alfano, Giovanni Angioni, Michele Bolla, Alessandro Brioschi, Bianca Brunori, Pier Paolo Creanza, Federico Marri, Elisa Serri.

To finally bear fruit, book projects require not only time, but also fertile soil to grow in. I am grateful to Bocconi University, and particularly to the Dondena Centre of which I have been a proud member since its foundation, for providing such an environment. My gratitude extends to the many colleagues and friends there for their continuous support and encouragement and for constantly reminding me that in the social sciences, 'There are more things in Heaven and Earth . . .'. A special thanks to Francesco Billari, who provided some crucial help in the early phases of the project.

Part of the book was written during a sabbatical period spent at the Department of Economic History of the London School of Economics and Political Science, in the autumn of 2019, and the first draft was completed during a visiting period at Trinity College Dublin in the summer of 2022. I am grateful to both institutions, and to all the colleagues who welcomed me in London and in Dublin, for providing ideal research environments. Unfortunately, the onset of the COVID-19 pandemic interfered with my plans to also spend a research period at the Stone Center on Socio-Economic Inequality, New York, in the spring of 2020, specifically to work on this book, but I remain grateful to the Center for having offered me this opportunity, and for having welcomed me (remotely) as an Affiliated Scholar. Interactions with, and intellectual admiration for, the colleagues there have contributed to shaping my own work on inequality and social mobility for years now, and this book has also benefited from this.

Special thanks go to the Bocconi Library and the staff of the interlibrary loan service. From the very beginning of my academic career, their competence has been crucial to my research, as has been their willingness to accommodate my 'special requests' during the writing of this book, of which the piles of books on loan currently in my office are proof. They will all be returned. Very soon. I promise.

But my biggest thanks go to Elisa, my wife, and to our fantastic kids Flavio and Giulio, who over the last few months have had to endure the fact that their respective husband and father had a book to finish. To them goes all my love.

AS GODS AMONG MEN

Introduction

TODAY, WESTERN SOCIETIES seem obsessed with the rich: who they are, how they became wealthy, how they behave or misbehave. Admired and flattered, and at the same time blamed and scorned, the rich and especially the super-rich are an ever-growing object of discussion among civil society. Some of them choose to become celebrities, a task made easier than ever by new communication technologies and the spread of social media. So much seems to have changed from the Middle Ages, when the rich were required *not to appear* to be wealthy (or at least not to show the full extent of their wealth), as the excessive accumulation of material resources was considered intrinsically sinful and even damaging to the correct functioning of a perfect (Christian) society and of its institutions, especially the political ones. As argued by some medieval commentators, if given apparently 'equal' access to political institutions, the super-rich would have de facto acted 'as gods among men', which was obviously not desirable.

And yet, how much has really changed? The very fact that the rich are the object of so much discussion, today *as* in the past, suggests that they struggle to find, or to be attributed, a proper place in society, again, today *as* in the past. These connections between past and present, hidden but at the same time clearly visible as soon as we look for them, are the main object of this book. This is not a simple account of the lives and deeds of the rich or super-rich, nor yet a book moved by personal fascination or distaste for them, but an attempt at a general history of the wealthy across the ages. Many examples will be given, and there is something to say for including brief narratives of the lives of certain extraordinary individuals (such narratives, beyond being scientifically illustrative and useful, are often quite entertaining), but these examples will be embedded in a general and systematic discussion.

Much has changed over time, and today's rich certainly did not come into their wealth in exactly the same way as the rich of the Middle Ages (Elon Musk is not Alan the Red), let alone those of the Classical Age, but the questions that we might wish to answer about them, for both past and present societies, are largely the same. From the point of view of social science, including that of an economic and social historian such as myself, these common questions are what makes it meaningful to attempt a sweeping analysis which systematically covers the period from the Middle Ages until today, with the addition of frequent incursions into the Classical Age. And this approach is necessary if one wants to address the deeper and crucial questions. What continuities exist across time? What makes the rich today similar to those of the past? How do these similarities help us to better understand the social unease at their very presence, an unease which appears to be a characterizing trait of Western societies of all times? To answer, we must take a *historical* approach. First, because if we do not pay attention to the historical context we risk comparing pears with apples, so to speak. Second, because if we do not look at the past, and specifically at the long run, we will never become aware of some of the more relevant and interesting issues to be explored.

This is not a book 'against' the rich but one 'about' them. There is no a priori intention to levy charges against their current behaviour, or to tap into societal discontent in order to attract attention. The origin of the book is, instead, rooted in a genuine scientific interest in who the rich were in the past, born almost by chance from a more general scholarly interest in long-term trends in economic inequality. The sudden realization that the rich as a specific category have rarely been the object of proper scientific study, especially for pre-industrial times, slowly grew into an ambitious project.[1] As the project is admittedly ambitious, one might wonder why this is not an even more ambitious book—why not a *global* history of the rich, instead of a history of the rich *in the West*? The main reason is that the focus on the Western rich is a direct requirement of the hypothesis that there are historical continuities in the way in which Western societies perceived (and perceive) them, in the kind of role that they attributed to them and in the behaviours that they expected of them, continuities which are deeply enrooted in Western culture and which from the Middle Ages on have also been shaped by the Christian religion. A second reason is that, to the best of my knowledge, there is no substantial literature specifically on the rich for any other world area. A general history of the rich in, for example, East Asia would be most interesting to read and would help to complete the puzzle, finally leading, potentially, to a global history. But for now, the focus must be on the better-documented West, defined along both a geographic and a cultural axis, thus including Europe, North America and other 'Western offshoots' whose culture is largely derived from European culture.

Studying the History of the Rich So Far: A Brief Overview

A defining characteristic of this book is that it focuses on the rich (or the wealthy; the two terms will be used as synonyms) as a *social-economic group distinguished by affluence*, not on specific wealthy individuals or dynasties or on social classes (not even just on the 'privileged' classes) or, finally, on wealth inequality. These other possible objects of research have attracted the attention of scholars much more frequently than the rich, and consequently, we must begin by briefly clarifying the differences between, and the connections with, what is attempted here.

Studies of wealthy individuals, families or dynasties are abundant in the historical literature; after all, something which makes the wealthiest stand out from all others is that they tend to leave behind a much larger amount of documentation, a disproportion that grows quickly when moving from recent to more remote epochs. These studies, however, very rarely have a comparative character, and when they do, they tend to favour biographical detail and historical contextualization over the analysis of commonalities across case studies and their interpretation in view of the broader picture. This is by no means a limitation of these precious works, but simply a difference in their objectives compared to what is attempted here. This book draws heavily on this literature as a provider of useful historical details and examples.[2]

Regarding the literature on social classes, while it has the useful feature of having paid due attention to preindustrial societies and not solely to modern ones, nevertheless it is set apart from our study by its object of analysis and by its main research questions. First of all, the definitions of 'class' traditionally used tend to reflect multidimensional social, political and cultural hierarchies which are much more complex than the simple economic hierarchy which sees the rich at the top. Much of this literature, or at least the part of it involving long-term analyses, has been produced by the Marxist schools of economic history which ran strong in many continental European countries until the 1970s or even the 1980s. These schools shared a specific research agenda: establishing who owned the means of production across time and more specifically, for preindustrial times, unearthing the historical processes that fuelled 'proletarianization' through the progressive dispossession of small owners, allowing for the parallel rise of the bourgeoisie. This agenda led to distinctions between very broad classes: the nobility, bourgeoisie and peasants, sometimes also singling out the clergy. Class definitions of this kind, unfortunately, are not useful for our study, for the same reasons that they are not useful for a study of economic inequality at the household or individual level, as, for example, it is a well-established historical fact that not all nobles were rich (as discussed in chapter 3), and most attempts to distinguish precisely who were the members of the 'bourgeoisie' across history have been roundly criticized. This caused this specific avenue of historical enquiry to dry up even before the fall of the Soviet Union in 1991.[3]

In this book, the rich are defined solely based on their affluence; they might be nobles or commoners, well-educated or utterly ignorant, bourgeois (in the original etymological meaning of coming from a '*bourg*' or city) or rural dwellers, they might own mostly land or mostly capital and so on. The change, across history, of the relative prevalence of rich individuals with specific characteristics, including the path which led them to great affluence, the composition of their wealth and the kind of privileges and entitlements to social, political *and* economic resources from which they benefited, will be the object of considerable attention throughout the book. In other words, focusing on a classification of the rich as a social group distinguished by one single trait—affluence—and allowing all other characteristics to vary, allows us to avoid the rigidity that tends to characterize class-based studies of long-run developments and allows the exploration of this very *variance* in substantive ways.[4]

Finally, studies of wealth inequality have flourished in recent years. Before the Great Recession beginning in 2008, economic inequality was still a relatively under-researched topic, and the few studies dedicated to its long-run tendencies had usually looked at income, not wealth. Across the West, the onset of the Great Recession tended to make civil societies more acutely aware of the relatively high levels of economic inequality that had been reached on the eve of the crisis (as this book will argue, it also tended to bring to the fore some unresolved issues concerning the role of the rich in society). It is in this context that the publication of economist Thomas Piketty's book *Capital in the Twenty-First Century* (2014) brought wealth to the centre of the conversation. Piketty made a compelling case that high returns to capital lead to continuous increases in inequality of *both* income and wealth; furthermore, he made the case that high returns to capital ensure that those who own more of it (the 'wealthy') will dominate the pyramid of total income (which is the sum of labour and capital income), as even those who earn very good wages, but have no property to begin with, will find it increasingly difficult to improve their relative position beyond a middling level. Shifting the attention from income inequality to wealth inequality tends to lead to a less optimistic view of the ability for economic growth to create opportunities and benefits for all. And it redirects our attention to complex and potentially controversial issues, such as the role of inherited wealth in defining the economic hierarchy of a given society and the role fiscal systems could, and probably should, have in ensuring an acceptably even playing field for all members of society—all issues which will be the object of in-depth discussion at various points in this book.[5]

An important characteristic of the work done by Piketty, his co-authors and many of the other scholars who in recent decades have concentrated their research efforts on inequality is their focus on the long run, as only by observing historical developments in wealth and income concentration can we truly understand the underlying drivers of inequality change, assess the degree to which a given situation, including that experienced by Western countries today, should be considered exceptional (or not) and discern whether it should be cause for concern. However, until recently, 'long run' in this context practically meant from the onset of the Industrial Revolution, as few had attempted to reconstruct wealth or income inequality trends in earlier epochs. Fortunately, even before the onset of the Great Recession some research teams had been busy collecting new data about economic inequality in preindustrial times, mostly of wealth because, as will be discussed in chapter 1, the historical sources available for this period allow us to observe the distribution of wealth much more directly than that of income. For at least some areas, especially in central and southern Europe, these studies could push as far back as the fourteenth century, leading to a substantial change in the way in which we look at the history of inequality in general. All of these new data are of crucial importance to this book, as they allow us to set the stage for subsequent analyses by looking, for example, at what share of the overall wealth was concentrated at the very top across time and space and at how many could be considered 'rich' in a given context.[6]

While there is clearly a strong connection between the purposes of this book and those of the recent literature on the history of economic inequality, a study of the rich as a specific social group offers a different, and in some respects a broader, perspective. While studies of the distribution of income or wealth tend to focus on quantification and on the reconstruction of time series of homogeneous measures of inequality, as well as on the interpretation of the causes and the social-economic effects of inequality, studies of the rich—as they are studies of people, not of material assets—need to have a stronger qualitative side and grounding in the historical context. They also require quantification, but of a somewhat different kind, for example, when they move from a consideration of how affluent the rich were to a consideration of who they were and of the social, economic and possibly cultural features that prevailed among them across history. This kind of quantification, however, is difficult to accomplish due to the relatively limited amount of useful documentation. While for the last few decades the spread of published 'rich lists' has made the task of studying the wealthy considerably easier, nothing similar is available for periods earlier than the late nineteenth century. This is why, so far, the few systematic studies of the rich have basically ignored the long preindustrial period, beginning in the early nineteenth century at the earliest. This is a limitation that this book intends to overcome, placing the preindustrial period on a par with more recent epochs. In fact, as has been shown by the burgeoning research on economic inequality, assuming a very long-run perspective tends to radically change our perception of the past *and* of the present and allows us to observe features of society that would otherwise remain hidden.[7]

A second limitation of earlier works on the rich is their lack of international comparison. They have tended to focus on specific parts of the West and especially on the United States. Already in 1925, the American-Russian sociologist Pitirim Sorokin, who is usually considered to have been the first to dedicate a modern scientific study to the rich, after pointing out that 'Wealthy men as a specific social group have been studied very little,'[8] focused on American millionaires and multimillionaires. Many other studies of the American rich have followed, reflecting both a practical situation which sees, from the late Gilded Age on, an exceptional concentration of super-rich individuals in the United States, and an apparently greater-than-normal attention to the role that they play, for better or worse, in modern societies (early encompassing reflections on the American rich include that of billionaire Andrew Carnegie and that of economist Thorstein Veblen, both authors who will be repeatedly mentioned throughout the book). This American focus on the rich appears to be the consequence of a historical path that diverges from that of other Western countries, especially the European ones, but the cultural, social and economic differences between Europe and the United States are always at risk of being overstated a priori and, indeed, here they will be subjected to analysis and discussion. Apart from the United States, the other Western country whose rich have been studied systematically is the United Kingdom, in part thanks to the substantial efforts in data collection conducted by historian William D. Rubinstein. However, no comparative studies exist, other than a few which cover only the last decades and are based on published rich lists.[9]

A third limitation of the existing literature is the excessive focus on the *super*-rich, which is largely the consequence of an over-reliance upon rich lists that usually include only the very top of the wealth distribution. While it is undoubtedly useful to pay particular attention to the super-rich, in part due to their potentially oversized impact on certain areas of human activity (in politics even more than in the economy), it is also clear that the conclusions that can be reached regarding, for example, the way in which they acquired their wealth could be different if one extended the analysis to the 'merely' rich. This book strives to do exactly this and also, whenever possible, to compare analyses conducted on narrower or broader definitions of the rich (for example, those belonging to the top 5%, 1% or 0.1% of the wealth distribution).

A fourth limitation of earlier studies is implicit in Sorokin's statement reported above: in a study of 'wealthy men', there appears to be little space for women. Unfortunately, this limitation is more difficult to overcome, and admittedly, this book mostly considers men. Although women appear among the examples provided and are included in my analyses wherever possible, wealth was usually kept in male hands and managed by men. As will be seen in chapter 5, until relatively recently the juridical framework did not easily allow women to 'act' in the economic arena. In such a context, the best opportunity for a woman to become formally entitled to manage her household wealth was to become a widow with underage children, and indeed, since early modern times, widows have played an important role in finance and in a few other sectors of the economy. Otherwise, the role played by women, for example in the context of merchant or entrepreneurial families or dynasties, tends to remain hidden, both in the available historical documentation and in the studies built upon them.

The Structure of the Book and Its Main Arguments

Who then are the rich? An intuitive answer would be: those who have considerable wealth. But how considerable and, more importantly, what do we mean by *wealth*? These and other essential definitory questions will be answered in chapter 1, which introduces the first part of the book ('In the Hands of the Few') whose general purpose is to set the stage for the subsequent analyses. Here, wealth is meant as material wealth (excluding other possible components, such as human capital or relational wealth), usually measured as household 'net worth', and the rich are those who have an abundance of it.

More precisely, two different and integrating definitions are used: one which simply looks at the apex of the wealth pyramid, taking as 'rich' those who belong to at least the top 5 per cent, and one which considers the whole of the distribution and sets the bar for affluence in relation to the median level. As I will argue, the most convenient threshold is ten times the median; the rich are those placed above this level. An advantage of the second definition is that it allows for a meaningful study of the prevalence of the rich over time, as the percentage of individuals or households placed above the threshold can vary depending on the shape of the wealth distribution. This is an innovative kind of analysis, which is not usually pursued for modern societies and which, to the best of my knowledge, I have pioneered for preindustrial ones.

However, we also want to know just how wealthy the rich were, a sort of information that, in recent studies of economic inequality, is usually presented in the form of the wealth share of the top percentiles—think of the 'one-percenters'. In chapter 2, these various definitions are applied to historical data to provide an overview of the concentration of wealth and of the prevalence of the rich across Western history, systematically covering more than seven centuries, as the longest time series that can be produced begin circa 1300. The factors shaping the wealth distribution in the long run and at a 'macro' level are also discussed. A crucial finding is that the underlying historical tendency towards increasing wealth concentration *is not* simply a by-product of economic growth. This leads us to focus on human agency and particularly on the behaviour of the economic elites (directly or through their command of key institutions), an aspect which will be the object of more in-depth exploration in subsequent chapters. In actual fact, across Western history, the only phases of substantial and long-lasting decline in wealth inequality appear to have been triggered by terrible catastrophes, and particularly by the Black Death pandemic of the fourteenth century and the World Wars of the twentieth, and this in large part due to the fact that they took the economic elites basically unawares (an issue debated further in chapter 11).

If, then, historical phases of (usually) wealth inequality growth or (rarely) decline can be identified with accuracy, phases during which the rich became *at the same time* relatively more abundant and proportionally much wealthier than all other components of society, we could wonder whether there was also any detectable change in the prevailing paths towards affluence. This is the object of the second part of the book ('The Paths to Affluence'), which begins with a series of three chapters (3 to 5) dedicated to what appear to be, historically, the main paths towards great wealth: that of becoming (or being born) a noble, the 'entrepreneurial' path closely connected to the ability to innovate and to exploit new economic opportunities and, finally, finance. Regarding the nobility, a crucial theme is that, apart from a first phase (typical of the Middle Ages, but not limited to it) in which noble status was acquired, often by means of some individual virtue (frequently, a martial virtue), thereafter it became just an inherited condition. It would be wrong simply to claim that all the descendants of the founders of a rich, noble dynasty did not 'earn' their privileged economic status. Across history, we have abundant examples of patrimonial mismanagement leading to impoverishment and even to the loss, or the suspension, of titles of nobility; in other words, it also requires effort and skill to manage an inherited fortune. Nevertheless, there is a clear difference between those few nobles who moved 'from rags to riches' and the multitude who were born to social-economic privilege. The inheritance of wealth and status is a topic introduced in chapter 3 and then discussed further, in its various aspects, in other chapters.

If, from nobility strictly meant, we move to the consideration of 'aristocracies' in general (defined as social groups holding high status and privileges), we bring to the fore behavioural tendencies that can also characterize members of dynasties that made their original fortunes in other ways. In chapter 4, the focus is on the merchants and entrepreneurs who, across history, were able to grow rich by exploiting innovations in products or procedures, often in connection with technological change. Of the three paths to riches that have been singled out, this appears to be the least controversial. Who could deny that a bold entrepreneur should be rewarded for her or his audacity? And yet, there are also dark sides to this story, for example when economic success was built upon the exploitation of non-Western people (or on outright slavery), which was a frequent occurrence from the very onset of European colonial and commercial expansion across the Atlantic. Additionally, after the first generations, even entrepreneurial wealth becomes more inherited than 'made'. In time, new money unavoidably becomes old, and those who own it are apt to acquire aristocratic tastes and behaviour or decide to directly pursue a path of formal ennoblement. Apart from discussing these general issues, chapter 4 singles out specific historical phases during which becoming wealthy by means of entrepreneurship/innovation was relatively easy: from the onset of the Commercial Revolution in the eleventh and twelfth centuries, to the opening of the Atlantic trade routes at the turn of the sixteenth, to the Industrial Revolution of the eighteenth and nineteenth and, finally, to the Age of Information which began in the second half of the twentieth century.

These phases of economic efflorescence also required innovations in finance, generating abundant opportunities for growing rich by lending and by providing financial services of various kinds (chapter 5). Although it is often difficult to distinguish whether a fortune is entrepreneurial or financial in its origin, singling out the path of finance is important because, from preindustrial times until today, it is the one that has led to the greatest concerns and suspicions. Our medieval ancestors struggled with the idea that money could be used to generate money in ways which were not sinful or socially reprehensible, but across the ages, a deep suspicion of finance has continued to characterize Western culture and it resurfaces regularly, most recently with the Occupy Wall Street movement. As the chapter argues, compared to that of nobles and entrepreneurs the claim to riches of bankers and financiers has always been considered somewhat weaker and socially troubling. If the current tendency towards the financialization of Western economies, and the related growth in the prevalence of fortunes with financial origins, continues, this long-unresolved social issue can only be expected to become more sensitive and urgent.

This part of the book concludes with two chapters (6 and 7) that bring together the evidence and findings from the separate analysis of distinct paths to wealth, in order to provide a general discussion of some key issues as well as a final overview of the prevalence of different kinds of rich individuals across the ages. Chapter 6 begins by focusing on what is apparently a narrow topic: the saving and consumption habits of the rich. Central to the chapter is the consideration that the rich are criticized alternatively for their lavish expenditure and for their tendency to accumulate ever larger fortunes, which the chapter dubs 'the curse of Smaug', after the dragon asleep on its treasures in Tolkien's *The Hobbit*. Again, clear elements of continuity can be found across history, from medieval sumptuary laws imposing constraints on a large range of 'visible' expenditures (for clothing, travel, celebrations and feasts and so on) to Thorstein Veblen's criticism of the 'conspicuous consumption' of America's Gilded Age and beyond. The chapter explores this key issue from a variety of angles, including the actual levels of expenditure and saving of the rich across history, the motivations behind their observed choices (among which is the urge to leave a large bequest and to found a wealthy dynasty) and the social and institutional constraints that they faced.

To save, then, or to consume? There appears to be no clear solution to this social conundrum: while conspicuous consumption (the show of wealth) is what usually leads to social anger against the rich, from a historical perspective what appears to be most problematic are the high saving rates which tend to characterize the wealth elite, leading to the establishment of dynasties and compromising social-economic mobility by ossifying the top of the wealth pyramid. This process is also shown in chapter 7, where the way in which phases of relatively easy social-economic promotion, obtained through one's merits, finally *come to an end* is discussed; the enrooting of dynasties with overbearing economic power plays an important role in this story. The chapter provides some quantitative evidence about the relative historical prevalence of fortunes inherited or 'made', as part of a broader discussion of the relative importance of various paths to affluence across history, including, beyond the three main ones outlined previously, others such as practising a liberal profession or holding top posts in public administrations and institutions. The overall picture is one of alternating phases during which it has been relatively easy, or difficult, to make it to the top, on which is superposed an overarching change in the main paths towards wealth: from the dominance of the path of nobility during the Middle Ages (with a probable peak around the thirteenth or fourteenth century) to the progressive strengthening of the path of entrepreneurship (peaking at the time of the First and Second Industrial Revolutions). In parallel, the path of finance also tended to become relatively more prevalent, a process which continues to this day, as, in recent decades, the acquisition of considerable wealth by means of finance has probably been easier than at any other moment in history.

Due to the mistrust of finance deeply enrooted in Western societies, it is no surprise that the financialization of wealth is causing growing concern, especially as we live in an age which seems plagued by recurring crises. This and other aspects are treated in the third, and final, part of the book ('The Rich in Society'). Chapter 8 begins by highlighting the wariness with which the West has always viewed the very rich, struggling to find them a specific social role to play and even to justify their very existence. Like a pearl in an oyster, the rich have been recognized as the product of an active society but at the same time have been regarded as somewhat extraneous to it. In the medieval Christian tradition, well represented by the thirteenth-century theologian Thomas Aquinas, the very accumulation of wealth was considered to be sinful. This led the rich to be scorned and, at the same time, generated in them a constant worry about the afterlife. A century later, political thinkers such as Nicole Oresme even claimed that in cities governed 'democratically', the super-rich should be expelled, since otherwise they would enjoy overbearing political power, being among the people 'as God is among men' (the expression to which this book owes its title). This is not very different from what, almost seven centuries after Oresme, was claimed by economist Thomas Piketty, who argued that an excessive concentration of wealth might be incompatible with the correct functioning of the characterizing institutions of Western democracies: a clear 'red thread in history', hidden in plain sight.

And yet, from the fifteenth century, when after the levelling imposed by the Black Death economic inequality began to grow again, theologians and philosophers modified their discourse to match a mutated reality, finding two specific roles for the rich: making the city splendid in everybody's interest by means of their 'magnificence' and acting as private reserves of financial resources into which the community could tap in times of crisis by means of taxation or of extraordinary contributions. In early modern times, the Protestant Reformation, and especially its Calvinist component, only gave some extra lustre to the rich, insofar as it hinted that material success might reflect being destined to salvation. But something continued to be expected from them, especially in times of crisis: until at least the 1907 banking crisis in the United States, 'solved' by the direct intervention of J. P. Morgan (who consequently came to be hailed as the saviour of his country from financial ruin, exactly as had happened to Cosimo de' Medici in fifteenth-century Florence), the super-rich were both able and willing to fulfil their traditional function of 'savers of last resort'.

While chapter 8 introduces many points of reflection, the three subsequent chapters thoroughly develop some of the most important ones. Chapter 9 begins by exploring the notion of magnificence, which literally means 'doing great deeds', as part of a more general discussion of the historical role (and aims) of the rich as patrons, benefactors and donors. Beginning with the Classical Age, when the willingness to do (that is, to pay for) great deeds for the benefit of the collective was both clearly expected from the rich and instrumental to their social and political ambitions, and continuing in the late Middle Ages when the likes of Cosimo de' Medici came to own the resources needed to achieve patronage and magnificence on a scale unseen since Roman times, the reasons why many among the rich used vast amounts of resources in this way were quite clear. Things got muddier when magnificence became confused with munificence, that is, a free act of generosity with nothing owed by the rich and nothing required in exchange. This is the tradition that, through the development of the notion of philanthropy in the late eighteenth century, led to today's 'giving'. And yet, many wonder if modern giving is truly disinterested, as the rich can use it to dodge taxation or even amass political influence.

Chapter 10 takes over the analysis of the connection between wealth and politics, focusing in particular on the super-rich: precisely those that some medieval thinkers (themselves inspired by the Greek philosopher of the Classical Age, Aristotle) believed should have been expelled from 'democratic' cities. Indeed, the case of Cosimo de' Medici, who was recalled from exile to save his country from war-induced financial ruin and quickly became its de facto ruler, perfectly illustrates the dangers that the extreme concentration of wealth could pose to relatively 'open' political institutions in a preindustrial setting. Given the highly sensitive nature of the question, the chapter, after a brief historical introduction, focuses on modern times, beginning with the Age of Revolutions when the principle of the equality of political rights became a characterizing feature of Western societies. Arguably, for a period during the twentieth century politics became less dependent upon wealth, but, in the final decades of the century, we also have signs that this phase might have ended. Were the political fortunes of billionaires such as Silvio Berlusconi in Italy and Donald Trump in the United States the direct consequence of their wealth? In the other direction, can involvement in politics be used to pursue personal enrichment? A final, crucial question posed in the chapter is whether a (probable) greater grasp of the rich on Western political systems explains their current ability to prevent the introduction of tax reforms aimed at making them contribute more, even in times of dire crisis.

The behaviour of the rich during crises is the subject of inquiry in chapter 11. Across history, catastrophes of many kinds (plagues and other pandemics, famines, wars, financial crises and so on) have affected the wealthy, sometimes damaging their economic fortunes and sometimes creating specific opportunities for further enrichment. For example, during wars the rich were, and still are, both the most coveted prey and the apex predator, that is, those best placed to profit (in part due to their political connections and their privileged access to information) from the economic needs created by the crisis. Beginning with the Black Death of 1347–52 and ending with the most recent crises, the 2007–8 financial crisis and the ensuing Great Recession and the COVID-19 pandemic (ongoing at the time of writing), the chapter analyses in detail the behaviour of the rich during these troubled times, how they adapted by making their patrimonies more resilient against future shocks and how their actions were judged by the rest of society. A crucial underlying theme of the chapter concerns how the wealthy were required to provide financial help, fulfilling a function that, as seen above, has played a key role historically in making the very presence of the rich more acceptable to Western societies. And yet, the more recent crises stand out from previous ones: first, they have been exceptionally gentle towards the rich (their financial losses after the 2007–8 crisis were quickly recovered, in stark opposition to what happened after the 1929 stock-market crash and the ensuing Great Depression), and secondly, the rich themselves have been exceptionally unwilling to contribute, even through only temporary increases in taxation, to supporting societal responses to crises. To what degree, and for how long, can the rich excuse themselves from something that the West has for centuries considered to be their specific duty without making their position socially untenable? This question underpins this entire book and is addressed directly in the concluding remarks.

PART I

In the Hands of the Few

1

What Is Wealth, and How Much Is Needed to Be Rich?

INDIVIDUAL MEMBERS of any human society, both present and past, tend to have an intuitive understanding of the concept of wealth. However, what they consider to be wealth can change significantly: is a wealthy person the owner of many cattle, or of elaborate and difficult-to-get or otherwise 'precious' equipment needed for his or her activities, or of a string of apartments in a city centre or, finally, of substantial but immaterial financial assets? While in most societies the patrimony of the rich is usually of mixed composition, its main components differ according to the epoch. Defining wealth is the unavoidable first step in a book such as this, and it will be immediately followed by a second step, that of defining who could be considered rich. Just as any society has an intuitive understanding of wealth, so it is also able to approximately identify who belongs among the rich. This is because, across history, wealth has always been unevenly distributed, and it is by looking at the unequal access to its different components that the rich can be properly defined in *relative* terms. While the vast majority of the citizens of today's Western societies could be considered 'wealthy' compared to their remote ancestors (in terms of their *absolute* access to goods and services), this is not very helpful for studying the rich as a specific economic and social category across history: any human society, bar theoretical examples of hyper-egalitarian ones, has had its rich as well as its poor. Analysing the composition of wealth and its distribution across history, however, is a complex task based on the limited sources available, from medieval manuscripts to today's wealth surveys and 'rich lists'. Discussing the difficulties posed by these sources is the third, and final, step taken in this chapter.

Defining Wealth across the Ages

What is wealth? We know from anthropological studies that the possession of assets has different meanings and consequences in different societies. Take the *kula*, a ritualized exchange system used in the Trobriand Islands in Melanesia. Two kinds of articles are traded, moving in opposite directions along a ring of islands with a circumference of several hundred kilometres: red shell necklaces (moving clockwise) and white shell armbands (moving counter-clockwise). These items have no practical use and have relatively limited intrinsic value. So, should they be considered part of the wealth of their holders, and how should they be evaluated? On the one hand, the holder can't keep them forever, as the *kula* have to be regularly circulated along the ring, so it would be inaccurate to say that they are 'owned' by anybody (save for the relatively exceptional case of valuables, known as *kitoms*, which are temporarily removed from the flow). On the other hand, the *kula* are roughly ranked so that their exchange, even in the absence of haggling, must take place on the basis of a perceived equivalence. Consequently, as a first approximation, we could say that the articles circulated in the *kula* trade can be considered to be valuable *simply because they are evaluated*. Looking deeper, we find that for their holders *kula* articles are a source of great individual prestige and trading them leads to the building up of personal renown or fame, so that being included in the *kula* trade means having privileged access to other economic (and relational, political and so on) resources. After all, voyages related to the *kula* often carry additional goods as well, to be bartered through hard bargaining. From this perspective, then, the *kula* articles, or maybe one's systematic involvement in their trade, *can* be considered part of the wealth of whoever holds them at any given time, and consequently it should come as no surprise that they are very unevenly distributed and concentrated in the hands of a few.[1]

Recent studies of small-scale societies (that is, societies composed of few individuals who interact face-to-face with virtually all others) have distinguished among three 'classes' of wealth: material, relational and embodied (the latter includes physical strength, practical skills, knowledge and so on). From this perspective, the *kula* trade, while having some connection to material wealth as the articles exchanged are valuable in themselves, is most clearly connected to relational wealth. Material wealth is the most important class in agricultural and pastoral societies, while for hunter-gatherers embodied wealth dominates, closely followed by relational wealth, and material wealth is of little import (as will be seen in chapter 7, this is also why agricultural and pastoral societies tend to be considerably more unequal than hunter-gatherers, given that material wealth can more easily be transferred from one generation to the next, leading to more substantial accumulation over time).[2]

We might believe that these difficulties in defining what wealth is pertain only to relatively 'primitive' societies, but it is not so: the problem exists even for the economically advanced societies found today across the West. Indeed, economic theory is yet to produce an entirely convincing definition of wealth. First of all, if we wanted to consider the distribution of *all* economic resources, then we should include human capital in our wealth definition, as has been suggested by some economists, and maybe social capital as well, which would be basically equivalent to taking into account embodied and relational wealth. In practice, though, the vast majority of studies focus on 'nonhuman capital' only, that is, material wealth (real property and financial assets). One theoretical justification for this is that material wealth can be easily bought and sold, while human capital cannot (although in some historical settings this was partly possible due to the slave market[3]). The other, and more important, reason for this choice is eminently practical: non-marketable wealth is difficult to observe and to evaluate for any society. Consequently, throughout this book the focus will be on material wealth only—although its connection to, and reciprocal influences with, human and social capital, including with political power, will also be explored in detail.

The notion of material wealth is closely connected to that of 'net worth', that is, the value of assets minus debts. For a study such as this, given its comparative intent and the long period covered, net worth might appear to be the most obvious and effective operational definition of wealth, and indeed it is—but only after clarifying that, in practice, the actual elements which contribute to determining net worth tend to be defined based on what can be observed. As aptly synthetized by economists Jesper Roine and Daniel Waldenström, for modern industrial and post-industrial societies there are three main categories of 'problematic assets', difficult to observe and/or to evaluate: (1) pension and social security wealth (or, more precisely, the present value of entitlements to the related future payments), which is, generally speaking, not marketable, cannot be converted freely into other forms of individual consumption and consequently cannot be uncontroversially defined as 'private property'; (2) consumer durables, like cars, furniture or clothing, which are usually missing from tax assessments and thus remain unobserved but overall might have significant value (it has been estimated that in Sweden, from 1810 until today, durables might have accounted for, in value, 10%–20%

of all non-financial assets); and (3) foreign wealth holdings, which tend to be missing from domestic fiscal assessments and have always been relatively easy to hide from tax officials—perhaps even more so today, given the high mobility of capital in an advanced, globalized economy.[4]

The problems we encounter in studies of modern societies, which cannot really observe all the components of a hypothetical overall net worth, are mirrored in studies of preindustrial societies, although possibly to a lesser degree. We are used to thinking that the information available tends to decrease as we look back towards the most ancient epochs. However, when we consider wealth specifically, it appears that late medieval and early modern societies were much more focused on measuring and evaluating wealth than the average Western country of today, for the simple reason that wealth tended to be the main item of personal taxation. When, especially from the second half of the nineteenth century, taxation began to move from wealth to income, we observe an increase in the information available for studies of the level and distribution of income, but a parallel decline in the information about the level and distribution of wealth. But even in areas and historical periods for which the information about wealth is relatively abundant, the problem remains that the components of wealth that were recorded for the purpose of taxation could vary. And yet, across the West, from medieval times and throughout the early modern period and beyond, until the spread and generalization of the personal income tax changed the situation entirely, some regularities are found, the most important one being the focus on real estate as the main component of taxable wealth. In the property tax records which were so widespread in southern and central Europe and which constituted the main basis upon which the fiscal burden was divided among households, lands and buildings always constituted the bulk of the recorded goods and with good reason: in the very rare circumstances when we can observe all (or almost all) components of wealth, we invariably discover that real estate constituted the vast majority, in value, of all properties.

For example, in the Florentine State (Tuscany) in 1427, when a truly exceptional effort was made to fully evaluate the fiscal capacity of all households, real estate accounted for 53.4 per cent of overall wealth, movables (including business investments) for 29.5 per cent and shares of the public debt for 17.1 per cent. These state averages, however, hide a reality in which real estate was an even more prevalent component of wealth. In 1427, Florence was one of the richest cities in the world and one of the main financial hubs of the continent, and consequently it held an enormous amount of financial capital for the time.

But this was concentrated in very few, and almost exclusively urban, hands: in the countryside, where the vast majority of the Tuscan population lived, real estate accounted for 90.6 per cent of overall wealth, movables for 9.3 per cent, and investment in the public debt was negligible (0.1%). The composition of the Tuscan rural patrimonies reflects well the conditions prevailing across the West in the late Middle Ages, at least outside the main cities.[5]

In the rural areas of Europe, then, the rich invariably had control over large lands—but even in cities, where the richest individuals often also owned considerable financial capital, they were *at the same time* the main owners of real estate: not only splendid urban mansions, but also farms and lands scattered around the countryside surrounding the city. In the rare instances when we can measure the correlation between the ownership of movables and of real estate, it invariably tends to be extremely high in rural settings (0.98 in the 'Three Hundreds' of Aylesbury in England in 1524–5), remaining strong even in those urban settings where financial capital was the most abundant (0.64 in Florence in 1427).[6] Indeed, the very fact that the taxation of wealth in pre-industrial Europe tended to focus on real estate (England is a partial exception) tells us something about what those societies thought really mattered for defining the fiscal capacity of a household: in absolute terms and, even more importantly, in relative terms, as more often than not property tax records were used to distribute a pre-determined amount among the households, which had to contribute to the levy proportionally to their assessed wealth. As late as 1847, even in a large and important city such as Paris, and even looking only at the composition of the fortunes of the richest (patrimonies above 1 million francs of the time), real estate amounted to 66 per cent of the fortunes of the nobles and 51.3 per cent of those of the bourgeoisie. In another large city in continental Europe, Milan, in the second half of the nineteenth century real estate remained even more prevalent in the patrimonies of millionaires (in lire): 83 per cent for nobles and about 60 per cent for non-nobles, with some variation depending on the specific category considered. In Paris, it is only from the turn of the twentieth century that we have evidence that real estate had become a minority component of millionaires' wealth. In 1911 it represented 37.4 per cent of the patrimony of nobles and just 25.6 per cent of that of the bourgeoisie. For both, stock (including governmental bonds and industrial shares) represented almost 50 per cent of the total.[7]

Based on the evidence above, the fact that for preindustrial times we mostly observe one specific component of wealth (real estate) does not compromise our ability to identify properly who the rich were in a specific area and period or to establish their approximate level of command of the overall economic resources relative to the rest of society. The situation, of course, would be different for modern times, and increasingly so the closer we get to the twenty-first century, because movable wealth, and particularly financial assets, has tended to become more prevalent as a component of sizeable patrimonies. According to the most recent estimates, in 2020 financial assets alone represented 73.2 per cent of gross wealth in the United States, 61.2 per cent in the Netherlands, 55.5 per cent in the United Kingdom and usually less in other large European countries, the continental average being 45.7 per cent.[8] The fact that the main components of wealth (or of net worth) change when moving from preindustrial societies to industrial and even post-industrial ones is something that we must be aware of but which does not prevent a meaningful comparison of wealth distribution across time, let alone a study of the rich across history. On the contrary: changes of this kind reflect transformations in the main paths towards personal enrichment, which are the object of Part II of this book. Indeed, if we intended to directly compare the level of wealth of individuals far removed in time—say, the Roman Marcus Licinius Crassus and the American Jeff Bezos—we would be in trouble, which is why, for the purposes of historical comparative studies, the most proper definition of who was rich is a relative, not an absolute, one, as is discussed in the following.

Who Can Be Considered 'Rich'?

Who could be considered rich in a given society? In the earlier section, the *kula* trade was introduced. Are the main protagonists of the *kula* trade rich? Yes, most definitely—if our definition of wealth includes relational wealth (or social capital) beyond material wealth. But as our focus is on material wealth, it appears that we must define the rich as those who have an abundance of it. While across history many among the 'materially' rich were also very well connected and held considerable political power, it would be incorrect to assume that *all* the rich had these characteristics. To give a fictional example, consider Ebenezer Scrooge, the protagonist of Charles Dickens's *A Christmas Carol*, who was very wealthy but also very unhappy and lonely, with no family other than a nephew and no friends to count upon. Indeed, an advantage of our definition of wealth is that it allows us to explore the connection between having privileged access to material (economic) resources and having privileged access to other kinds of resources. Is wealth a path to political power, or is political power a path to wealth? Questions of this kind will recur in this book.

A rich person, then, is somebody who has valuable possessions. But how many, and how valuable? In other words, how wealthy should somebody be in order to be considered rich? The answer to this question is less clear-cut than it might first appear and leads directly to an important divide in how social scientists, and particularly economists and economic historians, have looked at wealth in the long run. On the one hand, many have tried to directly compare the levels of wealth prevailing in different societies. There are many problems with this. First of all, if we look at the ease of accessing specific amenities, we might conclude that at least the vast majority of people in the past (say, in preindustrial times) were much poorer than the vast majority of people today. As clarified by economist Branko Milanović:

> The logic . . . is as follows. Take the example of artificial lighting or voice recording. For Julius Caesar to read a book overnight, easily move at night around his palace, or listen to the songs he liked would have required perhaps hundreds of workers (slaves) to hold the torches or sing his favorite arias all night. Even Caesar, if he were to do that night after night, might, after some time, have run out of resources (or might have provoked a rebellion among the singers). But for us the expense for a similar pleasure is very small, even trivial, say $2 per night. Consequently, some people come to the conclusion that Caesar must have had tiny wealth measured in today's bundle of goods since a repeated small nightly expense of $2 (in today's prices) would have eventually ruined him. Other people at Caesar's time had obviously much less: ergo, the world today is incomparably richer than before.[9]

The problem with the kind of reasoning that Milanović criticizes is that Caesar *was* rich: he was perceived as such by his contemporaries, because his command of economic resources was much larger than that of the average Roman. He did not have access to certain amenities that we take for granted today, but that is not because he was poor but because the relevant technology did not exist. It is definitely useful to explore how the availability of certain goods and services to the common people changed across the ages, but at the same time it would be a mistake to use the same basket of goods and services to compare the affluence of individuals from different societies. One might think that, in order to make this kind of comparison, it suffices to find an 'objective' standard of wealth. Early modern mercantilists, such as William Petty and Richard Cantillon, thought that this standard could be the amount of land and labour required to produce things. Later, Adam Smith argued that labour alone could be used in such a way. Milanović in his book *The Haves and the Have-Nots* followed Smith's approach, defining and comparing the rich based on the amount of labour that they commanded. The conclusion was that, circa 2010, the Mexican telecommunications magnate Carlos Slim was the richest man in the world—and maybe the richest man who had ever lived (in Milanović's evaluation, he was about fourteen times wealthier than Marcus Licinius Crassus, presumably the richest Roman of Caesar's time).[10] And yet, as Milanović admits, this approach remains full of pitfalls, as it does not truly solve the problem of comparing societies structured in very different ways, in which, for example, the ability to command the work of many people might come from political power rather than from what can be reasonably considered private wealth. The conclusion is that absolute comparisons of individual wealth make full sense only when looking at relatively similar societies (say, today's Western democracies), but their usefulness quickly deteriorates when moving to societies with different characteristics that are distant in space and/or in time.[11]

While it might seem interesting to compare the wealth of the nineteenth-century American financier J. P. Morgan to that of the fourteenth-century Florentine banker Cosimo de' Medici and while estimates of this kind undoubtedly arouse the curiosity of the general public, they are of limited use for a proper study of the rich. Virtually all relevant scientific questions that we might wish to answer about the rich, their characteristics and their role in society *do not* require us to directly compare their level of affluence across the ages. What we want to establish is who could be considered to have been rich in *any given society*, at *a given point in time*. In other words, we are interested in a definition which is not absolute, but relative, in two main senses: relative to a specific social setting, and relative in terms of the wealth of the rich compared to the other members of society. Helpfully, the most common measures of the affluence of the rich that we have grown familiar with (say, the wealth share of the 'one-percenters') are relative in nature.[12]

Before discussing these measures, though, it is important to clarify a further aspect. Focusing on relative measures of affluence implies focusing on distribution. In a society of equals, nobody is rich (in relative terms), although in principle everybody could have equal access to abundant resources and assets. This means that the very existence of the rich is the product of some degree of inequality in the distribution of valuable assets. But focusing on inequality is precisely what a certain scholarly tradition in economics has actively tried to avoid, in stark contrast with the classical economists, from David Ricardo to Karl Marx, who placed distribution at the centre of their analyses. And it is in connection with this scholarly tradition that a discourse of the kind criticized by Milanović could develop—only to be met with a strong scientific reaction in recent years, especially from 2008 when the beginning of the Great Recession heightened the perception of inequality across the West (would anybody seriously contend that in today's Western societies everybody is rich simply because everybody can read at night or listen to music while walking, while the Romans couldn't do either?). An important aspect of this reaction is the renewed attention paid to wealth (previously neglected in favour of income, which is *not* a scientifically neutral choice, as has already been discussed in the introduction).[13]

Having clarified that the best definition of the rich for a study such as this is a relative one, the next task then becomes to identify, if possible, a consensus or at least a broad agreement about where to draw the line between the rich and the rest. In practice, the most widespread approach appears to be that of looking at the top percentiles of the wealth distribution: say, the richest 10 per cent, 5 per cent or 1 per cent of the population. This is a 'relative' measure because, whatever the average level of affluence of a society, somebody will always be placed at the top of the distribution.[14] From an operational point of view, defining the rich as those belonging to a fixed percentage of the distribution allows us to explore their composition—with one word of warning: looking at larger or smaller percentiles potentially affects the composition of the rich significantly. This is why this study does not consider percentiles larger than the top 5 per cent, and whenever the available information allows, the features of larger or smaller percentiles are compared.[15]

Interestingly, the composition of the top wealth percentiles is something which can be compared much better across the ages than the absolute affluence of the rich. For example, the progressive rise of finance as a major path towards great wealth is something that can be observed and roughly quantified from the Middle Ages until today, precisely by looking at the origin of the affluence of those belonging to the top percentiles of the wealth distribution— the only problem being, of course, the availability of sufficiently detailed historical data. Additionally, defining the rich as those belonging to the top percentiles makes it easy to couple the analysis of who they were with the analysis of how large their wealth share was in different historical settings. This second objective is the one which has mostly drawn the efforts of scholars working on wealth inequality. For this reason, the evidence that we have available about the wealth share of the rich, particularly in preindustrial times, is relatively abundant.[16]

While defining the rich as those who belong to top wealth percentiles presents many advantages, it also has significant drawbacks, the main one being the impossibility of meaningfully comparing how many there were in different epochs—as by construction their absolute numbers will be a fixed proportion of the total population; hence they will reflect purely demographic developments. To address this problem, we need some sort of 'headcount' index, that is, an index which allows us to count how many are placed above a specific threshold: the 'richness line', also called the 'affluence line'.[17] This approach is entirely analogous to that followed by poverty studies, which use either absolute or relative poverty lines. Setting an absolute richness line is a tricky exercise, given that there is no consensus among scholars or among civil society about its placement. A recent study of the Netherlands established, based on a sociological survey conducted in 2018, that the average Dutch person considered a household with total wealth above 2.2 million euros (2.6 million U.S. dollars) 'rich', but individual answers ranged from 1 to 3 million euros. Unfortunately, no comparable in-depth studies appear to exist for other Western countries, and the researchers involved admitted that their results were heavily context-dependent. How would the citizens of a country with a welfare state system structurally different from the Dutch have answered? Also note that a threshold of 2.2 million euros might be too high for many Western societies today. A recent study of Germany in 2005–14 considered households with a net patrimony above 1 million euros (1.3 million U.S. dollars) to be 'high net worth' and those between 500,000 and 1 million to be 'affluent'.[18]

Fortunately, for the reasons discussed previously, we are primarily interested in defining a relative, not an absolute, richness line. In studies of contemporary societies, the most common value for the richness line is twice (200% of) the median *income*. Given the intrinsic differences between distributions of income and of wealth—the second tends to be characterized by a much greater distance between maximum and minimum values and more generally has a heavier right tail, which also reflects the tendency for wealth to be more concentrated than income—it would be wrong to set the wealth-based richness line at the same level as the income-based one. Few studies, however, have discussed the proper placement of a relative richness line based on wealth, simply because we usually lack good data about the complete wealth distribution of contemporary societies. It should not come as a surprise, then, that the rare attempts to estimate the prevalence of the rich based on a relative wealth threshold have to do with preindustrial societies. A particularly suitable richness line appears to be ten times (1000% of) the median wealth, which leads to estimates of the prevalence of the rich placed between 1 per cent and 10 per cent of the population: conveniently close to the top percentiles normally used for studying the wealth share of the rich.[19]

The relative measures introduced above will be used systematically in chapter 2, where an overview of the available quantitative evidence about the prevalence of the rich and their grip on the overall economic resources will be provided. They will also remain a constant reference throughout the book, whenever the need arises to provide some additional quantification, for example concerning the composition of the rich (chapter 7). However, in many instances, the only available information concerns the richest of all. Sometimes these are defined as even smaller percentiles (say, the top 0.01% of the wealth distribution), but more often they are set in absolute terms, taking as a reference their wealth measured in the relevant historical currencies (say, 1892 U.S. dollars) or, more rarely, converted into today's currencies. This is the case of the various 'rich lists', such as *Forbes'* 'billionaires lists', which are available for some Western countries from the nineteenth century on and which have become particularly widespread in recent decades. As this information is highly valuable for a study such as this, it will also be used, but an effort will be made to clarify which percentile of the relevant population is singled out by adopting a specific absolute threshold. Rich lists are only one of many sources of historical data used in the book.

The Historical Sources for Studying Wealth and the Rich: An Overview

Those historians and economic historians who are used to exploring the archives and perusing centuries-old original handwritten documents know the thrill of discovering something unknown and which, based on the cumulated knowledge of generations of scholars, should not exist. This is what happened to the author of this book on a cold winter morning about twenty years ago when, during one of his regular visits to the town archive of Ivrea (a small city in Piedmont, north-western Italy), he decided to request for inspection a document catalogued as a census and dated 1613: that is, well before any public administration of medieval or early modern Europe had developed a known interest in recording the population for the simple purpose of discovering who their citizens or subjects were. As it turned out, the document (a large leatherbound book) did exist and the date indicated in the catalogue of the archive was accurate. However, it was not just a population census, but something more revealing: a list of all households in Ivrea, with the details of their 'real estate, including feudal property, mills, ovens or furnaces, credits, economic activities, trades, capitals, offices, live-stock and food reserves'.[20] In other words, the city residents were required to provide details about each and every component of their wealth—and, by and large, they complied.

Of course, not all that glitters is gold, and the practical use of this historical source is more complicated than it might appear at first glance. It might be fascinating to discover that Antonio Ressia, who operated the White Cross (*Croce Bianca*) inn, owned four mares and one pig and held sizeable food reserves amounting to fourteen sacks of wheat and about 1,000 litres of wine (presumably for the activities of the inn: as the wine reserves are classified by the source as invested capital), but no indication of the monetary value of these assets is provided. Fortunately, Antonio's credits and debts are properly evaluated (his net debt position was negative for 125 scudi), as well as his real estate. Despite the difficulties of using it, the Piedmontese 'census' of 1613 is precious in offering us an overview of all the components of wealth of an early modern society, and as such, throughout the book it will sometimes be used as a source of examples and insights. Indeed, this source contributed significantly, many years ago, to reinforcing my personal interest in the historical distribution of economic assets, as well as to sparking a specific interest in who the rich were in a preindustrial setting—so, in a sense, its unexpected discovery contributed to the origin of this book. For the purposes of this chapter, however, the question that must be answered is the following: why did this source exist at all, and why was it previously unknown to scholars? The physical document preserved in Ivrea's archive is a copy made from the original upon its completion, and it includes a letter from the central authorities of the Sabaudian State[21] which was sent to *all* communities of Piedmont, requiring them to collect the aforementioned information and to send it to the state capital, Turin. As such, then, the document found in Ivrea is the local outcome of a large-scale and historically quite exceptional attempt to collect detailed information about the total wealth of all the households physically present in the duchy. Surprisingly, before my research on Ivrea this attempt was entirely unknown to modern scholars, and this was for a simple reason: after meticulous searches in the central archives of Turin, no information whatsoever concerning the 1613 'census' was found, as if it had never existed. Years later, as part of a large-scale study of wealth distribution in northern Italy which led to a systematic exploration of the local archives of Piedmont, other examples were sought. Copies of the originals which were sent to Turin (and have entirely disappeared) have been found for two additional cities, Moncalieri and Susa, as well as for a part of Turin itself.[22]

The fact that the original records have not survived and that no additional information could be found in the central archives of the state, strongly suggests that the initiative was a fiasco—hence quickly and purposefully forgotten. The fact that only in a few cities is there any information about this strongly suggests that the fiasco was due to the unwillingness of the communities to cooperate with the central state. And given the nature of the information that they had been required to send to Turin, it seems highly probable that they were reluctant to cooperate because the request seemed preliminary to some sort of fiscal levy, presumably in the form of an exceptional contribution initially (the letter does mention a 'subsidy due to His Highness')—but a characteristic feature of early modern fiscal systems is the tendency of exceptional, 'extraordinary' taxation to become 'ordinary', or yearly. In other words, the local communities, while they were generally ready to help the duke financially, were probably scared by the prospect of allowing the central state to know so much about the overall fiscal capacity of their residents.[23]

If the motivation behind the 'census' was, in fact, to build the basis for future taxation, then its purpose was entirely analogous to that of the 1427 Tuscan *catasto*. While the 1613 Piedmontese 'census' used to be entirely unknown to scholars, the *catasto* is, in contrast, one of the better-known European historical sources of the late Middle Ages and quite unique in providing information about almost all components of wealth for an entire state. Notably, in the early fifteenth century, Florence appears to have been much more able than Turin two centuries later to impose compliance upon the local communities of its state. In spite of its exceptional state capacity, however, in practice Florence also *failed* in its attempt at sweeping fiscal reform: as, after the very first survey of Tuscan wealth, it quickly abandoned all aspirations to record anything beyond real estate, which incidentally was the wealth component easiest to observe and to measure (also because lands and houses could not be hidden). Consequently, the 1427 *catasto* remains an *unicum*, although of exceptional value.

From the end of the Middle Ages, across Italy but more generally across southern Europe (from north-eastern Spain to the Adriatic domains of the Republic of Venice), and also across much of central Europe, real estate, recorded in property records with broadly similar features (called *estimes* in Catalonia, *cadastres* in France, *estimi* or *catasti* in Italy and similarly elsewhere), was the main basis of direct taxation. As such, real estate can serve as the minimum common denominator in what can or cannot be observed of household wealth in different preindustrial settings (the main variation being the inclusion or not in the records of capital invested in trades and in entrepreneurial or artisanal activities: what in Italy was usually called the *capitale dell'arte* or 'capital of the art'). A growing literature about long-term trends in the distribution of wealth has clarified the virtues and limitations of these sources. Among the virtues, the high comparability across time and space must definitely be mentioned, as well as the fact that, as argued in the 'Defining Wealth across the Ages' section of this chapter, these sources provide fairly complete and reliable information about what was by far the *main* component of wealth (additionally, as previously argued, the distribution of real estate appears to be strongly correlated with the distribution of movable wealth).

The main limitation of the *estimi* is, frequently, the entire absence of the propertyless, defined as those households which did not own any taxable property. However, even households with tiny properties, like a small orchard or a fraction of a vineyard, were recorded. This is why, in the relatively exceptional cases when the propertyless are included in the *estimi*, they are found to be very few: 3–7 per cent of all households. In practice, this means that inequality levels measured on the complete wealth distribution, or on the distribution excluding the propertyless, will be very similar (the measures including the propertyless will tend to suggest a slightly higher overall inequality than those that include them). The quantitative measures used in this book to analyse the rich, like the wealth shares of top percentiles, are even more robust to the presence of small issues at the bottom of the distribution, and some numerical examples will be provided in chapter 2. Given that the *estimi* tended to change little across time,[24] they allow us to reconstruct very long time series of quantitative indicators, dating back to the early fourteenth century in the luckiest instances and continuing until the mid-eighteenth century or even the early nineteenth, when the spread across Europe of the so-called modern *cadastre* system basically interrupts the series.[25]

While property tax records are by far the kind of historical source most used in recent studies of preindustrial inequality, they are generally quite rare or entirely unavailable for northern European areas. For the Low Countries, a historical source which has been used systematically by studies of inequality are the records of the rental value of the house in which each household resided. However, based on the current literature, the distribution of the houses' rental values reflects the distribution of income more closely than that of wealth (although admittedly, in a preindustrial context, the two can be expected to be highly correlated), and so it is not very useful for our purposes. Consequently, for the Low Countries we have to rely on more sporadically available sources, which provide us with information about the distribution of land and, as such, are fairly comparable to the sources used for southern and central Europe.[26]

Another northern area which stands out in a broader European comparison is England. There, from 1207, direct taxes (the 'lay subsidies') were levied on movable wealth, including coin and circulating capital, household furnishings, livestock and so on. The English system of fiscal levy of the central state was an exceptionally 'unified' one by the standards of medieval Europe. From circa 1290 on, these sources have survived for a good number of English counties, making it possible to explore the distribution of wealth in the decades immediately preceding the Black Death plague, which reached the British Isles in the summer of 1348. Other sources with broadly comparable characteristics exist for the early sixteenth century, particularly the 'Tudor subsidies' of 1524–5. Interestingly, these sixteenth-century sources calculated the expected fiscal revenue from three alternative tax bases: the lands, the wages and the movable goods. Each household was taxed on the base which ensured the highest revenue to the state. The vast majority of households were taxed on movable goods (up to 88% in Warwickshire) and just a small minority on lands (3.3% in Warwickshire, but the observed minimum, 0.8%, relates to Dorset). Usually, only the highest revenue was recorded so that for each household we have the evaluation of only one of the three bases. But in some very exceptional cases, like that of the Three Hundreds of Aylesbury in the county of Buckinghamshire, the evaluation of land is quite systematically provided alongside that of movable wealth. The correlation between the two distributions is found to be almost perfect, which is why, while for most of continental Europe we can take the distribution of real estate as an acceptable proxy for total wealth (real estate plus movables), for England we can take movable wealth for the same purpose.[27]

A major limitation of both the lay subsidies and the Tudor subsidies is that the bar for fiscal exemption was set at a relatively high level, and households below the bar were not recorded. In the worst cases (and systematically for the medieval lay subsidies) this can lead to the loss of more than half the overall population, so that specific statistical techniques have to be adopted to infer from the observed portion of the distribution some indication about the whole of society. An additional problem is that after 1524–5, the usefulness of the lay subsidies for a study such as ours quickly declines, as the records become increasingly unreliable. A new fiscal system introduced in 1662 also proves quite unsuitable for exploring the distribution of wealth, as the new 'hearth taxes' required each household to pay a fixed sum for every chimney located in the place where they lived.[28]

Given the intrinsic difficulties of using English fiscal sources to study how wealth was distributed, sources of other kinds might be considered. In particular, probate inventories (which result from the judicial process through which a will is accepted as the legal testament of the deceased) could allow us to sample the non-realty wealth of large strata of the population, and, at least in the case of England, they could be used to cover the entirety of the early modern period. So far, the best such attempt has been made by economic historian Peter Lindert, who used probates (plus clues as to the ownership of realty, that is, of real estate) to estimate the wealth shares of the richest 1 per cent and 5 per cent in England and Wales from 1670 to 1875.[29] Probates have also been used to estimate wealth inequality in the United States in 1774, on the eve of the Revolutionary War.[30] More recently, they have been used to reconstruct the wealth distribution of Scandinavian countries—namely, Sweden and Finland—in 1750–1900.[31] Although probates are clearly a very promising avenue for future research, they also have some obvious limitations. Firstly, producing acceptable national samples of probates, especially for early modern times, requires a vast amount of archival research. Secondly, and most importantly, such samples will never provide a coverage of the population (at the local or national level) as complete as that which, at least in principle, could be obtained from property tax records. A major problem is that probates 'present specific challenges related to sampling—as . . . they often reflect the richest part of the population far better than the poorest, and require assumptions about mortality rates by age, sex and socio-economic status to move from the distribution of wealth of those dying in a given period to the hypothetical distributions characterising living cohorts in earlier periods.'[32]

An advantage that probates do have over property tax records is that of allowing us to seamlessly connect the eighteenth century to the nineteenth: a particularly important period, as it saw the onset of industrialization across the West. For the nineteenth century, a better alternative is represented by the estate tax (or inheritance tax[33]), at least for countries where it was introduced precociously and where it had universal or almost universal coverage, such as France, where it was established by the revolutionary National Assembly in 1791 and has remained in place ever since. For this reason, France is currently the Western country for which we have the best and most systematic information about the wealth share and the composition of the rich during the nineteenth century.[34] Unfortunately, other countries introduced a universal estate tax much later. The United Kingdom did so in 1894 and the United States only in 1916. Italy was more precocious, introducing it in 1862, immediately after national unification (some pre-unification states had already been following the French model for a few decades). The spread of the estate tax from the late nineteenth century and the summary tabulations that were often compiled by the state administration based on individual declarations help to significantly expand the availability of good-quality data for the most recent periods. Although it remains very far from being universal, the information about wealth inequality and top wealth shares that we have for the twentieth century is vastly superior to the scattering of information available for the nineteenth.[35] Moreover, for the most recent period, there are excellent international databases, constantly checked and updated, which we can rely upon to provide most of the needed estimates. In particular, for the twentieth and twenty-first centuries, the *World Inequality Database* (WID) has been used,[36] with some integrations (for the most recent period) from the yearly *Global Wealth Databooks* (GWD) and additional scholarly works for specific countries.[37] For this reason, and also due to the availability of excellent surveys of the information on wealth distribution available for the twentieth century, the sources for this most recent period will not be discussed further—with one exception: rich lists.[38]

Before briefly discussing the rich lists, a couple of further clarifications are needed. First of all, there might be a concern regarding the unit of observation. Medieval and early modern property taxes, like most other wealth taxes (including modern ones) and most recent survey-based estimates of the wealth distribution (which are conducted for statistical purposes), have the household as their unit of wealth assessment. In contrast, probate and estate taxes concern individual wealth. As most of the data available for long-term analyses of the wealth distribution concerns households, this will be the preferred unit of analysis in this book (there is also a theoretical justification for this preference: all household members can benefit from the property, such as real estate, formally owned by just one of them). When only information about individual wealth is available, this will be clearly spelled out. The ensuing partial dishomogeneity in the data is dictated by the sources and, as such, it is a well-known feature of many comparative studies of wealth distribution. This being said, in practice, top wealth shares calculated on distributions of households or individuals tend to offer fairly similar contrasts—for example, in Sweden and the United States during the twentieth century.[39]

Another general concern with *all* fiscal sources from any country and epoch is the level of tax avoidance and evasion. This is invariably difficult to quantify, although some of the components of wealth, and particularly the main one in a preindustrial setting (real estate), are relatively difficult to hide or to dramatically misevaluate. In preindustrial times, in all those instances (which prevailed in southern and central Europe) when a fixed fiscal burden was distributed by each community proportionally to the tax assessment, there was a high degree of social and administrative control over the fairness of the evaluations: open revolt could erupt locally in the face of perceived injustice in the distribution of the burden. Arguably, the opportunity for wealth tax evasion and avoidance has tended to increase from the nineteenth century on—for example, because in the current global economy it has become easier to hide movable wealth by means of tax havens or other methods. Another relevant factor is that, when the amount of tax due from each household or individual is set directly by the tax administration of the central state, the social control over what *other* households or individuals are required to pay will tend to weaken, due to a weaker perception of the link between one's allotted tax and what has been paid by others. For the purposes of this book, tax evasion and avoidance can be presumed to have only a limited impact on the quantitative evidence presented—but at the same time, the possibility that the richest strata of society have more opportunity to escape taxation, including by means of strategic giving or charity, will be properly discussed (particularly in chapters 9 and 10).[40]

The information coming from fiscal sources and wealth surveys will be integrated with that from the so-called rich lists. Most (but not all) such lists are produced by important newspapers or magazines. Internationally, the best and most comprehensive rich list is *Forbes' The World's Billionaires* list, published yearly (the historical collection is available to researchers as the *Forbes* Billionaires Database, which covers the period from 2001 until today; the last year considered for this study is 2021). Nationally, some well-established lists include those published yearly by *The Sunday Times* for Britain and by the *Manager Magazin* for Germany; *Forbes* also publishes a national list for the United States, the *Forbes 400*. However, the *Forbes 400* is a less comprehensive list than *The World's Billionaires*, as the entry point is higher—in 2021, the poorest Americans in the *Forbes 400* were worth 2.9 billion dollars each. For the United States, some nineteenth-century rich lists also exist and can be used, for example, the list of 'millionaires' published by the *New-York Tribune* in 1892. These lists provide useful information about the characteristics of those placed at the very top of the wealth pyramid and so are potentially useful in fleshing out certain analyses; in this book they will be used to discuss the composition of the super-rich regarding the origin and nature of their wealth (inherited or self-made; coming from industry/commerce, finance or real estate and so on).

Admittedly, data from rich lists have many limitations, the main ones being the difficulties in identifying those who should be included based on public records and the high degree of guesswork that unavoidably goes into the evaluation of their assets.[41] Despite these limitations, rich lists (whose quality appears to have improved over time) are increasingly recognized as a useful source of information for social science research. This is even more clearly the case for those rich lists which have been pieced together by scholars based on archival evidence, such as economic historian William D. Rubinstein's *Biographical Directory of British Wealth-Holders*, a multi-volume *magnum opus* that, once completed, will include all the British people who died between 1808 and 1914 and left at least 100,000 pounds. These and other scholarly lists will be used both for the quantitative analyses presented in chapter 7 and to provide qualitative evidence in other parts of the book, together with a range of other historical sources (personal letters, chronicles, household budgets and so on) which could not be discussed in detail here. The time has come, in fact, to apply definitions to sources and to provide a first overview of how many in history were rich and how large their share of wealth was.[42]

2

Wealth Concentration and the Prevalence of the Rich across History

AN OVERVIEW

ALL HUMAN SOCIETIES, from prehistory through today, have been characterized by some degree of economic inequality. Arguably, complex societies would not even exist if they had been unable to concentrate and redistribute resources. In the early stages of human civilization, the ability to achieve more—to dig a network of irrigation canals in Mesopotamia's 'fertile crescent' and thus improve land productivity for all farmers, for example—went hand-in-hand with growing inequality. Therefore, it is obvious that somebody will loom above all others in terms of wealth and overall access to resources. The real historical question, and also a possible cause for concern today, is how great a share was this economic elite able to concentrate in its hands? The historical evidence currently available suggests that wealth concentration is a continuous process that has progressed almost without pause from ancient Babylon to the Middle Ages through to today. And the pauses that did occur have the troubling feature of being triggered by some of the most devastating catastrophes in human history, like the Black Death in the fourteenth century or the World Wars in the twentieth. This chapter provides an overview of the information about wealth concentration in the long run which has recently become available, integrating it with new evidence. Building upon the definition of the 'rich' discussed in chapter 1, we begin by looking at the wealth share owned by the top 1 per cent and 5 per cent. The general reported trends are briefly discussed in the light of the ongoing debate about the causes of changing inequality in human history. The final section of the chapter takes a different approach, defining the rich not as a fixed percentile at the top of the wealth distribution, nor as those above a specific wealth threshold, but based on their position relative to the median of the distribution. This allows us to ask different questions: how many across history were rich (at least ten times the median)? And did their prevalence change together with overall wealth inequality? The evidence presented and discussed here provides the basis upon which, in the second and third parts of the book, the main historical paths towards affluence and the changing position of the rich in society will be explored.

From the Black Death (and Earlier) to the American Revolution

Recent research has explored inequality in so-called primitive societies, from prehistory to the few surviving tribes of hunter-gatherers. Even these relatively simple societies, living just above mere subsistence levels, were economically unequal. Wealth concentration, through the inheritance system, was key to reproducing and deepening inequality across generations, a constant feature of human history which was only strengthened by the introduction of agriculture, leading to a greater relative importance of material wealth (and especially land and cattle) over other, less inheritable components. Thereafter, inequality deepened further in association with the development of early governmental institutions and the appearance of the first states.[1] Our ability to observe and to measure ancient inequality improves somewhat when we reach the Classical Age. In Roman-dominated areas wealth concentration seems to have increased steadily from the second century BCE to the first century CE, a period during which the size of the largest fortunes rose by a factor of 80, from 4–5 million to 300–400 million sesterces. At the time of Emperor Nero (who reigned from 54 to 68 CE), six men were said to have owned about half of the province of Africa, roughly corresponding to present-day Tunisia and the coast of Libya—at least before the emperor had their properties confiscated. The richest man of the period, however, was probably Marcus Antonius Pallas, an ex-slave of Greek origins who rose to top positions in the imperial government, serving as secretary of the treasury under Nero as well as under his predecessor, Emperor Claudius. According to the Roman historian Tacitus, Pallas's personal wealth amounted to 300 million sesterces, significantly more than the 250 million owned by the imperial household at the time of Augustus (and maybe of Nero as well, until the emperor rectified the ranking by ordering that Pallas be poisoned and acquiring much of his fortune) and the 200 million owned by Marcus Licinius Crassus, who in the late Republic was considered to be fabulously wealthy and who in 60 BCE joined forces with Julius Caesar and Gnaeus Pompeius to form the First Triumvirate, in a bid to transform his vast wealth into political pre-eminence. According to an estimate, the yearly income generated by Crassus's fortune was sufficient to command the work of 32,000 average Romans.[2]

Measuring wealth concentration properly for prehistory and the Classical Age is complicated by the limitations posed by the surviving documentary and archaeological sources; in fact, no measures of overall wealth inequality or of the share owned by the top percentiles are currently available.[3] The first good-quality estimates we have, at least for a few areas, date to the Middle Ages and are based on property tax records, as discussed in chapter 1. Italy is probably the European area with the best documentation for the earlier periods, and it is not by chance that much research has focused on some of the Italian pre-unification states. The Florentine State, which covered most of present-day Tuscany, is one of the few areas for which we have information pre-dating the Black Death plague of 1347–52. Around 1300, on the eve of the pandemic, in the city of Prato the top 1 per cent owned 29.2 per cent of the overall wealth, while if we extend the analysis to the top 5 per cent, the share of the rich was 55.3 per cent—more than the poorest 95 per cent of the population. Wealth inequality was somewhat lower in rural communities. For example, in the village of Poggibonsi, the top 1 per cent and 5 per cent owned 19.9 per cent and 39.2 per cent of all wealth respectively. In another Italian area, the Sabaudian State (roughly corresponding to present-day Piedmont), the estimated pre-plague share of the top 1 per cent was 22.3 per cent, and 47.4 per cent for the top 5 per cent, in urban settings. To place these measures in context, in Italy as a whole in 2020 the top 1 per cent owned 22.2 per cent of all wealth, and the top 5 per cent had as much as 40.4 per cent.[4]

In Italy, and probably across most of Europe, wealth concentration today is not very different from the period preceding the Black Death. This is an interesting finding per se; it suggests that contemporary societies cannot be presumed to be less unequal than medieval ones. But it should not hide the long-term fluctuations that occurred in the share of the rich. The Black Death itself caused one of two such swings that have been reported for the last thousand years (as will be seen, the decline and fall of the Roman Empire appears to have triggered an earlier, and comparably large, swing). The plague, which returned to Europe in 1347 after about six centuries of absence, was a momentous event not only for the resulting mortality (it killed between one-quarter and one-half of the population of Europe and the Mediterranean), but also because it had vast consequences for human history.[5] Among them, we must include wealth and income redistribution on a vast scale. This was found in all areas for which we have information about pre-plague wealth inequality. In Piedmontese cities, in the immediate post-plague years the share of the top 1 per cent had declined by more than 5 percentage points. The urban one-percenters suffered even more in Tuscan cities, where in the same period the drop exceeded 18 percentage points. The fall in the share of the rich grows if we consider the top 5 per cent, who released their grip on almost 8 per cent of the overall wealth in Piedmont and on over 23 per cent in Tuscany.

Something similar happened in the other areas for which we have information for such an early period, like southern France. In the city of Toulouse, the top 1 per cent owned 24 per cent of the overall wealth in 1335, but their share was just 10.8 per cent in 1398. Between the two years, the decline in the share of the top 5 per cent was even more dramatic: from 52.7 per cent to just 29.8 per cent. We also have some hints about a decline in income inequality, particularly in the Low Countries. Overall, a decline in inequality after the Black Death is something we should expect, given that we know from other sources that it triggered a phase of rising real wages. This led to a reduction not only in income inequality, but also in wealth inequality, as higher real wages gave a larger share of the population the means to acquire property in a context in which there was much more real estate than usual on the market, in part due to the patrimonial fragmentation induced by mass mortality, leading to cheaper prices.[6] The decline in inequality continued in the following decades, as seen in Figure 2.1 where the long-run (1300 to 1800) wealth inequality trends for a range of Italian pre-unification states are compared to those of Germany and England. As an example, take Germany. There, the shares of the richest 5 per cent and 1 per cent declined significantly from 1350 to 1450 (from 41% to 35.1% and from 21% to 16.8% respectively). Unfortunately, we do not have pre-Black Death information about the wealth distribution in Germany, but it is entirely reasonable to assume that, like in Italy and France, wealth inequality had been much higher before the pandemic.[7]

As a consequence of this long, plague-induced phase of declining inequality, by the first half of the fifteenth century much of Europe seems to have experienced an exceptionally low level of wealth inequality, surely much lower than anything that would follow. As is shown graphically in Figure 2.1, from the

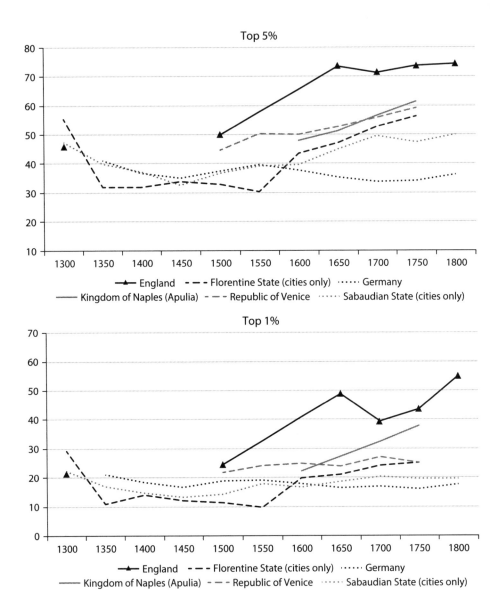

FIGURE 2.1. Long-term trends in the wealth share of the rich, 1300–1800.
Notes: For England, the figures concern movable wealth only until 1500 and
total wealth thereafter. For all other areas, the figures are based on property
tax records (see chapter 1 for further discussion).

sixteenth to the eighteenth century the growth in the share of the top 5 per cent was almost monotonic everywhere (except Germany: see below). The same is true for the top 1 per cent, although in some areas the growth in the share of the richest seems to slow down during the eighteenth century. If we focus on the longest time series, we find that in both the Sabaudian State and the Florentine State the share of the richest 5 per cent reached pre-plague levels only in the eighteenth century, and the share of the richest 1 per cent reached pre-plague levels even later. Overall, a tendency for wealth inequality to grow throughout the early modern period is to be found also in a range of communities spread across Spain and southern France. The only (partial) exception to this trend is Germany, which during the seventeenth century experienced a second phase of declining inequality, as a consequence of the devastating Thirty Years' War (1618–48) and of the terrible plague of 1627–9: a very specific situation which affected the German rich badly, as is discussed in detail in chapter 11.[8]

Compared to the centre and the south, the information currently available for the north of Europe is more limited, mostly due to differences in taxation systems. The case which has been studied most thoroughly is that of England, thanks to the pioneering works on early modern probates by economic historian Peter Lindert as well as some recent research based on the abundant fiscal sources available from the late thirteenth to the early sixteenth century.[9] If we assume that the earlier estimates, which reflect movable wealth, can be meaningfully connected to the later ones, which reflect total wealth (net worth), then it is possible to hypothesize that in England too the wealth share of the rich increased considerably in the first centuries of the early modern period. The increase continued, although at a reduced pace, during the eighteenth century. This trend is especially clear for the one-percenters, whose wealth share was 24.1 per cent around 1500 (it had been 21.5% circa 1300), doubled to 48.9 per cent by 1650 and finally reached 54.9 per cent by the end of the eighteenth century. While until the beginning of early modern times wealth inequality in England was relatively high but comparable to that of Italy and Germany, from the seventeenth century on it stands out as systematically the highest by far.

The difference between England and the continental European areas discussed above has two possible explanations (or a combination of them): one technical and one historical. The technical explanation has to do with dishomogeneity in the kind of wealth being considered and in the population coverage of the estimates. First, 'wealth' in the Italian and German estimates is basically real estate (lands and buildings—the 'immovables'), which was by far the main component of wealth in a preindustrial context but was not the only determinant of net worth and by definition did not coincide with movable wealth. This being said, based on the available information, the distribution of land and that of movable wealth were highly correlated, which suggests not only that they are directly comparable but that, even taken singularly, their distribution can be considered roughly indicative of that of total wealth. Chapter 1 offered supporting evidence and further discussion of this point, as well as of the second technical difference in the estimates: population coverage. The figures for England have been produced in such a way that they reflect all the households of the country, while those for Italy and Germany have been standardized by removing the propertyless. As the propertyless are the zeroes in the distribution, excluding them automatically lowers the estimated wealth share of the top percentiles. While this distortion can undoubtedly explain part of the reported difference between England and the other areas, the propertyless were few, usually 3 to 7 per cent of all households; therefore the distortion is limited. In the case of Germany, for which we also have estimates available of the top shares which include the propertyless, in 1500 (when the propertyless were 2% of all households) adding them to the distribution leads to an increase of the wealth share of the top 1 per cent from 18.8 per cent to 19 per cent and of the top 5 per cent from 37.5 per cent to 37.7 per cent, while in 1800 (when the propertyless were a more substantial 7.3% of all households) adding them increases the wealth share of the top 1 per cent from 17.6 per cent to 17.9 per cent and that of the top 5 per cent from 36.3 per cent to 36.7 per cent.[10]

Based on the above, it seems reasonable to presume that dishomogeneity in the underlying data could explain only a small part of the substantial differences in measured inequality between England and Italy or Germany. The historical explanation is maybe more promising, as it is based on the relative levels of development (hence, of overall wealth) of these areas. According to the most recent reconstructions, already by the beginning of the eighteenth century the English per-capita GDP had overcome that of central-northern Italy and of Germany, and the gap tended to increase as the Industrial Revolution unfolded. In principle, a higher per-capita GDP allows for the inegalitarian redistribution of resources on a larger scale. This is because in a normal situation everybody must be guaranteed the minimum to survive, which places a cap on the percentage of total resources that can be concentrated in the hands of the few. This is the reasoning behind the recently introduced 'inequality extraction ratio' approach. While this concept refers to income, it also has implications for wealth distribution as, in time, income inequality will produce wealth inequality through the mechanism of saving and inheritance, as discussed in chapter 6. Eighteenth-century England, then, might have been more unequal than continental Europe simply because *it was wealthy enough to afford it.* Another way of looking at this is to consider that the exceptional economic dynamism shown by this country from the time of its Atlantic commercial expansion and from the onset of the Industrial Revolution offered plenty of opportunities to daring individuals to grow rich and to the already-wealthy to become wealthier still. These processes of relatively easy personal enrichment also led to relatively high wealth shares of the top percentiles.[11]

Beyond England, we only have scattered information for northern Europe. In particular, for the southern Low Countries (roughly corresponding to present-day Belgium) in the early modern period, a range of case studies suggest levels of wealth concentration analogous to those found in central-northern Italy, with a long-run tendency towards inequality growth.[12] For Scotland in 1770 we have an approximate estimate of 27 per cent for the wealth share of the one-percenters (real estate only), which is again in line with central-northern Italy. For Sweden in 1750 a recent estimate places it at 43 per cent, which instead is comparable to England, but Finland is highest of all at 63.2 per cent (for both Sweden and Finland the figures refer to net worth).[13] Finally, beyond Europe, we have an estimate of wealth inequality in America in 1774, on the eve of the Revolution. In the territories of what would soon become the United States, the richest 1 per cent owned 16.5 per cent of the overall wealth, while the richest 5 per cent had about 41.1 per cent. It is an interesting historical fact that, in this early phase, America was much less unequal than most European countries. The relative positions would invert during the twentieth century.[14]

Wealth Concentration in the Modern Age

The tendency of growing wealth concentration that has been reported for the early modern period continued during the nineteenth century. According to all accounts and based on the data currently available, wealth inequality reached its historical maximum on the eve of World War I. In France—the country whose wealth distribution during the nineteenth century has been researched most thoroughly—in the immediate pre-war years the share of the top 1 per cent oscillated in the range of 54–56 per cent, at least 10 percentage points more than in 1807 (the first year for which we have information) when it amounted to 44.4 per cent. In the early twentieth century, a continental European country like France was still characterized by a considerably more uneven distribution of wealth than the United States. In 1913, the richest 1 per cent of Americans owned 46.6 per cent of all wealth or about as much as the richest Frenchmen had owned a century earlier. Indeed, in that year, the United States was characterized by a less uneven wealth distribution than almost all European countries: the share of the top 1 per cent is reported to have been 66.6 per cent in the United Kingdom in 1913, 56.5 per cent in the Netherlands in 1914 and 53.8 per cent in Sweden in 1908. Among the European countries for which we have information, only Norway was characterized by less wealth concentration at the top (the richest 1% had a share of 37.2% in 1912). However, the most egalitarian situation has been reported for the other northern American country, Canada, where in 1902 the richest 1 per cent had 36.4 per cent of all wealth (an estimate that refers to the Ontario area only).[15]

North America, then, continued to stand out for its relatively egalitarian situation, as it had done on the eve of the Revolution, a picture confirmed by Table 2.1. However, during the nineteenth century, American inequality was also on the rise. In the United States the share of the top 1 per cent was 26.7 per cent in 1870, considerably less than the 46.6 per cent reported for 1913 but much more than the 16.5 per cent estimated for 1774. Unfortunately, no in-between estimates are available, but it seems safe to presume that the overall secular trend was orientated towards a growing concentration of wealth in the hands of the rich. If we connect the three dates linearly, we get the tendency shown in Figure 2.2, which also makes it clear how the inequality gap between the United States and France tended to decline over time as a consequence of slower inequality growth in the latter. A tendency for inequality to grow similarly to that in America was found in some other European countries for which we have information, like Sweden. But it was in the United Kingdom that nineteenth-century wealth concentration was the highest, continuing a tendency already seen in the data for the eighteenth century: the wealth share of the top 1 per cent was 54.9 per cent in 1810, 61.1 per cent in 1875 and 70.7 per cent in 1900.[16]

The two World Wars, and the troubled period between them, led to a very significant decline in the share of wealth owned by the richest across Western countries. This can be seen both in Figure 2.2 (note the somewhat different trend followed by Sweden, which stayed neutral during World War I and where the decline in inequality intensified only from the mid-1930s) and in Table 2.1. There, for Canada, the United States and a selection of European countries— including all those for which we have information since the nineteenth or early

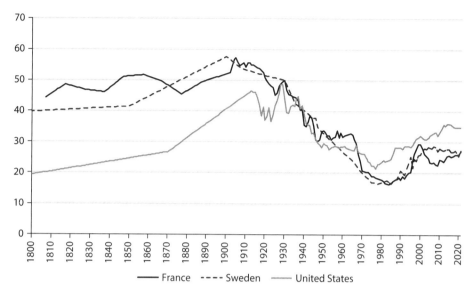

FIGURE 2.2. The share of wealth of the top 1 per cent in France, Sweden and the United States, 1800–2021.

twentieth century—the shares of the top 1 per cent and 5 per cent are provided every fifty years from 1850 to 2000, as well as 2020. So, for example, between 1900 and 1950 the richest 1 per cent released their grip on 27.7 per cent of the overall wealth in the United Kingdom. While this was the country characterized by the largest reduction in wealth inequality, almost everywhere the richest 1 per cent lost 16–20 per cent of the overall wealth (only Canada and Norway, which were relatively egalitarian to begin with, and neutral Switzerland experienced a less intense process of equalizing relative wealth). This, however, was due more to the damage suffered by large patrimonies (war hyper-inflation and the stock-market crashes of the 1920s destroyed financial capital; the wars, and especially World War II, significantly affected physical capital; many overseas properties and investments were lost) than to a trickling of wealth from the top downwards (see the next section for further discussion). Interestingly, the interwar period is also the moment when the United States finally caught up with continental European levels of wealth inequality.[17]

After the end of World War II and for thirty years or so, wealth inequality (and also income inequality) remained relatively low, and in many cases it fell even further, especially in continental Europe. This came to an end from the late 1970s/early 1980s, partly as a consequence of tax reforms across Western

TABLE 2.1. Share of the Top 1 Per Cent and 5 Per Cent in Europe and North America, 1850–2020 (Net Household Wealth. Data Clustered around Fifty-Year Breakpoints, with Actual Year—if Different from Breakpoint—in Parentheses)

	Top 1 Per Cent						Top 5 Per Cent					
	1800	1850	1900	1950	2000	2020	1800	1850	1900	1950	2000	2020
Europe												
Denmark			46.3 (1908)	29.6	27.2 (1996)	23.5			78.0 (1908)	56	53 (1996)	43
Finland	68.9	74.4	50.2	19.4 (1967)	21.2	28.5	85.2	89.2	76.1	46.8 (1967)	40.2	48
France	44.4 (1807)	51.1 (1847)	52.5 (1902)	33.7	29.3	22.1						41.8
Germany	17.6		46.7 (1899)	22.8 (1953)	14 (2002)	29.1	36.3				36 (2002)	50.4
Italy	32.7				17.2	22.2	66.7				36.4	40.4
Netherlands			54.0 (1894)	34.0 (1951)	22.2	20.4			79.0 (1894)	60.0 (1951)	43.6	40.5

Norway	39.7	41.5	37.2 (1912)	34.6 (1948)	19.6	27.7			69.2 (1912)	62.4 (1948)	37	48
Sweden			57.6 (1913)	32.8	21.9	34.9*	61.6	66.8	76.4	60.6	44.4	59.6
Switzerland			46.7 (1913)	37.8 (1949)	34.8 (1997)	28			73.6 (1913)	65.7	58 (1997)	51
United Kingdom**	54.9 (1810)	61.1 (1875)	70.7	43	18.5	23.1	74.3 (1810)	74.1 (1875)			30.0	43
North America												
Canada			36.4 (1902)	28.7	22.9 (1999)	23.8			65.1 (1902)		42.3 (2005)	43.6
United States	16.5 (1774)	26.7*** (1870)	46.6 (1913)	29.6	32	35.3	41.1 (1774)	49.4*** (1870)			57.7 (2001)	63.2

Notes: (*) For Sweden in 2020, the estimates of the wealth share of the top 1 per cent from the *Global Wealth Databook* (GWD) are much higher than those from the *World Inequality Database* (WID): 34.9 per cent versus 25.5 per cent. GWD is preferred here because WDI does not provide estimates of the wealth share of the top 5 per cent, while WID is used for Figure 2.2. (**) For the United Kingdom during 1900–2000 the figures refer to individual wealth, not household wealth. (***) Measure referring to gross wealth.

countries (see the next section). This is also when a difference seems to emerge in distributive dynamics between English-speaking countries and other Western countries. The point has been convincingly made that, if we look at the income share of the top 1 per cent, English-speaking countries followed a 'U-shaped' curve during the twentieth century, with the income share of the top 1 per cent growing quickly after 1980 (it rose by about 135% in the United States and the United Kingdom in 1980–2007), finally reaching or coming close to pre–World War I levels. In contrast, continental European countries followed an 'L-shaped' path, with a much lower tendency for income inequality to grow, at least until circa 2010.[18] A similar difference in distributive dynamics also seems to characterize wealth, at least if we focus on the United States, which, by 2000, when the richest 1 per cent owned 32 per cent of the overall wealth, was more unequal than any continental European country except for Switzerland. However, the same is not true for other English-speaking countries, such as Canada and the United Kingdom, where the richest 1 per cent owned 22.9 per cent and 18.5 per cent of the overall wealth: a middling level relative to the Western standards of that time. Indeed, they were much more 'egalitarian' compared to France, where the top 1 per cent owned 29.3 per cent of the overall wealth, although they were considerably more unequal than either Germany or Italy, where such shares reached 14 per cent and 17.2 per cent, respectively. The same conclusions could be reached by extending the analysis to the top 5 per cent (see Table 2.1). The relatively unequal situation of the United States is confirmed by looking at more recent estimates, as in 2020 the richest 1 per cent owned 35.3 per cent of all wealth, while the richest 5 per cent had 63.2 per cent. Almost everywhere, though, the share of the richest increased significantly between 2000 and 2020, in spite of the financial crisis of 2007–8 and the ensuing Great Recession. Indeed, the resilience of the rich during the most recent crises (including that caused by COVID-19) is impressive and will be discussed in detail in chapters 5 and 11.

To a large degree, American exceptionalism comes from its relative abundance of super-rich citizens and, as such, it is also apparent when focusing on increasingly smaller percentiles of the wealth distribution, like the top 0.1 per cent and 0.01 per cent. Unfortunately, wealth shares of this kind are available for very few countries. Figure 2.3 compares the United States with those countries for which we have the longest time series: Denmark and Norway. We find, again, an inversion in the relative positions, with the United States becoming the most unequal in the group from the late 1950s, which contributed to the creation of a U-shaped path which is even more clearly visible than when look-

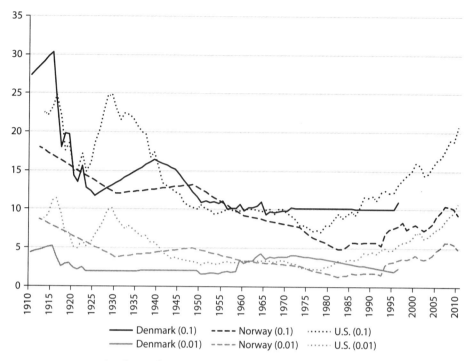

FIGURE 2.3. The share of wealth of the top 0.1 per cent and 0.01 per cent in Denmark, Norway and the United States, 1910–2010.

ing at the top 1 per cent or 5 per cent. Indeed, in the United States in 1914 the richest 1 per cent owned 44.1 per cent of all wealth, while the richest 0.01 per cent had 9.2 per cent. By 1980, those shares had declined sharply, to 24.3 per cent and 2.6 per cent respectively—which means that of the 20 percentage points of the overall wealth lost by the top 1 per cent, about one-third relates only to the top 0.01 per cent. However, if the richest of the rich were the chief 'victims' of the decline in wealth concentration in the first part of the twentieth century, they were in turn the main beneficiaries of the growing inequality in the distribution of material resources that started in the 1980s and continues today. By 2010, the wealth share of the richest 0.01 per cent of Americans was, at 10.8 per cent, more than double that found in Norway (4.9%). A few years earlier, in 2005, it had been 7.4 per cent, versus 4.7 per cent in Norway, 3.7 per cent in Sweden and 1.4 per cent in Spain.[19]

As a conclusion to this overview of long-term dynamics in wealth concentration, it is useful to recall that although Western countries have become more and more unequal in recent decades, wealth concentration is found to be even higher if we take a global perspective. In 2020, across Europe the richest 1 per cent and 5 per cent owned 29.4 per cent and 52.7 per cent of all wealth, respectively, while across North America such figures rose to 34.8 per cent and 62.1 per cent. But looking at the world population as a whole, the richest 1 per cent were found to own almost half of the overall wealth (44.9%), rising to 70.1 per cent for the richest 5 per cent.[20]

Why Does Wealth Concentration (Almost) Always Grow?

If we connect the long-term trends that have been reconstructed for some areas with the evidence available for the last two centuries, we get the clear impression that, in the long run of history, wealth inequality has tended to grow almost continuously. In the last seven centuries or more, a significant decline in wealth inequality—reflected in the shrinking of the share of the richest 1 per cent—can be detected only after large-scale catastrophes, especially the Black Death in the fourteenth century and the two World Wars in the twentieth. This is clearly visible in Figure 2.4, where the overall trend characterizing medieval and early modern Italy is continued by the European 'average' estimated by economist Thomas Piketty for the nineteenth and twentieth centuries using data on France, Sweden and the United Kingdom. The case of the United Kingdom is also singled out, as some information is available for the early modern period as well, while North America is represented by the United States. Note that the gap that seems to have existed between Italy and the European average around 1800 (when the share of wealth of the top 1% was 32.7% and 51.4%, respectively) would almost disappear if we considered the share of the richest 10 per cent. According to Piketty, around 1810 the top 10 per cent owned 82 per cent of the overall wealth, while at the endpoint of my estimates for preindustrial Italy, in 1800, the top 10 per cent owned 79 per cent of the overall wealth. The most important finding, though, is that the rate of growth of the share of all top percentiles—1 per cent, 5 per cent or 10 per cent—in Europe during the nineteenth century seems to have been almost exactly the same as that found in Italy in the period 1550–1800.[21]

The impressive continuity in the long-term tendency for inequality to grow raises many interesting questions about its causes. It would be impossible to provide an exhaustive account here of the current debates about the deep causes of long-term wealth (and income) inequality growth. A brief survey will suffice to provide some useful background information.[22] Some of the factors mentioned here will be developed in detail in other chapters, with a

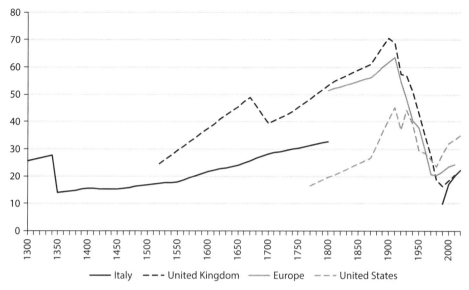

FIGURE 2.4. The share of wealth of the top 1 per cent in Europe, 1300–2020.
Notes: the series 'Italy' is an average of the Sabaudian State, the Florentine State, the Kingdom of Naples (Apulia) and the Republic of Venice (the estimates have been adjusted to include those with no property). Before 1500, only information about the Florentine State and the Sabaudian State is available. The series 'Europe' is an average of France, the United Kingdom and Sweden. The series 'United Kingdom' refers to England only (plus Wales from 1670) until 1875. Data shown per ten-year intervals.

specific focus on those that are more clearly related to the reported increase in wealth concentration at the very top.

The first aspect to consider is the equalizing power of large-scale catastrophes. Many scholars made this point for the twentieth century, when the World Wars caused wealth inequality to decline, first and foremost, through the destruction of capital (physical and financial), as argued in the earlier section. So the decline of inequality was not primarily the consequence of redistribution from the top to the bottom, but simply of the shrivelling of the wealth of the rich without anybody gaining from their losses. This being said, some redistribution did occur. In Western countries, this was associated with the extension of income tax and with a significant increase in estate tax, together with an overall increase in the progressivity of the fiscal regime (in a 'progressive' fiscal regime, those earning/owning more experience higher effective tax rates than those earning/owning less); I will return later to the crucial issue of taxation. Moreover, war hyper-inflation (including in the years following the end of war itself) was crucial for containing the public debt—but as the public debt had been owned mostly by the richest part of the population (those having capital to invest) this process was akin to 'expropriation by inflation'.[23]

In many respects, the case of the Black Death was entirely different from that of the World Wars. The destruction of physical and financial capital was minimal at most—what was destroyed was human capital. That is, people. This had 'egalitarian' effects, through the mechanisms which have been briefly recalled in the opening section of this chapter, and will be the object of in-depth discussion in chapter 11. The fact that the Black Death reduced inequality was an important discovery of my project *EINITE—Economic Inequality across Italy and Europe 1300–1800*, which reversed the earlier conventional wisdom that suggested an *increase* in wealth inequality after the pandemic.[24] Later, these findings were generalized by historian Walter Scheidel, who argued that in the course of human history—from the collapse of the Roman Empire during the fifth century CE and the disintegration of the Tang dynasty in China in the late ninth century CE, to the World Wars of the twentieth century—only large-scale violence (wars, revolutions, collapse of states or civilizations) and other catastrophes like exceptionally severe epidemics could lead to significant inequality decline.[25] Fortunately however, this interpretation is probably too extreme as it seems to underplay the ability of human beings to shape inequality levels and trends through institutions (especially inheritance and tax systems) which could foster egalitarian redistribution in normal times—although admittedly, depending on their design, institutions could also foster *inegalitarian* redistribution, which was usually the case for preindustrial societies as seen in the following, and even *prevent* catastrophe-induced levelling.[26]

Although Scheidel does point to state-building and the development of an elite controlling political power as drivers of the progressive concentration of wealth across history, his focus appears to be more on the causes of inequality decline than of inequality growth. In a sense, this is also a problem in another recent encompassing explanation of long-term inequality growth: economist Branko Milanović's theory of a historical succession of 'Kuznetsian waves', that is, alternating phases of rising and declining inequality. Of these phases, three would be visible, fully or partially, in Figure 2.4 if we include the current phase of increasing inequality that, in Milanović's view, will one day reverse, generating its own inverted-U. Kuznets's and Kuznets-inspired explanations will be briefly commented upon in the following; however, the problem with the notion of Kuznetsian waves is not whether or not waves occurred—the available historical evidence strongly suggests that they did—but that they were not 'necessary' historical developments. The Black Death occurred by accident, not because of internal developments in the European and Mediterranean economies. Moreover, the presence of phases of inequality decline does not prevent wealth (and income) from becoming ever more concentrated over time. Surely this was not the case in preindustrial times. Around 1800 in Italy, the share of the richest 1 per cent was almost 33 per cent, significantly higher than the pre-Black Death peak of about 23–25 per cent, and the most recent trends suggest that in many countries pre–World War I wealth inequality levels might be reached again in the not too distant future. This seems to be the case for the United States especially, although this is also a consequence of the relatively egalitarian situation that America enjoyed in the early twentieth century.[27]

What, then, are the factors leading to long-term inequality growth? No single factor seems to be able to explain this process in each period and in all areas. A theory that held great sway for a long time was proposed by economist Simon Kuznets in a seminal article dated 1955. He argued that income inequality followed an inverted-U path through the industrialization process (the so-called 'Kuznets curve'), with a rising phase at the beginning of industrialization. This path would be the consequence of economic development and particularly of the transfer of the workforce from a traditional (agrarian) sector to an advanced (industrial) one. Western countries would have experienced inequality growth during the late eighteenth and nineteenth centuries and inequality decline from a certain point during the twentieth century. Kuznets's hypothesis referred to income inequality; however, it can also be applied to wealth. Indeed, many studies of Western areas reported an inverted-U path in wealth inequality during the Industrial Revolution, with a decline from the two World Wars; this is also clearly visible in Figure 2.4. However, if Kuznets's argument still stands as a description of the historical paths followed by inequality in Western countries, its broader implications have now been proven wrong: both if we look at the left-hand side (the long preindustrial period) and at the right-hand side (from circa 1980 until today) of the Kuznets curve.[28]

Regarding preindustrial times, Kuznets seemed to imply that before circa 1800 or 1750 at the earliest, inequality was relatively low and stable over time. However, this was not the case. The first attempt to measure inequality growth for a large area during the early modern period focused on the northern Low Countries (roughly corresponding to the present-day Netherlands) and found evidence of a much longer phase of inequality growth, beginning from the sixteenth century and continuing without pause throughout industrialization.

This phenomenon was first interpreted as the consequence of preindustrial economic growth, an explanation that was 'Kuznetsian' in character.[29] The picture, however, became more complicated as soon as more information about long-term inequality trends, in both income and wealth, became available. For many European regions during the early modern period inequality was also found to grow in phases of economic stagnation or decline. This was the case, for example, in the Sabaudian State in the seventeenth century and the Florentine State, the Republic of Venice, the Kingdom of Naples and the southern Low Countries during the seventeenth and eighteenth centuries. Therefore economic growth, although it might well have favoured inequality growth in certain periods and areas—like the northern Low Countries throughout early modern times—could no longer be accepted as the only explanation for what seemed to be a general process.[30] Many other factors were then considered, from urbanization and demographic growth to the complex social-economic process of the erosion of small ownership usually referred to as 'proletarianization' to institutional change and particularly the rise of the fiscal-military state (see below).

Even if some factors played a general role at least in certain epochs, it is probably wrong to look for a single unifying cause of long-term inequality growth. Instead, in preindustrial times, there was no *necessary* cause of inequality growth, but a number of *sufficient* causes. This means that if one of them was active (even in the absence of all others), inequality tended to increase. These sufficient causes include economic growth, demographic factors, institutional change (increasing regressive fiscal pressure), proletarianization (that is, the crisis of small ownership) and so on. An additional implication of this way of looking at the sources of inequality growth is that in the long preindustrial period it was much easier for inequality to grow than to decline, so inequality growth was able to continue without pause, as per inertia. Indeed, only the aforementioned large-scale catastrophes were able to (temporarily) stop it.

It is beyond the objectives of this chapter to provide an in-depth discussion of all the possible causes of preindustrial inequality growth. One, though, requires some extra attention: the rise of the fiscal-military state, that is, the progressive emergence of the 'modern' state with its deeper capacity and much greater ability to impose taxes on its subjects, chiefly to pay for the ever-increasing costs of war and defence. This process, which intensified markedly from the sixteenth century, was associated with considerable growth in the fiscal burden per capita and involved all European areas independent of their economic conditions, as they all had to play the same game if they were to protect themselves or be able to project power outside their boundaries. The reason why an increase over time of the fiscal burden per capita could lead to further inequality growth is that preindustrial fiscal systems were regressive: the effective tax rates paid by those at the top of society were lower (and considerably so) than those suffered by those at the bottom. This was the consequence of a regime of systematic privilege, enrooted in law and institutions as well as in a culture that favoured nobles over commoners, urban over rural dwellers and so on. With a regressive fiscal regime, post-tax inequality is higher than pre-tax inequality, and the greater the fiscal pressure, the greater the difference between pre- and post-tax distributions. Of course, greater income inequality will also produce, over time, more wealth inequality, by means of saving and investments (see chapter 6); hence the growth in per-capita taxation associated with the rise of the fiscal-military state can be taken as a co-cause of the growth in inequality of both income and wealth.[31]

At some point between the second half of the nineteenth century and the first decades of the twentieth, fiscal systems turned from being regressive and inequality-enhancing overall into being progressive and inequality-reducing. The exact timing is unclear because we lack specific studies of this fundamental transition.[32] As we have seen, we do have hints that fiscal reform ought to be included among the factors leading to inequality decline in the interwar period. Then, during World War II, the progressivity of fiscal systems increased to levels never experienced before or since.[33] More importantly, fiscal redistribution seems to have been a major reason for the lull in inequality growth in the post-war decades. In 1975, the top rate on earned income was 83 per cent in the United Kingdom, 70 per cent in the United States, 72 per cent in Italy, 60 per cent in France, 56 per cent in Germany and 47 per cent in Canada. Twenty-five years later, at the end of a long series of fiscal reforms, the situation was inverted, with a top rate of 61 per cent in France, 60 per cent in Germany, 54 per cent in Canada, 51 per cent in Italy, 48 per cent in the United States and 40 per cent in the United Kingdom. The top rates of estate and inheritance taxes, which directly affect wealth distribution, followed a similar pattern. In 1980, the top rate was 75 per cent in the United Kingdom, 70 per cent in the United States, 35 per cent in Germany and 20 per cent in France, but in 2013 the highest rate was found in France (45%), followed by the United Kingdom (40%), the United States (35%) and Germany (30%). It is not possible to discuss here the reasons for and possible merits of tax reform. What needs to be underlined, though, is that the progressive simplification of the fiscal systems and the reduction in the top rates provided fertile ground for an increase in inequality. In a sense, these fiscal reforms contributed to 'causing' inequality growth, both because they led to less-progressive fiscal systems overall (hence their ability to reduce post-tax inequality declined) and because they favoured behaviours, for example in wage negotiation, that led to increasing within-company wage differentials.[34]

Of course, changes in fiscal regimes were not the only factor leading to growing wealth concentration. The argument against mono-causal explanations that has been proposed for the preindustrial period stands for the modern age, too. In a recent masterful study of American inequality from 1700 until today, economic historians Peter Lindert and Jeff Williamson identified a range of concomitant causes favouring (income) inequality growth from the late 1970s onward, which include, beyond political shifts (leading to the aforementioned tax reforms, as well as to the restricting of the welfare state and so on), skill-based technological change, increasing competition in international trade, growing imbalances in levels of education and the rise of the financial sector. Some of these factors will be explored in the second part of this book. However, in a period like the current one, when fiscal reform and the simplification of the tax structure have again become central to the political debate in many Western countries (from the United States to Italy) but wealth and income inequality are already at historically high levels, it seems important to pay particular attention to the possible distributive impact of changing fiscal systems. This will be a recurring theme throughout the book.[35]

How Many Were Rich across Time?

So far, the wealth shares of the top percentiles have been used to get an impression of the relative position of the rich compared to the rest of society. In fact, when the share of the top 5 per cent or 1 per cent increases, not only does wealth become concentrated in fewer hands, but the wealthy tend to become ever more distant from all others in terms of their overall command of economic and social (and, maybe, political and cultural) resources. And yet, the picture that we get by analysing wealth shares is unavoidably incomplete because, by definition, these indicators do not tell us how many were rich in a given area and period. To explore this other aspect, we can rely upon a different kind of relative definition of the rich: those whose wealth is at least ten times the median level. In principle, the bar for affluence could be placed even higher (say, fifty times the median), but our chosen threshold has the useful characteristic of bringing, for most of the period considered here, the estimated prevalence of the 'rich' close to the percentiles used in the earlier analyses.[36]

This is clearly visible in Figure 2.5, which includes all of the countries that were already present in Figure 2.1 except for England.[37] Until the mid-sixteenth century, with the sole exception of the Florentine State in 1500, the prevalence of the rich remained between 1 per cent and 6 per cent. Only from circa 1600, across Italy, did the rich start to become a larger percentage. For example, in the Republic of Venice, where they had been 2.8 per cent of the population circa 1500, they were 7.1 per cent in 1600, 9.3 per cent in 1700 and 12 per cent in 1750. Interestingly, this growth was even more pronounced in the Florentine State, while it was less intense in the Sabaudian State (see below for further discussion). Germany, which is the only other area of Europe that can be explored systematically in this way, differs from the Italian states in two respects. First, just as found when looking at the wealth shares of the top percentiles, from the seventeenth century Germany follows a diverging path compared to other areas of the continent: instead of growing, the prevalence of the rich tends to decline throughout the century (from 3% in 1600, to 1.2% in 1700). This decline is the direct consequence of the devastations of the Thirty Years' War, which not only proved exceptionally damaging to the largest fortunes (as is reflected in top wealth shares) but also remodelled the overall wealth distribution in such a way that it became markedly less polarized than it had previously been, with fewer people placed very far from the median values, as, indeed, the reduction in the prevalence of the rich is matched by a parallel reduction in the prevalence of the poor.[38]

Had it not experienced the Thirty Years' War, Germany would probably have found itself much more unequal at the beginning of the nineteenth century, and its rich would have been far more numerous. While there is no doubt that this terrible conflict helps to explain why, towards the end of the early modern period, Germany stands apart from all other European areas for which we have information, where the prevalence of the rich is concerned Germany appears to have been different from a much earlier period. From the Middle Ages it already had relatively few rich compared to Italy, while at the same time, as will be remembered from Figure 2.1, the wealth share of the top 5 per cent was comparable and that of the top 1 per cent even higher. A technical explanation for this is that those placed above the median value tended to cluster close to it, except for relatively few individuals (basically the 'one-percenters') who concentrated in their hands an exceptionally large amount of the overall wealth, at least until 1600, after which their fortunes were ruined by war. This explanation, however, is not fully satisfying as it does not tell us anything about why German wealth distribution had such characteristics to begin with. In part, this comes from comparing urban distributions for the Sabaudian State and the Florentine State with overall distributions for Germany, as the wealth distribution in cities tended to be more polarized, with a larger percentage of both very poor and very rich households compared to the countryside. But even looking at the periods for which overall distributions are also available for the Italian states, the difference remains, as, for example, in 1500, when in Germany the rich were 1.9 per cent of the population, they were 2.7 per cent in the Sabaudian State as a whole and 5 per cent in its cities and 4.8 per cent in the Florentine State as a whole and 7.5 per cent in its cities. Future research will be needed to clarify the reasons for this structural difference between Germany and other European areas, a difference which had hitherto gone unnoticed.

Figure 2.5 also shows the trend followed by the southern Low Countries. Although this case must be interpreted with extra care as the data refer to income, not wealth (hence the threshold for affluence is set at a lower point: five times the median[39]), the general pattern matches that of Italy. This confirms that the German case is exceptional, standing out in comparison both with southern and with northern European areas. Finally, the relative movement of the Italian states merits some comment. The early modern period saw the onset of economic stagnation in many parts of Italy, including the most economically advanced ones. This was the case for the Florentine State from the sixteenth century and for the Republic of Venice from the mid-seventeenth. Towards the end of the early modern period, only the Sabaudian State was showing considerable economic dynamism. There, from the turn of the eighteenth century, proto-industry was booming and the agrarian sector was also experiencing intense innovation. For both sectors, the recently introduced silk industry played a key role (from the farming of silkworms to the production of silk thread and fabric), as it did in promoting the expansion of the financial sector. Additional proof of this divergence between the Sabaudian State in north-western Italy and the other pre-unification countries covered by Figure 2.5 comes from urbanization rates which, from the seventeenth century (and earlier for the Florentine State), were found to be declining everywhere except for the Sabaudian State where the share of the population living in cities with at least 5,000 inhabitants grew from 22.5 per cent in 1650 to 26.1 per cent in 1800. The conclusion is that, looking at the prevalence of the rich, we find no connection with economic growth. The Florentine State, which had set

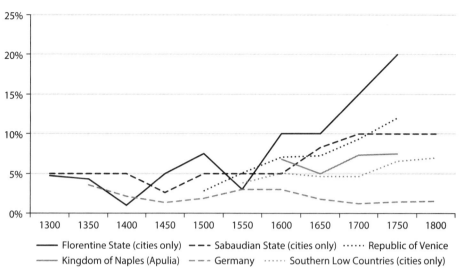

FIGURE 2.5. Long-term trends in the prevalence of the rich, 1300–1800.
Notes: the richness line is set at ten times the median value of the distribution.
For the Southern Low Countries, for which only information about the
income distribution is available, the richness line has been set at five times the
median instead.

upon a path of relative decline precociously, is the Italian area where early
modern growth in the prevalence of the rich was the most intense. In the Sabaudian State, whose economy was burgeoning, this tendency was much
slower, especially during the eighteenth century when economic growth intensified. This is because economic growth tends to increase the *average* income
and wealth, but their distribution is shaped by a broad range of factors, which
together determine *how many* will benefit from growth. In the Sabaudian State,
the benefits appear to have been distributed in a relatively equitable way. In
the Florentine State, where there was no growth, the wealthy elites were nevertheless able to improve their relative position by acting in an increasingly
rapacious way towards the poorest strata, a process which was only made
worse by the increasing numbers of the 'rich'. Imagine a cake that shrinks in
size, while the number of exceptionally hungry guests at the party continuously increases—soon, the other partygoers will only get crumbs.[40]

Unfortunately, for the modern age we lack the kind of complete wealth
distributions used above for preindustrial times and, consequently, it is impossible to estimate the prevalence of the rich in the same way. What we do have

is some information about how many were placed above fixed thresholds—say, the dollar millionaires or billionaires. This kind of information will be extensively used in chapter 7 to quantify the relative importance of different paths to wealth across history. Here, however, it is of somewhat limited interest, as it tends to cover very small percentiles of the overall population. Only from 2012 do we have any estimates of the prevalence of broader segments of the population. In that year, those with a net worth above 1 million U.S. dollars were 1.6 per cent of the adult population of Europe and 4.5 per cent that of North America (4.7% in the United States alone). This stark difference between continents markedly reduces when focusing on western Europe only: dollar millionaires were 3.3 per cent of the population in the United Kingdom, 2.4 per cent in Italy and 2.2 per cent in Germany. France, with 4.8 per cent, even beat the United States by a slight margin. However, by 2020, the gap between America and western Europe had increased significantly, as dollar millionaires were 8.8 per cent of the population of the United States and 5.6 per cent that of Canada but were just 4.9 per cent in France, 4.7 per cent in the United Kingdom, 4.3 per cent in Germany and 3 per cent in Italy. At that time, of all the Western countries, only Switzerland (14.9%) and Australia (9.4%) had a prevalence of millionaires higher than the United States, while Luxemburg matched it exactly. In the United States and Canada, as well as in many other European countries and most notably in the United Kingdom and Germany, the prevalence of millionaires has increased in recent years, despite a financial crisis, a 'Great Recession' and a pandemic.[41]

The factors which led the rich (however we define them) to become exceptionally abundant in the twenty-first century and the roots of their current exceptional resilience to shocks of all kind will be discussed at many points in the book. Here, it is important to highlight that this happened in a situation of growing inequality, which is not necessarily also one of a 'rising tide that lifts all boats' in spite of what many politicians—and many economists—like to argue. If we take a broader historical perspective, the ability of the wealth elite, which was often also a political elite, to expand its control of the overall economic resources even when economic growth was lacking is a stark reminder that, across the ages, not all paths towards affluence have been forged by means of merit or virtue. Regarding personal enrichment too, the human experience is multifaceted and needs to be considered with care. Undoubtedly, in some historical phases, economic opportunities have been relatively abundant and it has proved easier to become rich. The evidence presented in Figure 2.5 suggests that the early modern period was relatively more favourable to fortune-building than the Middle Ages, and this is connected to important phases of economic change and innovation, from the opening of the Atlantic trade routes to the onset of the Industrial Revolution. Similar phases are also found in more recent periods, for example in the late twentieth century, at the onset of the computer and information age. And yet, there are many ways in which wealth can be accumulated, and indeed neither economic growth per se nor the emergence of new economic opportunities are necessary conditions for new rich individuals to emerge. The different paths which, across history, have led to personal enrichment are the object of the next part of this book.

PART II

The Paths to Affluence

3

On Aristocracy, New and Past

ACROSS THE CENTURIES, wealth has tended to become ever more concentrated and the ranks of the rich have become larger and larger. This finding is important in itself, as arguably there is something which is common to all of the rich and super-rich just because their wealth sets them apart from the rest of society. And yet, wealth has not always been accumulated in the same way, and it seems reasonable to imagine that the sometimes quite momentous changes that led to the rich becoming richer and more numerous are also associated with changes in how their fortunes came into existence. Were the rich brilliant (or just lucky) entrepreneurs, great financiers or members of the nobility? Was their wealth mostly self-made or inherited? These are the questions to which we now seek answers, because the composition of the rich in terms of background, occupation and social-juridical status has important implications for the role that they play in society. We begin by distinguishing some different paths towards great wealth, starting with what is probably, in the collective mind, the prototype of the rich who acquired privileged status by birth, not worth: the noble aristocrat. As will become clear by the end of this chapter, being a member of the nobility did not have quite the same meaning in the Middle Ages as it has today, and the relationship between noble status and wealth is much more complex and varied than is often presumed.

What's in a Noble? Some Initial Definitions

While the concepts of nobility and aristocracy seem intuitive, they present many layers of complexity. So, it seems proper to begin our analysis with some definitions, starting with the most restrictive concept: nobility.

We can define the nobility as a privileged social group holding hereditary titles and/or other hereditary signs of distinction. This definition, again apparently intuitive, points to two characteristic features of nobles: the fact of enjoying a formally recognized condition of 'privilege' compared to other social groups and the hereditary nature of their high status. As inheritance is always one of the most strictly regulated (formally or informally) features of any human society, the transmission of noble titles across generations requires a specific institutional framework—as does the very existence of the nobility, given that in many Western countries today it has been abolished. What our definition does *not* require is for nobles to stand out from other individuals because of their wealth.[1]

In our definition, the nobility is just one specification of a broader concept, that of aristocracy. Following a scholarly tradition started by the German sociologist Max Weber, aristocracy is, again, defined not by its wealth nor by its control of economic resources, but by its high social status (itself based upon non-economic qualities like prestige or honour), by enjoying certain privileges and by the ability to concentrate power (military and/or political).[2] As is also the case with the concept of nobility, the practical characteristics of an aristocracy varied widely across space and time.[3] Indeed, if we look for a definition covering Western history from Antiquity until today, we have to recognize that the *only* necessary characteristic of an aristocracy is to have high social status, conferring on its members some sort of privilege.[4] Hence, we can simply define the aristocracy as 'a social group holding high status and privileges', of which hereditary nobility is the most obvious example.

The reason why it is important to underline that great wealth is not a necessary condition for being a noble or an aristocrat is that historically we find many examples of impoverished noblemen. Weber himself pointed out that when, from the beginning of the early modern period, the economic position of the landed nobility (which he referred to as the 'patrimonial lords') began to be challenged by new groups, a tacit or even an explicit compromise tended to arise whereby the landed nobility agreed to renounce at least part of their economic dominance but were guaranteed a range of juridical and economic privileges, including fiscal exemptions. At least initially, this tacit agreement also preserved the nobility's control of political power, control which, however, in most areas tended to erode over time.[5] While this way of portraying European history does capture a major historical process, we also know that the nobility was not uniformly affected by a path of economic decline and that new and usually very rich members continuously joined its ranks. After all, in countries, like England, where the nobility still exists, its members remain an important component of the rich and super-rich.[6]

If the hereditary nobility can be taken as the best example of an aristocracy, we might wonder why we need to distinguish between the two. The reason is that in some countries that do not currently recognize, and in some rare instances like the United States that have *never* recognized in their history, the existence of a hereditary nobility, it remains possible to discuss the existence of a high-status, privileged class: hence, of an aristocracy. Additionally, there is growing concern about the possibility that a new 'global aristocracy' is on the rise today. This is an important issue because it leads to many relevant questions about current paths towards great wealth. Therefore, we will pay some attention to modern aristocracy(ies), but only after providing a historical overview of how, across Western history, entering the nobility or being born into it affected individual chances of being very rich.

The Enrooting of the Feudal Nobility in Medieval Europe

At the end of September 1066, the son of a Breton count looked hopefully at the English shores. With little chance of inheriting his father's title, destined for his older brother, young Alan—known as Rufus or 'the Red' because of his beard—had answered the call of his second cousin, William of Normandy, who was planning to lead an invading army across the Channel. Together with his brother Brien, he was part of a contingent of 5,000 Breton soldiers and 100 ships that his father, Count Eudon, had sent to join William's army. Alan was highly motivated for the enterprise, as he was keenly aware of having a much better opportunity to improve his personal position and make a fortune in a foreign country than in his native Brittany, where he would have been constrained by succession laws and would have had to compete with his six brothers for resources and honours. Indeed, Alan seems to have played an important role at the Battle of Hastings, fought on 14 October 1066 in the hills of South Sussex, as commander of the left wing of the invading army.

Hastings proved a decisive victory for the Normans and their allies, with the Saxon army crushed and their king Harold dead on the field. So, as William readied himself to be crowned king of England in Westminster Abbey, Alan Rufus also received his reward in the form of many towns in Cambridgeshire, including quite a few expropriated from Harold's widow. But this was just the beginning of Alan's ascent to immense wealth. Unlike many others who had followed William across the sea, Alan had come to stay. While many of William's original companions soon returned to Normandy with their plunder, including in time Alan's own brother Brien, he remained and played an increasingly important role in completing the conquest of the country. He developed a specialization in crushing revolts, first in 1069 when he helped his brother to subjugate the city of Exeter which had rebelled against the extortionate taxes imposed by the conquerors and had joined forces with an army led by Harold's sons. Then, and most importantly, from the summer of 1069 to 1072, he joined William's campaign against the rebellious earls of northern England and their Danish allies. Alan was also involved in the brutal repression which ensued, the so-called 'Harrying' of the north which may have led to over 100,000 deaths due to violence, famine and other afflictions. As rebellious Saxon nobles were dispossessed, William doled out 'honours', or lordships, to his most loyal followers. A crucial step in Alan's ascent was the award of the honour of Richmond which comprised no less than 199 manors. Alan immediately set out to build Richmond Castle in a strategic and easily defensible position. It became the symbolic centre of Alan's domains. These continued to increase in the following years, largely thanks to Alan's ability to take the winning side from early on in the frequent revolts against William and his successor, William II. By the 1080s, Alan Rufus was without doubt one of the richest men in England. According to an estimate that should only be taken as indicative given the intrinsic limitations of the available information, the revenues from his huge landholdings may have amounted to about 7.3 per cent of the entire net national income of England at the time, and Alan could perhaps be considered the richest man that ever lived in Britain (monarchs are not to be included in this kind of ranking). Importantly, several others among William the Conqueror's early companions appear in a recent list of Britain's richest people of all time.[7]

The case of Alan Rufus allows us to highlight an important point: not all rich and super-rich members of the nobility inherited their fortunes. Alan was born a noble but, if we go further back in time, we find a moment when the system to which landed nobility pertains was little more than a work-in-progress. In Europe, nobles existed in Roman times, as surely the patricians, who were supposedly descendants of a small number of original Roman families (a condition which was obviously hereditary) and who in the early Republic monopolized public offices, fit our definition.[8] Interestingly the *nobilitas*, from which the word 'nobility' originates and which refers to a new aristocratic group that began to emerge from the late fourth century BCE and acquired increasing relevance in the late Republic and under the Empire, was always a much more permeable group than the patriciate.[9] This social system, however, crumbled together with the Empire from the fifth century CE and was replaced by a scattering of different nobilities emerging from the retinues of the local

Roman governors and of the chieftains of the 'barbaric' populations that settled within the boundaries of the old Empire.[10]

The emergence of the kind of hereditary nobility that was in place by the
time of Alan Rufus is closely associated with the emergence of early states and
in particular the development of their administration, which usually over-
lapped (in full or in part) with the household of the sovereign. In this context,
'office holders strove at permanent and hereditary positions. Instability of the
early medieval states helped them. So in Carolingian times "count" (Latin:
comes) was a judge that accompanied the Emperor. In the twelfth century
emerged other *comites*, provincial governors, and "viscounts" as their representatives. Border provinces of the Empire were governed by the "mar-
quesses".'[11] In time, this process gave rise to the 'feudal' nobility, regulated by
more precise and juridically defined rules of interpersonal relationships between a ruler and his vassals. This social and economic system was already
recognizable in France in the twelfth century and continued to develop during
the rest of the Middle Ages, together with the idea of society divided into
distinct orders or 'estates': those who pray (the clergy), those who fight (the
nobles) and those who labour (the commoners or the 'Third Estate').[12]

A more detailed discussion of the emergence and the enrooting of the feudal nobility in Europe is beyond the objectives of this book. From our perspective, what matters is that at some point in time, a certain high-status position
which had probably been acquired (in many if not in most circumstances)
because of the competences or capability of a specific individual—either a
skilled administrator or a brave military leader—became the object of hereditary transmission. At the risk of over-simplification, we can then state that the
founder of a noble dynasty is intrinsically different from his descendants, as
he *made* his position, while they simply *inherited* it. In some respects, then, a
possible issue with the nobility as a path towards wealth is that in the vast
majority of cases (but not nearly all of them) it was an *easy* path and did not
involve any specific competence or attitude on the part of the noble rich except, perhaps, refraining from excessive expenditure and from overly risky
endeavours. But, of course, this is only part of the story, as the way in which
belonging to the nobility, or more generally to an aristocracy, might favour
enrichment does not depend only on inheritance but also on access to exceptional opportunities. This is quite clear in the context of the medieval feudal
system, as there the nobility had a strong grip on the political system, controlled substantial coercive means and used them to maximize the tribute
extracted from the lower social strata, consequently increasing their (and their

descendants') wealth.[13] Additionally, nobles had privileged access to remunerative military commissions, not only in the Middle Ages but throughout the early modern period, in association with the expansion in the size of armies and in the level of state military expenditures.[14]

As belonging to the landed nobility developed into a kind of hereditary position, a notion also developed that the noble's condition (and wealth) was *justly* passed on to descendants, because this was in accordance with some sort of divine design. In other words, the hereditary transmission of privileges and feudal patrimonies, while it obviously tended to lead to considerable inequalities, was not perceived or conceptualized as problematic because it was believed to correspond to God's plan, in the context of a society that understood itself to be structurally unequal, for example because of the existence of juridically distinct estates.[15] This is what Weber described as hereditary charisma: a condition in which recognition is no longer paid to a charismatic individual (for example, to the founder of a dynasty) but to the legitimacy of a position acquired by inheritance, even in the total absence of personal charisma or, one would say, of any other virtue.[16] As will be seen in chapter 8, in medieval Europe this general recognition of the privileged position of the nobility made the existence of super-rich nobles within society much less problematic compared to that of 'sinful' super-rich commoners, even those who were known to have built their own fortune.

Becoming a Noble, from the Early Modern Period to Napoleon's Time and Beyond

In a sense, the golden age of the European feudal nobility was already ending by the fifteenth century. This was because of increasing tensions among the nobles themselves—a problem of soaring within-group inequality, including of wealth, leading to a decreased capacity for effective collective action—as well as because of growing competition from other social groups (or, to use a different terminology, other 'classes') and particularly from the bourgeoisie. This resulted in deepening distinctions between a higher and a lower nobility, as well as between old and new nobility. While the precise characteristics of these processes vary considerably across Europe, it is worth recalling the example of France, where the 'nobility of the sword' (*noblesse d'epée*) with ancient medieval origins felt increasingly threatened by the 'nobility of the robe' (*noblesse de robe*). The latter was made up of commoners who had acquired a kind of noble status attached to specific offices, for example that of member of a *parlement* or provincial court. In early modern times, these offices could simply be bought and were hereditary, at least until the French Revolution of 1789 put an end to them. To further complicate the matter, many nobles of the robe were wealthy enough to buy landed titles (*fiefs de dignité*), adding the name of their new fief to their own.[17]

Take the case of the French dynasty of the Crozat. Antoine I Crozat, a merchant from Albi, was the first in the family to harbour ambitions of ennoblement. In 1652, after the death of his first wife, he moved to Toulouse in Languedoc, where he immediately prospered to such a degree that he could begin activity as a banker in addition to being a merchant. He then bought at the discount price of 10,000 livres the fief of Barthecave, which had been ruined during the Wars of Religion of the late sixteenth century. His new title of *seigneur de Barthecave et Préserville* surely helped him to arrange his second marriage, this time into the local nobility. To demonstrate the acquisition of noble status, Antoine I started to wear a sword and act like a noble; he also restored the *chateau* of Barthecave and even invented a new genealogy for his family. But he finally overstepped the mark: the old nobility took offence at the parvenu, and the governor of Languedoc repeatedly fined Antoine I for 'usurpation of nobility'. He had, however, traced the path which would thereafter be followed by his descendants, the most well-known of whom, also called Antoine, managed to become one of the most important men in France.

Like his father, Antoine II made his fortune as a merchant and banker but with much greater success, especially when he started to act as a tax farmer: in 1689 he became general collector (*receveur général*) for the entire Generality of Bordeaux. Even more importantly, he became involved in overseas trade, first investing in tobacco from Saint-Domingue, then in the slave trade: in 1701 he acquired a monopoly on this trade in all the Spanish colonies. Finally, in 1712, he was awarded a 15-year trade monopoly in Louisiana (then a French colony) for which he created the *Compagnie de la Louisiane*.

In 1714, Antoine II started a resolute campaign to elevate his status and strengthen his claim to nobility. He began by buying the Barony of Thiers for 200,000 livres and for 500,000 the Duchy of Saint-Fargeau. While buying a duchy did not technically allow Antoine II to use the title of duke, he could however call himself *seigneur du duché de Saint-Fargeau* (albeit briefly, as due to some difficulties he had to sell the duchy in 1715). The largest investment, however, was in the Barony of Châtel, for which he paid the enormous sum of 1,100,000 livres. The expense was worth it, as soon afterwards he managed to convince the old king, Louis XIV, to make him *Marquis du Châtel* in recognition of his services as lender to the crown. At this moment, Antoine II was probably the richest man in France, and Voltaire, the famous writer and member of the French Enlightenment, called him 'Crozat Cresus'. But in spite of all the honours awarded to him, the nobility continued to consider Antoine II a parvenu like his father. The family ennoblement strategy, also pursued through systematic marriages into more consolidated noble families, finally paid off in the third generation as Antoine II's children seem to have been well-integrated into the French nobility.[18]

From our perspective, the situation typical of the nobility in early modern times leads to two questions. First, how permeable was the nobility to new members, especially to rich commoners who, like the Crozat, constituted the vast majority of the new nobles of the time? And secondly, why would a rich commoner want to sustain potentially very high expenditure just to add a title to his name? Throughout Europe, we find repeated attempts to restrict access to the nobility. This tendency was also quite clear in a merchant republic like Venice, the relatively rare case of a European polity where feudal nobility never had a strong grip on economic and political power. Even Venice, however, considered it necessary to clearly identify the members of the patriciate who, from 1297, had sole access to the main political body (the famous closure, or *serrata*, of the *Maggior Consiglio* or Great Council). Soon, lists were made of those who were eligible for the *Maggior Consiglio*, and from 1323 it was clearly established that inclusion had a hereditary basis: only the descendants of previous Council members were to be admitted. In this way, membership of the *Maggior Consiglio* became the real line of demarcation between the Venetian patriciate and the rest (among patricians there were no further formal hierarchies).[19]

Highly restrictive rules of this kind, which in time came to be common across Italy, in practice did not prevent the occasional inclusion of new members into urban patriciates, most notably of the very rich. In the Republic of Venice during the seventeenth century we find many examples of wealthy provincial families, like the Zambelli from Padua or the Ottolini and Zenobi from Verona, who after acquiring great wealth through their commercial activities were allowed into the patriciate.[20] This had become possible due to a law introduced in 1646, which required the payment of an admission fee amounting to the enormous sum of 100,000 ducats but imposed hardly any additional restrictions.[21] In other Italian states, for example Milan, it seems that becoming a member of the nobility was somewhat easier than in Venice, partly because the regulations in place to limit the process were not fully applied. In fact, 'the only absolutely indispensable requirement in order to follow the path which led to [the patriciate,] the pinnacle of Milanese society, . . . seems to have been wealth'.[22] Beyond being able to pay the extortionate fees required to be included in the urban patriciates, in many parts of Europe the rich could simply buy fiefs and acquire the related titles. Indeed, new fiefs were sometimes created in order to satisfy exceptional financial needs of a sovereign, for example in the Sabaudian State in north-western Italy where in 1618 a large number of new fiefs were created and the corresponding titles were sold to replenish the coffers of Duke Charles Emmanuel I, exhausted because of the First War of the Montferrat Succession of 1613–17. A similar need to fund military efforts and the expenditure on an oversized army is found in eighteenth-century Prussia, where each king ennobled a much larger number of burghers than his predecessor for the lofty price of 400 thalers, equal to about 7 kilograms of silver, each.[23]

Beyond buying their way into the nobility, commoners could also follow other paths to achieve a similar result. One possibility was to be ennobled because of services to the state. The case of the French *noblesse de robe* mentioned above can be considered an example of this kind, but the practice was widespread. For example, the king of Spain, Philip V, during his reign (1700–46) created over 200 new titled (landed) nobles among his ministers and members of the high administration of the state, as well as conferring 'mass grants of ordinary nobility' which, however, had little practical import.[24] Another way was to marry into the nobility. This served both to cement one's shaky claims to noble status and to improve the social standing of one's descendants. The case of the Crozat family is again emblematic of a general phenomenon. Both of these eventualities—ennoblement through service to the state and marriage into the nobility—are closely connected to affluence, first because building a career within the high administration was itself a possible path towards great wealth (see chapter 4 for further discussion), and second because why else, if not for their wealth, would a respectable noble family condescend to establish a marriage alliance with a commoner? In early modern times, many families of the old nobility had become impoverished and often needed an injection of fresh resources and to be on good terms with some members of the otherwise despised new rich, simply to prevent loss of status. Consider the example of two prosperous early modern French financiers who acted as lenders to the crown, Pierre Jacquet and François Sabathier. They are fairly rare examples of financiers who, as commoners, managed to marry into high nobility. Their respective wives, Anne de Saulx-Tavanne and Marie-Lucie Chasteignier, brought meagre dowries: the first 30,000 livres, and the second the 'hope of her inheritance'. These were dwarfed by the gifts required from the husbands: a total of 146,000 livres in the first case and 243,000 in the second (although of this sum, 200,000 livres was to be paid only after François's death).[25]

Given the high costs that wealthy commoners had to sustain on the often slow path towards ennoblement, we might wonder why they were so keen to pay them. The concept of nobility must undoubtedly have exerted a strong psychological attraction on the rich and super-rich of preindustrial Europe, an attraction akin to being admitted into an exclusive club.[26] In certain social contexts, like that of nineteenth- and twentieth-century America where nobility was not recognized by law, building relationships with the European blood aristocracy, and in particular marrying a noble bride or groom, might have represented a specific form of what the American economist Thorstein Veblen called 'conspicuous consumption': basically, the consumption of exceptionally expensive goods for the simple purpose of demonstrating one's high social status (conspicuous consumption will be discussed in greater detail in chapter 6).[27] However, in the European context, up until the early twentieth century at least, the very rich also saw ennoblement as a way to secure social recognition: the more so, the more recent their wealth. But more importantly from our perspective, it seems certain that becoming a noble opened additional opportunities for business—certainly in the context of public administration and service to the state, as is apparent in the case of the ascent of the Crozat in France. This is a complex topic since ennoblement could also bring obligations which instead constrained the ability to do business, as will be discussed later. However, the fact remains that belonging to the nobility constituted, in early modern times, a fundamental path towards great wealth not only because it could simply lead to the inheritance of some ancestor's feudal fortune but also because it helped already rich commoners to become even richer.

Across continental Europe, affluent commoners' aspirations to ennoblement did not disappear with the spread of the new ideas promoted by the 1789 French Revolution. Notwithstanding the initial revolutionary furore, which did in fact considerably damage the relative position of the nobility in France and put an end to the spread of the *noblesse de robe*, the establishment of the French Empire under Napoleon (1801–14) led to a new wave of ennoblements in France but also, for example, in Italy. This was part of a conscious effort to get rid of the old nobility through the compulsory partition of their estates at the moment of inheritance, as established by the new 'egalitarian' *Code Civil* (also known as the Napoleonic Code) and, at the same time, create a new nobility supportive of the imperial government, a point already highlighted by Weber.[28] After the fall of Napoleon and the onset of the Restoration, the Bourbons (1815–30) were as keen as the *Empereur* had been, and for much the same reasons, to create new (and supposedly loyal) nobles, again selecting them from the groups which could offer greater material help to the ruling dynasty. The very rich were, again, first in line. This is why, as will be seen in chapter 7, the prevalence of nobles among the richest actually increased considerably in France during the first decades of the nineteenth century. Only from the late 1850s do we find a tendency towards decline,[29] that is, immediately after the privileges connected to noble status, already much reduced after 1789, were entirely eliminated by the 1848 revolution and the establishment of the Second Republic. Hereditary titles continued to be recognized by law until 1870; thereafter in France the nobility, as we have defined it, ended, and noble titles only remain as accessories of the surname. While the French example would in time be followed by many European countries, in others a formally recognized nobility survives to this day, as discussed in the following section.

The Survival of the Nobility in the Twentieth and Twenty-First Centuries and the Emergence of New Aristocracies

In much of the West, the nobility no longer exists. The United States was the first to get rid of it: the constitution ratified in 1788 explicitly prohibited the federal or state governments from granting any 'title of nobility'.[30] France completely abolished nobility in 1870; Austria, Hungary and the other countries born from the fragmentation of the Habsburg Empire, as well as Germany and Poland, did away with it after World War I, when they became republics. Italy did the same after World War II, as did some eastern European countries that fell into the Soviet sphere of influence, like Bulgaria and Romania. Many other European countries, especially in northern Europe, stuck to constitutional monarchy as a form of government; hence, they continue to possess a formal nobility. This is the case for Belgium, Britain, Denmark, Sweden and the Netherlands as well as, in southern Europe, for Spain, although almost everywhere current constitutions do not recognize any substantial legal privileges of the nobles (the main exception is Britain). In North America, the case of Canada is somewhat peculiar: the country recognizes the monarch of England as sovereign, but there has been no legal nobility since the 1917 'Nickle Resolution' required the sovereign to refrain from bestowing British hereditary honours (titles of nobility or even hereditary peerage) on Canadian citizens. While the Resolution never became a formal law, it did constitute the basis for the policy followed in Canada.[31]

At least in those countries where the nobility has strong and ancient traditions, the nobles continue to be an important component of the rich, while their position among the super-rich seems to be declining. This is surely the case in Britain, where in 1990 15 per cent of the richest hundred individuals came from the landed nobility, but only 4 per cent did in 2005.[32] Based on the 2020 rich list of *The Sunday Times*, the figure has remained stable to this day (the richest of the British nobles, holding the tenth absolute position in the list, is the Duke of Westminster whose patrimony amounts to 10.3 billion pounds or 13.2 billion U.S. dollars).[33] Here, something more needs to be said about the way in which nobles have (or have not) been able to preserve their wealth across generations.

Key to the perpetuation of noble wealth are laws regulating inheritance. In particular, to serve the purpose of avoiding the dispersion of patrimonies, some sort of impartible inheritance system is required.[34] As has already been mentioned, in France and in other European areas the introduction of partible inheritance for (ex-)feudal property at the turn of the nineteenth century tended to destroy the wealth of the old nobility. As this process was closely connected to the introduction of the Napoleonic Code in 1804 (which required that each child should be given a share of the inheritance which could not fall below a specified minimum), it is clear that a distinction arose between those European areas that were more or less directly influenced by the French Empire, like Italy, the Low Countries and parts of Germany, and the others—beginning with the greatest rival of France during the Napoleonic Wars: Britain. There, primogeniture—an inheritance system under which the oldest surviving son receives a larger share, including the feudal estate in the case of the nobles—remained the default rule in the absence of a valid will from the Norman Conquest of the eleventh century until 1925.[35] Furthermore, it remains valid to this day for the high nobility or 'peerage' (which includes dukes, marquises, earls, viscounts and barons), at least in some form, as inheritance of the title follows a male-preference primogeniture rule.[36] While in theory a modern British peer could give a fair share of inheritance to all his children (sons and daughters alike), in actual practice (male) inheritors of the title tend to receive the vast majority of their father's estate.

While some sort of unequal rule regarding inheritance should probably be considered a necessary condition to ensure the survival of nobles among the rich and super-rich, it is by no means sufficient. This is confirmed by the recurrent injections of new wealth that many noble families required to stay afloat due to their expensive lifestyle and even, in certain settings like twentieth-century Britain, due to legal systems which, for a period at least, became relatively adverse to great landownership.[37] Marriages with rich commoners, including foreigners, became commonplace among the British nobility in periods when their fortunes were waning, especially from the 1880s, when a combination of declining prices for agricultural products and a relatively high cost of labour brought many large estates to the brink of bankruptcy. In this scenario, marrying a commoner seemed an acceptable alternative to selling vast amounts of land or precious art collections on the market. An indicator of this is the proportion of women with commoner origins presented at court, which grew from about 10 per cent in 1841 to over 50 per cent by the end of the century. Many of these were the daughters of rich American industrialists. These developments mirrored those in continental Europe: take, for example, the 1895 marriage of the French marquis Boni de Castellane, a key figure of the Belle Époque renowned as a master of refinement and taste, to Anna Gould, the daughter of the New York railroad magnate Jay Gould. The event caused a sensation on both sides of the Atlantic as this was one of the very first instances of a French noble marrying an American heiress—and equally sensational was the subsequent divorce (1906), after Boni had dissipated about 10 million dollars of Anna's patrimony (about 297 million in 2020 U.S. dollars).[38]

In other instances, the wealth of the nobility survived because it was well-administered and/or because some among the nobles were able to profit from the new opportunities offered by the Industrial Revolution and subsequent developments (see the next section), maybe with a touch of luck as in the case of the Grosvenor family, to which the aforementioned Duke of Westminster belongs. This family is of relatively recent ennoblement compared to others who can trace their ancestors back to the Norman Conquest: Richard Grosvenor, High Sheriff of Cheshire and later an active member of parliament, was only made a baronet in 1622. The family was destined for enrichment from 1674, when Thomas Grosvenor married the young heiress to the manor of Ebury. This comprised the so-called '100 acres' north of Piccadilly (most of the current area of Mayfair in London) and the 'Five Fields' (Belgravia and Pimlico). While the area was composed of bog and marshland at the time, it is now some of the most valuable real estate in the world. Indeed, the rapid expansion of London ensured that the heirs to the Grosvenor family, who since 1874 have carried the title of Duke of Westminster granted by Queen Victoria, have been among the very richest people in Britain since at least the mid-nineteenth century, and in many years they were the richest of all. Other super-rich noble families of Britain who were inordinately advantaged by the booming prices of urban estates, especially in London, include the Cadogan family (earls), the Portman family (viscounts) and the Howard de Walden family (barons).[39]

Beyond the survival, in some Western societies, of quite a few rich nobles, we also find a much more general process of consolidation of national and international wealth aristocracies. This process also involved countries that strongly rejected nobility, beginning with the pioneers: the United States. Alexis de Tocqueville's view, expressed in the mid-nineteenth century, that the American 'republican democracy' was characterized by a form of social hierarchy that would prevent the establishment of aristocracies (because of high social mobility, the openness of the elites, the clear separation between wealth and power and the massification of education)[40] seems to have been rather too optimistic. Many studies have reported that, as soon as wealthy dynasties had become well-established, a clearly identified group with all the characteristics of an aristocracy tended to develop. During the nineteenth century, this was especially clear in the great cities of the East Coast, beginning with Boston where many among the richest descended from merchant clans, like the Amorys and Cabots, who had initially risen to prominence fifty years or so before the Revolution. They created trading houses structured around the family, which favoured the transmission of both business practices and wealth across the generations.[41]

By the first decades of the nineteenth century, Boston's rich elite already seemed much more conservative compared to that of the booming rival city, New York, notwithstanding the recent diversification into textile manufacturing. As historian Frederic C. Jaher argued,

> unlike Boston the New York mercantile [and banking] community did not develop long-term family continuity. . . . The result of the New York population boom [during the nineteenth century] was that New York's older elite, faced with the more rapid rate of social and economic change could not recruit from its own members the numbers necessary to fill positions of metropolitan leadership. The slower growth of Boston permitted its

leading families to stabilize themselves over several generations while more abundant opportunity in New York beckoned new men to wealth, status and power.[42]

Quite clearly, the very open character of New York's economic elite and the relatively good opportunities for upward social mobility hindered, to some degree, the development of an aristocracy which perpetuated its own status by exploiting privilege. This was the characteristic trait of American society that so impressed Tocqueville.

However, this was not the *only* modality through which American elites had emerged. In many parts of the country—certainly in the south, but not only there—some components of the pre-independence 'manorial' elite survived as well, in part by mixing with the new industrialists,[43] and Boston was not the only city where a more conservative, dynastically connoted attitude had already emerged; see, for example, the case of Philadelphia.[44] What is more, by the end of the nineteenth century even in New York the self-made man had become a rarity among the richest, replaced by simple inheritors of large fortunes who increasingly behaved as members of a patrician group: 'inheritance, the basic dimension of aristocratic wealth, facilitated the formation of, and entry into, the patriciate. Great fortunes also promoted unions with old families or eased entry into the cultural and charitable activities and institutions which marked the rites of passage from family founder to Knickerbocker and Brahmin', 'Knickerbocker' and 'Brahmin' being terms sometimes used to indicate the members of the traditional old upper classes of New York and Boston respectively.[45]

Compared to other old cities of the East Coast, however, the New York elite always remained more open to new members and somewhat more fragmented, notwithstanding some explicit attempts during the 1880s and 1890s to give greater social coherence to an aristocratic group identified along the axes of wealth, birth and style. Interestingly, this process was led by women like Alva Erskine Smith Vanderbilt and Caroline Schermerhorn Astor. The latter introduced a name for this aristocratic group, the 'Four Hundred'. Among these, members of the old Knickerbocker families were by far the largest group, but they remained just a strong minority. Indeed, the only common trait of the Four Hundred was great wealth, which in about 50 per cent of cases had been acquired simply through inheritance or marriage.[46]

In a sense, the emergence of the East Coast aristocracy of wealth mirrors, although without the trappings of the feudal system, the story of the new nobility established in England after the Norman Conquest: the generation of the founders is characterized by heroic attainments and bold moves to seize exceptional opportunities, but the generations of their descendants look increasingly different with the passing of time. There usually comes a point when inheritance seems to be the only real basis of one's claim to high status, a moment, in the development of a rich dynasty, when it is quite difficult to imagine that 'merit' might justify its high standing within society. This is crucial to understanding why the presence of very rich or even super-rich individuals tends to lead to social concerns. The case of the East Coast aristocracy of the nineteenth century also helps us better understand current worries about the emergence of a new 'global aristocracy'. Before focusing on this point, though, it is important to go back to the narrower concept of nobility and to discuss some further aspects of the complex relationship between nobility and wealth.

Nobility and Wealth: Some Further Reflections

Throughout Western history, entering the nobility, by right of birth or by means of ennoblement, represented one major path towards great wealth. However, if we observe the whole group of the nobility, we must also recognize that not all nobles were particularly wealthy—indeed, some of them were quite poor.[47] This was, for example, the case for many Spanish *hidalgos*, who often had no rich ancestors but were simply the final beneficiaries of phases of mass ennoblement dating back to the so-called reconquest (*reconquista*) against the Moorish Iberian kingdoms. Poverty did not prevent the *hidalgos* from thinking highly of their status and from looking at the recently ennobled with disdain, even when they enjoyed much better material conditions. This kind of situation was recurrent in areas of Europe where historical vicissitudes had led to blanket grants of nobility, like those awarded by the Polish kings in the fifteenth and sixteenth centuries to smooth territorial expansion.[48] In other instances, however, nobles had become impoverished because their ancestral wealth had been squandered or had simply evaporated due to unlucky turns of events—think about the wave of poor nobles flocking to Venice after they had been forced to abandon their domains on the island of Crete, which the Republic had lost to the Ottomans after the lengthy and hard-fought war of 1645–69. Sometimes, specific categories of impoverished nobles came to constitute well-defined social groups like, again in Venice, the *barnabotti*. These patricians, although they had no significant patrimony left, continued to maintain their seats in the *Maggior Consiglio*.

Beyond profligacy and vicissitudes, in the Old Regime there were other menaces to the preservation of noble wealth: the need to maintain a certain (very expensive) standard of living and the prohibition of practising professions or activities considered lowly. Together, these two aspects were the essence of the requirement, which nobles had to satisfy to avoid losing their status and privileges,[49] of *vivere more nobilium*, a Latin maxim which means 'to live like a noble'. In other words, *appearing* to be a noble was a necessary condition for *being* a noble or even for aspiring to become ennobled as the case of Antoine I Crozat discussed earlier shows very well. For example, in Italy, in the main cities of the Papal States during the seventeenth and the eighteenth century—when the boundaries between classes had become more rigid than in earlier periods—living nobly entailed owning an urban palace with a private chapel, a villa in the countryside or at least a hunting lodge and a family tomb; being the beneficiary of one or more *fideicommissa* (entails) and of other benefices; and refraining from practising any sort of mechanical (that is, manual) art or other lowly occupation.[50] Across Europe, maintaining this kind of lifestyle without compromising the ancestral patrimony became increasingly difficult, basically because the expenditure deemed necessary to live nobly was increasing, the revenues from land struggled to keep pace and the nobles had very limited opportunities to supplement their revenues with income from other activities. As noted by French historian Roland Mousnier,

> The problem is that the career options available to a gentleman are not numerous and are usually ruinous. In the army, in the fleet—careers truly worthy of him—, at the Court, in the high offices of government, the gentleman spends more than he earns. Some gentlemen, belonging to the middling and the lower nobility, join the judicial magistracies. . . . They are a small proportion of the body of the nobility, as all these functions, even if they have the dignity of justice and of service to the king, are tainted by some sort of 'bourgeois character.'[51]

In some settings, in order to stay afloat, impoverished nobles resorted to somewhat questionable activities—albeit not tainted by even a whiff of bourgeoisie—like the aforementioned *barnabotti* of Venice who were prone to corruption whenever they obtained a public office and who systematically sold their vote in the *Maggior Consiglio*, a practice which increasingly affected the inner workings of this crucial institution, mostly to the advantage of a few super-rich patricians.[52]

The noble lifestyle was so expensive that it often proved excessive even for rich and recently elevated families. Take the case of the French family Tristan from Beauvaisis who, from the first decades of the seventeenth century, grew rich through their offices in the regional administration and through lending to nobles. When the unfortunate nobles could not repay their debts, the Tristan took their lands and fiefs as their own. At the beginning of the eighteenth century, they officially acquired noble status themselves, by buying the important office of notary and secretary of the king. Shortly afterwards, Nicolas Tristan, *seigneur* of Hez, Juvignies and Verderel, decided that the time had come to move further up the social ladder. He disdained the offices traditionally held by his family, acquiring a post in the military instead, and adopted the noble lifestyle in full—until, in 1762, his finances became so ruined that he suffered the same fate that his family had inflicted, generations earlier, on other nobles: he was forced to sell his family domains to repay his debts.[53]

This, however, is only one side of the coin. On the other side, we find new opportunities opening up to rich commoner families who managed to become nobles—opportunities that might have exerted an even stronger pull than the psychological factors discussed in the earlier section (the sheer attraction of joining an exclusive social elite and the pleasure of buying something that very few could afford) in inducing many to set out on the expensive path towards ennoblement. As seen, gaining access to offices in the highest echelons of the state and court administration, offices usually reserved for the nobility (even the very recent nobility), offered excellent opportunities for further enrichment. But more generally, what appeared to be very alluring was the integration into a political system. Such integration created new opportunities, if only because it gave access to restricted information and to a certain degree of control over the risks involved in financial activities. For whereas it was usually considered unbecoming for a noble to invest in industry, the same could not be said for lending to the state.[54] Prudent investments in the public debt could solve the problem of keeping up with expensive (and semi-compulsory) consumption habits, as has been argued, for example, in the case of England, although as the Industrial Revolution progressed, this might not have prevented the nobility from losing relative financial status compared to the capitalists.[55] Investment in the public debt was an even better opportunity in those polities, like the Republic of Venice, whose form of government gave the patrician elite some real control over public finances or at least some early warning of possible trouble. It is not by chance that the Republic never defaulted on its debt, notwithstanding recurring and enormously expensive wars against a military giant like the Ottoman Empire—those who would have been responsible for the default were also those who had lent the resources to the state.[56]

Somewhat paradoxically, from the point of view of the wealthy commoners of continental Europe, becoming a noble might have offered greater economic advantages during the nineteenth century—that is, when the nobility is usually considered to have been in decline everywhere—after the spread of the reforms inspired by the French Revolution and codified by Napoleon. In fact, while nobles lost many of their privileges, they were also freed from many obligations, especially those aimed at preventing them from pursuing unbecoming activities and investments. In other words, they progressively acquired an advantage that until then had been reserved for non-noble aristocracies and chiefly the American one. This was because, as perfectly elucidated by Weber, being accepted into a circle of 'esteemed families' led to many favourable consequences including, in modern times, easier access to high-level, high-paying positions in corporations and administration and, even more importantly, useful social contacts through which to further one's financial and economic objectives.[57] This seems to have been the case in the German area, where the formal prohibition against nobles engaging in industrial endeavours was lifted in 1806, following Napoleon's victory at Austerlitz and the end of the Holy Roman Empire. Although much of the old nobility continued to observe the traditional boundaries of socially acceptable activities, the newly ennobled could act quite freely.[58] This became more relevant after the Unification of Germany in 1871 as the economic elites of Hanseatic cities like Hamburg, where status and political power had always depended much more on wealth than on nobility, were faced with the challenge of devising ways to profit from the opportunities offered by the new imperial context—a task which could be better accomplished by having some sort of contact with the emperor or at least with members of his court. This problem, however, was far more general: businessmen across Germany could no longer rely upon their established contacts with the local political elites but needed to approach the new rulers based in the (relatively) aristocratic new capital, Berlin.

Approaching the court milieu could prove very difficult for commoners, as a banker active in the late nineteenth and early twentieth centuries, Karl von der Heydt, stated in his memoirs:

As members of the bourgeoisie we were excluded from the court, which also meant that we could not belong to court society, by which is to be understood that exclusive circle assembled around the court, consisting of the higher nobility, the diplomatic corps, the highest court officials, and some very wealthy noble families.[59]

To overcome the obstacle, von der Heydt successfully sought ennoblement. In doing this, he followed a tendency that had intensified from the 1850s or 1860s. If in Prussia in the mid-nineteenth century the share of entrepreneurs among the newly ennobled was 6–7 per cent, during the reign of Emperor Wilhelm II (1888–1918) it had grown to 14–15 per cent. Of these new nobles, 40.5 per cent came from industry (often from the arms industry), 29.7 per cent from trade and 29.1 per cent from finance (the residual is unknown).[60] And yet, it has also been argued that the German business elites were relatively uninterested in merging with the nobility, possibly in part due to the presence among them of a strong Jewish component, preferring to form their own aristocratic elite instead.[61] This said, the growing presence of entrepreneurs and especially of industrialists among new nobles seems to have been a European trend. For example, in Britain, they were 11.5 per cent of the total in 1868–80, then peaking at 40.9 per cent in 1900–9.[62] In the case of Britain, however, the most striking feature is probably the relative willingness of nobles at least in the Victorian era to become involved in new businesses opportunities, at their own conditions, as will be seen in the next chapter.

Has a 'Global Aristocracy' Arisen Today?

The presence of a legally recognized nobility is not a necessary condition for the development of a well-defined aristocracy; the emergence of an American aristocracy during the nineteenth century is an excellent example. It is in this light, then, that we should understand recent concerns about the emergence of a sort of global aristocracy, functionally similar (from the distributive point of view) to national aristocracies of the past but defined on a much wider, and indeed global, geographic level. As an early example of this concern, consider what Stephen Haseler, a social scientist, argued somewhat emphatically in the late 1990s: 'New global capitalism is giving birth to nothing less than a new global aristocracy—a largely family-based class, or caste—which, through a variety of mechanisms, controls the huge accumulation of private capital—increasingly through inheritance', although as Haseler also admitted, this emerging global aristocracy might not be as 'rigidly entrenched' and 'not nearly as restricted' as past ones.[63] Some of these worries, and especially those about the growing importance of inheritance (as opposed to work) as a way of accumulating wealth, are central to more recent reflections on the limits and dangers of capitalism today, most famously those proposed by Thomas Piketty. Truly, inheritance is a crucial topic in a study of the rich and will recur in this book. We have already discussed its importance in allowing for the historical development of aristocracies. As today there are many signs that inheritances are becoming a larger and larger component of overall wealth in much of the West, it seems that the ground is fertile for the development of new aristocracies.[64]

However, there is more to an aristocracy than raw wealth. So, asking the question of whether a new global aristocracy is on the rise is not exactly the same as asking whether or not wealth inequality is growing (as seen in chapter 2, it is). Other factors, like the existence of some degree of social cohesion within an exclusive group, a cohesion originating from and continuously strengthened by social contacts and by some shared views and objectives, also play a role. There are many signals that point exactly in this direction. Consider for example the persistence of the practice of elite schooling, which involves sending children to a limited number of highly prestigious schools (and later, universities: think about the Ivy League in the United States or Oxford and Cambridge in Britain) which are overwhelmingly attended by the next generation of the elite. As the American sociologist Charles Wright Mills made clear in the 1950s, the shared experience of attending such institutions and perhaps being a member of their highly exclusive clubs played a critical role in establishing social, as well as psychological, affinities in the 'power elite' of the United States.[65]

More recently, evidence has been provided about the persistence of an 'old boy' culture in Britain. For example, it has been estimated that pupils from the Clarendon schools, a group of nine elite institutions designed as 'Great Schools' by the Clarendon Commission in 1861, are today ninety-four times more likely to take up prestigious positions than students coming from other schools. Interestingly, two recent British prime ministers, David Cameron and Boris Johnson, attended Eton College, the most prestigious of all the Clarendon schools (Rishi Sunak attended another, Winchester College). This is notwithstanding changes that have occurred in recent decades, mostly due to educational reform,[66] and the adoption of a new 'language of talent, merit, and hard work' which masks, but does not in any way counter, the ability of elite schools to create inequality in Britain as in the United States and elsewhere in the West.[67]

Those same changes, by making elite educational institutions somewhat more open to students from different backgrounds, have also offered an opportunity for wealthy foreigners to have their children educated in the same culture. In early 2020, just before the onset of the COVID-19 crisis, about

43 per cent of boarders in British boarding schools were the children of non-British parents residing overseas (children of immigrants are not included in the calculation). This implies a large increase from the 31 per cent of 2007, the first year for which these data are available. In 2020, 46 per cent of foreign pupils came from mainland China and Hong Kong. Germans (6%) followed, at a distance. The prevalence of foreigners, however, appears to have been rather lower in Clarendon schools, at least judging by the small percentage of students who took English as an additional language (less than 6% at Eton in 2019).[68] At Yale, which will be taken as exemplary of Ivy League universities, the international student population has increased by over 50 per cent in the last decade. In 2019–20, international students represented 22 per cent of the total enrolment, with Chinese students leading by a wide margin: they accounted for 32 per cent of all international students, followed by Canadians (8.4%), Indians (7.7%), South Koreans (5%) and Britons (4.6%). Surely today not all students from elite educational institutions come from a privileged background, and the international mobility of students is, generally speaking, a very positive development. At the same time, however, the growing prevalence of non-Western students in highly prestigious institutions can also be taken as indicative that a global aristocracy, itself the inheritor of pre-existing national aristocracies, might truly be in the making.

Prestigious educational institutions are also one of the means through which

> valuable extracurricular interests and practices [are nurtured], particularly in terms of sport, cultural participation, and taste. These dispositions and practices do not necessarily guarantee entrance to the elite, but they do smooth trajectories, especially in hypercompetitive settings where informal notions of cultural fit are used to distinguish between candidates who are otherwise similar in terms of credentials and experience.[69]

The 'smoothing of trajectories' is exactly why worries about the emergence of a global aristocracy are justified. As with national aristocracies of the past, belonging to today's global aristocracy leads to some de facto privileges: like being preferred for a top post over equally or even better qualified competitors simply because of a specific background (coming from a very rich family, having attended the right schools and universities) and of *appearing* and *being perceived* to belong to a social elite. In this kind of situation, 'merit' becomes nothing more than a rhetorical expedient.

The tendency of the rich and super-rich to create their own aristocracies, or to join pre-existing established aristocratic groups like the nobility, is one of the reasons why a condition of high wealth inequality can give rise to social concern, as will be discussed in Part III of the book. It is clear, though, that not all the rich were born into great wealth, and surely not all of them made their fortunes by exploiting aristocratic privilege. Indeed, Western history is full of examples of brilliant individuals who managed to acquire great wealth thanks to their abilities; it is to this category that we must now turn our attention.

4

On Innovation and Technology

THE HISTORY OF THE WEST is punctuated by brilliant individuals who climbed to the top of the wealth pyramid thanks to their exceptional skills (and, almost invariably, to a bit of luck). There is a clear historical path towards wealth built on merit, competence and courage. Of all possible paths to personal enrichment, this is today the least controversial, although the same is not necessarily true in the case of past societies. This chapter focuses on those individuals who became rich as a result of their ability to innovate or to correctly identify the new opportunities provided by changes in markets and economic structures or in technology. However, the opportunities open to economically ambitious individuals have not been the same throughout history, which is why we will begin with the Middle Ages, then move to early modern times, when the opening of the Atlantic trade routes created a radically new situation, and finally to the heroic phase of the Industrial Revolution(s). As with noble dynasties, in the case of merchant or entrepreneurial dynasties the fact of being born into great wealth is no guarantee of possessing valuable personal qualities; in other words, within those dynasties, after the generation of the founders, great wealth tends to become increasingly unrelated to merit. This is a major reason why, across the world, resentment against the very wealthy is building up, and consequently it will be given particular attention. The chapter ends by looking at a more recent period, when the beginning of the computer age and the advent of new information technologies offered exceptional opportunities for rapid enrichment, but also when inequality became enrooted in many countries.

As a conclusion to this brief introduction, it is worth recalling that, by definition, entrepreneurship is closely connected to innovation, at least if we adopt the popular view originally introduced by the Austrian economist Joseph Schumpeter. According to him, an entrepreneur is whoever is willing and able to apply an innovation to economic processes. This might involve transforming an invention into a commercial product, establishing new commercial routes or simply improving production processes or forms of business organization. To make something new, however, more often than not the entrepreneur needs to break what existed before: something Schumpeter referred to as 'creative destruction'.[1] This is one reason why, while arguably society profits from the rise of entrepreneurial innovators, this process is not without its victims, as will become clear in the course of this chapter.

Brilliant Sinners: Traders and Merchant-Entrepreneurs in the Middle Ages (and Before)

Opportunities to become rich through entrepreneurship and innovation have been relatively more abundant in some epochs than in others. In European history, a consolidated historiographical tradition holds that the Roman Empire did not constitute a setting particularly favourable to technological (and business) innovation. In addition long-range commerce was stifled by the tendency of all provinces to converge towards substantial uniformity in the goods produced and consumed (think of the well-known Roman habit of trying to plant their preferred vegetables and trees, like grapevines and olive trees, wherever they went, thus preventing the large-scale import-export of related goods such as wine and oil) and by the social disapproval with which those involved in trade were met, including (albeit less so) at the largest scale of operations. There were, of course, exceptions, and even some senators were known to use, or were suspected of using, strawmen to pursue 'disreputable' business activities. We should also account for some degree of variation across space and time and remember that the imperial setting also offered substantial advantages to business, for example, a large unified market and a common currency and language. For this reason, in the centuries following the fall of the Empire and the crumbling of its economic and commercial system, the entrepreneurial path to wealth became even more difficult to tread and the wealthiest individuals tended to belong to a different category: the nobility.[2]

Things started to slowly change from the eleventh century, when the so-called 'Commercial Revolution' of the Middle Ages began. Starting in Italy, which had been the core of the old Roman Empire, and in the Byzantine domains in the eastern Mediterranean area, a new commercial economy developed which would soon involve the rest of Europe. In this story, the Italian 'maritime republics' that grew around important trading cities like Amalfi, Genoa, Pisa,

Venice and, on the other side of the Adriatic Sea, Ragusa, played a crucial role, as did, with a delay of a century or so, the northern European cities of the Hanseatic League, a commercial and defensive confederation. It is in these very specific social, economic and cultural environments, so different from the prevailing conditions of the time—'*illa gens non arat, non seminat, non vindemiat*', that is, 'that people do not plough, nor sow, nor harvest grapes' an amazed eleventh-century writer from Pavia (a city right in the middle of the Po Plain) observed, referring to the Venetians—that bold individuals could devise ways to profit from growing business opportunities. Among them, those who managed to rise to the greatest wealth were merchants specializing in international trade, the same economic elite that, according to the French historian Fernand Braudel, played a crucial role in the early emergence of Western capitalism.[3]

This economic elite prospered especially in places which, from the political and institutional point of view, were exceptional: a merchant 'republic' clearly does not belong to the system of medieval feudalism (notwithstanding its ability to generate, in time, an urban patriciate sharing crucial characteristics with the nobility, as seen in chapter 3). If we look at the exceptional character of the main medieval merchant cities, including the 'free cities' of the Hansa League, from our specific perspective focused on the rich, we must come to the somewhat surprising conclusion that it was here, much more than in the main body of the continent where an agrarian economy and feudal structures prevailed, that income and wealth inequality could grow without check. This point was also made, with usual acumen, by Max Weber: 'Feudalism, with its closely delineated rights and duties, does not only have a stabilizing effect upon the economy as a whole, but also upon the distribution of individual wealth'.[4] In other words, although it enrooted a fairly high degree of economic inequality, feudalism, precisely because it constrained the ambitions of the emerging groups, tended to prevent economic disparities across societies from reaching even higher levels.

However, Weber seems to have failed to notice the other side of the coin: the rise of commoners' wealth could not have occurred *without* the presence of the nobility, because it was precisely to service the needs of the nobles that the Commercial Revolution had started. Given the high transportation costs, long-distance medieval trade tended to be profitable only for highly valuable goods which, in the eleventh or twelfth century, were demanded almost exclusively by the ruling classes and their immediate subordinates (bureaucrats, high officials and officers and so on). It was their desire to consume luxury goods that led to the initial emergence of a network of long-distance trade routes, which whenever possible mirrored those that had been used in Roman times. Most of these luxuries were produced in southern Europe, and in some cases (like that of fine glass from Venice) they were an Italian monopoly or almost one, while other goods (particularly pepper and other exotic spices) had to be sourced from the Levant and north Africa but still required the intermediation of southern European merchants. Additionally, the dietary preferences of the nobility, for example regarding the consumption of white bread and of wine (wheat and grapes are difficult to cultivate in northern Europe), generated a need for other trades, offering new opportunities to keen merchants.[5]

So it was in the main trading cities, with their relatively ample economic freedoms, that capable and bold individuals could rise to such heights of wealth to become, compared to their fellow citizens and in the words of the French theologian Nicole Oresme, 'as God among men'. Yet notwithstanding the opportunities offered by the Commercial Revolution, the Middle Ages were certainly not an epoch particularly conducive to entrepreneurial enrichment. According to medieval Christian theology the rich were all sinners, heading towards eternal damnation because of their avarice. This issue is fundamental to our understanding of the cultural unease generated by the presence of the very rich within society and will be developed in detail in chapter 8. For now, suffice it to say that in the Middle Ages there was considerable cultural resistance to the rise of commoners to great wealth.[6] This was not a problem for the nobles who were recognized as having a right to rule over non-nobles and to have privileged access to resources (although only within the complex of mutual obligations typical of the feudal system). But rich merchants, let alone the despised bankers discussed in the next chapter, at the start of the Commercial Revolution were considered an anomaly.[7]

Cultural and religious pressure against great wealth weighed so heavily upon the minds and souls of many members of medieval merchant and entrepreneurial families that some repented and stripped themselves in full or in part of their worldly possessions. The most striking cases became renowned and were the object of veneration. The best example is probably that of St Francis, the scion of a rich merchant family from Assisi in Italy who renounced his father's wealth to pursue a life of poverty and prayer, ultimately founding a mendicant order. While St Francis radically changed his way of life when still in his twenties, others made similar decisions only after achieving entrepreneurial success, sometimes rather unscrupulously.

Take the case of Godric of Finchale, born towards the end of the eleventh century to a family of poor peasants from Walpole in England. His origins were so humble that he started as a beachcomber, sifting sand hoping to find salvageable goods from shipwrecks. His first move up the social ladder was to become a peddler in his own town, but the real turning point in his career was joining a group of itinerant merchants who travelled from market to market. Based on the surviving accounts, Godric was an exceptionally able and successful merchant and soon accumulated enough resources to play the great game of international trade, sailing along the shores of Britain, Flanders and Denmark.[8] According to some sources, he might also have been involved in acts of piracy—indeed, he might even have been the English pirate Goderic who in 1102 helped Baldwin, first king of Jerusalem, during the First Crusade, although this is highly uncertain. And then, at the peak of his success and having achieved great wealth, the conversion: Godric—reportedly after a visit to the holy island of Lindisfarne and a vision of St Cuthbert—chose to become poor again. He gave away all his goods to charity and started to live as a hermit in Finchale. He was soon recognized as a saint, known (as St Francis also was) for his kindness towards wild animals.[9]

The cases of St Francis and St Godric are indicative of the unease which accompanied the building of great merchant fortunes for most of the Middle Ages. They remain, however, exceptional cases: in most instances successful merchants found a way to combine their economic ascent, the building of a family fortune to pass on to their descendants and their fears of the afterlife. An excellent example is that of the merchant from Prato, Francesco di Marco Datini, whose economic activities are well known due to the survival of his enormous personal archive, which includes 130,000 business letters, 500 books of accounts and several thousand documents of other kinds. Born in 1335 to a middling family, in 1348 Datini was made an orphan by the Black Death. His father (a retail seller of food who probably also worked as a moneylender) left him a small house, a piece of land and the sum of 47 florins. In what his contemporaries must have regarded as a very bold move, probably even rash, Francesco Datini, aged fifteen, sold the land for 150 florins and left Prato for Avignon in southern France. The city, which at that time hosted the Papal Court, was an important centre for trade, where Italian and Flemish merchants met and their interests intertwined. Within a decade Datini was well established, forming partnerships with other Tuscan merchants and specializing in the trade of metals, arms and armour. For some idea of his success, consider that when in 1367 he renewed a partnership with Toro di Berto both merchants contributed capital of 2,500 florins. Datini's shops in Avignon traded in a large variety of goods, which soon included cloths, spices and silk. Datini also started exporting fine French enamels to Florence and developed a very profitable trade in religious pictures. By now, from his base in Avignon, he managed a thick network of business relationships spanning beyond Provence, Catalonia and many Italian cities, including Rome and Naples. And yet, when Pope Gregory XI returned to Rome, Francesco Datini decided to return to his native Tuscany as well, after having spent more than thirty years in Avignon.

In Italy, Datini's activities flourished further. He made a decisive move into the cloth market, establishing manufactories in Prato, joining the Florentine *Arte della Lana* (the guild of wool manufacturers and merchants) and becoming a major importer and distributor of foreign wool and rough cloth to be finished locally. In 1386 he opened a warehouse in Florence proper and formed companies with local merchants, focusing on the wholesale trade and distribution of luxuries and bulk commodities. Whenever possible, he diversified: in the textile sector he started trading silk as well and established ventures in a range of cities including Pisa, Genoa, Barcelona and Valencia. This careful diversification strategy seems to have been Datini's trademark: he was capable of bold moves to seize new market opportunities but was also markedly risk-averse, favouring an incremental strategy of accumulation. Each of the companies that he started operated as an independent enterprise, and he was in the habit of insuring all his merchandise even when risks were deemed minimal. His business practices were very innovative for his time—he was a genuine Schumpeterian entrepreneur—and influenced many others. Indeed, Francesco Datini might have been the inventor, or at least one of the first promoters, of a new form of business organization: the partnership system, which provided owners with some protection from financial ruin due to unlimited liability and also allowed easy diversification into multiple markets.[10]

Almost until the moment of his death, in 1410, Datini continued to work and to increase his patrimony (in 1403 he was the tenth richest resident of Florence, a remarkable achievement, given his relatively humble origins and the wealth of the city). However, upon his death he had no surviving son to continue his activities, a circumstance which might have made it easier for him to pursue a very long-term kind of investment in eternal salvation. He left a yearly sum of 100 florins for the sustenance of his widow and assigned 1,000 florins to his daughter, but the bulk of his estate (which overall amounted to almost 100,000 florins: 500–600 times his initial inherited capital) was destined for the foundation of a hospital for the poor, the *Casa del Ceppo dei poveri*.

Francesco was also an innovator in charity, as a much smaller sum (1,000 florins) was destined for the establishment of the *Spedale degli Innocenti* in Florence, the first orphanage specifically for abandoned children.[11]

Francesco Datini's charity upon his death is simply an exceptional case of a practice which was quite common among medieval merchants and, as will be seen, continued in some form in early modern times and beyond. Indeed, this seems to have been a conscious attempt to balance the risk of eternal damnation with the urge to accumulate wealth: a proper 'strategy for the afterlife', in the words of historian Samuel K. Cohn.[12] But his story offers more to our understanding of the specificities of the paths to wealth that were open during the final centuries of the Middle Ages. Francesco was, in a sense, 'freed' from his duties to family and from social constraints by the Black Death, which allowed him to inherit much earlier and without having to share (in addition to his parents, two of his three brothers died during the pandemic), and to emigrate to France without a second thought. In the post-plague decades, the social-economic context became favourable to the rise, both political and economic, of new families.[13] Francesco Datini profited from this relatively open society, despite the fact that the Black Death caused considerable harm to many members of the 'old wealth' of the time, descendants of those who had prospered in the heyday of the Commercial Revolution,[14] which is entirely coherent with the picture of sharp decline in wealth inequality after the pandemic discussed in chapter 2. Changes in social and economic structures, but also in consumption habits, triggered by the Black Death allowed for the easier introduction of innovations. For example, the boom in the silk industry in Italian cities like Lucca or Bologna from the second half of the fourteenth century has been explicitly connected to the new situation created by the plague.[15] Now, we must move to the early modern period, when the forces for change that the Black Death had helped to liberate brought bountiful fruits— for those who were ready to collect them.[16]

A New World of Opportunities

The progressive expansion of a European and Mediterranean trading network during the Middle Ages set the scene for the boom in international trade that accompanied the opening of the Atlantic trade routes. At the onset of this story, Portuguese and Spanish explorers and traders played a key role. Initially they had pursued different objectives: the Portuguese had been trying for most of the fifteenth century to open a sea route circumnavigating Africa, with the intention of reaching the source of the precious spices that were in high demand across Europe and thereby replacing the Italian merchants (chiefly the Venetians) as the main suppliers to northern Europe. The Spanish, on the other hand, jumped at the chance to find a shortcut—reaching China by crossing the Atlantic, as proposed by Columbus—both for their own profit and to undermine the efforts of their Portuguese neighbours and potential rivals. Both of these projects were accomplished by the end of the fifteenth century: in 1492 Columbus reached Hispaniola in the Caribbean, while in 1498 Vasco da Gama reached Calicut in India. This gave southern European merchants a head start.[17] Importantly, the Italians were not excluded from the early business opportunities provided by the Atlantic routes. After all, Columbus was Genoese—as was much of the capital that funded many of the early expeditions to the New World.

Soon, however, northern European economic actors (the Dutch and later the English) entered the game, and in time they managed to cut for themselves a very large part of a continuously increasing pie. In this, they were considerably helped by a crucial innovation, the privileged trading companies, beginning with the foundation of the Dutch East India Company or VOC (*Vereenigde Oostindische Compagnie*) in 1602. These companies were established to exploit the commercial opportunities offered by the new trade routes but also to make up for lost time in comparison with the Portuguese and Spanish 'first comers'. They possessed special privileges, such as the exclusive right to use certain routes or to trade in specific goods. The major ones were also given some state-like powers, such as the power to maintain a fleet and army and to govern the bases and territories they obtained outside Europe. Altogether, the privileged companies represented an excellent new investment opportunity for the wealthy, including for rich nobles who could become shareholders without dirtying their hands with 'bourgeois' activities.[18]

The emerging situation also opened up new paths for enrichment for all those bold enough to face the many dangers (personal as well as economic) inherent in this kind of trade. As an example, consider the Dutch trader Jan Pieterszoon Coen, born in 1587 to a relatively modest family from Hoorn, a port city in northern Holland. His father, who had started off as a brewer and later moved into commerce, seems to have fully understood that a new golden age of trade was approaching. He sent his young son to Rome for a seven-year apprenticeship with a Flemish-Italian family of bankers, the Visschers. There, Coen was to learn the accountancy and trading techniques used in southern Europe, like double-entry bookkeeping, which at the time were more advanced than those used in the north. When he returned to Holland, Coen was ready for the kind of ambitious merchant expeditions that the VOC was planning in the East Indies. In 1607 he joined one of the very first of these expeditions as an assistant merchant. To appreciate the kind of personal risk that he was willing to take, consider that, according to one estimate, mortality among the Dutch leaving for the East Indies could easily have reached 50% in the first voyages organized by the VOC.[19] Coen's first trip, however, was successful, and by 1612 he was ready for a second one, this time as a senior merchant.

Coen's rapid rise to higher office is explained not only by his personal skills, which were considerable, but also by VOC's rapid expansion. This allowed Coen to become the head of all of the VOC's trading and plantation activities in Bantam (west Java) in 1615, director-general of the company shortly thereafter and finally, in 1617, aged thirty, governor-general of the East Indies. As governor he was responsible for planning and executing the overall strategy of the VOC's commercial and economic expansion, as well as for managing its military power, given that this new golden age of international trade was rife with conflict: with local potentates and with what remained of the Portuguese domains, but also with their increasingly ambitious English rivals. It was Coen who advocated that the VOC should try to secure spices directly from the producers in Asia, forcefully keeping rivals out of the trade and avoiding price increases at the source from which the natives might have benefited to the detriment of the Europeans. This led to a focus on a few highly profitable commodities and in particular cloves, mace and, the most profitable of all, nutmeg. Nutmeg originated in the Banda Islands in Indonesia and was much sought after not only as a cooking spice, but also as a drug with many medical uses, including as protection against the plague. Given that nutmeg could not be cultivated outside the Bandas, the VOC was in a position to control the entire trade, reaping enormous profits: it has been estimated that in the early seventeenth century the selling price in Europe was 840 times the price at the source.[20]

Jan Pieterszoon Coen served as governor-general of the East Indies for two terms. In-between, he returned for a few years to Europe, where he married a woman from a prominent family, Eva Ment, probably with the aim of consolidating his social ascension and possibly with a view to strengthening his political clout before returning to the Indies. In fact, Coen repeatedly had to fight to impose his views upon the company's top ruling body, the *Heeren XVII* or 'Gentlemen Seventeen', composed entirely of members of very wealthy and already established families. These had looked down on Coen, with the condescension always reserved for the nouveau riche, however capable they might be. Additionally, some among them had reservations about the ruthlessness with which Coen had fostered the VOC's interests in the Indies.[21]

Before focusing on this aspect, and more generally on the 'dark side' of early modern commercial and colonial expansion, we need to look more closely at the whole range of different paths towards wealth that it created. There were many of these, as could be expected given the dramatic increase in international trade that was associated with this early phase of globalization and the substantial stimulus that it provided to the European economy by triggering 'a virtuous circle of increased trade, growth of purchasing power, consumption, work ethics, institutional change and innovation'.[22] First, there was the opportunity to become directly involved in the Atlantic business, as an independent trader or as the employee of a privileged company. The latter situation, which was the case of Coen, was by far the most frequent for the longest routes, due to the exclusive rights granted to, and enforced by, such companies. Within them, offices were often very remunerative, due to good salaries and abundant opportunities to make extra profit through private trade, corruption and theft. This is how a governor-general of the VOC, whose nominal salary amounted to 700 florins per month, could end up earning 10 million florins. Although opportunities for lining one's pockets increased steadily from the bottom to the top of the company's hierarchy, the practice was ubiquitous and explains why so many were ready to take on even the humblest positions on privileged companies' ships, suffering terrible living conditions for years at a time. But for those who had capital to invest, the privileged companies offered excellent opportunities without leaving the comforts of Amsterdam or London; the VOC, for example, since its founding paid an average yearly dividend of 18 per cent. Despite the obvious risks (many a privileged company went bankrupt), the most careful and luckiest investors saw their capital multiplied in a matter of years.[23]

There were also those who simply preyed on the labour of others. In the sixteenth and seventeenth centuries, far from European eyes a merchant could easily turn pirate if the effort looked worth the risk. Beyond this, the conflicts which were generated by commercial and colonial expansion, as well as the spillovers from disputes over European affairs, led to the spread of the practice of granting 'letters of marque' to corsairs or privateers. These letters basically allowed the beneficiary to perform legal piracy, attacking the vessels of enemy countries (but often preying on noncombatants during peacetime as well) and taking them and their cargo as prizes.[24] Some corsairs became fabulously rich, such as Sir Francis Drake, an English privateer with modest origins (he was the son of a farmer) who from the 1570s to the 1590s preyed upon Spanish ships and coastal towns. His most successful operation was the capture of *Nuestra Señora de la Concepción*, a Spanish 'treasure ship' which had been following the Manila route with its cargo of 36 kilograms of gold, 26 tons of silver and chest upon chest of other treasures.[25] According to a somewhat bizarre list of 'top-earning pirates' published by *Forbes* in 2008, Drake's lifetime earnings from piracy would have amounted to 115 million dollars (138 million in 2020 U.S. dollars), making him the second most successful pirate of all time. The first place goes to 'Black Sam' Bellamy, an English pirate active in the early eighteenth century who specialized in capturing Spanish and French ships off the Atlantic coasts of America and whose reported lifetime earnings reached 144 million in 2020 U.S. dollars.[26]

The flourishing of piracy is just one among many questionable—yet entrepreneurial—practices that became widespread with the opening of the Atlantic routes. A recent synthesis of those predatory behaviours that can be grouped under the heading of 'raiding' distinguished among three main categories: piracy, the exploitation of natives and slaving.[27] All of these, and especially the last two (as piracy mostly pitted European against European), are highly relevant to recent attempts to re-interpret the rise of the West to global dominance along lines somewhat less flattering to the Europeans. Historian Kenneth Pomeranz's famous book *The Great Divergence* (2000) is an excellent example. Here, we will briefly focus on how these practices generated their own paths towards enrichment, beginning with the exploitation of natives. It is useful to go back to the case of Jan Pieterszoon Coen, whose behaviour in the Indies led to some raised eyebrows even among his superiors, as he did not hold back from very harsh treatment of native populations whenever they opposed him or seemed guilty of some misdemeanour against the Dutch. The best-known examples are, first, the razing of the Indonesian city of Jacatra (today Jakarta) with the subsequent expulsion of the native population.[28] Second, there was the 1621 attack on the natives of the Banda Islands, who had allegedly violated a contract with the Dutch which prevented them from also trading with the English. Due to the impossible-to-meet conditions imposed on the defeated, over 90 per cent of the population died. Of the 1,000 or so survivors, 800 were forcibly relocated to Java. The workforce was then replenished by importing Asian slaves to serve under Dutch planters. Although some of the victims might have died of disease, the behaviour of the Dutch in the Banda Islands has been rightly considered a form of ethnic cleansing. This is why the historical figure of Coen, who from the end of the nineteenth century, after a long period of oblivion, had been portrayed as a heroic character in Dutch history, has been the object of much controversy in recent years.[29]

The exploitation of natives was recurrent in all European colonial empires, beginning with the first phase of European expansion, dominated by the Spanish and the Portuguese. Many *conquistadores* came from a relatively poor background, which is why they were ready to take part in such dangerous voyages of exploration and conquest to begin with. They had every intention of making a great fortune in the New World, and the easiest way to achieve this was at the expense of the natives. Take the case of Francisco Pizarro, exemplary of an entire generation of poor adventurers from the Spanish region of Extremadura. The illegitimate and illiterate son of a second-order noble, he travelled for the first time to the Americas in 1502, when he was already in his late twenties. So, for him, real success was relatively slow in coming, but when it arrived it was truly spectacular: in 1532, notwithstanding the enormous disparity in the forces on the ground, he managed to capture Atahualpa, emperor of the Incas. After inducing him to collect an enormous ransom (reportedly, Atahualpa promised 85 cubic metres of gold and double that amount of silver for his own freedom), he ruthlessly put him to death after a mock trial and proceeded to secure the whole of Peru for the Spanish crown, putting an end to the Inca civilization. At the same time, together with his brothers, he tried to establish a strong personal grip on as much Peruvian wealth and resources as possible. Although in time the Spanish crown tried to seize most of the possessions of the Pizarro family in the New World (especially after their feud with the Almagro family, which cost the lives of both Francisco Pizarro and his old associate, Diego de Almagro), they managed to preserve considerable wealth, having reinvested much of the revenue from Peru in Spain as was common among the *conquistadores*. Francisco's brother, Hernando, was particularly keen to establish the conditions in which his descendants would become respected components of the Spanish upper class, which is why he created a *mayorazgo* (an entail) in favour of his son, to preserve the integrity of the family patrimony across generations. Indeed, in 1629, another member of the family, also called Francisco, was made Marquis of Castile and was granted a substantial yearly income in exchange for renouncing some of the residual family claims in the Americas.[30]

The stories of many Spanish *conquistadores* show remarkable similarities to the processes of conquest, ennoblement and enrichment discussed in chapter 3, for example those that followed the Norman Conquest of England. But here, what needs to be underlined is that the initial plunder represented only a tiny part of the overall exploitation of the natives. This continued for centuries under a variety of systems, like the Spanish *encomienda* which allowed the European beneficiary (the *encomendero*) to impose tributes upon specific groups of locals, to be paid in gold, in kind or in labour. Indeed, with the passing of time and the exhaustion of treasures ready for the taking, people—the labour force—became the most sought-after commodity. As written by a late conquistador, Bernardo Vargas Machuca, at the turn of the seventeenth century, 'The Spaniard does not settle or inhabit deserted lands, however healthy and rich they may be in gold and silver; he inhabits and settles where he finds Indians'.[31]

And yet, as a consequence of the demographic collapse suffered by American populations, the Indians soon became scarce.[32] This development played a pivotal role in promoting the third and final kind of raiding: slaving. There are two distinct aspects to consider here. First, the use of slaves was widespread in European colonies. Going back to the case of the Pizarro family, Francisco's brother Hernando, who played a key role in managing the exploitation of the recently discovered silver mines of Potosí, imported black slaves for the heaviest duties from 1536.[33] Slaves, most of them of African origin, soon became ubiquitous in the European plantations in the Americas and were fundamental in enriching both the nascent colonial elite and their relations back in Europe. Slavery was also present in East Asian colonies, although its spread was more limited. Jan Pieterszoon Coen, who considered it expedient to substitute slaves for difficult-to-control local populations in key producing areas (remember the case of the Banda Islands), tried to promote slavery but with limited success, given that many native governments of the area considered it a repugnant and immoral practice and were not ready to provide the Europeans with slaves.[34]

The second aspect to highlight is that the slave trade itself remained a profitable business for most of the early modern period. The transfer to the Americas of at least 12 million enslaved Africans from the sixteenth to the nineteenth century (of whom about 1.5 million died during the trip), to which we should add about 6 million slaves destined for Asian colonies, was initially built upon a network established by Portuguese merchants from the fifteenth century to import slaves to Europe.[35] The Portuguese were the first to profit greatly from this new opportunity and monopolized the Atlantic slave trade throughout the sixteenth century. From the early seventeenth century, however, the Dutch, the British and the French entered the trade to service their own colonies as well as to divert part of the revenues from the Portuguese, revenues which remained conspicuous throughout the early modern period.[36] In chapter 3, the case of the French trader and financier Antoine II Crozat, who obtained the monopoly on the slave trade in the Spanish colonies, has already been discussed. The British proved particularly successful slavers, especially from the mid-seventeenth century when the growing demand for sugar in Europe led to a boom in production on the plantations of the Antilles, which relied heavily upon a slave workforce.[37]

Granted, the new opportunities for enrichment from the opening of the Atlantic trade routes towards the Americas and Asia were not exclusively cases of exploitation, nor were all those who benefited from the new opportunities personally involved in practices that would appear questionable or altogether repugnant to modern observers and certainly not to Europeans of the past, who had a much lower bar for acceptable behaviour, especially regarding non-white people. And yet, the fact remains that the dark side was strong; as suggested by historian Kenneth Andrews, referring in particular to the British case, trade, plunder and settlement (including in lands forcefully stolen from the natives) were all part of an inextricable bundle of practices. Pomeranz goes further, arguing that slavery and the exploitation of non-European areas were fundamental in placing western Europe on its rising path compared to other relatively advanced areas of the world (the 'Great Divergence').[38] As will be seen, this contrasts directly with the views of those who argue that the phase of exceptionally rapid progress characterizing much of the West from the nineteenth century was mostly the result of innovation, and hence of the efforts of ambitious entrepreneurs aiming to improve their material conditions. Before focusing on this period, more needs to be said about the opportunities for enrichment that, in early modern times, opened up in the Old World and were only indirectly affected by the European expansion to other continents.

New Opportunities in the Old World

While the paths towards enrichment offered by the economic use of the resources of the New World tended to attract unscrupulous individuals, or at least led many to resort to questionable practices, developments in the Old World provided opportunities to achieve great wealth that better fit the modern ideal of success built upon 'merit'. From the very beginning of the early modern period some industrial sectors, like large-scale mining, the fishing industry and of course the complex and composite textile sector, underwent spectacular transformations that offered keen entrepreneurs plenty of opportunities for success.

Take fishing for example, and more specifically the development of large-scale and 'industrial' herring fisheries in northern Europe. Here, huge profits came from exploiting a crucial innovation, the invention of the herring buss, a specialized deep-sea vessel. The herring buss was developed in Dutch ship-yards during the fifteenth century and was the culmination of a centuries-long process that had seen Dutch fishermen struggling to impose their cured her-rings on the internal market and in the broader Baltic area, which for most of the Middle Ages had been dominated by the higher-quality (and better-tasting) produce of southern Sweden.[39] Basically, the herring buss was a factory-ship: a direct ancestor, together with whalers, of today's fish-processing vessels with facilities for freezing. Compared to earlier ships the herring buss was able to remain at sea for longer periods at a time (five to eight weeks) and to process the product onboard, which involved other innovations to speed up the gutting and salting of fish. This allowed it to fish farther away from port, roaming the open North Sea searching for schools of herring since they had been dwindling close to the coast.

Although the initial development of the herring buss dates to the fifteenth century, many improvements were needed to perfect the numerous techno-logical innovations involved, and to make this new sector function smoothly additional innovations were required in business organization, financing (es-pecially the *partenrederij*, a form of partnership which allowed groups of urban capital-holders to make joint investments in specific ships, limiting the expo-sure of each single investor) and institutional support for the industry, for example to monitor quality control: a complex and incremental process that was completed only by the second half of the sixteenth century. Thereafter, the number of active herring busses boomed, reaching peak numbers in the first decades of the seventeenth century when 500 ships were operational in Hol-land alone. This resulted in an almost fourfold increase in production com-pared to the mid-sixteenth century and established the basis upon which the Dutch Republic succeeded in monopolizing the market, which they continued to do until the end of the seventeenth century.[40] As most fishing firms owned only one or two herring busses (although some had up to ten), the number of entrepreneurs active in the field was quite large. If one considers that even greater profits could be made by trading salted herrings instead of directly producing them and that this became the main Dutch export in the Baltic area, it is clear how the little 'herring revolution' experienced by the Dutch Republic created widespread opportunities for enrichment.[41]

The case of the Dutch fishing industry is exemplary of the transformative power that technological innovation could have well before the beginning of the Industrial Revolution. Another good example is the silk mill, invented in Italy during the thirteenth century.[42] As has been explained for the fishing industry, technological innovations could be fully exploited only after they were accompanied by other kinds of innovation, in business practices, in labour organization and in the relevant institutional framework. Innovations of this kind were also crucial to the success of those who aspired to profit from one of the major historical developments of early modern times: the dramatic increase in the strength and reach of the state and the accompanying expansion of its bureaucracy.

Beyond offering opportunities for enrichment 'from within', that is, from holding well-paid offices, early modern states needed to outsource a broad and expanding set of services. Many had to do with a key function, collecting taxes. Indeed, tax farmers regularly appear among the very richest members of pre-industrial European societies, as will be further detailed in the next chapter. In other instances, states acquired innovative services developed by private entrepreneurs, some of which in time came to be considered so important and strategic that they decided to internalize them. This is precisely what happened with postal services, which in their modern form were developed by an Italian family, the Tasso (or 'de Tassis' in the Latinized version), who in time would become a prestigious and super-rich component of the German nobility: the Thurn und Taxis.

Francesco Tasso, born in the Italian village of Cornello in northern Lombardy in 1459, plays a key role in this story. He built upon the expertise accumulated in earlier decades by other members of his family who had helped to set up the *Compagnia dei Corrieri* in Venice, a private corporation that provided postal services to the Republic, while a distinct branch of the family (the Sandri) had provided similar services to the Papal Court in Rome. In 1489 an older brother of Francesco, Iannetto, had become director of the postal service of the Holy Roman Emperor, Maximilian I of Habsburg, and towards the end of the century had received as compensation for unpaid services some mines and a fief in the Austrian region of Carinthia (mining would remain an important side-activity for the Tasso). But it was Francesco who brought the family business to an entirely different level and in the process radically reformed the way in which postal services were organized across the European continent. In

1501 in Bruges, he was appointed *Maistre et Capitaine de Postes* ('Master and Captain of the Post') of Maximilian's son, Philip the Handsome, an episode which is usually considered the turning point in the development of a pan-European postal system.[43] Originally, Francesco Tasso was asked to reorganize the postal services of Philip's domains in the Low Countries and in Bourgogne, basically acting as a private contractor. In 1505, shortly after the young duke had become king of Castile (Philip I) through his spouse Juana, a new contract was stipulated by which Francesco had to secure the postal connections between the main post office in Brussels and Spain, to the southern city of Granada, as well as with a range of French cities in-between. Finally, postal connections were established with the imperial court of Innsbruck, and it must be highlighted that the composite and territorially fragmented character of the Habsburg domains in sixteenth-century Europe played an important role in establishing the need for a new kind of regular postal service, spanning the continent (in 1516 the service was extended to include Italy, reflecting Habsburg expansion in that area). The 1505 contract provided Francesco with a yearly allowance of 12,000 Flemish livres to ensure a high-quality service, which he dutifully provided: in those years, post from Brussels reached Innsbruck in five days and Granada in fifteen (six and eighteen in wintertime).[44]

Francesco Tasso proved to be such a capable postal entrepreneur that in 1515 Emperor Maximilian awarded him new fiefs and the illustrious title of count palatine. The family had just made a decisive move towards high noble status. Francesco died without direct descendants in 1518, but his place was taken by a nephew, Giovanni Battista Tasso (one of his many family associates) and passed on across generations. The services provided by the family continued to expand, and new postal routes were opened and administered by the Tasso based on a range of agreements with local governments, which allowed them to acquire and to hold a semi-monopoly in the sector for centuries. The service, which had initially been provided to rulers and high state officials only, by the beginning of the seventeenth century was open to all those who could afford to pay the fees established by the Tasso, a development which vastly increased the scope of their business. The family reached its maximum power in the seventeenth century, after another Holy Roman Emperor, Rudolph II, had progressively made all postal services an imperial privilege, granting it as exclusive to the Tasso family in a move aimed at strengthening the emperor's pre-eminence over the rest of the imperial nobility. In a turn of events which might seem bizarre to modern eyes, matters evolved even further in favour of the Tasso family, as in 1615 the high charge of imperial postmaster was enfeoffed to Lamoral Tasso and his descendants: medieval feudal institutions were bent to serve modern needs.[45] In 1624 the Tasso family was elevated further, becoming *freiherren* of the Empire. Around that time, to consolidate their claim to noble status and maybe to better integrate into the German elite, they started to call themselves Thurn und Taxis, adding to their name that of a Milanese family with ancient Longobard origins, the della Torre (tower, or *turm* in German), from whom they now (rather questionably) claimed to descend. In 1682 the Thurn und Taxis became imperial princes and in 1754 were even admitted to the Imperial Diet, the most exclusive political body of the Holy Roman Empire. The family hold over postal services in central Europe continued in the following decades. Although it was increasingly compromised by the new political situation of the nineteenth century, the service survived until the Prussian occupation of Frankfurt, where the Thurn und Taxis had their headquarters, during the Austro-Prussian War of 1866. The family, however, remains to this day one of the richest in Germany.[46]

The case of the Tasso/Thurn und Taxis is yet another good example of how the accumulation of wealth led to the acquisition of high status—in this case, even to formal acceptance into the highest nobility—as well as of political power. It is also indicative of how brilliant individuals can ensure the fortune of their family for centuries to come. Although in the case of the Tasso, business remained in the family DNA until events prevented them from continuing their traditional activities, the historical development of wealthy dynasties gives rise to many problems if we try to identify the exact degree to which the possession of great wealth has been the result of personal capabilities. Before looking at this aspect, however, we need to focus on what is traditionally considered one of the phases of Western history most favourable to innovation: the Industrial Revolution(s).

The Boon of Technology: Becoming Rich in the Industrial Age

If in early modern times innovations in technology and business organization already had the power to transform entire sectors, offering in the process excellent opportunities to would-be entrepreneurs, circumstances became even more favourable to bold innovators with the beginning of the Industrial Revolution, when the pace of technological change increased significantly. Today, it is much discussed whether the First Industrial Revolution, which is traditionally considered to have begun in England in the middle of the eighteenth century, was truly 'revolutionary' or whether it was simply the prosecution of a much more incremental process. But from our perspective, which is focused on the opportunities for enrichment through innovation that opened up in different epochs, there is little doubt that from a certain point in time new technologies began to be experimented with and applied to new processes and new products at an unprecedented pace. After all, as argued by economic historian David Landes in his classic book *The Unbound Prometheus*, 'The heart of the Industrial Revolution was an interrelated succession of technological changes. . . . Concomitant with . . . changes in equipment and process went new forms of industrial organization.'[47] However, it is the so-called Second Industrial Revolution, which began in the mid-nineteenth century and continued up to the eve of World War I, that stands out as the real golden age of innovators. This is due to the different nature of technological change during the First and Second Industrial Revolutions: more incremental and 'applied' in the first, and more scientific and based on theoretical principles that could be acquired only through extensive study and education in the second. As a consequence, while the First Industrial Revolution was strictly connected to traditional sectors (steam is the exception) such as iron and textiles, where many a fortune had already been made from the Middle Ages on, the second featured entirely new sectors, like industrial chemistry and electricity, while some pre-existing sectors, for example steel, were radically transformed. Additionally, while the First Industrial Revolution had been mostly restricted to Britain and a few other small areas of continental Europe, like Belgium, and then spread to some other Western countries (including the United States and partially France) from the early nineteenth century, the second gave latecomers the opportunity to catch up. The best-known cases are Italy and Germany, both recently unified countries (in 1861 for Italy and in 1871 for Germany), and, beyond Europe, Japan.[48]

There are different views about the nature of the Industrial Revolution and the overall role played by innovation. Contrary to those who have argued that the Industrial Revolution was the ultimate consequence of a centuries-long accumulation of capital,[49] others have focused on innovation and ideas, themselves the result of a new cultural climate more open to change and 'progress', as the main drivers of these socially and economically transformative processes. In recent years, these views have been strongly defended by Joel Mokyr.[50] Another economic historian, Deirdre McCloskey, has focused on related topics: the importance of new ethics and of the socio-cultural transformations through which the pursuit of economic success and of wealth, which had been the object of scorn in earlier centuries among the social elite, now incited admiration, giving rise to the much more positive and even heroic view of the successful entrepreneur that survives to this day.[51] We will return to this topic in the final section of this chapter.

While it seems proper to highlight the importance of innovation and technological change, as well as the new cultural and social climate that accompanied the Industrial Revolution, this should not obscure the fact that many successful entrepreneurs of the nineteenth century and beyond saw ennoblement, or at the very least aristocratization, as the ultimate objective of their ascent. In other words, a society which no longer looked 'down' on entrepreneurs did not necessarily stop looking 'up' to aristocracy. Secondly, in terms of attitudes, ethics and culture broadly meant we often find a difference between the generation of the founders and those of their descendants; once again, we encounter the problem of dynasties, which is also the problem of whether wealth was or was not acquired by merit (or by the application of 'bourgeois virtues', à la McCloskey).

Before exploring this problem, we need to offer a few examples of the innovation-led paths towards wealth that can be considered typical of the Industrial Revolution. For the early, English-based phase, it seems natural to look at innovators in the textile sector. Richard Arkwright, for example, was a man of humble origins with little education who started out as a barber and wig-maker in Lancashire. Despite this unpromising start, Arkwright was clearly a highly ingenious individual, as in the 1760s he invented a waterproof dye which could be applied to the wigs in fashion at the time. But the invention for which he occupies a place of honour in both the history of technology and economic history is that of the spinning frame, used for the first time in 1765 and patented in 1769, when Arkwright was 37 years old. The machine made it possible to dramatically reduce the cost of cotton spinning, especially from the 1770s when Arkwright adapted it to use water power instead of horses. The result was the famous water frame, able to spin 96 threads at a time and to produce the strongest yarn then available. Additionally, the purpose-built mills where water frames were installed represented a key step towards the development of modern factories geared towards mass production. Arkwright obtained an all-embracing 'grand patent' in 1775 and set out to maximize the profit from his inventions. In this, he was eminently successful: already by 1782 his personal capital amounted to 200,000 pounds and his businesses employed 5,000 people. By the time of his death in 1792, he had moved further up the social ladder (he had been knighted in 1786), and his fortune had grown to

500,000 pounds or about 80 million in 2020 U.S. dollars. In spite of this, he felt under constant threat from unlicensed competitors driven to act outside the law by the high fees required to use Arkwright's patents. Arkwright waged a years-long legal battle against them, which he continued with other means even after the patents had expired, trying to monopolize the business to the outrage of his most stubborn competitors.[52]

If Arkwright's innovations were mostly in machine technology and in factory organization and had to be defended tooth and nail, others focused on introducing new products and new practices of sale and distribution, to serve the ever-growing cohorts of potential consumers of medium- and high-quality goods. A particularly interesting example is that of Josiah Wedgwood; although perhaps less known as an individual than Richard Arkwright, his legacy lives on in the celebrated Wedgwood porcelain. His beginnings were not very promising either. The thirteenth son of an undistinguished potter from Staffordshire, young Josiah started out as a thrower, that is, a maker on a potter's wheel. However, a bout of smallpox left him lame and unable to work the wheel; later in life his leg even had to be amputated below the knee. Consequently, he became a modeller, which proved fortuitous as seemingly the new specialization suited his natural propensity for experimentation. And experiment he did, developing in 1759, when he was approaching thirty years of age, a new green ceramic glaze that allowed him to set up his own business. After that, Wedgwood introduced innovation after innovation: new earthenware, stoneware and finally, from the mid-1760s, a richly glazed creamware which Queen Charlotte graciously allowed him to call 'Queen's Ware' and which was a great success in Europe and America. But possibly his most successful product was jasperware, refined after scientific experimentation with many thousands of samples and which required the development of a pyrometer to measure oven temperatures, a feat that in 1783 led to Wedgwood's election to the Royal Society: no mean achievement given his lack of formal education.

Wedgwood's creations, however, were easily copied, and in this regard he took the opposite path to Arkwright. Instead of fighting a never-ending defensive war he continuously launched new products, with a keen eye for changes in the tastes of the nobility, which remained the uncontested leader in fashion, and he also adopted innovative marketing strategies. He invested in fashionable shops, showrooms and temporary exhibitions and built upon his renown as a supplier to royalty (beyond the English crown, he supplied Catherine II of Russia with the unique 'green frog' service, worth 2,700 pounds or about 446,000 in 2020 U.S. dollars) to bathe his products in an aura of exclusivity and to charge prices much higher than those of his rivals. He conquered foreign markets, in an era when it was exceptional for a Staffordshire potter to sell even in London. Finally, in Etruria, the specialized factory that he had built near Stoke-on-Trent, he introduced new forms of labour organization that increased efficiency and at the same time guaranteed the high level of flexibility needed to achieve product diversification (he also built a model village for his workers by the factory and set up an insurance scheme for them). When he died in 1795, he left a fortune of 500,000 pounds, which matched Arkwright's, an impressive achievement given that the inherited capital he had started with was just 20 pounds.[53]

If during the First Industrial Revolution it was possible for brilliant individuals with no education or any other advantage to achieve great success and become rich and sometimes even super-rich, things were quite different during the Second Industrial Revolution. Although, as has already been argued, potential innovations 'for the taking' were even more abundant, to identify and perfect them, as well as to apply them to practical use, a much stronger background was needed, especially regarding education and skills that could not be easily acquired in the field but had to be fine-tuned in specific places—universities, polytechnics—which were not easily accessible to the poorest strata of society. Or at least, young scions of established entrepreneurial dynasties needed to be wise enough to build research and development teams and recruit trained chemists and engineers. Even those innovators who had not completed higher formal studies possessed, almost invariably, solid scientific knowledge.

Such was the case of the Belgian chemist and entrepreneur Ernest Solvay, born in 1838, who was forced out of school at the age of 16 by poor health. So, while his parents had intended for him to go to university, he was obliged to pursue his interest in chemistry by studying at home. This, however, was more than enough for him to glimpse opportunities for innovation: a few years later, as an apprentice-manager in charge of ammonia waters at his uncle's gas company, he devised a method to produce sodium carbonate (soda ash) from salt brine and limestone (a carbonate sedimentary rock), recovering and recycling ammonia as well. Soda ash was used copiously in the production of soap, glass and bricks. Young Solvay immediately spotted the commercial opportunities offered by the new chemical process. In 1861 he filed his first patent, and in 1863 he created a start-up with his brother using capital provided by family and friends (he had a lifelong dislike of banks). The new company, Solvay & Cie, was conveniently located near Charleroi, at the centre of a wide network of transportation routes (road, railroad and the Sambre river) and close to the source of many important raw materials. By 1868, the company was the main manufacturer of soda ash in Belgium and, from the 1870s, it started to open plants across Europe, Russia and the United States, developing an internationalization model that relied heavily upon partnerships with local entrepreneurs. By the early twentieth century, Solvay's company had a 90 per cent share of the global production of soda ash and had diversified into other branches of industrial chemistry. He was probably the richest Belgian of his time. He was also a particularly socially conscious employer: his company introduced the eight-hour workday well before it became compulsory, and employees were provided with healthcare and paid vacations. In his final years (he died in 1922), Solvay retired from active management of the company and focused on scientific research and philanthropy, especially through scientific patronage. He also became involved in politics: twice a senator, in 1918 he was appointed 'Minister of State' by the king of Belgium.[54]

Of those who profited most from the Industrial Revolution, not all were as socially conscious as Solvay or Wedgwood. In this respect, a particularly well-known group is that of the American 'robber barons'. This derogatory definition was introduced in the mid-nineteenth century to indicate a group of individuals who had accumulated immense wealth, allegedly through unscrupulous and amoral behaviour, just like the *Raubritter* of medieval Germany, impoverished knights who charged tolls to cross their lands or to navigate the Rhine river without imperial authorization or even resorted to downright banditry.[55] Some members of the group, like J. P. Morgan, focused on finance and will be introduced in the next chapter. Others, however, made their fortunes in new industrial sectors: oil in the case of John D. Rockefeller, but more often the steel and railroad sectors so famously expanded by the entrepreneurship of the likes of Andrew Carnegie, Jay Gould and Cornelius Vanderbilt.[56] All three came from rather humble origins, as did most robber barons (J. P. Morgan is the main exception).

Andrew Carnegie, for example, was the son of a Scottish handloom weaver who migrated to America with his family in 1848. His first job, in a factory in Pittsburgh, earned him 1.2 dollars a week, but in 1901, when he was persuaded to sell his shares in the steel industry to the newly constituted United States Steel Corporation, he was paid 225.6 million dollars in gold bonds (7.1 billion in 2020 U.S. dollars). At that moment, he was the richest living American and possibly the richest man on the planet. Carnegie was a peculiar character. On the one hand he did not baulk at exploiting his employees (in his steel mills, twelve-hour workdays were imposed, and even twenty-four hours on alternate Sundays so that workers had one day of rest every two weeks) or at using violence and blackmail against trade unions or at eluding government regulations. He even developed a theory, drawn from social Darwinism (Carnegie paid special tribute to the American philosopher, sociologist and biologist Herbert Spencer), to justify his predatory behaviour. On the other hand, in his later years he became a great donor and wrote a manifesto, *The Gospel of Wealth* (1889), in which he argued that the only worthy behaviour for a rich man was to give away the fortune he accumulated during a lifetime.[57]

While Carnegie might have been somewhat troubled by the enormous wealth that he had amassed, others were not, for example Jay Gould, father of the Anna Gould introduced in chapter 3 as exemplary of the many rich American women who married into the European nobility. After beginning in the tannery industry in the 1850s, from 1859 Gould began to speculate in railroad shares and soon became a very successful railroad entrepreneur, particularly after he acquired Union Pacific in 1873. By the early 1880s he controlled, through a network of companies, 15 per cent of U.S. railways, and on many important routes he was able to extract huge monopolist rents, although a more positive interpretation of Gould's entrepreneurial activity would highlight his role as a catalyst for the national integration of the fragmented American railroad network.[58] But the monopolistic instinct was by no means his only misdeed. During his career, Gould was repeatedly involved in bribery; attempted to kidnap an impostor, 'Lord' Gordon-Gordon, who had tried to cheat him and had subsequently fled to Canada, leading to an international incident; and even caused a gold panic, 'Black Friday' of 1869, because of a botched attempt to manipulate the market. Although he has been often portrayed as 'the supreme villain of his era', as noted by business historian Maury Klein, there is little doubt that he was also a businessman of genius.[59] Unlike Carnegie, he was not much interested in philanthropy, and he started a dynasty of financiers and railroad entrepreneurs.

Before turning to dynasties, some final clarifications are needed. The cases of entrepreneurial success described in this section are all related to the achievement of truly enormous fortunes. But the opportunities offered by the First and Second Industrial Revolutions also allowed many others to get rich, even if not super-wealthy. Each new great company that emerged was in need of effective managers, who had to be recruited largely from outside the family circle. These managers earned high salaries, often becoming co-investors in the companies, and built a sizeable patrimony which was usually at least in part passed on across generations (beyond paying for the better education of children to improve their chances of further economic achievements).

And yet, this picture of abundant opportunities for many should not be understood as one of improvement for all. The frequently made claim that modernization and industrialization improved material conditions across the West should be taken, as the Romans said, with a grain of salt, as during this historical phase wealth inequality tended to increase quite significantly in many countries, as seen in chapter 2. This was surely the case for the United States: as the number of millionaires reached unheard-of levels (in 1892, an inquiry by the *New-York Tribune* found that there were 4,047 of them), American society was becoming increasingly polarized, diverging from the relatively egalitarian and open conditions praised by Tocqueville in the middle of the nineteenth century.[60] Vast masses of factory workers were exploited by their employers and experienced very limited improvement in standards of living during their lifetime. They had little or no opportunity to escape their humble conditions by means of their personal capabilities and efforts. This nagged at the conscience of at least some of the new super-rich, including Carnegie, who in his *Gospel of Wealth* warned that 'rigid castes' had started to appear, separating workers from employers—and in the end, the poor from the rich.[61] He set out to limit the damage, for example by opening libraries for workers in the towns which hosted his factories in a paternalistic attempt to create the conditions for their personal improvement. But such improvement was difficult to achieve: Carnegie himself had contributed to the establishment of a somewhat exploitative social and economic framework that limited the chances of entering the well-to-do strata of society. This is also why, in the United States as elsewhere, the exceptional opportunities for enrichment typical of the Second Industrial Revolution finally dried up and were not encountered again for a long time.

The Problem of Entrepreneurial Dynasties: From Merit to Privilege?

Throughout history, the foundation of entrepreneurial dynasties is so recurrent, and it is so important to define the character of the rich and the super-rich component of any given society, that it requires some specific attention. In chapter 3, the point was made that there exists a structural difference between the founders of a noble dynasty and their descendants: the latter inherited their privileged social and economic position, while the founders often had to struggle to rise from obscurity. In the case of entrepreneurial dynasties, the problem appears to be somewhat reduced as many among their members continue to practice the original family activities in commerce, industry or finance. Additionally, for them the process of inheritance is not so explicitly arranged to ensure the perpetuation of privilege as is the case for the nobility. But in practice, it is clearly possible for rich commoners to manage the transmission of wealth across generations in ways not altogether different from those used by the nobility. Indeed, the institutions used to this end are often very similar if not exactly the same.

If the creation of entrepreneurial dynasties resembles the establishment of noble lineages, the passing on across generations of social and economic privilege is all the more troubling in societies, like ours, where at least in some influential milieux the belief is widespread that great wealth should not be regarded as a problem but as a simple reward for merit. This meritocratic argument is stronger when made for the dynasty founders or for the first generations, than when looking at older wealth. And by now it should be clear that new wealth naturally tends to become old wealth, increasingly removed from the ideal of status acquired through exceptional personal abilities and closer to a de facto situation of inherited privilege within an aristocratic group with or without formal nobility.[62] Along similar lines Veblen, inspired by direct observation of America during the Gilded Age, warned about the tendency for the progressive development within human societies of any epoch, of a 'leisure class' which, by definition, is idle and does not partake in the business activities on which their inherited fortunes were built: 'The occupations of the [leisure] class are . . . diversified; but they have the common economic characteristic of being non-industrial. These non-industrial upper-class occupations may be roughly comprised under government, warfare, religious observances, and sport.'[63]

A fuller account of some of Veblen's views will be provided in chapter 6, which focuses on two economic processes that are essential to the transmission of wealth across generations: saving and inheritance, balanced against consumption including that of the 'conspicuous' kind. Here, we will provide some practical examples of how entrepreneurial dynasties came into being. We will also highlight how, at a macro level, these processes became widespread in periods when new opportunities were relatively abundant but were also instrumental in bringing such historical phases to an end. When new wealth becomes old it is inclined to assume a defensive stance against new entrants which goes beyond simple disgust for the nouveau riche and includes (according to the specific context) a tendency to try to keep them away from the levers of economic or political power and to crush in their infancy, or to absorb, innovative start-ups that might compromise the position of well-established companies.

Consider, for example, the Dutch Republic during its Golden Age.[64] In the first decades of the seventeenth century, commercial and colonial expansion across the oceans and a wave of important innovations in the mainland had led to rapid economic growth and to widespread enrichment. At a later stage, however, the combination of increasingly complex circumstances (especially due to repeated wars over dominance of the seas and colonial spheres of influence with England) and of the simple desire to enjoy their own riches and social advantages without too much trouble led Dutch society to become progressively more closed and less socially mobile. At the individual level, it made perfect economic sense for families that had become rich in the 'heroic' phase of the Golden Age to avoid the high personal and financial risks that beset those involved in Atlantic trade, but when this became a collective behaviour, it had serious consequences. This is particularly apparent in the political sphere. The regents (*regenten*), a category that covers all kinds of rulers of the Dutch Republic (including city leaders and heads of organizations) and whose members originally came from the richest and most successful merchant families of each locality, became an increasingly specialized class, anxious to preserve its position. This is confirmed by the spread, from the mid-century, of the 'contracts of correspondence' that committed groups of closely related regents to appoint each other to the most important and best-paid posts. As a result, by the early eighteenth century 83 per cent of the newly appointed city councillors of Rotterdam and 79 per cent of those of Hoorn were a close relation (son, son-in-law, brother-in-law, uncle or brother) of another councillor. At the same time, members of the regent class became less and less active in trade and in other sectors of the economy. This transformation represented a specific step in the development of wealthy dynasties.[65]

The case of the Teding van Berkout family, from the city of Hoorn, is telling. Originally, they were called Berkout; in the mid-sixteenth century, Pieter Janszoon Berkout was referred to simply as a 'cheese merchant at Hoorn'. Pieter, however, was also a magistrate and a member of his city council. His son Jan married into a well-born family, the Teding, whence came the second part of the family name. He was also a merchant and a member of the local council. The third generation, that of Adriaan Teding van Berkhout, departed from this pattern as Adriaan was made to study and attended university, becoming a doctor of law. Immediately afterwards he obtained a public office, that of 'pensionary' of Monnickendam, a position that required him to accompany city delegates to the assemblies of the states of Holland. This post led to another, at the National Auditing Office. In 1604 he married Margaretha Duyst van Beresteyn, the daughter of a powerful and wealthy regent of Delft. In 1613, Adriaan was appointed to the Council of State. His descendants would continue to hold high office in Holland and in the state institutions until the end of the Dutch Republic in 1795.[66]

In many respects, the closure of the Dutch elite towards the end of the Golden Age mirrored developments in Italy at the beginning of the seventeenth century, that is, when this area began its relative decline partly due to fierce competition from the Dutch Republic. In Italy too there was a tendency towards the oligarchic closure of city councils, with families of the local elite attempting to ward off intruders by erecting legal barriers to their eligibility for public office.[67] And here, too, we observe a shift in investment from trade and industry towards land. While this shift did have some aristocratic connotations, it was often based on sound economic reasoning: in the new circumstances, and given the relative disadvantage suffered by Italian merchants in accessing Atlantic trade routes directly, land offered a more stable and somewhat 'protected' kind of investment. This was especially the case after the terrible plague of 1629–30 had all but destroyed the residual chances of the most economically advanced Italian states, and particularly of the Republic of Venice, to keep up with their northern European competitors.[68] These processes also tended to increase and to entrench inequality in land ownership, which in the context of what remained mostly agrarian societies was likely to have far-reaching anti-egalitarian consequences, because land was at the same time the main component of wealth and the main source of income. So, when capital-rich families decided to divert their ample resources from industry and trade to real estate, often profiting from times of crisis and particularly from famines, when starving small owners were forced to sell their properties at an unfavourable price, they established distributive conditions that tended to lock the lowest strata into a disadvantaged economic (and political) situation.[69] Similar effects were produced in Spain by the efforts of the *conquistadores* to make their social and economic rise permanent and to become fully-fledged members of the Iberian nobility.

If cycles of social-economic opening and closure can be clearly identified in medieval and early modern times, the same seems to hold for the period of industrialization. In England, for example, Josiah Wedgwood founded an entrepreneurial dynasty which also became involved in national politics (some relatives had other focuses, most famously the naturalist and biologist Charles Darwin, the son of Josiah's older daughter, Susannah, and the husband of Josiah's granddaughter—hence Charles's own cousin—Emma).[70] Richard Arkwright was likewise a dynasty founder: his son, Richard II, was a skilled businessman and had probably become, by the time of his death in 1843, the richest commoner in England.[71] Subsequent generations of Arkwrights, however, were usually happy just to enjoy the riches accumulated by the first generations, living the life of country gentlemen.[72]

Another interesting case is that of the Whitbreads. The dynasty founder, Samuel Whitbread, was an entrepreneur who revolutionised the brewery sector in eighteenth-century London, being one of the very first to experiment with large-scale production. He came from a family of the lesser gentry which had a tradition of holding public office: Samuel's father and grandfather had both been collectors ('receivers-general') for the land taxes in Bedfordshire. Although he came from a well-off family, Samuel Whitbread was the first to amass considerable wealth, as already by 1762 the capital invested in his brewery in London amounted to 116,000 pounds (about 23 million in 2020 U.S. dollars). From the 1760s, however, he also started to buy land and property in his native Caddington and adopted an aristocratic lifestyle, setting the stage for a clear change of direction in the family's activities. This tendency only intensified after his son, Samuel II, had come of age and made it clear that he was not interested in brewing. Samuel Whitbread made the decisive move in 1795, when he acquired the estates of Viscount Torrington in Bedfordshire.

At the time of his death the following year, Samuel Whitbread was the second-largest land owner in the county, after the Duke of Bedford. This shows up in the structures of the revenues enjoyed by his successor, Samuel II: in 1803–9, 73 per cent came from his estates and 27 per cent from the brewery. Although he was an efficient manager of his properties, Samuel II's main interest was in politics. After all, he had been schooled at Eton and had attended university at Oxford and Cambridge, so he did not lack connections. In 1806 he was offered a peerage but declined, as he thought that he could have greater political influence as a prominent commoner than as a second-rank noble (he had, however, married into the nobility). He was elected to parliament for the first time in 1790, holding the post for 23 years and promoting social reforms: he championed the establishment of a system of national education, the introduction of a minimum wage and the abolition of slavery. In this, he followed in the wake of his father, who had also been a member of parliament and an abolitionist, and in time was followed by a long list of Whitbreads who served in the British parliament. An entrepreneurial dynasty had morphed into a political dynasty, whose success was underpinned by a large accumulated family fortune.[73]

Although each case has its own specific features, it is clear that industrialization in Britain led to the emergence of a massive number of wealthy dynasties, which typically started out as entrepreneurial but often quickly took a different direction after the founders had passed away, for example by pursuing politics and high office and/or merging with the nobility. This issue is also related to the debate about the relative importance in different periods of industrial capitalism and of so-called gentlemanly capitalism, as well as about the relative importance of industry, trade and finance for the British economy in general and for paths of personal enrichment in particular.[74]

The same tendency for entrepreneurial dynasties to be born in the favourable climate of the Industrial Revolution only to move to sectors of activity other than industry, or to join Veblen's 'leisure class', is also to be found outside Britain. But most importantly, even if we look only at those whose fortunes remained clearly connected to business, during the century and a half of the First and Second Industrial Revolutions members of wealthy dynasties founded by brilliant entrepreneurs who had profited from early opportunities tended to be an increasingly large share of the total, cluttering the roster of the rich and making it more difficult for new entrants to join the economic elite. Take the case of Germany. Here in 1910–12, of all businessmen worth at least 2 million marks, 46.9 per cent were active in the service sectors (27.3% in banking alone) and especially in traditional subsectors, as for example those owning department stores—a great commercial innovation of the nineteenth century—made up just 1.6 per cent. Of the 49.8 per cent active in the industrial sector (and leaving aside the 3.2% active in both services and industry), those who can be assigned to the new industries typical of the Second Industrial Revolution (chemicals, electricity and machinery) were a fairly small minority: to be precise, 10.2 per cent of all multimillionaire German businessmen. According to historian Dolores Augustine, 'This demonstrates that there was a noticeable time lag in the conversion of economic success into wealth'.[75]

If we look at the figures from another angle, the case of Germany also demonstrates the resilience of the fortunes built in earlier phases and passed on within families involved in relatively traditional activities, industrial or otherwise. Something similar can be found in the United States: although almost invariably the successful entrepreneurs of the Gilded Age founded dynasties of their own (Andrew Carnegie is the notable exception), in numerical terms they remained, by the end of the nineteenth century, a minority component of those who could be considered to be very affluent. But even if they were a minority (although accounting for an inordinately large share of the overall wealth), the nouveau riche of the second half of the nineteenth century added to those whose fortunes had earlier origins. By the turn of the twentieth century, this helped to create a social-economic context which does not seem to have been very favourable to the rise of a new generation of innovators and entrepreneurs. This was also because many key economic sectors had become increasingly dominated by powerful trusts and cartels that actively stifled competition, as will be discussed further in chapter 5. The tragic events of World War I (1914–18) make it difficult to tell precisely, but there is every reason to believe that once again in Western history a cycle of great opportunities for enrichment had come to a close. The very success of the early innovators who proved able to accumulate their wealth and pass it on to their descendants, founding dynasties, had contributed to its end. This is a lesson to bear in mind when considering the most recent wave of brilliant innovation and great enrichment, which is often considered to be a characteristic feature of the (still ongoing) Age of Information.

Achieving Great Wealth in the Age of Information: Opportunities for All?

During the First Industrial Revolution, and even more during the Second which involved a much broader portion of the West, it was relatively easy for newcomers who had a good command of the relevant technologies and an eye for new opportunities to become very rich, very quickly. By the turn of the twentieth century, however, the well of opportunities had already started to run dry; thereafter the World Wars all but sealed it for a few decades. In some countries, and especially those which had previously lagged behind, the years immediately following World War II were again an epoch when the path to wealth by means of entrepreneurial innovation was relatively easy. This was the case in Italy during the so-called economic miracle of the 1950s and 1960s: what until then had remained a mostly rural country transformed into a modern industrial nation, a process to which a blossoming of new small- and medium-sized enterprises, for example in the consumer goods sector, contributed greatly. These enterprises, which were usually family-run, allowed the accumulation of significant wealth, often starting entrepreneurial dynasties which, although with some difficulty, have survived to this day and remain typical of Italian capitalism.[76]

This being said, if we think about relatively recent phases during which it was definitely possible to go all the way 'from rags to riches' simply by possessing some knowledge and skills in new technologies, even without many years of expensive formal education and/or a sizeable initial capital and the backing of a well-established family, the most striking instance is surely that of the computer and information age, especially from the 1970s to the early 2000s. Some of the protagonists of this phase have become very well-known due to their high profile in the media and because many have been the subject of popular biopics or biographies and books. A first generation of innovators made their fortunes in the early years of personal computing; Bill Gates and Steve Jobs belong to this group. Innovations involved hardware, but more often software due to much lower barriers to entry at least until companies like Microsoft (founded by Gates and Paul Allen) made their bid to gain stable control of a number of crucial markets, beginning with that of operating systems. A second generation profited from the advent of the internet: Amazon's founder, Jeff Bezos, and Google's Larry Page and Sergey Brin all belong to this group. Amazon was incorporated in 1994, Google in 1998, but up until at least the beginning of the twenty-first century it was still possible to achieve immediate success by applying intuitions about how the internet and other information technologies could be used to provide new services. So, a third generation of innovators is perfectly represented by Facebook's co-founder, Mark Zuckerberg.[77]

After so many American names, one might wonder whether the phenomenal opportunities of the period were limited to the United States. The answer is yes and no. It is most definitely 'yes' if we look at those who have achieved really extreme wealth, as is consistently shown by all available lists of the richest living individuals (both Gates and Bezos have, at various times, been reported to be the richest man in the world; in *Forbes'* list of the richest people in 2020, Bezos was first, Gates second, Oracle's co-founder Larry Ellison fifth, Zuckerberg seventh and Page and Brin thirteenth and fourteenth respectively). But the answer is negative if we take a broader look at individual paths of enrichment. Consider the case of the Italian Federico Marchetti, who in 2000 founded Yoox, a company which pioneered online fashion retail and in 2018, when it was bought by Richmond, was evaluated at 5.3 billion euros (6.3 billion U.S. dollars). Or the Swiss Guillaume Pousaz, who in 2012 founded Checkout.com with the aim of providing online payment services to shops around the world. Like many other companies focusing on online services and e-commerce, Checkout.com thrived during the COVID-19 pandemic, and the value of Pousaz's assets (who at that time owned about two-thirds of the company) skyrocketed, allowing him to enter *Forbes'* 2021 list of the richest people in the world with an estimated net worth of about 9 billion dollars. This being said, the fact remains that paths towards enrichment generated by the age of information in Europe did not lead to the same levels of individual wealth. To some extent this is probably a reflection of an institutional framework less favourable to extreme accumulation (due for example to fiscal systems that weigh relatively more on the rich: see chapter 10), but it also seems due to the fact that the subsectors where Europe proved most innovative and competitive required greater initial investments and were usually exploited by pre-existing and well-established companies. This is the case of the mobile telecom industry, which saw the emergence of hardware producers like Ericsson in Sweden and Nokia in Finland, both of them active from the nineteenth century, and of service providers like Omnitel in Italy (Omnitel was a new company, but it was founded by Olivetti, a computer company which had earlier been a leading producer of typewriters).

Although the information age led to enrichment on the two sides of the Atlantic in different ways, this does not necessarily mean that opportunities were better spread across society in Europe than in the United States. While this might seem to be the implication of the different trends in wealth concentration followed from the 1970s by the United States and by continental European countries, as reported in chapter 2, looking at the super-rich should not lead us to overlook how the rise of large innovative companies created opportunities for many others—smaller companies born to service them or specializing in exploiting niches created by the very rise of those large companies, executives or simply early employees of exceptionally successful businesses. A famous example, oft-recalled by the media, is that of Microsoft which, due to the company habit of providing its employees with stock options, between the initial public offering in 1986 and the rise in share prices of the following decades seems to have created about 12,000 new millionaires.[78] Many founders and stock-owning employees of other companies achieved great wealth because of Microsoft's increasingly aggressive strategy of acquisitions, which is where the interpretation of the company's behaviour as provider (or not) of opportunities for enrichment becomes rather more nuanced.

Gates and Allen founded Microsoft in 1975, with the mission of developing and distributing commercial software. Gates, in particular, was a young man of twenty from a wealthy family from Seattle who had left Harvard without graduating to focus on computer programming. Microsoft's fortunes began to soar in the early 1980s, when the company signed a contract with IBM to provide the operating system for its computers, MS-DOS. In 1985, Microsoft Windows was released, which extended MS-DOS by adding a graphical interface. The company, now controlled by Gates alone (Allen had resigned in 1983 due to poor health), was already the market leader in operating systems, which is why when it went public in 1986 Gates, aged thirty-one, became the world's youngest self-made billionaire. In the following decades, Microsoft continued to consolidate its dominant position in the market and expanded into new internet services, beginning with internet browsers. This led to the 'browser war' with Netscape, whose Navigator was the most widely used browser in the mid-1990s. By the end of the decade, that was no longer the case: Microsoft Explorer, provided as part of the Windows package from 1995, had assumed a dominant position and Netscape was in rapid decline. Microsoft had moved very aggressively against Netscape, and in 1998 it was taken to court in the United States accused of anti-competitive behaviour. In 2000 it was found guilty of violating the Sherman Act, the famous antitrust law introduced in 1890, which in time brought about the forced breakup of many semi-monopolists; for example, in 1911 this was the fate of Standard Oil, the company founded by John D. Rockefeller. However, Microsoft settled the case with the American government and suffered very mild consequences. Based on subsequent difficulties Microsoft encountered with public regulators—most spectacularly with the European Union, which in 2004 fined it 497 million euros, which for the time was a record sum corresponding to about 847 million in 2020 U.S. dollars—the company was not exactly repentant. While with Netscape it elected for war, in other instances Microsoft found it more convenient to simply buy off established rivals in sectors where it planned to expand. A recent example is the acquisition of another successful start-up of the early twenty-first century, LinkedIn, in 2016.[79]

Microsoft is just one example of a practice which is common among the largest companies born of the information age. Some of them have attracted the attention of antitrust regulators; for example, by 2020 the European Union had repeatedly fined Google an overall amount of almost 10 billion euros, and in November that year it levied formal antitrust charges against Amazon.[80] Indeed, Jeff Bezos has sometimes been compared to Gates due to his penchant for uncompromising and aggressive behaviour towards potential rivals.[81] From our perspective, the most relevant consequence of the expansionist and acquisitive tendency of the information technology giants is that such behaviour can be expected to reduce opportunities for others, both in terms of preventing the formation of new companies and of condemning potential competitors to early failure or to be bought before the founders and their associates have had the chance to reap all the benefits that could have been their due. This is, indeed, an added theoretical justification for the existence of antitrust laws and authorities, beyond that which concerns the negative consequences that uncompetitive markets have for consumers. But if we take a long-term perspective, the problem is that the extreme level of concentration of certain key services which has been reached today, coupled with the willingness of the tech giants to expand into new areas and to stifle potentially threatening external innovations, is one of the factors that might lead to the end of a historical phase during which it was relatively easy to become rich through entrepreneurial innovation. This is exactly what happened towards the end of the Second Industrial Revolution.

Another somewhat troubling development is the tendency in recent decades for an increase in income disparities within companies. According to many scholars, this is the outcome of dramatic reductions in top income tax rates, especially in Anglo-Saxon countries, which provided the incentive for more aggressive bargaining behaviour at the top. Indeed, this might be an important contributing causal factor of the diverging patterns in income inequality observed in different groups of Western countries from the 1970s on.[82] At first sight, this process might seem to favour the enrichment of employees and therefore to be 'egalitarian' in the very specific sense of extending the opportunities to accumulate wealth to broader groups of executives and other categories of very well-paid employees. On the other hand, there is reason to fear that this may lead to the establishment of a system of within-company extraction, advantageous for a few but detrimental to many others. Even if this is a contentious issue, it cannot be denied that growing intra-company inequality does not bode well for the chances of upward mobility of those who enter occupations at the lower levels of the income pyramid who, although not necessarily less brilliant and potentially capable, are usually less educated and not particularly well endowed with social and relational capital.[83]

Beyond all this, another development might loom in the future: the establishment of dynasties, whose negative consequences for social-economic mobility across society have already been discussed based on historical evidence from earlier epochs. According to one estimate, of all the billionaires alive in continental Europe during 2001–14 about half had inherited their wealth, and the same was true for about one-third of those from Anglo-Saxon countries (Canada, the United States and the United Kingdom),[84] although interpreting these figures as 'high' or 'low' is not as straightforward as some seem to think.[85] Admittedly, many of the new rich and super-rich of the information age are simply too young to have already bequeathed their position to descendants or relations, so we are still a long way from a situation in which the high prevalence of dynasties could systematically prevent new actors from moving up the wealth ladder. And yet, across history, that is exactly the kind of situation which has tended to bring phases of intense entrepreneurial innovation to an end, which seems reason enough to be wary. From this perspective, it is important to consider the attitudes, especially among the super-rich, towards the intergenerational transmission of wealth. In 2010 Bill Gates, together with his then-wife Melinda and Warren Buffett, created the 'Giving Pledge', committing to divesting themselves of over half of their wealth before death. Zuckerberg was one of the original forty billionaires who signed the pledge (by the end of 2020, the signatories had grown to 216). Historically, even among the rich the idea that wealth should not be accumulated per se or simply be passed on but should be put to the service of humanity is not new: in American culture, it has strong roots in Andrew Carnegie's view, expressed in 1889, that 'The man who dies rich, dies disgraced'. But Carnegie was influenced by early Christian doctrine and consequently was connected to a much older tradition which, as seen, was fully operative in the Middle Ages when a very wealthy merchant, Francesco di Marco Datini, prescribed in his will that the vast majority of his fortune be used to establish new charitable institutions, for the poor and for orphans. Surely, the society and culture in which Carnegie lived, and most definitely that in which Gates and Buffett live, is much more tolerant of the presence of super-rich individuals compared to medieval societies which regarded them as sinners *tout court*. However, it also seems clear that to many super-rich themselves the enormous size of their patrimonies, almost godly compared to the meagre possessions of the man in the street, is somewhat troubling. This consideration holds even when taking into account that philanthropy can also be considered an investment to increase one's social, cultural and symbolic capital; therefore it is not always truly selfless.[86]

These are complex and highly relevant questions, worthy of specific attention. And surely the striking continuities that we have highlighted in the role of the rich in society, and especially of those who do not have 'title' to their great wealth beyond the fact of having accumulated it in time (the case of nobles is different), are not the only ones that could be identified: think about the persistence across history of a strong connection between wealth and political power. All these issues will be discussed in detail in the third and final part of this book. But now, it is time to complete our analysis of the major historical paths towards great wealth with a consideration of finance, which is also the path that, across the ages, has led to the greatest disapproval and social anger.

5

On Finance

THROUGHOUT HISTORY, the shrewd management of money has always offered great opportunities for personal enrichment to those with certain highly
specialized skills. Bankers, financiers and investors occupy a prominent place
among the rich in any epoch. Sometimes they focused single-mindedly on
finance in the strict sense, but often they were also active in capital-intensive
sectors of the 'real' economy, like international trade. Although the boundaries
are often blurred, it is important to focus on finance as a distinctive path to
wealth because across history it is the one that has invariably been considered
the most problematic: in many settings, those who made the commerce and
the management of money per se their main activity faced social scorn.
From the medieval condemnation of usury (which originally included all
forms of moneylending), to nineteenth-century distaste for profiteers and
ruthless financiers, to Occupy Wall Street and other movements protesting
against growing inequality stemming from an excessively financialized
economy, the world of finance has always been viewed with some suspicion,
including by those who were in the greatest need of the services that it was able
to provide.

Indeed, Western societies have always considered bankers' and financiers'
claims to riches to be rather weak compared to the nobility, whose right to
wealth came to be established by birth in accordance with deeply enrooted
social and cultural norms as well as formal law, and compared to innovators
and entrepreneurs, who could be seen as reaping the profits of their intuition
and their ability to bring innovations to economic fruition. Paradoxically, this
remains true even under those juridical systems, like most current ones, that
have made the possession of large financial assets the least assailable, including
by means of taxation. And yet, in other respects, like the possibility for women
to operate relatively freely even in social contexts that actively tried to limit

their legal capacity to act, or in allowing for economic interactions across religious barriers, finance has always tended to be a remarkably open world. This chapter aims to make sense of all these apparent paradoxes.

Usurers or Bankers? The Commerce of Money in Medieval and Early Modern Times

Towards the end of the fourteenth century Francesco di Marco Datini, the famous Tuscan merchant whose ascent to a position of absolute prominence in European international trade has already been traced (chapter 4), informed some of his close business associates that he intended to move into banking. This led to considerable worries in his inner circle, as his partners feared that he might lose his good reputation. For example, his friend and associate, Domenico di Cambio, wrote to him in August 1398:

> I have to inform you of what I hear being said. Many people told me: 'So Francesco di Marco wants to lose his name as the main merchant of Florence, to become a moneychanger [*chambiatore*]: and there is none among the moneychangers who does not make usurious contracts'. In your defence I replied that you want to be more merchant than ever and that, if you opened a bank [*banco*] you would not do it for usury. And they replied: 'This is not what everybody will say: they will say instead that he is a usurer [*chaorsino*]!' And I answered them: 'he would not do this to be a usurer; as he will leave all that he has to the poor'. And the other replied: 'Do not presume that he will ever again be considered the great merchant that he was, nor with such a good reputation [*buona fama*]'.[1]

Datini stubbornly went through with his idea and opened a *banco* with a junior partner. However, the *banco* was shut down only a couple of years later due to the premature death of his partner before, it seems, having caused any permanent damage to Datini's reputation, and maybe it is not too far-fetched to imagine that by then the great merchant had a better understanding of what he risked by diversifying into finance. But the concern of his friends and associates illustrates the general disapproval of banking and of other financial activities that was deeply enrooted in medieval societies. This had a double origin: first, the condemnation of the accumulation of wealth as avarice, a deadly sin. In this, bankers and financiers faced the same problem and the same psychological pressure as wealthy merchants (see chapter 4). Second, they were under the constant suspicion of usury, because any form of interest on debt was considered to be usurious, due to a certain interpretation of the Bible[2] further reinforced by Scholastic theology and particularly by Thomas Aquinas. Based on the classical Greek philosopher Aristotle, he stated that money does not generate money (*nummus non parit nummos*).[3] It was not profit from economic transactions in general that was under suspicion, but the possibility of reaping a profit from the mere lending of *money*: 'usury occurs where there is no production or material transformation of real goods.'[4]

Unlike the accumulation of wealth, which was frowned upon but not forbidden, usury was formally prohibited (firstly, by the Church) or heavily regulated, at least in theory, which created more than a few frictions in the inner workings of an increasingly complex economic system. The problem was partially solved by tolerating it when practised by Jews, as they were not part of the Christian community. But more importantly, lending for interest found a way into the system by means of the flourishing of a range of practices against which, in time, resistance proved to be in vain, which is also testimony to the practical importance of this kind of service. A typical example was to hide the interest in the exchange rate applied to different currencies. As a result, by the early thirteenth century the English cardinal Robert of Courçon, who also served for a period as chancellor of the University of Paris, claimed in his treaty *De usura* that, together with heresy, usury was to be considered the great evil of his time. This view was shared by others, if we consider the plethora of official condemnations of the practice and their increasing severity from the mid-twelfth to the mid-thirteenth century.[5] On the other hand, the very same developments seem to reflect the ever-greater diffusion of the commerce of money which went *pari passu* with the Commercial Revolution of the Middle Ages. Large-scale banking was not born out of the small-scale activities of moneychangers, but of the great commercial companies that sought a way to easily reinvest their bountiful profits.[6]

In time, theology had to adapt to the realities of economic life. This is reflected, first of all, in the progressive accumulation of 'exceptions' to the prohibition of lending with interest, as is clearly visible in twelfth- and thirteenth-century canon law. Among the very first exceptions to appear was a distinction between the illegitimacy of *private* moneylending and the legitimacy of *public* moneylending when it was aimed at preserving the wealth of institutions. So, for example, religious institutions (monasteries, religious orders like the Templars who provided financial services to the king of France and so on) were to be allowed to practice pawnbroking and to offer contracts of mortgage. This was just the first step towards the eventual recognition that certain services were of public utility and so had to be allowed, at least in some forms and especially if they were practised by the right people: well-respected professionals and not the 'manifest usurers' (*usurarii manifesti*) who shamelessly exercised their activities in public, servicing mostly the middling and lower strata of society.[7] Indeed, this was part of a more general process of cultural elaboration, completed by the fifteenth century, that finally gave the rich and the super-rich a purposeful role in society: they *saved* to the benefit of the community, as in times of crisis the community could tap into their personal resources by means of *borrowing*.[8] This crucial development in the social perception of the rich will be explored in detail in chapter 8.

Whatever the theory, in practice banking services were a booming business from at least the late thirteenth century, especially in Italy which played a pioneering role in great finance. The bill of exchange, issued in one place and payable in another, in a different currency, was the main technical instrument which allowed the prohibition of usury to be overcome.[9] Although most great bankers of the late Middle Ages were well-respected (they could not have remained in the market otherwise), the suspicion of usury continued to weigh heavily upon many of those active in the financial sector, as is shown by the concerns of Datini's friends as well as by the enduring prejudice and social disapproval experienced by Jews, who in the collective European imaginary came to be considered the prototypical example of usurers.

In the earliest phases, Florence was clearly one of the main financial centres in Europe; a group of three families—the Bardi, the Peruzzi and the Acciaiuoli—dominated the continental financial markets in the late thirteenth and early fourteenth centuries. Each of these families had started its activities in international trade and then moved into banking where they met with exceptional success and accrued what was, for the time, huge wealth. Their operations were on such a grand scale and so complex that they came to constitute, in historian Edwin S. Hunt's definition, the first 'super-companies' of Europe. They often acted as a consortium to meet the financial needs of princes from across the continent. It was in the risky business of lending to sovereigns that they finally came undone: while the Pope proved to be a fairly reliable borrower (one who was also extremely useful in protecting bankers from any accusations of usury), the same could not be said for the king of France, the king of Naples and especially the king of England. As the Tuscan consortium had financed the sovereigns of both England and France, but had to choose to service just one of the two when the Hundred Years' War (1337–1453) started to brew, they sided with Edward III of England, not only because he was their greatest borrower, but also to protect their access to English wool, a raw material essential to their other activities in textile manufacturing. This led to the loss of most of their French business and to problems in recovering the sums lent to the king of France. Edward III graciously offered to compensate them for their losses, but this never happened and indeed, a few years later, the king of England forced the Bardi and the Peruzzi to accept a large haircut on his debt. Losses incurred with England added to those incurred with France and were compounded by problems at home following Florence's defeat in 1341 in a costly war with its great rival of the time, Pisa, over control of the smaller city of Lucca. All three families had contributed to financing the endeavour and now had little hope of recovering their investment quickly, let alone in full. In the uncertain situation that followed, many depositors, especially foreign ones, began to withdraw their funds. As a result, in the early 1340s all three banks went bankrupt and had to be liquidated. These developments, together with the further damage caused by the Black Death of 1348, led to a restructuring of the Tuscan banking sector, creating the conditions which favoured the rise of the Medici family.[10]

The case of the Medici is the perfect example of a rise to a position of both great wealth and political power, built mostly upon finance. The origins of the family remain relatively obscure; however, in the thirteenth century they must have been involved in the trade of textiles and also in activities related to their rural properties in the Mugello area, north of Florence, from where they originated. What is certain is that they had no involvement whatsoever in either large-scale banking or international finance. The first members of the family to specialize in the sector started out as associates of a distant cousin, Vieri di Cambio, who from the 1370s onwards was considered one of the leading Florentine bankers. Francesco di Bicci de' Medici was taken on as Vieri's junior partner in 1382, showing great personal capabilities as, within eight years, he appears to have risen to the position of senior partner. Vieri and Francesco's bank had branches in other Italian cities, including Rome which from 1385 was directed by Francesco's younger brother, Giovanni. It was he who, around 1397, founded the *Banco de' Medici* in Florence and joined the *Arte del Cambio* (the moneychangers' guild). Although by Tuscan standards, the Medici were late comers to the banking business, their company immediately proved successful. Its early growth was slow but steady, which suited Giovanni's cautious attitude—surely a virtue in such a turbulent epoch, beset by recurring plagues and civil conflict (the established social order had been upset by the Ciompi revolt of 1378, led by wool carders and other workers who were marginalized by the guild system). By the time he retired, in 1420, the bank's initial capital of 10,000 florins had generated profits of over 151,000 florins, three-quarters of which were assigned to Giovanni (upon his death in 1429 he seems to have left to his heirs an estate worth almost 180,000 florins). Giovanni's characteristic, lifelong reluctance to involve himself in politics, which was certainly not shared by some of his descendants, nevertheless seems to have influenced, at least to some degree, his son Cosimo, who in time would became the real ruler of Florence while taking great pains to lead from behind the scenes.

Cosimo de' Medici (or Cosimo 'the Elder') was brought up to become the leader of the family bank, and his personal life was shaped by the needs of the company. To this end he married Contessina de' Bardi, the niece of one of his father's minority partners and a member of an 'old money' (although much diminished) Florentine family. This was just the beginning, as in time Cosimo came to be 'multiply embedded in complicated and sprawling Florentine marriage, economic, and patronage elite networks'.[11] This was instrumental in his rise, which was not only economic but political as well. Economically, he brought the profits of the Medici bank to unprecedented levels. In 1420–35, the bank produced profits of over 186,000 florins, that is, about 12,000 yearly: almost double the yearly profit typical of Giovanni's time. Profits escalated further in the following years, as they amounted to 291,000 florins overall in 1435–50: over 19,000 yearly. Of these profits, two-thirds went to Cosimo and his brother Lorenzo, a share which grew to three-quarters from 1443. By 1457, Cosimo's household was the richest in Florence (therefore one of the richest in Europe); indeed, it was over four times as rich as the second richest one, based on the *catasto* (a property tax register) drafted that year. His father Giovanni di Bicci had never got beyond third place in the ranking.[12] Much of Cosimo's fortune came from the Rome branch, which profited from a privileged relationship with the Pope that lasted for most of the fifteenth century, as the manager of this branch usually also held the position of Depository General of the Papal Court. The Medici's business relations with the Church went much further, as the various branches of the bank regularly made loans to cardinals, bishops and other high-ranking prelates. As noted by historian Raymond de Roover, an advantage of this was that ecclesiastics tended to be more reliable debtors than laymen, as they had more to fear from the threat of excommunication because of their debts, a threat to which the Medici, emboldened by the support they received from an indebted Pope, made regular recourse.[13]

Politically, Cosimo was originally seen as a champion of the 'new men', invariably very rich, who seemed to be trying to acquire a more prominent position in the city. As such, he was also perceived as a threat to the established order of an oligarchic Republic, which is why there was an attempt to oust him in 1433. The Florentine government, stirred up by a coalition of powerful old families, and chiefly by the Albizzi, charged Cosimo with aspiring to rise above ordinary citizens and thus upturn the republican government. Based on this accusation, Cosimo was briefly incarcerated, at risk of being put to death (as requested by the Albizzi) and was finally exiled. Paradoxically, this was the prelude to his rise to the status of de facto ruler of Florence (achieving precisely what his enemies had accused him of trying to obtain) as the following year the city, broke after another unsuccessful war against the Republic of Lucca, exiled Rinaldo Albizzi and recalled Cosimo. As reported by the great Florentine political philosopher of the Renaissance, Niccolò Machiavelli, upon his entrance into the city Cosimo 'was hailed as the benefactor of the people, and the father of his country'.[14] This is traditionally considered the beginning of the Medici's 'hidden lordship' of Florence: although Cosimo maintained tight control over the city government, he rarely assumed any official public position and never for long, and he also abstained from delivering public speeches.

Cosimo de' Medici saved Florence from financial catastrophe in 1434. From that year, his activities as a philanthropist and patron of the arts and culture greatly increased, especially after the Council of Florence of 1438–9, aimed at reconciling Western and Eastern churches in an attempt to protect what was left of the Byzantine Empire from Ottoman expansion. Cosimo, who had been instrumental in bringing the Council to his city, developed a great interest in the Neoplatonic ideas expressed by some of the eastern representatives at the Council, which ultimately led him to sponsor the Platonic Academy in Florence and to found the Medici Library at the Dominican Convent of San Marco (often considered to have been the first public library in Renaissance Europe) and others. This way of giving back part of the huge wealth that he had accumulated (which surely also helped to consolidate his political grip on Florence), however, was not sufficient to reassure him that his sins had been properly atoned for, because he was the first to suspect that at least some of his gains had been ill gotten. As was common in the Middle Ages, when he felt that his life was coming to an end (he died in 1464) he intensified his charity. Additionally, as was possible only for somebody who had always maintained close business connections with the Church, he managed to obtain a papal bull of absolution for his sins, paid for by endowing the Monastery of San Marco in Florence.[15]

After Cosimo's death, leadership of the Medici family and bank was assumed by his grandson, Lorenzo 'The Magnificent', who was much more
interested in politics (both local and international) than in business and completed the family shift away from Giovanni di Bicci's stance of non-involvement
in government. Like Cosimo before him, Lorenzo did not formally become
the lord of Florence, but his descendants did, obtaining in 1532 the hereditary
title of Dukes of Florence with the support of Pope Clement VII (who himself
happened to be a Medici). The way in which the Medici used their wealth to
reach ambitious political objectives will be further discussed in chapter 10.
Here, a final consideration is needed: by *becoming* princes, the Medici found
a way to overcome the risks implicit in *lending* to princes, which was almost
an unavoidable necessity for those who aspired to reach the highest positions
in European late medieval international finance. In Florence, this had already
brought about the downfall of the Bardi and Peruzzi banks, but the history of
the continent is full of examples of this kind, becoming only more numerous
in early modern times.

Consider for example the case of the German bankers from Augsburg, another prominent financial centre of late medieval and early modern Europe. If
the Medici had profited greatly from their relationship with the Pope, German
bankers like the Fuggers and the Welsers owed their considerable success in
large part to their connections to the Holy Roman Emperor and the Habsburg
family. They opened branches in key junctions of the Habsburgs' vast domains, in particular the city of Antwerp in the Low Countries which, during
the first half of the sixteenth century, came to be the economic capital of the
continent. Indeed, Antwerp was probably the European city that profited most
from the early phases of the new Atlantic trade, in part thanks to the fact that
it was a Spanish possession. Growing quantities of spices from Africa and Asia
(pepper and nutmeg), sugar from the Antilles and non-colonial goods like
English cloth (finished and dyed in Flanders) arrived in the city, together with
large quantities of American gold and silver, transferred by the Spanish to finance their activities in continental Europe and to buy massive quantities of
goods for their developing American colonies. All this required the availability
of large capitals and access to refined financial services to balance the trade, to
move funds across the continent (and increasingly, across the seas) and more
generally to allow the booming commercial and industrial activities of Flanders to expand smoothly. The Fuggers and other German bankers played this
game very successfully, especially during the reign of Emperor Charles V. This
changed under his son, King Philip II of Spain, who in 1557 went bankrupt

causing considerable damage to Antwerp's (and Augsburg's) financial sector. Shortly afterwards the king of France, Henry II, also arbitrarily reduced, and then temporarily suspended, interest payments, further complicating the situation for many Augsburg firms and leading to a wave of bankruptcies. Things went from bad to worse after the beginning of the rebellion of the Low Countries against Spanish rule, in 1566.[16]

The case of the Fuggers, who can be considered lucky as they survived the crisis (albeit far from unscathed), is exemplary of the dangers, as well as of the opportunities, which came with being the bankers of the great ruling nobility of Europe. The Fuggers had moved to Augsburg in 1367 and were originally active in the textile and goldsmithing sectors. Slowly they expanded their businesses: from working and trading gold and jewellery, in the second half of the fifteenth century they entered the lucrative international business of transferring to the Papal Court in Rome the sums collected for the procurement of church benefices and the sale of indulgences. The family reached its greatest wealth under Jacob 'The Rich' (1456–1525), who proved an exceptionally successful entrepreneur in the mining sector (in copper-rich Neusohl in present-day Slovakia he developed the largest mining centre of the time) and also reaped huge profits from international trade in spices and other goods. The mining activities were closely dependent upon the goodwill of the emperor (initially, Maximilian I) and other feudal lords, paid for by the provision of financial services.[17] This close connection between financial and political power was further demonstrated by the imperial election of Charles V, which was won against a very strong rival (the king of France, Francis I) for a huge price: 852,000 guilders were spent in gifts (technically, bribes) to the seven prince-electors. Of this sum, 544,000 guilders were raised by Jacob, a sum that in time he was able to recover in full: no small feat, given the circumstances.

On his death, in 1525, Jacob the Rich was surely one of the wealthiest men in Europe and even, according to some of his contemporaries, the wealthiest of all. He had also proved an innovator in charity, founding in Augsburg the *Fuggerei* which is usually considered the oldest social settlement in Europe (see chapter 9). His nephew Anton, who succeeded him in directing the family's activities, focused even more on providing loans to the Habsburg dynasty and, indeed, played a key role in financing Charles V's wars against the spread of Protestantism. Anton was also very successful in international trade (less so in mining) and by 1546 had increased the company assets to about 5.1 million guilders (from the 2 million inherited from Jacob's directorship). Shortly before his death, however, Anton had to face a serious financial crisis when, in 1557, the king of Spain defaulted on his debt. This sent German bankers into disarray, including to some degree the Fuggers (Anton's nephew and business partner, Hans Jakob Fugger, had to declare personal bankruptcy) whose losses must have considerably exceeded 1 million guilders.[18]

By Anton's death in 1560, the family net worth may have shrunk to about 260,000 guilders, an estimate obtained by subtracting liabilities of 5.4 million from total assets of 5.66 million guilders. Additionally, many assets consisted of Spanish and Dutch debt claims that were difficult to collect. The family company, however, survived and even continued to lend to Philip II, although after the crisis Genoese bankers replaced the Germans as the main providers of financial services to the Spanish crown. After Philip II's second default in 1575 the Fuggers (who on that occasion were the only ones excluded from the discontinuation of payments) considerably reduced their exposure to the king, probably due to a mixture of fear and a declining interest in risky businesses. The family had begun the process of ennoblement: Jacob the Rich had been made a count by Emperor Maximilian I, a title shared by Anton who, in addition, had married into the old nobility. If they had remained financiers and merchants at heart, this was not the case for their descendants who gradually moved what was left of the family riches to land (the company was completely dissolved in 1658), diversifying into three branches fully belonging to the nobility and pursuing an aristocratic lifestyle.[19] Yet again, new money had become old, but more interestingly here, what remained of a fortune made to a large degree in finance had been enshrined in land and other stable assets, which has allowed it to survive to the present day.

Tax Farming, a Necessary Evil

The Bardi and Peruzzi were ruined by their involvement with kings, and the Fuggers were seriously harmed, but the Genoese who dominated the European financial markets of the sixteenth and early seventeenth centuries found a way to tame even the kings of Spain: from their point of view, the four defaults of Philip II looked more like a negotiated restructuring of the crown's long-term debt than unavoidable and 'disordered' bankruptcies. Notwithstanding the Spanish defaults of 1575 and 1596, in 1566–1600 the typical Genoese family bank made annual returns in the range of 7.3 per cent (the basic long-term rate on renegotiated Spanish sovereign debt) to 20 per cent. Indeed, the Genoese managed to turn a profit even from the funding of the *Invincible Armada* which was meant to invade England in 1588.[20] Slowly, the European financial system was becoming more stable, at least in terms of a progressive reduction of the risks to which those financial players who had dealings with governments and ruling lords were subjected, which also means that, as a path towards great wealth, finance was becoming a much safer one. In part, this reflects innovations in financial techniques. If the Fuggers had been 'among the first of a new breed of financiers who began to mobilize credit for governments by floating bonds for investors rather than by direct lending',[21] the Genoese made an art of the careful drafting of loan contracts and contingency clauses. But to a large degree, the increasing safety in financial activities reflects the growth in the size of states and public administrations: to the greater needs of the public, fuelled mostly by the escalating financial needs of war or defence associated with the so-called 'military revolution' in early modern Europe,[22] corresponded a need for a more stable and organic provision of financial services, and hence the practical need to preserve, and allow to flourish, the specialized operators that provided them. Direct lending to governments and princes, however, was just one facet of a bundle of financial services which was closely connected to other, equally important ones, beginning with tax farming.

In preindustrial Europe, tax collectors were among the most hated individuals, and they were also consistently counted among the richest individuals, both at the local and state level. They were not usually employees of the administration, but were tax 'farmers' who provided an advance of money in exchange for the right to collect the leased tax revenues. In this respect, medieval and early modern European states were considerably less 'modern' than the Roman Empire of old, which had employed public officers to collect direct taxes (in contrast, private contractors, the hated *publicani*, had been common in republican times).[23] Often, the right to collect was simply auctioned to the highest bidder, so that farmers needed to maximize the revenues collected, which surely contributed to their real and perceived ruthlessness. Indeed, from the point of view of the state, here lay an additional advantage of tax farming: beyond guaranteeing the agreed-upon revenue and assuming all of the risks implicit in tax collection, the tax farmers shifted attention away from the true promoter of the fiscal levy (the state and/or a local government or territorial body), carrying the blame for extortionate taxation themselves. This approach has been well-documented for some European polities, for example the Republic of Venice, where the ruling city often managed to appear as the protector of the provincial subjects *from* the rapacious collectors.[24]

On the other hand, for those being taxed, tax farming led to an altogether nastier and less fair system because the collectors were prone to cede to the pressure of local notables, whom they often knew well because they lived in the area and belonged to the same local elite, leading to unequal treatment to the disadvantage of the weaker social strata. It should come as no surprise, then, that in the Dutch Republic during the seventeenth and eighteenth centuries the system of tax farming was a major cause of social discord, often leading to riots, or that in France during the Revolution many saw an opportunity to make tax farmers pay for their presumed misdeeds, leading to twenty-eight executions in 1794—including Antoine Lavoisier, an important administrator of the *Ferme générale* better known as one of the fathers of modern chemistry.[25]

From our specific angle, the spread of tax farming, associated with the continuous increases in per-capita taxation and the diversification of fiscal instruments that is typical of early modern Europe (the period of the rise of the fiscal state[26]), provided additional opportunities for rapid personal enrichment. At the highest levels, we find tax farmers who contracted fiscal revenues across entire states. A typical example is France, where tax farming was the domain of a small number of trusted courtiers like Antoine II Crozat who, as seen in chapter 3, was one of Louis XIV's tax farmers in the late seventeenth and early eighteenth centuries, possibly becoming the richest man in France. In France, the relatively high degree of centralization of tax farming allowed the monarch and his government to play one bidder against the other, to the point of soliciting offers from reliable connections simply to increase the price of the concession. Although the profits of tax farmers were somewhat constrained (to the benefit of the state, not of the taxpayers), due to the large scale of the concessions they remained potentially huge.[27] At this level, it is obvious that those who had the financial means to advance the sums required for securing the tax farms tended to be among those more generally involved in large-scale banking, in part because in many instances tax farms were used as a substitute for collateral in loans to governments.[28] For example, in the early fourteenth century it was the Florentine families of the Bardi, Peruzzi and Acciaiuoli who formed a syndicate to collect the taxes of the Kingdom of Naples. About a century later, the Medici acted in a similar capacity for the Papal Court, and the Fuggers did the same for the king of Spain, collecting the revenues of the three great ecclesiastical orders of Spain (a farm they had been awarded to repay them for the financial support they had provided for the imperial election of Charles V).[29]

Across Europe, however, opportunities for tax farming were widespread and not limited to those who negotiated directly with crowns and central governments. Locally, we find financial operators involved in the collection of regional and town tributes as well as subletters of portions of larger farms. In early modern times, whenever we are able to analyse lists of the richest individuals in a given community, we usually find tax collectors at the top. Take the example of the Sabaudian State (Piedmont) in north-western Italy: there, based on an exceptional source dated 1613 which details the overall wealth of all heads of households in a range of communities, we know that the richest individual in the city of Susa was a certain Bernardino Sestrono, recorded as an innkeeper (*oste*) but whose considerable wealth of 11,200 scudi came mostly from his other activities. He was a leaser of the properties of the priory of Susa, as well as the tax collector for the *dacito*, an indirect tax on the transit of goods through the Susa valley, a business for which he directly employed two agents. Clearly, he was well endowed with capital (the source also informs us that he had many credits in the Dauphiné, just across the Alps, which had, however, been seized by the king of France during past wars with the Sabaudian State), which is what allowed him to act as a financial entrepreneur. Similarly, in another Piedmontese city, Ivrea, the collector of the salt tax, Battista Guido, was the sixth richest individual.[30]

If we also count these smaller-scale operators, tax farmers appear to have been ubiquitous in preindustrial Europe, as were taxes of various kinds, many of which had been inherited from medieval times and went hand in hand with what remained highly fragmented jurisdictions, while others were introduced as states became hungrier for resources and better able to extract tribute. The rise of the fiscal state, then, had inequality-promoting effects that went beyond those resulting from regressive taxation to include the opening of new paths through which considerable fortunes could be accumulated, for example, by the concentration in a few pockets of resources extracted from the collectivity by tax farmers to repay loans due to private financiers. This topic will be further discussed in chapter 10. Here, it will suffice to recall that the provision of financial services of various kinds (lending, tax farming) to states whose scope and functions were continuously expanding is simply a component, albeit a particularly important one, of a more general process as those same states were in need of a broader range of innovative services (remember the development of the first continental postal system by the Tasso/Thurn und Taxis family). Moreover, their expanding administrations and bureaucracies offered many additional opportunities for increasing one's wealth thanks to well-paid public offices.[31] This path to wealth was particularly important for the hereditary nobility, which as seen in chapter 3 was always looking for socially acceptable ways to preserve or restore its fortunes (in addition to being one of the possible paths *towards* the acquisition of noble status). Nobles also profited from the early modern expansion of the financial sector by acting as investors, as is discussed in the following section.

On Investors, from Preindustrial to Industrial Times

An important development typical of early modern finance was the spread of contractual arrangements and of financial instruments that allowed for capital to be invested without any direct involvement of the investor in the ensuing activities. This presented a range of advantages, for example, diversifying the investment across sectors and companies in order to reduce the risk and facilitating the pursuit of profit in innovative enterprises by economic actors who had to avoid dirtying their hands with bourgeois activities in order to preserve their status or who were simply unwilling or unable to assume a more entrepreneurial role. In time, as the titles corresponding to these investments became progressively easier to trade in specialized markets, *trading* stock itself became one possible path for personal enrichment, albeit a somewhat shaky one considering that soon the first financial bubbles would develop—and burst.[32]

Some of these new investment opportunities have already been mentioned in chapter 4: think of the privileged companies set up to profit from the Atlantic trade, beginning with the VOC and the WIC founded in 1602 and 1621 in the Dutch Republic[33] and the English East India Company (EIC) founded in 1600. The VOC was the first to issue public stock or, more precisely, it was the first to start a process that would soon lead its stock to become fully public. At the moment of its establishment, over 1,800 individual investors contributed to the initial capital of 6.4 million guilders. Of these, only seventy-six (the *bewindhebbers*) were accorded some managerial authority, and from their numbers the seventeen active directors, the *Heeren XVII*, were selected. Importantly, and marking a clear difference from the merchant companies that had been set up before the establishment of VOC's monopoly on the East Indies trade, none among the investors (not even the *Heeren XVII*) had unlimited liability for the debt of the company. Instead, investors were responsible only to the extent of their own investments. In modern parlance, the VOC was entirely a limited liability company: another important step in making the world of finance safer for both specialized actors and occasional investors.[34] In 1609, it was decided that the invested capital was non-refundable. Investors, however, were allowed to sell their shares to others, which gave a boost to the activities of the Amsterdam stock exchange, established by the VOC specifically for this purpose. It is commonly considered to have been the first institution specializing in the formal trade of securities. A further boost to the stock exchange was given by the increasing amount of medium-term debt issued by the company to fund its expeditions. In 1610, the VOC paid its first dividend. Although this was in kind (pepper and mace), it was substantial: according to the company, a return of 125 per cent on the initial investment, but, since many shareholders protested that they could not sell the spices at the price needed to realize such a return, it was probably less. They asked for cash dividends instead, which in time would lead to a shift in company policy making the ownership of VOC shares even more 'friendly' to investors.[35]

For some hundred years after its foundation, the VOC was the largest joint-stock company in the world. At least in principle, investment in it was open to large strata of Dutch society and, although the largest 10–11 per cent shareholders owned half of the overall stock, most initial investors had contributed only small sums, as little as about 20 guilders. Additionally, as the *Heeren XVII* were nominated by, and answered to, the public authorities of the Dutch cities that had helped to create the VOC and consequently were largely sheltered from the influence of shareholders, there were basically no restrictions on who could purchase company shares; even foreigners were welcome. The open model of financing established by the VOC was only slowly imitated abroad. In comparison, the English EIC started out with a much more traditional character. All shareholders were part of the General Court and played a direct role in running the company, as well as electing the directors from among their fold.[36] A crucial distinction remained between those investors who had no intention of participating in the management and shaping of the company's commercial decisions but simply aspired to substantial returns, and those who instead sought from their participation in the EIC benefits for their other activities; this was the case for many merchants of the 'city' of London. But the company always managed to restrict the number of shareholders, in order to maximize the advantages of the monopoly for a relatively small number of investors, who were usually very rich and influential to begin with.[37] Among these, the nobility played a key role: in the early seventeenth century, about 20 per cent of all those who invested in the English overseas trade belonged to the gentry. While many among the nobility viewed this with scorn, the advantages of financing Atlantic trade ventures were so clear that by the early eighteenth century attitudes had already changed radically, not only in England but also in European countries, like France or Spain, that had narrower views about what was proper for a noble.[38]

This was a fundamental, albeit slow, shift. Before it was completed, the European nobility had become deeply involved in another financial novelty of early modern times: government bonds.

In the Republic of Venice, whose patricians were never averse to profiting from interesting economic opportunities, a consolidated debt existed from 1262 (the *Monte*) which paid an annual 5 per cent. It was the first arrangement of this kind in Europe, quickly imitated by other Italian cities beginning with Genoa in 1274. As the Republic of Venice was an extremely reliable borrower (in its long history, it never defaulted), sovereign debt provided the social and economic elites with exceptional opportunities for investment, especially when, in early modern times, expensive wars generated a need for more substantial borrowing on the part of the state. So, during the seventeenth century, the size of the Venetian public debt increased manyfold because of the expenditures for the long War of Candia (1645–69) against the Ottoman Empire. Debt shares were acquired mostly by patricians, merchants and other members of the economic elite and paid an annual nominal rate of 7–8 per cent and sometimes even higher. Although other social strata also invested in the public debt, this was by no means an opportunity for all because in the Republic of Venice, as in the Dutch Republic, the existence of minimum entry sums for subscribing to public debt effectively restricted it to the richest part of society. This arguably contributed to the tendency towards an increasing concentration of wealth. The distributive injustice of the system was further increased by the fact that while interest rates were high, very low risks were incurred. It was well known that the patricians who controlled the government had invested in public debt themselves; therefore, it was considered highly unlikely that they would endanger one of their main and most stable sources of income.[39]

Considered from this angle, it is clear that the expansion of sovereign debt during the seventeenth century, which was also connected to the establishment of public banks (for example, the Bank of England in 1694), had an impact on overall inequality that remains to be explored in full. It surely helped to consolidate the position of the old rich, as well as leading to further increases in their wealth share. For example, in the Dutch Republic by the first decades of the eighteenth century, through the continuous purchase of bonds, the wealthiest families came to concentrate a much larger share of the public debt in their hands than they had ever had before. This was reflected in the composition of their patrimonies: in Delft in 1706–30 almost 60 per cent of the wealth of the richest 5 per cent of households was composed of bonds of all kinds (indeed, the richest 5% owned 85% of all bonds held by non-institutional owners of

Delft; by the 1770s the share had grown to 91%). This also reflected an aspiration to retire from commercial and entrepreneurial activities, consolidating their grip on politics instead. According to historians Jan de Vries and Ad van der Woude, 'The existence of a gigantic public debt concentrated in the hands of families of great wealth, and the direct access of many of those families to political office, established the basic framework in which the "oligarchization" of political life . . . became intensified'.[40] So the development of financial markets was instrumental in creating the conditions that allowed Dutch families with a mercantile past to morph into non-entrepreneurial, politically powerful dynasties, a process already described in chapter 4.

If in some periods and settings the availability of more and better opportunities for financial investment might have deprived the economy of substantial capital (not to mention irreplaceable human capital), in others it fuelled the opposite process, for example by allowing the nobility to invest their wealth in entrepreneurial activities. Seventeenth- and eighteenth-century investments in privileged companies are one example, but similar circumstances were to be replicated at the time of the Industrial Revolution. Especially in England, the actual extent of the involvement of nobles in providing the capital needed to fund crucial investments is much debated. A particularly important case is that of canals. These were built by joint-stock companies that made public calls on shares before beginning their activities; thereafter shares could be sold on the secondary market. Canal securities offered good returns, although they were subject to considerable risks given that not all canals turned out to be profitable. According to a view popular in the 1950s and 1960s, landowners (most of whom were nobles of some sort) supported the development of facilities for communication with their economic and political resources because this benefited their agricultural enterprises and the exploitation of the mineral assets that might be present on their estates. The fact that the nobility's interest in canals and similar investments was not purely speculative led to an interrelation of the interests of landowners and industrialists that was not usually found in continental Europe. However, later studies have argued that landowners had no special interest in canals and simply participated in the new business in proportion to their share of national income.[41] But as many of the wealthiest individuals of industrializing England were nobles, the fact remains that they represented a significant share of all investors and were often among those who invested the largest sums: in canals or, as shown by recent research, in turnpike roads where large landholders tended to be the only investors wealthy enough to diversify their portfolio by buying bonds from multiple turnpike trusts, thus achieving a significant reduction of risk.[42] There also seems to have been huge regional variation in how the nobility contributed to the investments of the Industrial Revolution: while in the north it played an active and positive role, this was not necessarily the case in the south.[43] This being said, in parts of continental Europe, like Germany, the nobility also appears to have been heavily involved in financing the railroads and other infrastructure of the (Second) Industrial Revolution,[44] which suggests that we should be careful when considering claims of English exceptionalism in this regard.

Bankers of the Modern Era: Continuity and Change

If we consider the opportunities for enrichment offered by finance in the first century of the modern era and onwards, the first thing to highlight is the impressive continuity with earlier phases. This is clear when looking at investment opportunities (in that case, the really transformative innovations date to early modern times) and even clearer when looking at banking. Bankers of the early nineteenth century (and beyond) still operated in ways which were not too dissimilar from those that had developed in late medieval times. Although by now it was no longer necessary to hide interest in exchange rates, the substance of the bankers' activities remained basically the same, grounded, as it was, in complex networks of kinship and family relations and in the cultivation of social contacts with governments, aristocrats and entrepreneurs active in trade and industry. Even one of the main novelties to occur in banking, the spread of joint-stock institutes with limited liability beginning from the second half of the nineteenth century, saw the very active presence of established banking dynasties, like the Rothschilds who in 1864 contributed to the foundation of the *Société Générale*.

The Rothschild family originated from Frankfurt am Main in south-western Germany, another important European financial hub although never the main one until the European Central Bank was established there in 1998. The Rothschilds were devout Jews who prospered in the trade of wool and silk in the face of antisemitic prejudice and legislation. Trading in silk, for example, was formally prohibited for Jews but the Rothschilds were never easily stopped. The founder of the banking business, Mayer Amschel Rothschild, had begun in 1757 as an apprentice of the Oppenheim bank in Hannover, which counted among its customers many noble families and where he could refine his expertise in rare coins and medals. These skills brought him to the notice of Wilhelm IX, the hereditary prince (landgrave) of Hesse-Kassel, and in 1769 he became the 'court Jew'. His brief was to provide the prince with a variety of financial services, and the appointment greatly enhanced his social status. By dint of paying an ad-hoc tax, he was even allowed to leave Frankfurt's ghetto on Sundays.[45]

Mayer Amschel had founded the first branch of the Rothschild family in Frankfurt. In 1798 his third son, Nathan Mayer, moved to England with his father's blessing in order to expand the international operations of the family. He was given a capital of about 20,000 pounds (2.8 million in 2020 U.S. dollars). Initially he settled in the industrial city of Manchester where he traded, with great success, in cotton cloth. A few years later he was ready to move to London where, with his increased capital, he began to deal on the stock exchange and shortly afterwards opened a branch of the family bank. In his early activities he was helped considerably by the strong connections that his father had established with the Jewish economic elites of London, connections further strengthened in 1806 when he married Hannah, the daughter of a leading merchant of the city (Levi Barent Cohen) who also brought him an ample dowry of 3,248 pounds. From the outset, Nathan played the great game of government finance, including by funding Wellington's campaigns in Europe against Napoleon, nothing new for an upper-tier international banker (remember Anton Fugger's financing of Charles V's wars against the Protestants). His other specialties at the time included speculating in gold and smuggling English goods to the continent, in open violation of Napoleon's Continental Blockade. Because of these anti-Napoleonic activities, the Rothschilds hoped to profit from the opportunities that opened up after the *Empereur*'s defeat, in part because they had loaned 5 million francs to the 'restored' king of France, Louis XVIII, so that he could make a dignified return from exile. Initially, however, they were excluded from major transactions as they were met with the collective hostility of the local financiers, who were partly envious and partly driven by the antisemitic prejudice that remained strong in France, although not as much as in central European areas. Nevertheless, the Rothschilds eventually overcame such resistance (and exacted financial vengeance upon their enemies), and the Paris branch of the family, established by Nathan's younger brother James (né Jakob) shortly before the death of the patriarch Mayer Amschel in 1812, prospered.

In the following years, through its three main branches, the Rothschild bank strengthened its dominant position in European international finance. The leadership remained concentrated in the hands of the male line of Mayer

Amschel's descendants, following his explicit recommendation (enshrined in his will) that brothers-in-law were never to be integrated into the family bank; for good measure, Mayer Amschel also excluded all his daughters from any participation in the company. Partly for this reason, and partly because the founder had also admonished his descendants to remain faithful to the Jewish religion and not to marry outside the faith, in the following decades the Rothschilds systematically intermarried: of the eighteen marital unions entered into by Mayer Amschel's grandchildren, sixteen were between uncle and niece or between first cousins. Apart from the religious preoccupations of the founder, it must be noticed that the practice of marrying across different lines of descent also served to avoid patrimonial losses due to the payment of sizeable dowries to outsiders—and to this end, it had been quite common in medieval and early modern times. Nothing new, then, although admittedly the Rothschilds went to some lengths to remain faithful to the founder's will, at least until the death of Nathan Mayer in 1836; thereafter the family marriage practices became rather more open (and troubled). In perfect continuity with the preindustrial past, the family became increasingly aristocratic. This was especially the case for the English branch, beginning with Nathan Mayer's son Lionel. Although he already held the Austrian title of baron, inherited from his father, he sought to enter the English peerage as well through the good offices of Prime Minister Gladstone, but Queen Victoria balked at the idea of bestowing such honour on a Jew and particularly a speculator. However, in 1885 she relented and made Lionel's son, Nathan Mayer II, the first Baron Rothschild. He was the first Jew to become a member of the House of Lords (Lionel had already been a Member of Parliament).[46]

In the initial phases of their ascent, the Rothschilds faced considerable social scorn: both as Jews and as financiers. As Jews, they began their banking operations in a period when it was just becoming possible for those of their religion to operate at the top level of international finance; as will be recalled, in earlier epochs most Jews had had to limit themselves to small consumer credit and to operating on a local scale. But even if they were now legally allowed to become involved in all sectors of finance, at least in countries like England and France, they continued to suffer from prejudice. In European culture Jewish lenders had unjustly become synonymous with usurers: not a good basis on which to pursue a profession in which interpersonal trust was pivotal, and for this reason in their initial activities they often had to operate through socially presentable 'silent partners'. As financiers, the Rothschilds suffered from the general mistrust with which other sectors of the economy and society viewed those who specialized in the commerce of money. This mistrust had not been blown away by societal modernization but continued to exist in new and mutated forms which had their origins in the medieval suspicion of all economic activities that did not involve the production or transformation of real goods. Take, for example, a late nineteenth-century thinker like Veblen. His distinction between 'industrial' and 'pecuniary' economic institutions (companies), that is, between those focused on the production of new things and those focused only on ownership or acquisition (like investment banks),[47] did not appear out of the blue but is connected to an enrooted and recognizable trait of Western culture. Veblen also referred to this opposition as one between 'industry' and 'business', to which corresponded radically different ways of behaving and thinking ('habits of thought'). Pecuniary institutions represented a risk for society at large because in the pursuit of profit per se their leaders acted like modern predators, disregarding the damage they might cause to others.[48] The kind of ruthless businessmen that Veblen had in mind were the 'robber barons' of Gilded Age America: in his *Theory of Business Enterprise* (1904) Veblen explicitly mentions the likes of Andrew Carnegie (see chapter 4) and J. P. Morgan.

Independently from Veblen's position, it seems fitting to conclude this section with a brief portrait of the Morgans, one of the main American dynasties to build a fortune on high finance. Indeed, some have argued that the Rothschilds' main mistake was to have failed to understand the full potential of the United States, avoiding founding a branch in New York notwithstanding the insistence of some of their associates.[49] The Morgan family had migrated from Wales to America in 1636, settling in Springfield, Massachusetts. By the early nineteenth century, members of the family were already quite wealthy, with activities in various areas. Joseph Morgan, the first to move to New York, made a fortune in the coffee house business and was also involved in many companies in the transportation sector (canals, steamships, railways and so on). On his death, in 1847, he left his son Junius Spencer a fortune of about 1 million dollars (about 32 million in 2020 U.S. dollars).

Junius, who a few years after his father's death had moved to London (while sending his son, John Pierpont, to complete his studies in Switzerland and Germany), became a successful entrepreneur in the national and international trade of raw materials, especially cotton, but more importantly, he was the first member of the family to become involved in banking. In 1854 he became a partner in George Peabody's investment bank in London. Ten years later, upon Peabody's retirement, the firm became J. S. Morgan and Co. For a while, the bank struggled against the traditional resistance of the financial establishment to newcomers (an establishment which, at that time, was perfectly represented by the Rothschilds, that is, by the newcomers of the earlier generation). Junius, however, had a stroke of luck with the Franco-Prussian War of 1870–1: the embattled French emperor, Napoleon III, was in urgent need of money, but the Rothschilds, who had strong connections to both France and Germany, hesitated to commit for political reasons, and in addition, like other major banks, they did not have much faith in France's ability to win the war (and to repay the debt). Then, the Morgan bank stepped in, granting a large loan in favour of the French government, although at an interest rate of 15 per cent: so high that it wounded the self-esteem of the country. With the fall of the government and the proclamation of the Commune in Paris the market value of the loan titles crashed, and Junius had to buy more shares himself to avoid further drops. This was perceived in France as further humiliation, leading, after the end of the war, to a financial dream come true for the Morgan bank: in 1873 a 'liberation loan' was launched, which was used to repay older loans at par. The bank turned a huge profit of about 1.5 million pounds (174 million in 2020 U.S. dollars).

Notwithstanding this episode, the early fortunes of the Morgans were not due to loans to governments and rulers to the same degree as the Rothschilds and other European financial dynasties. Instead, they specialized in industrial speculation (what Veblen would have called 'business'), an art at which Junius' son, John Pierpont, excelled. While his father remained in London, he was mostly active in the United States, where he proved an extremely successful businessman in many crucial sectors of the Second Industrial Revolution, like railroads or steel; it was he who managed to convince Andrew Carnegie to sell his assets in the steel industry in 1901, leading to the birth of the United States Steel Corporation (see chapter 4). In these endeavours, John Pierpont's aim was usually to favour industrial concentration and 'cooperation' instead of competition, which made it possible both to cut industrial costs and to establish monopolies, maximizing financial returns for the shareholders but also leading to the kind of societal damage indicated by Veblen. But J. P. Morgan was also ready to put his enormous financial means at the service of his country (although not entirely disinterestedly). In 1907, in a phase of economic recession, a panic triggered by reckless financial operations led to huge losses on the New York Stock Exchange, and a series of runs on banks ensued. The financial crisis seemed on the verge of spiralling out of control when John Pierpont intervened, leading a group of enterprises and financiers to save a range of companies which were at risk of bankruptcy, thus contributing in a decisive way to restoring confidence in the solvency of the financial system.

In a sense, John Pierpont Morgan had bailed out his country (a feat that he repeated later that same year, saving the city of New York from bankruptcy), fulfilling precisely one of those functions that late medieval theologians had attributed to the super-rich, as will be discussed in chapter 8. While these actions earned him much private and public approbation, they also fuelled increasing concern about the economic and financial power of the American super-rich. In 1912, Congress established the Pujo Committee to investigate the so-called money trust which, from its base in New York, supposedly controlled the nation's finances.[50] John Pierpont was required to appear before the committee, an experience which seems to have exhausted him (he never enjoyed very good health) and according to some, including his family, contributed to his death in 1913. Towards the end of that year, the Federal Reserve System was introduced so that the United States would never again need to be saved by private financiers. Paradoxically, the display of financial power used on behalf of the public by John Pierpont Morgan in 1907 led to the establishment of conditions that made it unnecessary for private bankers to cyclically contribute to the public good, thus freeing them from an onus they had carried since medieval times. This and other similar developments elsewhere in the West had long-term consequences which will be discussed in the concluding section of this chapter.[51]

A final point remains to be made about how the way in which banks came to be structured in the late nineteenth century allowed for excellent opportunities for enrichment that went far beyond the relatively small group of controlling families of well-established financiers. While for a long time the Rothschilds actively tried to keep all of the directorship functions within the family, the Morgans, in part because they were much fewer in numbers, always had a marked propensity for delegating important managerial tasks to growing cohorts of highly skilled individuals. Indeed, by the time of John Pierpont's successor, Jack, the family representative had a mainly supervisory function. The bank became increasingly open to the outside until, in the second half of the twentieth century, it became a fully manager-led company. In the meantime, it had been split up because of New Deal legislation (see the concluding section of this chapter), and the two resulting companies (J. P. Morgan & Co and Morgan Stanley & Co), like all traditional private banks, were facing increasing competition from, and pressure to merge with, the flourishing new joint-stock banks. But from our perspective, what should be highlighted is that from the second half of the nineteenth century the financial sector was much larger than it had ever been before and so consolidated its role as a major path towards wealth. This was a path that, importantly, was at the time relatively open to women, again in continuity with the preindustrial past.

Women in Finance: An Overview

As has been clarified in the introduction, any attempt to study the prevalence of women among the rich throughout history is confronted with two problems: the relative scarcity of information in some of the more systematic archival sources that we have available, like fiscal records, due to the practice in use until at least the nineteenth century of recording the details of heads of households only (usually males), and the limitations of women's legal capacity to act which were widespread across the West. Although we do know about women who played a pivotal role in the management of merchant enterprises, usually acting as close partners of their husbands and much more rarely on their own or with some sort of substantial operative and patrimonial independence, it is in finance that they found a relatively free space for action.

Take for example the Italian city of Milan, which has always been a major European financial centre. A detailed study of 1,902 *confessiones* (a kind of notary deed through which private individuals entrusted capital to bankers to be invested in financial operations) stipulated in 1575–1607 with the aim of investing in the international exchange fairs of Bisenzone reveals that, of 605 distinct customers, 509 (84%) were women. Of these, the vast majority (86%) were widows. This apparent over-representation of widows has a clear juridical reason: on the death of their husbands, women legally acquired a greater capacity to act independently, that is, without the express consent of their husbands. At the same time, in the absence of children, they gained access to sizeable assets, as they obtained the restitution of their dowry, as well as (at least in Milan) all of the other goods that they had received from their or their husband's family. Otherwise, more often than not they were named the usufructuary and administrator of the deceased husband's properties until the children came of age. Whatever the case, many widows found themselves awash with capital. Investing it in finance was relatively simple to pursue, socially acceptable and offered the hope of substantial revenues (often of the order of a net 7%–9% yearly for Milanese widows).[52]

The presence of juridical restrictions on women's capacity to act, which usually made them dependent upon the authorization of their husband or of some male relation, is a well-known feature of preindustrial Europe, one which seems to have strengthened during the early modern period. In much of the continent, these restrictions were further expanded and generalized at the very beginning of the nineteenth century by Napoleon's *Code Civil* and all the many codes that drew direct inspiration from it, leading, in many areas, widows to lose much of their economic freedom, at least formally.[53] The situation was no better for women in a common-law country like England, as there the doctrine of 'coverture' provided even less protection to a married woman (the *feme covert*) than was common in continental Europe, and her legal capacity to act was similarly constrained.[54] And yet, everywhere, women continued to feature prominently in certain sectors of finance. Indeed, their presence increased throughout the seventeenth and eighteenth centuries, and as a group they became more diverse and less dominated by widows.[55] Their activities, however, are not easy to follow, because they were almost exclusively involved in 'dark matter credit', intermediated by notaries and hence difficult to observe, which in preindustrial times had greatly facilitated the meeting of the offer of private capital with demand, and that had survived even when new kinds of banks, more open to the general public, began to appear during the nineteenth century.[56] For the historian, this means that information about women's financial operations has to be laboriously collected from vast series of notary deeds, which is why systematic studies remain rare and are restricted to only a few areas, including, again, Milan. There, it has been estimated that during the eighteenth century, women mobilized 11 per cent of global sums (as creditors or as debtors, but the first were markedly prevalent) and were involved in 17 per cent of all deeds. The tendency was for a continuous rise in their relative weight, as they were involved in 20 per cent of all deeds in the 1830s and in 24 per cent in the 1840s. In other northern Italian cities during the eighteenth century the share of capital mobilized by women was similar or even larger than in Milan, with estimates ranging from 11 per cent to one-third. This situation was not specific to Italy but was also to be found elsewhere, for example in France. In Paris women had accounted for 11.8 per cent of all lenders in private loans, mobilizing 16.1 per cent of capital in 1662, but their financial activities grew continuously over time and by 1740 they were 27.6 per cent of all lenders and mobilized 23.5 per cent of capital; in the same period they also accounted for almost 30 per cent of those lending to the state. Figures for provincial areas of France are similar.[57]

Of course, not all women involved in private finance were particularly rich, but a sizeable proportion of the lenders did have access to considerable capital, like the Milanese widow Paola Tartara who, in the late 1770s, loaned a total of 232,873 lire divided into ten deeds.[58] There are also cases, albeit quite rare, of women who even in preindustrial times managed to enter the much more exclusive world of high finance. An example is Gracia Nasi, a Portuguese woman born in 1510 among the *marranos*, that is, Jews who had converted to Catholicism, usually under the threat of persecution.[59] It is highly probable that her family had always remained faithful to the Jewish religion while outwardly conforming to Catholic practice. When she was eighteen she married her uncle, Francisco Mendes, the descendant of an important banking family who had also become a major participant in the international spice trade. In fact, the Mendes (also known by their pre-conversion family name of Benveniste) had played a key role in financing the expeditions which led to opening the sea route to India by circumnavigating Africa. This guaranteed the family company a very sizeable share of the imports of pepper. In 1538, however, Francisco died, splitting his fortune between Gracia and his brother and partner, Diogo, who was in charge of the branch opened by the family bank in Antwerp where it cooperated closely with the local branch of the Fugger firm.

Although Gracia had probably been responsible for managing the family operations in Lisbon during her husband's illness, upon becoming a widow she suddenly felt all the fragility of her position, that of a rich woman (and a *marrana* to boot) in a male-dominated world. Before being forced into a new marriage by some greedy suitor or becoming the object of religious persecution (the Portuguese Inquisition had been established in 1536), she moved from Lisbon to Antwerp with her daughter and younger sister Brianda. There, she enjoyed somewhat greater freedom than in Portugal (both as a woman and as a covert Jew) and, as Diogo appears to have openly recognized her talent, she became his close collaborator, a family deal that was sealed by Diogo's marriage to Brianda.

When Diogo died, probably in 1542, Gracia inherited half of the the family company's capital; and (as per Diogo's will) she became the administrator of the entire Mendes fortune. But again, she and her female relatives were perceived as easy prey; this time it was no less than the Holy Roman Emperor, Charles V, who tried to arrange a marriage between Gracia's daughter (then not yet ten years of age) and don Fernando, an illegitimate descendant of the House of Aragon. Don Fernando happened to have promised the emperor 200,000 ducats as a gift if his matchmaking proved successful, a sum that he could easily have accessed upon marriage into a super-rich family with no males. The Nasi-Mendes women fled once again (Antwerp was a Spanish domain, subject to the authority of Charles V), first to Aachen on the pretext of taking the thermal baths, then to Lyon and Venice, but finally it was in the Italian city of Ferrara, then capital of the duchy ruled by the Este, that Gracia found shelter, albeit temporarily. In all this time, she found a way to continue proficiently managing the financial and trading operations of the Mendes firm and also to help her fellow Jews escape persecution and preserve their cultural and religious heritage, a parallel activity that she had pursued since the time of her residence in Antwerp. In tolerant Ferrara she returned openly to the practice of the Jewish religion, although this exposed her to charges of apostasy by the Christians. This is one reason why in 1553 she moved to Constantinople, where she remained, held in great regard by the Sultan and continuing her efforts to help both the local Jewish community and persecuted Jews across Europe, until her death in 1569.[60]

The case of Gracia Nasi, which is usually, and rightly, presented as a great success story for a Jewish woman facing religious persecution and gender discrimination, can also be taken as representative of the extent of such discrimination, from which even a very wealthy and well-connected individual found it difficult to escape, having to repeatedly flee from unsought and greedy suitors and rapacious rulers. As a woman who played the big game of high finance in preindustrial Europe, then, she remains an exception. The cases of women involved in private financial activities, using intermediaries (notaries) but no less skilful because of this, are much more representative of the general situation. As has already been mentioned, the important position occupied by women among private lenders continued well into the nineteenth century, when the industrialization process offered them many additional opportunities. Take the business of railroads in Great Britain. According to a recent study, women had been an important but minority presence from the very beginning (they were over 10% of all shareholders in some railroad companies of the mid-nineteenth century), but by the early twentieth century they accounted for 30–40 per cent of shareholders in a large sample of companies. In the vast majority of cases they acted as solo investors, while men usually preferred joint shareholding. This seems to suggest that, for women active in the financial markets, preserving their independence was at least as important as the pursuit of profit; indeed, the very fact of investing their capital can be understood as a way to protect their (financial) independence. From this perspective, the higher risk of less diversified investments (a direct consequence of the choice to avoid joint shareholding) was more than compensated for by the lower risk of seeing others taking decisions concerning their own capital.

As a confirmation of this point, in the rare instances when they took part in joint shareholding women tended to avoid investing together with male relatives but had a marked preference for arrangements in which the lead investor was another woman.[61]

It is clear, then, how the development of stock markets further increased the space for women's independent action in the financial sphere. In Britain, as in America, from the mid-nineteenth century women were simply intensifying practices that were already well-established in earlier epochs. For example, women made up 11 per cent of shareholders of the East India Company in 1709 and 20 per cent of shareholders of the South Sea Company in 1723. Women, the vast majority of whom were widows or unmarried, also represented 20 per cent of the shareholders of the Bank of England in 1720. In the United States they were 14.5 per cent of the original shareholders of the Commercial and Farmers Bank of Baltimore in 1810 and 25 per cent of the shareholders of the Philadelphia Bank in 1812.[62] This being said,

> Before the Civil War, American women's investment opportunities were mostly local and somewhat limited: savings banks, farm mortgages, municipal bonds, canal companies, and insurance companies. This was to change dramatically as a result of postwar industrial and financial expansion. . . . For propertied women, investments in stocks and bonds became another way to support themselves without compromising their status through waged work or trade.[63]

This is not to say that a greater presence of women in the stock markets did not lead to public censorship and scorn fuelled by masculine prejudice—it did—but it is also clear that on Wall Street from the Gilded Age on women were a collective power to be reckoned with. Many of them were widows, but there was also a significant number of married women who had retained control of their properties by means of wedding contracts, in a juridical context that was slowly becoming more gender-balanced. Unfortunately, we lack overall quantitative assessments of the relative position of female Wall Street investors, but the surviving records of some stockbroker firms are indicative. For example, in 1886–7 women made up 24 per cent of the 188 customers of Morton, Bliss & Company. They were over-represented (38%) among those who held investment accounts for the buying and selling of shares, although overall they seem to have followed a more risk-averse investment strategy compared to men. By 1910, American women had further consolidated their presence among shareholders: they were probably about 20–25 per cent of all shareholders and were over-represented in some specific sectors like banking, where they may have amounted to one-third of all investors, and (as in Britain) railroads where they seem to have made up 40–50 per cent of all investors in at least some of the leading companies. Many, and probably most, of these women came from the upper-middle and high classes and would have to be counted among the rich.[64]

The Progressive Financialization of the Modern Economy

During the years preceding World War I, across the West financial capitalism probably reached a peak in its ability to exert control over the whole economy. Highly concentrated in a few family dynasties and institutions, financial capital played a key role in the organization and reorganization of the industrial sectors that had emerged from the Second Industrial Revolution. However, the financial system also showed signs of instability, the most serious of which was the 'bank panic' of 1907 which, having started in the United States, spread to a range of other countries, including France, Germany and Italy, with serious consequences. At the same time, and further fuelled by episodes like the 1907 crisis, consensus grew in favour of policies aimed at preserving competition in the face of industrial concentration, protecting the bank deposits of small savers and generally reining in the economic omnipotence of great financiers. All of this had a series of consequences, from the strengthening or the founding of national banks in order to free governments from the need to rely upon private capital in times of need, to antitrust legislation and laws that closely regulated banking activities. The United States, the country where the emergence of gigantic industrial and financial companies was the most pronounced, played a pioneering role in the introduction of regulations of this kind, beginning in 1890 with an antitrust law, the Sherman Act. Regarding finance, the key developments took place after the 1929 financial crisis, in a political context which capitalized on growing resentment against the rich, who supposedly had been spared (or had even profited from) the plight of the common people. As part of President Roosevelt's New Deal, regulations aimed at preventing insider trading and market manipulations were introduced and the Security and Exchange Commission (SEC) was set up to supervise stock-market activities. However, for the world of finance at large the most important novelty was the Glass–Steagall Act of 1933. This law separated investment banks (which underwrote and dealt in securities) from commercial banks (which took in deposits and made loans), leading, among other things, to the splitting up of the Morgan bank and delivering an almost-fatal blow to the 'money trust' that had dominated the U.S. economy of the early twentieth century.[65] Laws similar to the Glass–Steagall Act were soon introduced elsewhere, for example in Italy with the *Legge Bancaria* of 1936.[66]

Regulations introduced in the 1930s surely helped to contain the growth of the financial sector during the first half of the twentieth century, although in that regard probably the most important role was played by the general economic disruption and the destruction of financial capital caused by the two World Wars (and the ensuing hyper-inflation) along with the events of the troubled period in-between, like the stock-market crash of 1929. Indeed, economist Thomas Piketty has recently argued that damage to financial capital, especially that concentrated in large patrimonies, is one of the key historical reasons for the decline in wealth inequality observed from the onset of World War I until the 1950s, especially in Europe, as in the United States the size of capital compared to national income remained somewhat more stable.[67] However, from the 1980s the pendulum has started to swing again in favour of finance, leading to worries that today's economy is becoming too 'financialized'. As will be argued below, this process and these worries exert a strong influence on the way in which society at large perceives financiers and bankers.

It is commonly accepted that an important factor leading to the expansion of finance in recent decades has been the progressive deregulation of the sector, which began in the 1980s and was favoured by a political and ideological shift spearheaded by President Ronald Reagan (1981–9) in the United States and Prime Minister Margaret Thatcher in the United Kingdom (1979–90). In the increasingly competitive world of the late twentieth century and given the relative ease with which capital could now be transferred from one part of the planet to another, financial innovation spread largely by imitation and came to involve all Western countries. In Europe, this process was encouraged by the European Economic Community (EEC) through a series of 'bank directives' aimed at promoting economic integration and creating a continental level playing field. For example, in Italy, the 1936 *Legge Bancaria* was repealed by the *Testo Unico Bancario* of 1994, which applied the Second Banking Directive of the EEC locally and allowed, after almost sixty years, 'universal banks' to operate again in the country. In the United States, the repeal of the Glass–Steagall Act by means of the Financial Services Modernization Act[68] of 1999 was a symbolic episode. Arguably the new Act mostly ratified the status quo, as the provisions of Glass–Steagall had been much weakened by a series of court rulings and regulations in the preceding years, and yet some believe it did play a significant role in subsequent developments, including by paving the way for a new financial crisis.[69]

Many, including Paul A. Volcker, a former chairman of the Fed, have considered the weakening of rules aimed at limiting bank speculation to be one of the underlying causes of the financial crisis of 2007–8 which started in the United States, spread globally and triggered the Great Recession that in some countries lasted until 2013. Others have argued that the main causes of the crisis were different, like the international housing bubble created by the property boom of the early 2000s, or at least that on balance the financial deregulation of the 1980s and 1990s provided more benefits than costs.[70] It is beyond the scope of this book to explore this contentious issue further. What needs to be highlighted instead is that, without doubt, financial deregulation led to the dramatic expansion of the financial sector seen in recent decades across the globe. In western Europe, already by 2000 it could be argued that twenty years or so of progressive deregulation had led to a doubling of both the ratio of banking assets to GDP and the number of employees of financial institutions. As the size of the workforce had remained largely constant, this represented a significant change in the occupational structure.[71] The employment share of finance stopped growing in the twenty-first century in most Western countries, stabilizing at about 3.5 per cent of all hours worked in the euro area during 2001–10 (higher, 4.4%, in the United States with the United Kingdom in-between at 3.9%).[72] In terms of the contribution to value added, and notwithstanding the 2007–13 crisis, the share of the financial sector oscillated within a fairly tight band in the first decades of the century; in the euro area it was, on average, 4.9 per cent in the five years 2000–4, and 4.7 per cent in 2015–19, while in the United States it grew marginally, from 7.5 per cent in 2000–4 to 7.6 per cent in 2014–18. Only in the United Kingdom was there substantial growth, from 5.4 per cent in 2000–4 to 6.8 per cent in 2015–19.[73] But almost everywhere in the West the ratio of financial assets to GDP (the most commonly used indicator of the 'financialization' of an economy) has continued to grow.[74]

The generalized growth of the ratio of financial assets to GDP has led to worries about further increases in both income and wealth inequality, due to the tendency for the ownership of those assets to be highly concentrated.[75] But another important reason why finance has contributed to rising inequality during the last forty years or so is that since the 1980s this sector has tended to pay higher and higher wages: according to one estimate, finance occupations are responsible for 15–25 per cent of the increase in the wage inequality that has occurred in the United States between 1970 and 2005. What is more, finance tends to pay a relatively large number of very high wages: in the early years of the new millennium, in the United States, CEOs in finance earned on average three and a half times as much as CEOs in other sectors who had comparable education and qualifications.[76] These processes, which to some degree involved all Western countries, led to employees in the financial sector becoming a very sizeable component of top earners: in 2010, across Europe, financial sector employees accounted for 19 per cent of those receiving the highest 1 per cent of gross wages, a marked over-representation, considering that they were just 4.4 per cent of all employees.[77]

In recent years, then, finance has become relatively more important as a path towards great wealth.[78] Here, some further reflections are needed on recent shifts in the perception of bankers and financiers and on concerns that remunerations paid by financial institutions might be excessive or at least might provide the wrong incentives. Indeed, many have blamed the 2007–13 crisis on the bankers' supposed 'greed', spotlighting their earnings and renewing a tradition of suspicion which, as we have seen, has ancient roots: there is nothing new under the sun. A much-debated issue is whether or not the high wages paid in the financial sector reflect high productivity. The fact that, when controlling for education and qualifications, there are still large wage differentials between finance and other sectors suggests that they do not (or not solely). Some studies have provided substantial evidence supporting this view, for both Europe and America. But if higher wages in finance do not reflect productivity, it seems unavoidable that they reflect rents, which financial institutions might accumulate because of the existence of barriers to entry or by profiting from various forms of public support, such as government guarantees. Rents would then be transferred, at least in part, to employees mostly by means of wage premia.[79]

There is also substantial evidence that the rents distributed to employees of financial institutions tend to accrue to those placed at the top of the income distribution (top managers and so on). Importantly, fiscal innovations that occurred from the 1980s, and in particular the progressive reduction of top rates of income tax, probably contributed to the spread of practices of aggressive bargaining for higher wages, bonuses and various benefits. This happened in finance as in other sectors,[80] but it was in finance that the greatest opportunities for rent accumulation were to be found. Arguably, this also led to reckless behaviour and unnecessary risk-taking on the part of top managers, who were strongly incentivized to maximize profits (on which their overall compensation depended). It is in this way that bankers might have contributed to triggering, or to establishing the conditions that aggravated, the 2007–8 financial crisis. Whatever the real responsibilities of bankers and financiers, the fact remains that large strata of society have *perceived* them as responsible for the collective plight that ensued. Public resentment grew to new heights when it became clear that soon after the financial crisis bankers had returned to unethical or perhaps inappropriate practices, particularly regarding their readiness to bolster their own income with huge bonuses.[81] The Occupy Wall Street protests of 2011 are closely connected to this situation and are the expression of social anger about perceived injustice.

All these issues will be further discussed in the final part of this book, which is concerned with the position that the rich occupy in society. Now, some final considerations are needed about another troubling aspect of the most recent financial crisis: the impression that very few of those who might have played a role have met with some form of punishment. I am not referring here to judicial punishment in the form of fines or incarceration, although it is also a widely held (but impossible to demonstrate) belief that, worldwide, only a few of those who acted in violation of rules and regulations have been punished.[82] I refer instead to economic punishment, in the form of the failure of overbold institutes and damage to the patrimony and long-term incomes of those involved in questionable behaviour. The point here is not to pass any moral judgement, but simply to point out a relevant historical development: after Lehman Brothers was allowed to fail in September 2008, in what remains the largest bankruptcy in American history, the U.S. government, as well as other governments worldwide, realized that some institutes were really 'too big to fail'. Consequently, it was considered preferable for the public to step in, for example by injecting public capital or by facilitating mergers, because the cost of public aid could be reasonably presumed to be much smaller than what would otherwise have been suffered by the broader economy. This, however, raises concerns about moral hazard, as (for example) confidence that the government will step in in the case of trouble could lead to the under-pricing of risk and to suboptimal investments in monitoring risk-taking. For this reason, 'too-big-to-fail firms will tend to take more risk than desirable, in the expectation that they will receive assistance if their bets go bad', as argued by the Fed chairman, Ben Bernanke, in public testimony in 2010.[83]

There are other implications of the existence of too-big-to-fail companies, implications that have gone undetected inasmuch as they can be glimpsed only by taking a very long-term perspective; as discussed earlier in this chapter, one crucial reason why Western societies came to accept the presence of super-rich individuals was the silent understanding that, in time of dire need, *they* would help the community with their private resources. This was done, for example, by Cosimo de' Medici in fifteenth-century Florence, but there are much more recent examples: the last one probably being Pierpont Morgan's (and associates') rescue of the United States from the crisis of 1907. In the case of companies that are too big to fail, it appears that a U-turn has been completed: private individuals accumulate financial patrimonies of unprecedented size, but if their firms get into trouble they are saved with public money. If we remember the problems encountered by medieval lenders to sovereigns, we can describe this inversion as a passage from a situation in which the risk of public debt is privatized (as it was carried by lenders to states and sovereign lords), to one in which private risks are collectivized (as banks that are 'too big to fail' are bailed out with taxpayers' money). When seen from this perspective, the concerns about extreme wealth concentration which for several years have been growing across the West appear to have, at the very least, some historical and cultural justification. This point will be further discussed in chapter 8, but before that, we need to explore other aspects of the way in which, across history, large patrimonies could be built and passed on to descendants.

6

The Curse of Smaug

THE SAVING AND CONSUMPTION
HABITS OF THE RICH

IN THE LAST INSTALMENT of *Forbes*' 'Fictional 15', a ranking of the richest characters in fiction published in 2001–13, the dragon Smaug—the antagonist of Tolkien's *The Hobbit*—contended for first position with Scrooge McDuck. Both characters stand out for their pathologically high propensity to save and hoard wealth. Smaug, in particular, is representative of the infamous greed of his kind, serial accumulators and custodians of treasure according to fictional tradition rooted in ancient German folklore. So enthralled was Smaug with his own hoard that losing even a tiny part of it (a golden cup, stolen by Bilbo the hobbit) threw him into a rage, which led to his undoing.[1]

Across history, many wealthy individuals have been deemed avaricious, sometimes pathologically so. At the other extreme, however, we find as many who have been blamed for squandering their fortune in the pursuit of pleasure or for simple vanity. Indeed, the rich as a category stand out *at the same time* for their consumption habits and for their saving habits. This is one reason why it is proper, in our analysis of the rich, to focus directly on these aspects of their collective behaviour. But there is more: the ability to accumulate wealth across time depends on the propensity to save instead of consuming. As wealth can be passed on to future generations by means of inheritance, it appears that the hoarders will be better able than the profligate to originate dynasties and to enroot within society a condition of high wealth inequality potentially unrelated to any merit beyond parsimony pure and simple. As seen in the preceding chapter, parsimony of such a kind would have been considered sinful avarice by medieval societies. But those very same societies would have blamed, and tried to punish, those who made a show of their wealth. Indeed, the behaviour of the spendthrift was considered almost as sinful as that of the miser. So, to save or not to save, that is the question to which Western societies, when faced with the presence of very rich and especially super-rich individuals, could never provide a clear answer. Discussing the nature of this social conundrum, whose basic traits are remarkably persistent across time and which remains a highly sensitive issue today, is another key objective of this chapter.

The Consumption Habits of the Rich: From Medieval (Relative) Moderation to Conspicuous Consumption

Being rich is also a matter of behaving and spending as rich people do. Insofar as the rich, or a part of them, constitute a status group, they have to adopt a specific lifestyle.[2] From the Middle Ages to the nineteenth century, when becoming closer to, and finally entering, the nobility was a major ambition of the European new rich, such a lifestyle was modelled upon that of the nobles, which led to a defensive reaction on the part of the old nobility: how much money the rich parvenus were able to spend mattered less than the manner in which they spent it. These concerns about taste and culture, which caused much pain and humiliation to the preindustrial rich, were progressively abandoned when the balance of economic power swung more and more towards the bourgeois component of society and, across the West, wealth aristocracies began to appear which were no longer interested in gaining the approval of the traditional nobility.

The relationship between wealth and nobility, which has been analysed in detail in chapter 3, is a useful starting point for our discussion of the consumption habits of the rich. Indeed, it highlights a crucial feature of medieval societies which survived until later epochs: while the nobility, because of its formal and publicly accepted status, was entitled to privileged access to material resources (increasingly obtained through inheritance) and a more luxurious lifestyle than that of the commoners, this was not the case for rich non-nobles. The progressive emergence of the non-noble rich as a specific category, a process which was fuelled by the medieval Commercial Revolution, from at least the thirteenth century led to social resentment of their unwarranted luxury. This process was obviously clearer in the wealthiest areas of Europe, like Italy, and was evidenced by social reactions of various kinds. It is not by chance that St Francis, who at the turn of the thirteenth century began preaching the virtues of a lifestyle characterized by material poverty (a point on which he departed from earlier preachers, like Bernard of Clairvaux, the founder of the Cistercian monastic order, who had focused on poverty 'in spirit', that is, on a mental attitude), came from a wealthy merchant family from Assisi.[3] And it is surely telling that from about the same period we see the emergence of city regulations aimed at clarifying the limits within which those belonging to different social strata had to maintain their visible expenditure. Regulations of this kind are usually referred to as 'sumptuary laws'.

In the quite refined form that they had already acquired by the fifteenth century, sumptuary laws were explicit in proposing a hierarchic classification of society in which the legitimate level of consumption, and how much wealth could be exhibited, were a function of social position. In the Italian city of Bologna in the mid-fifteenth century, the group composed of knights, 'doctors' and gentlemen (the latter defined as those belonging to ancient families and who for at least thirty years had not exercised any 'art') had the right to the most expensive and ornate apparel. Only those belonging to four highly prestigious guilds or *arti* (those of the notaries, of the moneychangers, of the drapers and of silk—the last two on the condition that the individual in question was not involved in any manual activity) were allowed a similar level of luxury, although with some exceptions, like the prohibition on women wearing silk. Below this high social level, prohibitions quickly became more stringent.[4] Across Europe, sumptuary laws imposed limits not only on the precious items one could own and display, but also on the amount which could be spent in organizing events or on specific occasions, like marriages or baptisms. In the case of baptisms, for example, across Europe sumptuary laws defined whether it was allowed to throw a party at home after the event and, in such a case, how many guests could be invited, what food could be served and in what quantity; the acceptable value of the gifts offered by the godparents; the maximum number of participants at the procession carrying the newborn to church and how they should be dressed; and so on.[5]

Sumptuary laws were meant to be an instrument for disciplining society.[6] And yet, it would be incorrect to consider them a total impediment to the abundant consumption of luxuries and to showing off one's wealth. This is not so much because sumptuary laws were not generally respected—recent research has highlighted that in many historical settings, public authorities exerted much effort to this end—but because for those who really wanted to exceed the limitations, another path was open: paying a fine and having their way. Seen from this perspective, then, sumptuary laws resemble a tax on high levels of consumption, which of course many rich households were quite happy to pay. Indeed, some have argued that at least in some cases a redistributive intent (from the richest to the collectivity) was explicit, as in the French city of Montpellier, where those who violated the sumptuary laws introduced in 1255 were required to pay a fine of 1,000 bricks for the restoration of the city walls. In the Italian cities of Faenza and Rimini, the fines paid by the rich for their luxuries were used to increase the endowment of the *Monte di Pietà*, a public institution which provided consumer credit to the poorest social strata (in Parma the revenues from the fines were given over to the Hospital of the Misericordia).[7]

Arguably, sumptuary laws characterized societies deeply different from modern ones, which are 'consumerist' in the sense that they assign a high value to the *activity* of consumption and have achieved historically unprecedented *levels* of consumption. And yet it is tempting to draw some comparisons, as the propensity to break regulations and pay a fine to get one's way has surely not disappeared from the mindset of many rich, and especially super-rich, individuals. Take for example the wedding party thrown in 2013 in Big Sur, California, by Sean Parker, one of Napster's co-founders. His 364 guests were introduced to a campground where an imitation of a ruined stone castle had been erected along with Roman columns, bridges, an artificial pond, waterfalls and so on. This architectural pastiche had not received proper authorization (the party took place in an environmentally protected area), but Parker could easily afford to pay the ensuing fine of 2.5 million dollars. After all, he had already spent about 10 million on the wedding itself.[8]

Whatever their real nature, European sumptuary laws proved unable to prevent the spread of the consumption of luxuries and of the external show of wealth among the ever-richer economic elites. So much so that by the early twentieth century what was left of the European nobility had abandoned almost any hope of distinguishing themselves from the parvenus based on a more refined style of consumption and a better understanding of fashion. On the contrary, in countries like France some moderation in consumption and the self-imposed limitation of exhibiting wealth (like family jewels) only in 'appropriate' circumstances had become a crucial feature of the nobility, at least in terms of how members of that category perceived themselves and their position in society. Tied to this, it came to be considered disgraceful for a noble to even talk about money and wealth, with exceptions made only for very specific contexts, chiefly when inheritance was involved. In this regard, the French nobility seems to have differed from others, especially the English, who were not as socially and culturally constrained in their attitude towards money.[9]

As the nobility retreated, at least partially, from its traditional role as the top-spender in society, the new wealth aristocracy which emerged during the nineteenth century from the world of industry and finance did not suffer any such constraint. On the contrary, in order to belong to this status group, the show of specific, luxurious consumption habits was a necessity, something Veblen referred to as 'conspicuous consumption'. For Veblen, who had in mind first and foremost the American society of the late nineteenth century, many rich individuals purchased expensive and superfluous items in order to gain status or to make the status that they had already achieved apparent to all observers. Indeed, the rise to higher status of an individual set on a path of enrichment requires, for Veblen, a 'gradual amelioration . . . in the articles of his consumption'. In fact, '[s]ince the consumption of these more excellent goods is an evidence of wealth, it becomes honorific; and conversely, the failure to consume in due quantity and quality becomes a mark of inferiority or demerit.'[10]

For sure, examples of conspicuous consumption in the late nineteenth-century United States are not lacking: think of the legendary parties thrown by the Vanderbilts, a 'new rich' family which under Cornelius 'the Commodore' had made its fortune in the shipping and railroads sector.[11] Or think of the great hunting expeditions in the American West of which many prominent financiers and businessmen from New York, like Leonard Jerome, were so fond.[12] But even after Veblen's times, sociological research on the American rich of the twentieth and twenty-first centuries has confirmed that in many cases the acquisition of luxurious goods (for example, a collection of expensive cars) is used by the very rich, and especially by those new to wealth, to signal to society at large that a process of social promotion has taken place. On the other hand, many very rich individuals, especially those already familiar with great wealth, take pains to safeguard their privacy, partly for reasons of personal security. Even in this case, though, expensive consumption habits (like the acquisition of a palatial home) are usually the rule and part of the status strategy of the rich. The difference with those who consume more publicly is that 'these purchases tend to be designed to ensure their status within the upper class itself rather than to demonstrate it to ordinary (nonrich) people.'[13] Arguably, they also serve—together with the ability to display highbrow tastes or, more generally, 'a distinct way of being in the world' inculcated from infancy by family and schooling[14]—to isolate the wealth aristocracy from the rest of society, including from the new rich, in the United States as in the United Kingdom and elsewhere in Europe.[15]

If we look at the goods consumed by the rich and the poor, the bundles of consumption at the extremes of the wealth pyramid differed more in pre-industrial times and during the nineteenth century than they have from the early twentieth century until today (to clarify: almost all Western households today can afford a car of some sort, but only the richest households of the eighteenth century owned a coach). Before the twentieth century, the lower and lower-middle strata almost exclusively consumed the goods necessary to satisfy subsistence needs: food, housing, clothing and fuel to keep warm. In 1688 England, these categories of goods represented 98.8 per cent of the consumption of the bottom 41 per cent of the population. In contrast, if we look at the fairly rich (the 5% just below the top 5%, hence percentiles 91–5 of the income distribution), we find that the same categories represented 87.8 per cent of household consumption, which left space for a sizeable 12.2 per cent spent on other kinds of goods and services. If we compare this situation to that of the United States in the first half of the nineteenth century, a household with the same relative position as the English 'fairly rich' mentioned above would have dedicated about 39.5 per cent of its consumption expenditure to services and other goods beyond food, housing and clothing, for example home furnishings or children's toys (an American household belonging to the second decile—the next-to-poorest—could have afforded to spend only about 5.6% of its income on these categories of consumption).[16] Differences between the wealthier strata and the rest increase exponentially if we move from rich to super-rich status. So, in the United States of the late nineteenth century, the richest 0.1 per cent spent quite lavishly on yachts, luxury coaches and show horses, as well as on events and social activities like gala parties, box seats at the opera, club memberships and travels abroad.[17]

Estimates of proportional consumption by broad categories of goods of the kind presented earlier hide two crucial differences between the consumption of the rich and of the lower strata. First, within each category, even food, the kinds of goods consumed differed deeply. In the early nineteenth-century United States, for example, staple grain products represented 31.3 per cent of the budget of a household in the second decile and just 10.4 per cent of that of one in the percentiles 91–5, which could spend much more (in both absolute and relative terms) on luxury foods like beef, sugar and alcohol. The second crucial difference is that these figures describe consumption bundles but do not tell us what share of the household income was consumed and what share was saved.[18]

The Saving Habits of the Rich: A Historical Overview

Upon his death, on 21 June 1737, the Venetian patrician Piero Pisani Moretta left an enormous patrimony worth over 1 million ducats, including a villa in Montagnana which had been designed by the famous architect Andrea Palladio in the mid-sixteenth century. To grasp the size of Piero Pisani's bequest, consider that it amounted to about one-fifth of the overall yearly fiscal revenue of the Republic of Venice. While he came from a wealthy and politically important family, he had greatly expanded his inherited wealth by means of substantial savings: in 1703–5, on average he re-invested 86 per cent of his yearly revenues. Years after his death, in a poem composed on the occasion of the marriage of his grandson Pietro to celebrate the groom's ancestry, Piero was recalled as a man 'upright and of almost angelic behaviour [*angelici costumi*]', surely to indicate his famous thrift. Others, however, recalled his character differently. For example, Girolamo Cappellari Vivaro, who in the 1740s wrote a treatise on the most illustrious Venetian families, stated that Piero Pisani 'bequeathed immense wealth, accumulated through his mean parsimony [*meschina parsimonia*].'[19]

These contrasting views about the propensity of a super-rich patrician to save illustrate the basic ambiguity with which Western societies have always viewed wealth accumulation. In Christian theology, avarice/greed is condemned as a capital sin—even worse than squandering. And yet many among the wealthy and powerful of eighteenth-century Venice must have felt some sort of admiration for Piero Pisani, if only because he strengthened his lineage. Indeed, his only surviving daughter, who inherited most of his patrimony, married Gerolamo Pisani, the last descendant of another branch of the family—the Pisani *del banco*—whose fortunes had been mostly squandered by Gerolamo's grandfather, a certain Gerolomon.[20] It seems certain that in the extended-Pisani-family lore, Piero the miser was remembered more fondly than Gerolomon the spendthrift. After all, the Pisani did not have to consume conspicuously in order to establish their status among the Venetian economic and political elite: Piero was the last descendant of Vettor Pisani, the celebrated hero of the Republic who had led the fleet to victory against Genoa, Venice's arch-rival, during the War of Chioggia of 1379–81.

Cases of substantial wealth accumulation obtained through an exceptional capacity to save are not at all uncommon in Western history. Take Henry Cavendish for example, the English scientist and natural philosopher who, among other things, discovered that water was composed of hydrogen and oxygen and developed theories of heat and of electricity. Although he was born into a family from the high nobility (he was the eldest son of the third son of the Duke of Devonshire) he held no title and did not inherit any substantial land-holdings. However, in 1783, aged fifty-three, he inherited substantial funds from his father (161,100 pounds) and from an aunt (97,100 pounds), which were mostly invested in Bank of England annuities paying a yearly 6 per cent, as were the 17,388 pounds that Cavendish had owned from before the bequests. Given his monastic lifestyle, he saved this steady income almost entirely, re-investing it in annuities. Married to science, he was considered a misogynist (he died a bachelor) and was well-known for his frugality, his lack of interest in social life and his tendency to wear old and unfashionable clothes. His sav-ings piled up year after year, and at his death in 1810 he left a fortune of about 1.2 million pounds (112 million in 2020 U.S. dollars), four times what he had inherited twenty-seven years earlier, which is what we should expect consider-ing that a capital invested at a yearly 6 per cent and left to accumulate will double every twelve years. According to an early biographer, Cavendish was 'the richest of the wise and the wisest of the rich'. [21]

While Cavendish's spending behaviour went hand in hand with a markedly anti-social attitude, the same could not be said for many other wealthy or super-wealthy individuals, who took part in social life but at the same time cultivated an external image of relative modesty and parsimony and, while they spent substantial amounts, nonetheless saved the vast majority of their earnings. To some degree, this description matches many industrial tycoons of Gilded Age America: 'The public persona of the self-made man was based on a cult of outward modesty and respectability. As a rule, robber barons were puritanical, parsimonious, and pious'.[22] One could also note that a 'self-made man' (or woman) *could not* rise to a position of great wealth without a pen-chant for saving. But then, only a few among the robber barons were entirely self-made men, whatever their self-image or however they liked to be per-ceived by others. As seen in chapter 4, one who was truly able to rise from rags to riches was Andrew Carnegie, the steel tycoon. He is also a perfect example of a super-rich individual of the nineteenth century who resisted showing off his wealth in the form of consumption. Indeed, he even theorized, in his *Gospel of Wealth*, that 'a man of wealth' should 'set an example of modest, unostenta-tious living, shunning display or extravagance', and should provide only 'mod-erately' for 'the legitimate wants of those dependent upon him',[23] thus imposing a cap on the consumption level of his entire household.

Whatever the degree of actual moderation (external or domestic) of the rich, one fact remains: while across the West there seems to have been, and there still is, a widespread conviction that the 'typical' behaviour of the rich leads to exceptional levels of consumption, they have also always tended to distinguish themselves by their exceptional capacity to save. Without this feature, the rich and super-rich as a social group would have been historically much more limited in numbers, much less distant from the rest of society in their access to economic means and much more socially open and basically unable to create enduring dynasties (although this last point is also inextricably connected to the process of inheritance, as discussed in the next section). The rich, then, differ radically from the poor not only because of their much higher ability to consume, but also because of their even higher ability to save, as the poor across time and space have been characterized by the practical impossibility of saving. Those who are placed close to a level of subsistence by definition cannot save without compromising their survival and that of their families, which is one reason why dire poverty tends to become an unescapable trap no matter the aspirations and the commitment to hard work of those who fall into it.

If, then, the ability to save is a crucial distinctive feature of the very rich, it comes as something of a surprise that it has only rarely been the object of proper measurement for both past and modern societies. This is possibly because very few studies have been dedicated to the rich as a social-economic category, a point which has already been made in the introduction. For preindustrial Europe, the information currently available is very sparse, as the topic has rarely been explicitly touched upon by research on specific rich individuals and families. Sometimes, rough estimates can be derived from published data on family budgets. One notable case for which we do have information is that of the aforementioned Piero Pisani Moretta who, in 1705–35, was able to save and reinvest, in land and in financial assets, between 71 per cent and 97 per cent of his overall revenues, with an average of 86 per cent over the entire period. However, as seen above, Piero Pisani was an exceptional case, and very few Venetian patricians shared his *angelici costumi*. In another case for which we have good information, that of Andrea Barbarigo—a lesser noble, only distantly related to the main branch of the Barbarigo family—it is possible to calculate a yearly saving rate of approximately 60 per cent during the period 1431–49. This allowed Andrea to accumulate a considerable fortune, rising to a position of prominence among the Venetian merchants thanks to his trade (mostly of wine and cheese) with Crete and the Levant. A 60 per cent saving rate is substantially lower than Piero Pisani's 86 per cent, but Andrea Barbarigo never became as rich as him: upon his death, although surely among the richest 5 per cent of individuals in the Republic of Venice, Barbarigo was probably not among the richest 1 per cent (Piero Pisani definitely belonged to the top 0.1%). And yet, his propensity to save remained considerably higher than that of most people of equal social and economic standing. This is clear from Table 6.1, which reports the results from an exploration of the saving rate of rich Italian families in preindustrial times.

As can be seen in the table, based on a range of wealthy families in Piedmont (Sabaudian State) during the seventeenth and eighteenth centuries, it appears that the rich could save up to 80–83 per cent of their annual revenues. Interestingly, here we again find a tendency towards higher saving rates among the richest of all (the Ricci of Acqui, indicated by some contemporary observers as one of the four richest families of the Piedmontese nobility, saved 73% of their yearly income in 1740–9). As argued by historian Stuart J. Woolf, the families of the social-economic elite who resided in the capital city of Turin, whose members held some public office and who had at least some contact with the court, tended to have a fairly homogeneous level of ordinary expenditure, from which would automatically result a tendency towards a higher rate of savings as we move from rich, to very rich and finally to super-rich status.[24] The Piedmontese cases also remind us that in the context of family dynasties the attitudes and the motivations of specific generations could lead to large differences in saving rates. Consider the case of the Paesana family: in Carlo Maria's time (1670–1715) the yearly saving rate was over 20 per cent, but his son and inheritor Baldassare was seemingly unable to accumulate any further. At least he did not dissipate the family fortune. In other instances, members of a dynasty significantly diminished the family patrimony through their high expenditures, through business mistakes or through bad luck. This was for example the case for Piero Guicciardini, who in the early fourteenth century had inherited one of the largest fortunes in Florence but who, scarcely interested in business, relied on poor administrators who squandered it. According to his great-grandson Francesco (a famous historian and political writer), he died poor, although this statement must be qualified as he still left a fairly substantial patrimony of about 5,000 florins.[25] Unfortunately, based on the available information, it is impossible to precisely estimate Piero's saving rate, which was surely negative.

The sample of Tuscan families, like the Guicciardini, included in Table 6.1 basically confirms the results for Piedmont and extends them to an earlier period (the fifteenth to sixteenth centuries), particularly regarding an increasing propensity to save higher up the wealth ladder. This can also be observed in individual paths of enrichment. Consider the case of Giuliano Capponi, son of Pier Capponi, the merchant and statesman from Florence famous for standing up to the king of France Charles VIII in 1494, when he threatened to answer French trumpets with Florentine bells. In 1496–1530 Giuliano, together with his brother Niccolò, who left the financial management of their undivided patrimony mostly to him, achieved a yearly average saving rate of at least 53.6 per cent. In this period, the two were among the richest 5 per cent, but the constant increase of their patrimony was propelling them upwards. After Niccolò's death in 1529, Giuliano was able to save 69.4 per cent of his yearly income in 1532–44 and over 80 per cent in 1553–68. By then, Giuliano's fortunes placed him solidly among the richest 1 per cent.[26]

Table 6.1 also includes two rich women, Selvaggia Strozzi and Lucrezia Dionisi, who stand out for their relatively low saving rates. This, however, must be read in the light of their specific situations. Both were widows with underage children. In the case of Selvaggia, who in 1492–1502 maintained an average saving rate of 3 per cent, while she retained the management of her own household, most of her liquid assets were administered by her nephews. In the case of Lucrezia Dionisi (née Giustiniani), in 1853–61 she saved on average 7.8 per cent of her own income, but if one also includes the revenues and expenditure related to the part of the patrimony which was technically the sole property of her underage children but which she administered, the saving rate increases to a respectable 19.6 per cent.

And yet, one could argue that the sample of rich families reported in the table is somewhat distorted, either because scholars have tended to focus on the most successful cases and/or have provided less precise information about the squanderers, or because those rich individuals who managed to establish a dynasty which was not subsequently derailed by spendthrift descendants have left the best and most abundant archival documentation (*and* because of this have been the target of historical research). Based on considerations of this kind, in a recent attempt to roughly estimate saving rates across the whole of the wealth distribution of the Republic of Venice, Matteo Di Tullio and myself have argued that it can be reasonably presumed that the richest 5 per cent saved on average between 20 per cent and 40 per cent of their yearly income.[27] Although this estimate is based on just a subset of the cases reported in Table 6.1, it is basically confirmed by our additional data. Interestingly, it is also consistent with a tentative estimate for the Dutch Republic in 1600–1811,

TABLE 6.1. The Propensity to Save of the Italian Rich from the Fifteenth to the Nineteenth Century

Individual or Family	Period*	Area	Position in Wealth Distribution	Yearly Average Savings Rate (%)
Filippo Strozzi	1471–83	Florentine State	Top 0.1%	89
Selvaggia Strozzi	1492–1502	Florentine State	Top 0.1%	3
Piero Pisani Moretta	1705–35	Republic of Venice	Top 0.1%	86
Marquis Del Borgo	1740–9	Sabaudian State	Top 0.1%	73
Alessandro Gondi	1496–1516	Florentine State	Top 1%	≥55
Giuliano Capponi	1532–44	Florentine State	Top 1%	69.4
Giuliano Capponi	1553–68	Florentine State	Top 1%	>80
Carlo Lodovico Barolo	1664–1705	Sabaudian State	Top 1%	10.3
Carlo Maria Paesana	1670–1715	Sabaudian State	Top 1%	>20
Riccardi family	1690–1719	Florentine State	Top 1%	50
Gerolamo Barolo	1705–35	Sabaudian State	Top 1%	3.6**
Baldassare Paesana	1715–36	Sabaudian State	Top 1%	0
Marquis Ricci of Acqui	Early 18th century	Sabaudian State	Top 1%	80–3.3
Ricasoli family	1817–29	Florentine State	Top 1%	11
Andrea Barbarigo	1431–49	Republic of Venice	Top 5%	60
Giuliano and Niccolò Capponi (brothers)	1496–1530	Florentine State	Top 5%	≥53.6
Jacopo Guicciardini	1505–32	Florentine State	Top 5%	11.9
Bernardo Sacco	1548–69	State of Milan	Top 5%	22
Giacomo Antonio Odescalchi	1575–78	State of Milan	Top 5%	>70
Alberto Radicati di Passerano	1707–19	Sabaudian State	Top 5%	9
Giovan Francesco Dionisi	1813–29	Lombardo-Venetian Kingdom	Top 5%	36.8
Ottavio Dionisi	1848–52	Lombardo-Venetian Kingdom	Top 5%	0.1
Lucrezia Dionisi	1853–61	Lombardo-Venetian Kingdom	Top 5%	7.8
Dionisi family as a whole	1853–61	Lombardo-Venetian Kingdom	Top 5%	19.6

Notes: (*) The 'period' column reports the span of years used in the computation of the yearly average saving rate, depending upon the availability of good-quality data as well as the personal story of each rich individual. (**) When excluding pensions paid to his brothers, the saving rate of Gerolamo Barolo increases to 18.5 per cent.

which placed the saving rate of the rich at 25–40 per cent.[28] Consequently, while waiting for more research on this topic, it seems reasonable to assume that a saving rate range of 20–40 per cent reflects the situation of the richest 5 per cent well and that presumably this should be increased when focusing on the very top. In fact, a simple modelling exercise leads to the hypothesis that on average the richest 1 per cent saved 30–60 per cent of their income, which fits the empirical evidence collected in Table 6.1 reasonably well.[29]

One might expect that, when moving from preindustrial to modern societies, there would be a substantial increase in the available information, but this appears not to be the case, as the topic has rarely been the object of specific research. And yet, the few surveys we have suggest that the modern rich are on average no less parsimonious than the preindustrial rich. The actual saving rates characterizing them seem to be even higher. At the very least, it is possible to interpret in this way the findings from a survey of OECD countries during 2003–10 which reported a saving rate in the 20–40 per cent range for those belonging to the top 20 per cent of the income share, exactly the same range that we have attributed to only the preindustrial top 5 per cent. The range accounts for variation among countries. For example, the top 20 per cent saved slightly over 40 per cent of their income in the United States and in Mexico and about 30 per cent in the Netherlands and in France. Just to be clear, the same study also suggested that even in rich countries, the bottom 20 per cent were unable to save anything or even had to decumulate wealth and/or become indebted.[30]

There are probably two main reasons why the modern rich save more, in proportion to their income, than the preindustrial rich. First, with the financial innovations that went hand in hand with the Industrial Revolution and the expansion of public debts, the opportunities for investing in relatively safe assets guaranteeing good returns increased, and this might have acted as an incentive to save. However, good opportunities for investment had always been open to the rich—remember, from chapter 5, the case of the Venetian public debt or of the somewhat riskier investments in the Dutch and English privileged companies—and it is difficult to estimate just how much the expanded opportunities of early industrial times could really have strengthened their propensity to save. Perhaps the second reason is more important: higher saving rates may simply reflect a condition in which the population as a whole has grown richer and, at the same time, the gap in total income (and in wealth) between the top and the bottom of the distribution has increased. In this scenario, it seems reasonable to assume that the share of one's income that needs to be spent to signal status and satisfy one's aspirations of consumption, however expanded those might be in a modern consumerist society, will be lower compared to preindustrial times. Another way of expressing this concept is to argue that the marginal utility of consumption tends to zero as the level of consumption rises. After all, as Haroldson L. Hunt, an American oil tycoon of the early twentieth century, stated, 'for practical purposes, someone who has $200,000 dollars a year is as well off as I am',[31] and at that time he was the richest man in the world.

The relative lack of studies on the propensity of the rich to save is probably due to the fact that even asking this question seems to challenge influential ideas in economic theory, especially Milton Friedman's 'permanent income' hypothesis, according to which individuals tend to keep their levels of consumption smooth across time, so they adjust their saving rate over their life (bringing it below zero, thus becoming indebted, in phases of low income) to compensate for income fluctuations. Consequently, for Friedman, when measuring the correlation between current incomes and saving rates, the finding that at any given moment in time those earning larger incomes have higher saving rates *does not* imply that individuals who throughout their life earn a larger 'permanent income' save more than those who earn a lower one.[32]

While the logic of this statement is valid, Friedman's additional belief that the saving rate is about the same among those with higher and those with lower permanent incomes could only be proved or disproved based on empirical evidence. For decades, such evidence has remained inconclusive (as tends to be common in all ideologically charged debates in the social sciences). However, in the last twenty years or so, the few studies that have addressed the issue on the basis of new evidence have tended to report that those individuals or households with higher lifetime incomes tend to save more and also tend to be characterized by higher wealth. For example, Dynan, Skinner and Zeldes, who also provide a useful synthesis of the relevant literature, have analysed the case of the United States in 1984–94 and have argued that those among the top 20 per cent in the distribution of permanent incomes had a saving rate of over 25 per cent (with some indication that the rate would be much higher if measured for the top 5% or 1% only).[33] Saving rates declined sharply moving downwards in the distribution, reaching a level of zero for the bottom 20 per cent. These findings are in line with those reported previously for current incomes, although moving from an analysis of current incomes to one of permanent incomes does lead to some reduction in the estimates of saving rates at the top.[34]

The debate on permanent income has focused on modern societies. Undoubtedly, this is the proper choice, but this is not to say that thinking about the implications of this idea for a preindustrial society does not offer useful insights. Indeed, if we assume that the poorest strata are stably placed at, or very close to, subsistence levels (which was basically the case for most preindustrial European societies), then logically, when considering permanent incomes, the saving rate at the bottom of the distribution is about zero. Regarding the rich, the very existence of high wealth concentration at a certain moment in time is proof that in earlier years saving has occurred, which is the prerequisite of wealth accumulation; hence the hypothesis that saving rates do not depend upon the level of permanent income is untenable for preindustrial societies. This is also due to the tendency for the first-generation rich—whether they belonged to the nobility or were active in trade, industry or finance—to originate dynasties which is a clear feature of medieval and early modern societies (and arguably of modern ones as well) and in most circumstances would be an impossible feat without substantial savings. So the conclusion is that, if we take a long-term perspective based on the currently available data, which are admittedly not that abundant, the rich have always tended to have a stronger inclination (not to mention ability) to save than any other component of society. This immediately leads to another question: why do the rich choose to save?

The Rich, the Race and the Inheritance

If it is true that above certain levels of income any further increase has little or no impact on one's consumption level, as argued by billionaire H. L. Hunt, then the question becomes *why* do so many very rich, let alone super-rich, individuals seem to have the urge to save more and to accumulate ever greater wealth? The easiest explanation is that they are cursed with insatiable greed: the very curse of Smaug which gives this chapter its title. After all, as real estate tycoon Donald Trump stated in his book *The Art of the Deal* in 1988, well before becoming president of the United States, 'The point is that you can't be too greedy'.[35] But greed pure and simple, while it surely characterizes many among the rich and the super-rich, is nevertheless inadequate to explain their collective behaviour. Moreover, the view that avarice is the basic motivator of the rich has been enrooted in Western culture for so long that technically it constitutes a prejudice (as it is not based on the proper 'judgement' of specific cases). Like all human groups, the rich have complex motivations and psychology. So the fact that they appear to consider the accumulation of wealth an end in itself has different explanations for different individuals. One possible explanation has to do with what great wealth can bring beyond simple spending power: 'unspent wealth yields a flow of services (such as power or social status) which have the same practical effect on behavior as if wealth were intrinsically desirable'.[36] The connection between wealth, social status and power (including political power) has already been introduced in chapter 3, and some further aspects will be explored in chapter 10.

Another possible motivation driving many very rich individuals to thrift and wealth accumulation is the simple joy of competing in the race. The rich are driven to become even richer by the satisfaction derived from seeing their wealth increase and from rising to a higher position in the national or even the global wealth hierarchy. H. L. Hunt again provides us with one of the best formulations of this principle: 'Money's just a way of keeping score. It's the game that matters'.[37] Today, the World's Billionaires ranking by *Forbes*, and similar rich lists, help considerably in keeping score. Obviously, it is difficult to separate this psychological aspect from the aspiration of social-economic promotion (something which tends to be deeply ingrained especially in those rich who have humble origins) or from the intention of securing a flow of 'services' of the kind mentioned above. But, at the same time, it is important to highlight that many among the rich are also very competitive in the sense of seeing themselves in competition against other rich individuals, a behaviour of which we have many historical examples and fictional ones as well: suffice it to cite the eternal struggle for richest-of-all status between cartoon characters Scrooge McDuck and John D. Rockerduck (author Carl Barks modelled Rockerduck's name as a play upon that of real-life billionaire John D. Rockefeller). This competition also potentially has serious psychological downsides, especially among descendants of famously rich, and often very talented, individuals who struggle to free themselves from the shadow of their ancestors.[38] In other words, they feel compelled to take part in a race that they cannot win.

This same urge to continuously accumulate can be looked at from a different, and somewhat more positive, angle if one considers Weber's well-known idea that the very 'spirit of capitalism' consists in the drive to accumulate for the simple sake of accumulating more (the ceaseless pursuit of profit). While in contrast with earlier religious ethics—remember medieval Christian theology regarding the sin of avarice/greed—for Weber the spirit of capitalism was finally unleashed in the West in the sixteenth century by the Protestant

Reformation. Especially among the Calvinists, who believed in predestination and in salvation by grace, successful accumulation provided anxious merchants and early entrepreneurs with the confirmation that they belonged among the elect (hence they were often driven to accumulate *more* wealth than others, just to be sure). But, more generally, for the whole of the Reformation the accumulation of wealth acquired a religious significance, becoming a 'calling' (*Beruf*). Indeed, Weber considered this behaviour to be, at the individual level, irrational.[39] There will be other opportunities to return to this idea (and to the many critiques thereof). For the purposes of this chapter, the main point to highlight is that the drive to accumulate, competitive or religious as it might be, does not necessarily go hand in hand with a 'greedy' and miserly attitude. Indeed, there are some well-known cases where the final, declared aim of accumulation was to be able to 'give'. A perfect example of this attitude is Andrew Carnegie, for whom 'the man who dies ... rich dies disgraced' and who after retiring from the race for wealth invested the vast majority of his patrimony in charity of various kinds.[40] However, it could also be argued that, in doing so, he simply entered another race: that of conspicuous philanthropy.[41]

Historically, the accumulate-to-give attitude (be it truly altruistic or somewhat self-interested) has characterized just a small minority of the rich. Another kind of psychological, cultural and social-economic motivation has played a much more important role: that of accumulating a patrimony sufficient to originate, or to consolidate, a wealth dynasty. In previous chapters, many cases of wealth dynasties have been provided: from late medieval bankers like the Medici to early modern entrepreneurs like the Thurn und Taxis to dynasties emerging from the opportunities of the Industrial Revolution and expanding financial markets. And we should not forget the wealthy components of the nobility, for whom ensuring the survival of the lineage was an even more explicit objective.

Perhaps we should accept as an uncontroversial fact that many human beings are driven by the aspiration to ensure the fortunes of their descendants. But in the social sciences, and especially in economics, the idea of saving in order to bequeath a fortune to descendants is at odds with the 'life-cycle' hypothesis introduced by Franco Modigliani in the 1950s. In its simplest formulation, this hypothesis suggests that individuals make their decisions about how much to consume based on their lifetime resources. So, in order to keep their consumption levels fairly stable over time, they will not save anything or will even become indebted when they are young, they will save during their

working life, and during retirement they will dis-save the resources accumulated in their working life. As they smooth their consumption over time, during
their working life, the higher their current income, the more they will save. As
per Friedman's 'permanent income' hypothesis, this could lead us to believe
that higher saving rates for the 'rich' (defined here as those with higher incomes from labour and capital) are somewhat illusory, as across their lifetimes
both the rich and the poor will spend all of their accumulated resources. In
practice, however, this would happen only if individuals were able to perfectly
foretell the moment of their death; according to Modigliani, it is uncertainty
about death that leads prudent individuals to end up with lifelong savings,
resulting in undesired bequests.[42] But in this scenario there would be no reason to expect that the rich save *proportionally* more than the poor.

There is no need to discuss in detail here the debate about the life-cycle
hypothesis, nor all the possible extensions of the model, save to point out
that the evidence that has now become available for modern societies suggests that at least for the upper tail of the income distribution—the rich—
models derived from Modigliani's tend to systematically over-estimate
consumption in older age. In other words, the rich do not nearly spend all
their accumulated wealth before dying, which results in substantial bequests.
As shown by economist Christopher Carroll in what remains one of just a
few systematic attempts to model the saving behaviour of the very rich, one
way of solving the problem from the point of view of economic theory is to
assume that the very rich save intentionally in order to leave a bequest and
maybe to start or consolidate a dynasty. Another is to assume that they derive utility from wealth per se (or from the flow of services associated with
unspent wealth, as mentioned in the opening of this section), in what Carroll
calls a 'capitalist spirit' model which however can be taken to also cover accumulation due to a competitive urge (the race) or simply greed. This being
said, all these models predict that upon their deaths the rich bequeath a
fortune to their descendants, whether intentionally (because of an urge to
create a dynasty) or not.[43]

If we consider preindustrial societies, there is little doubt that strengthening
the dynasty (or the 'lineage' for the nobles) by passing on a healthy fortune
constituted an explicit ambition for many of the rich. This urge, in fact, reflects
a structural difference between today and past societies: in preindustrial times,
the survival of a specific rich individual, or of his descendants, was highly
uncertain. It was a recognized fact of life that an event might occur—such as
a major plague—that would lead to the death of many inhabitants of a specific

city, even the absolute majority of them in the worst cases. Even in ordinary times, a more or less sudden death due to illness or accident was a distinct possibility, including for the young. In a context such as this, individuals were acutely aware of their own mortality and tended to be relatively more focused on trying to ensure the welfare of their descendants. But as the survival of specific descendants was equally uncertain, they focused on protecting what they could: the patrimony. It is also in this sense that we are to understand the juridic motto, widely used in various formulations by southern European jurists from the fifteenth and sixteenth centuries: *familia, id est substantia,* meaning 'the family *is* the patrimony'.[44]

As will be seen in chapter 11, in the centuries following the Black Death the need to protect the patrimony against mortality crises in order to protect the family led to significant changes in the habits of the rich concerning inheritance, namely to the spread of practices aimed at ensuring the undivided transmission of the bulk of the family wealth across generations. But that was just a specific aspect of a much more basic and widespread urge to save and accumulate in order to leave bequests to one's descendants, an urge which obviously could be pursued mostly by the rich. As seen earlier, the saving rate increased dramatically moving up the social-economic ladder. Savings allowed the wealthy to preserve, and possibly to expand, the inherited patrimony before handing it on to their descendants. As at the bottom of the distribution saving was practically impossible and accumulated wealth (including that obtained from inheritance) was usually absent or extremely limited, it is clear how the propensity to save and bequeath contributed to strengthening the long-term tendency towards ever-growing wealth inequality which has been observed in many European areas. This situation, which characterizes medieval and early modern times, does not seem to have disappeared with the modern age, although it might have softened along with improvements in life expectancy at birth and the emergence of a different social-cultural context, which was more individualistic and less focused on family and kin. However, this hypothesis seems to run contrary to evidence suggesting that today the rich save a larger proportion of their income than was common in the past, although it is unclear whether this remains true when life-cycle resources (or permanent income) are considered. Admittedly, at present we lack the information needed to establish how much the modern rich differ from their predecessors regarding their attitude to saving and to accumulation. What is more, beyond these emerging differences there are also some enduring commonalities, to which we should now turn our attention.

To Save or Not to Save? A Social Conundrum

From a historical perspective, there is an apparent paradox in the attitudes of the rich towards saving and consumption. In the long run, it is the relatively high propensity for saving of the very rich that could constitute a social problem, whenever (through the mechanisms of inheritance) it tends to enroot hierarchies of wealth that prove difficult to upturn or even to substantially modify through 'spontaneous' processes of the upward mobility of the bold and capable. From this perspective, higher consumption rates at the top would be preferable, limiting accumulation, countervailing the tendency towards the emergence of dynasties and expanding the aggregate demand (thereby potentially improving the chances of rising through one's abilities and hard work across society). However, in public opinion it is conspicuous consumption—the show of wealth—that is usually considered the most damnable, leading to social anger towards the rich. Nowadays the excesses of the rich in the West make headline news and draw heavy criticism, which reflects the attitude of past societies: think of the medieval and early modern 'sumptuary laws', which were aimed at moderating the show of wealth and introduced explicit limits on conspicuous consumption, all in order to keep peace within the community.

In a sense, the rich are stuck between two kinds of behaviour that societies at large tend to consider vices (or sins, according to Christian theology): avarice and profligacy. In the *Divine Comedy*, Dante Alighieri, the great Italian poet of the late thirteenth century, even places the hoarders and the spenders together in the fourth circle of hell, where they suffer the same punishment under the watch of Plutus, the pagan god of wealth.[45] So, to save or not to save, that is the question to which we might wish to seek an answer.

In addition to all the individual motivations that they might have for saving, the rich could also be induced to avoid spending conspicuously by the fear of public reprobation. According to Machiavelli, in the fifteenth century this was the case for Cosimo de' Medici, who 'never transgressed the decent moderation of civil life; . . . for he was aware that a constant exhibition of pomp brings more envy upon its possessor than greater realities borne without ostentation.'[46] And yet, Cosimo's visible moderation was instrumental in pursuing a path towards the de facto lordship of Florence (see chapter 5). Furthermore, it is surely not true that moderation would invariably allow the rich, and especially the super-rich, to escape public criticism. A good example is Jay Gould, the railroad magnate and allegedly one of the most hated of the American robber barons of the Gilded Age. The press of the time disliked him for many reasons, including for his reserved attitude. According to historian Maury Klein, 'Gould's personal habits offered little meat for news-starved newsmen. His devotion to family and quiet leisures, however commendable, resisted efforts to humanize his public image through an inventory of his personal or moral eccentricities. . . . [H]e had no redeeming social vices upon which the public might fawn and forgive.' This is how he came to be considered 'the supreme villain of his era'.[47]

That somebody could be 'redeemed' from having super-rich status implies that the very holding of such status is considered a sin. That the sin of avarice might be redeemed by committing that of profligacy, as if the two cancelled each other out, is clearly an absurdity from both a theological and a logical point of view. But this very absurdity highlights the basic contradictions in how society perceives the behaviour of the very wealthy. The Anglo-Dutch philosopher Bernard de Mandeville pointed in the same direction in the famous satirical poem *The Fable of the Bees*, first published in 1705. In a prosperous hive, populated by bees selfishly driven by personal gain and by the pursuit of 'lust and vanity', the view spreads that they should instead adopt a virtuous lifestyle. The god Jove listens to the complaints and fills the hearts of all bees with 'honesty' (virtue). The ensuing economic collapse of the hive, due to a sudden drop in consumption levels, leads Mandeville to his famous conclusion, that 'Private Vices . . . may be turned into Publick Benefits.'[48] Over two centuries after the publication of Mandeville's poem, British economist John Maynard Keynes claimed that it had influenced him in developing his theory about the pernicious consequences of insufficient demand (Mandeville is also considered a forerunner of economic liberalism).[49]

In the opposite direction, one could argue that Mandeville's 'honesty' could help solve another possible economic problem, that is, scarcity of capital, as a high saving rate tends to increase the capital stock. But has capital been scarce historically? If we turn to classical economists such as Adam Smith, David Ricardo and Thomas Malthus, whose theories are particularly suitable for understanding the inner workings of a *pre*-industrial society (the kind of society that Mandeville also had in mind), we find that they agreed that of the three factors of production, that is, land, labour and capital, early modern Europe suffered from a relative scarcity of land, while both labour and capital were relatively abundant.[50] Consequently, this other possible justification for a strong saving attitude on the part of the preindustrial rich is weakened.[51] And the same is possibly true for the post-industrial rich: in the Age of Information, the initial capital needed by many of the most innovatory startups is relatively limited and easy to obtain. As argued by economic historian Bob Allen, even during the First Industrial Revolution in Britain capital was relatively abundant and cheap, which created an incentive to substitute capital for labour by mechanizing production.[52] There are, of course, many other interpretations of the historical significance of the accumulation of wealth (capital), and some of them will be discussed in chapter 8. For now, the tentative conclusion is that, from a long-term perspective, situations in which a high propensity for saving among the rich might have solved a problem of severe scarcity of capital were restricted to very specific historical settings.

Our question, then—to save or not to save?—has multiple possible answers. From the point of view of the working of the economic system and of the organization of society, there are at least some good reasons to argue that the rich should not save too much (except for historically rare phases of scarcity of capital). But from the point of view of social perception, the more the rich spend, the greater their (perceived) moral fault, and the greater the collective condemnation for high disparity in the access to economic resources: a situation that conspicuous consumption would, at least, help to soften. And there is more: if we move away from looking at the general perception of the rich across society to the way in which they and their societal role were presented in works of 'high culture' (which also influenced society, although starting from the upper strata) we discover that from the late Middle Ages until, arguably, modern times it was in their ability to *save*, supposedly in the interests of the collectivity, that the existence of super-rich individuals found its justification. This is material for discussion in the final part of this book, dedicated in general to the role played by the rich in Western societies. Before that, we need to complete our discussion of the historical paths leading to great wealth by providing some sort of tentative measurement of their relative importance and intensity over time.

7

Making It to the Top

AN OVERVIEW

THE PREVIOUS CHAPTERS HAVE FOCUSED on the different paths and on the personal attitudes that, across Western history, have allowed individuals to achieve wealthy status. As a conclusion to this part of the book, we now need to bring everything together in order to provide at least an impression, and possibly some tentative estimates, of the relative prevalence in time of different kinds of rich individuals—nobles/aristocrats, entrepreneurs of all kinds and financiers. Some phases of human history have been more favourable than others for making a fortune, although the means to do so have varied across time. This variation does not only have to do with the origin of wealth and with the specific social-economic status of the rich in a given historical context, but also involves a crucial divide: in some historical phases, it has been relatively easier to accumulate wealth from nothing, or at least to considerably expand a modest patrimony, while in others the highway to wealth has clearly been inheritance. The relative weight of inheritance in defining who can be classed as rich in a given society is a crucial aspect, which is also relevant to current debates about whether or not conditions of high economic inequality are compatible with how modern Western societies are supposed to function and be organized. Yet again, placing today's concerns in a long-term perspective allows us to consider the whole issue from a novel angle. This is why the chapter will begin by looking at the sources of individual wealth from a long-term perspective and will end with some reflections about current tendencies.

The Main Paths to Affluence in History: Summing Up

In this book, a rough distinction has been made between three major historical paths towards affluence: nobility/aristocracy, entrepreneurship and finance. Of course, other paths were also open—for example liberal professions, such as the medical or legal ones—but the relative movements of those three tell us a great deal about the very nature of the process of wealth acquisition across the ages and also allow us to directly tackle some of the most pressing questions about the rich in history. Taken together, all possible paths to enrichment have always been followed by a relatively small group of individuals; as will be remembered from chapter 2, the rich (defined in relative terms, that is, based on the ratio of their wealth to the median wealth of a given society and epoch) can be presumed to have been no more than 5 per cent of the population during the Middle Ages and the sixteenth century, and only from circa 1600 did they start to become more numerous, up to maybe 10 per cent of the population by the turn of the nineteenth century. And yet, there clearly have been historical phases during which each of these paths has been relatively easy to follow. These phases were specific to each path and did not overlap, or not fully, generating a complex pattern of which we know little. What follows is the first attempt to formulate some general hypotheses.

Overall, the historical literature discussed in chapters 3 to 5 gives the impression that each of the three paths (which were by no means hermetically separated) produced its own wave-like trend in the relative prevalence of individuals becoming rich. It is possible to summarize the previously discussed evidence as follows. During the Middle Ages, to be or become a noble was an important way to acquire great wealth, especially when the feudal system began to emerge and then to consolidate. The peak was probably reached by the thirteenth or the early fourteenth century. What seems clear is that by the fifteenth century the golden age of the feudal nobility was coming to an end. In early modern times, ennoblement continued to be pursued as a means for expanding one's wealth, in association with the growth of state bureaucracies whose top posts tended to be reserved for nobles (old or newly minted). Even in modern times we find some waves of new ennoblements driven at least partly by economic interest, for example under Napoleon's reign in continental Europe, and up to the nineteenth century being born into the nobility dramatically increased the chances of being born into wealth or of standing to inherit a substantial patrimony. This opportunity was greatly reduced from the nineteenth or the twentieth century, with some geographic variation associated with the disappearance or persistence of a formal, legally recognized nobility in each country. While some nobles and aristocrats continue to appear in all national lists of super-rich individuals, in relative terms their prevalence is probably lower today than at any other point in the last couple of thousand years.

If we turn to entrepreneurship, it seems clear that the early Middle Ages were not an epoch very favourable to enrichment through economic innovation. As this was apparently also the case in Roman times, we can tentatively state that for the first millennium of the Common Era this path towards wealth (and also the path of finance), while it always remained open, played a minor role compared to that of the nobility. This is especially the case if we remember that in the context of the Roman Empire, belonging to a patrician family or to the *nobilitas* ensured much greater economic opportunities, such as access to lucrative public offices, compared to those open to the general population. It was, then, only from the onset of the Commercial Revolution in the eleventh century that there began to be abundant (and, perhaps, unprecedented) opportunities for accumulating wealth through one's entrepreneurial ability. The tendency intensified with the opening of the Atlantic trade routes from the late fifteenth century, as this historical process created new opportunities for enrichment connected to the New World on top of those opening up in the Old World. Arguably, the peak in the relative importance of entrepreneurship as a path to wealth was reached at the time of the First and Second Industrial Revolutions. But by the turn of the twentieth century it had become difficult for outsiders to make inroads into markets dominated by powerful trusts and cartels whose constituent companies were controlled by super-rich families with an increasingly aristocratic character and attitudes. In many countries, enrichment through entrepreneurial innovation became easier in the years following World War II and again during the early phase of the computer and information age (from the 1970s to the early 2000s), while probably never returning to the relatively open condition typical of the Industrial Revolution. Indeed, in recent years it is finance which stands out as the emerging path towards wealth.

Like entrepreneurship, finance only played a minor role from Roman times until the early Middle Ages, a situation which began to change with the Commercial Revolution, when new financial services were needed to fuel commercial expansion across Europe and the broader Mediterranean area. As a path towards wealth, finance continued to grow in later epochs, following (at a distance) the tendencies already reported for entrepreneurship. The gap probably started to close during the nineteenth century, but it is only in recent decades that, for the first time in history, finance has become a truly major path for personal enrichment, a development whose historical significance will be discussed later.

The picture that has been drawn is hypothetical and ridden with problems, because it might be difficult to place a given individual squarely into one category (how to distinguish a merchant-entrepreneur of the late Middle Ages from a financier, when he was active in both commerce and finance?), because it focuses on major trends, losing sight of potentially important shorter-term fluctuations, and finally because it does not take into account the different chronologies that must have characterized different parts of the West. And yet, it is a useful approximation, especially considering that the prevalence of different kinds of rich individuals across time has so far remained uncharted territory. So, while waiting for more research on the topic, and referring to earlier chapters for additional details and for a thorough discussion of each path to affluence, it now seems proper to consider what supporting quantitative evidence we have.

The Composition of the Rich from the Late Middle Ages to the Nineteenth Century

The information available about the composition of the rich in medieval and early modern times is rather scarce, partly due to the relative rarity of the kind of historical sources needed to explore this topic and even more because of the lack of research on the rich as a distinctive social category. Yet we can obtain useful data from fiscal records and particularly from the property tax records widely used in southern and central Europe which in some instances specify the occupation of household heads. Among the most ancient sources with these characteristics is the famous *catasto* made in Florence in 1427. If we consider as rich those whose total net wealth was at least ten times above the median, which in this place and time was a relatively sizeable proportion of the overall population (13.2%), we find that 27.7 per cent of them were involved in some sort of entrepreneurial activity (including craftsmanship). The richest in this group were the members of the wool and silk guilds. Just 2 per cent were involved in financial activities, such as moneychanging. Professionals, especially notaries and doctors, amount to another 4.9 per cent. Unfortunately, for the others no occupation is given directly by the source. The situation does not change if we focus on a more restrictive definition of rich, that is, on the 489 households who constitute the top 5 per cent of the net wealth distribution. Among these, 'entrepreneurs' were 24.5 per cent, financiers 3.9 per cent and professionals 2.9 per cent.[1]

Albeit incomplete, this information does support two relevant conclusions: first, that those who made their fortune in finance tended to be more prevalent higher up the wealth ladder, and second, that even in Florence, which in the late Middle Ages was one of the main financial centres of Europe, the path to wealth through finance involved far fewer people than that related to the entrepreneurial exploitation of the opportunities offered by commerce and industry. However, the percentage of households for which no specific occupation is reported is so large that a substantial degree of uncertainty remains. For example, among the richest of all we find Giovanni di Bicci de' Medici, the founder of the family bank and father of Cosimo the Elder. Although he was a member of the moneychangers' guild, the *catasto* does not specify his occupation, possibly because his family was so well-known that any clarification was unnecessary (and maybe the tax officers found it difficult to classify the Medici, given the complex of economic activities in which they were involved). Something which the Florentine *catasto* does unequivocally confirm is that among rich household heads women were a small minority: less than 1 per cent no matter how we set the bar for being rich, and they were almost always widows. This does not mean that the prevalence of wealthy women was drastically lower than that of wealthy men, but only that given the way in which our sources are structured women tend to remain invisible.

Another typical fault of sources of this kind is that they do not allow us to clearly distinguish the nobility or the urban patriciate. This has to do partly with the communal traditions of many European cities and partly with the somewhat erratic way in which the titles of nobility were reported in the original sources, especially regarding the lower nobility. In the case of the Republic of Venice, which is the rare area where the composition of the preindustrial rich has been studied in a more or less systematic way, counts and marquises regularly appear among the very richest individuals. For example, in the city of Bergamo from the mid-sixteenth to the early-eighteenth century high nobles invariably accounted for four to five of the ten richest inhabitants. If we expand the analysis to the whole of the richest 5 per cent, the prevalence of nobles was at least 20 per cent in 1555, 49 per cent in 1640 and 55 per cent in 1704. These, however, are to be understood as lower boundaries, as they include only those whose title (as reported by the sources) identified them with some certainty as noble. What is more, we do not know anything about other activities that some of these nobles might have pursued or about the activities of Bergamo's non-noble rich, as the local property tax records do not detail occupations.[2]

It is in other cities of the Republic, like Verona and Vicenza, that we can get some information about who the non-noble rich were. In both cities during the fifteenth century their composition closely resembles that of Florence in 1427. Textile entrepreneurs featured heavily among them, like the *drappieri* in Verona who had a monopoly on the production and exchange of wool. In both Verona and Vicenza, the sources also show the growing prevalence among the rich of entrepreneurs in the textile sector or related sectors (like the tanners in Vicenza). In Verona, which can be observed from the early fifteenth century up until the eighteenth, it has also been noted that from the seventeenth century the *drappieri* were progressively replaced by the *mercatores* or 'merchants', who had an innovatory and more dynamic (more 'entrepreneurial') approach and who were active in a broader range of sectors, for example, the then-booming silk sector. From about the same time a change in the kind of professionals who more frequently became wealthy has also been reported, with notaries, who (as in Florence) had constituted a significant part of the medieval rich, being displaced by public officials involved in local and state institutions. In terms of the overall composition of the rich, the situation in the Republic of Venice in the early seventeenth century closely matches that reported by a study of the Sabaudian State in north-western Italy. An important aspect to highlight is that in most places during early modern times finance continued to be a decidedly minor path towards wealth as, barring major financial centres, it involved a much smaller proportion of the rich than in late medieval Florence (in the average town of the Sabaudian State, usually the only 'financiers' present among the richest 5% were the tax collectors).[3]

For Verona, for at least some dates it is possible to provide some tentative quantifications based on surviving property tax records. Figure 7.1 reports the percentages of the rich belonging to our three main categories, plus that of professionals and public officers, from 1409 to 1635, applying alternative definitions of the rich. In this place and period, those whose wealth was above ten times the median tended to make up 3–4 per cent of the overall population, so they can be treated as an intermediary category between the top 5 per cent and 1 per cent.[4] The figures confirm some general patterns. First, the prevalence of the nobles tends to grow when focusing on the richest of all; they never exceed 20 per cent of all households when looking at the top 5 per cent, but they are often above 30 per cent when the top 1 per cent is considered, with a peak of 38.1 per cent in 1409 (note that the same concerns expressed above

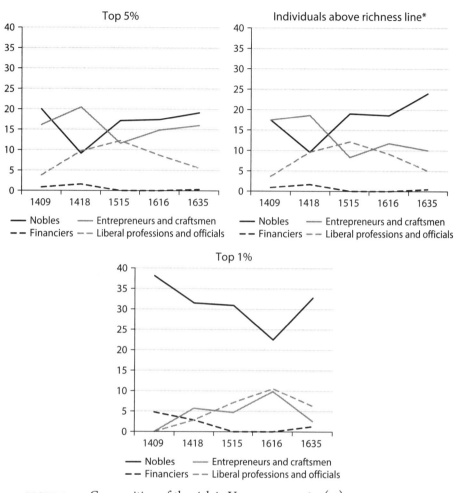

FIGURE 7.1. Composition of the rich in Verona, 1409–1635 (%).
Notes: percentages are standardized to take into account some changes in the
proportion of the rich which could be assigned to any category at different
dates. (*) Richness line set at ten times the median value of the distribution.

for the nobles of Bergamo also apply to the Veronese nobles). Second, the
prevalence of financiers is negligible, even more so than in Florence in 1427,
which is reasonable given that Verona was not nearly as specialized in financial
services as Florence. Verona's specialization was mostly in the production and
trade of textiles, which is reflected in a relatively high prevalence of entrepreneurs and craftsmen among the rich. This is especially true for the fifteenth
century, when they range between 16.2 per cent and 20.5 per cent of the top

5 per cent and between 17.4 per cent and 18.6 per cent of the top 1 per cent, with possibly some decline in the following centuries. With respect to rich entrepreneurs, however, the most important changes have to do with their internal composition, which confirms what has been discussed above: if in 1418 the *drappieri* alone account for almost 8 per cent of the richest 5 per cent and merchants of various kinds for little over 1 per cent, in 1635 the situation is inverted and merchants are 7.6 per cent of the richest 5 per cent while the *drappieri* have entirely disappeared as a category singled out by our sources. This is, of course, without forgetting that for most individuals no occupation whatsoever is indicated.[5]

Across Europe, from the late Middle Ages and throughout the early modern period, entrepreneurship became an ever more important path towards wealth. While the scattered evidence available for northern Italy is compatible with this conclusion, we should also consider that this part of Europe was not on the winning side of the Little Divergence, partly due to its geographic disadvantage in profiting from the opening of the Atlantic trade routes and the new economic opportunities related to them, as detailed in chapter 4. It was not by chance, as historian John Munro argued when analysing the emergence of new forms of entrepreneurship in England, that this process began in 1540–1640 but only fully developed in 1640–1740. In the Dutch Republic, which had preceded England by a few decades in becoming a major beneficiary of the new economic opportunities, during the seventeenth century merchants and entrepreneurs already accounted for about 42 per cent of the richest 250 inhabitants (about the top 0.015%), a proportion which remained almost unchanged in the following century.[6] While the very occurrence of the Little Divergence suggests that local differences must have been present (for example, an earlier expansion of entrepreneurial opportunities in Italy compared with England but also a relatively sluggish dynamic from around the early seventeenth century, as shown by the case of Verona, a divide which would increase with the First Industrial Revolution), the fact remains that the information currently available supports the view that in the West as a whole, during the early modern period, enrichment through entrepreneurship was becoming relatively easier than at any earlier time.

Before considering the situation during the Industrial Revolution, it is necessary to return briefly to the nobility. The rise of entrepreneurship as a path to wealth inevitably tended to erode the dominant position of the nobles among the rich, even though many aristocrats also found a way to profit from the new opportunities, as discussed in earlier chapters. And yet, at the begin-

ning of the nineteenth century, a very large share of the overall wealth continued to be held by the nobility. In parts of northern Italy, for example, it has
been estimated that in that period nobles owned at least a quarter of all real
estate.[7] The share of the nobility was larger in other European areas where the
feudal system had traditionally been stronger. On the eve of the 1789 Revolution, in provincial France, the majority of the nobles continued to be rich. In
Toulouse, where the nobility as a whole owned 63 per cent of the overall wealth,
it is possible to estimate that at least 75 per cent of them were rich, with a fortune above 63,000 francs, while that of the average worker or labourer was 389
francs; 2.11 per cent of all nobles owned more than a million francs.[8] The Revolution curtailed the patrimony of many nobles, but it did not remove them
entirely from the top positions in the wealth distribution. In Paris, a study
based on estate tax returns argues that in 1807 the aristocracy owned a sizeable
18 per cent of the wealth of the top 1 per cent (calculated based on those dying
that year), which, however, can be considered an exceptionally low share. Importantly, this estimate includes both the old nobility which had survived the
Revolution and the new nobility created by Napoleon and mostly composed
of chief military officers. As mentioned in chapter 3, new ennoblements during
the nineteenth century further complicate the picture, especially considering
that, in that period, the parvenu felt little or no constraint in continuing to
pursue 'bourgeois' activities. The nobility would recover some of the lost positions in the following decades:

> The share of aristocratic decedents among the very rich follows an inverted-
> U-shaped curve over the nineteenth century. That is, nobles became more
> and more numerous in top wealth fractiles from 1807 until 1847, then the
> trend reversed and their importance declined steadily. To be sure, aristocrats
> remain overrepresented throughout the period, including in 1902 (about
> 13 percent of nobles in the top 1 percent of estates, over 25 percent in the top
> 0.1 percent, versus less than 1 percent in the population as a whole). The in-
> verted-U pattern is yet another of the Revolution's legacies.[9]

In other words, the dynamics of the Revolution may have created a
U-shaped pattern in the prevalence of the nobility among the rich in France
from the mid-eighteenth century to Napoleon's times, followed by an inverted-
U pattern during the nineteenth century.[10] But overall, France fits the general
picture described earlier, as from the middle of the nineteenth century 'the
share of wealth held by aristocrats . . . was eclipsed by that of financiers and
industrialists.'[11] Importantly, the rise of fortunes made in finance and big

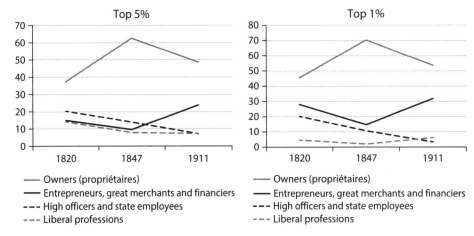

FIGURE 7.2. Composition of the richest 5 per cent and 1 per cent in Paris, 1820–1911. *Notes*: the figures refer to the richest 5 per cent and 1 per cent of Paris residents who died in 1820, 1847 and 1911.

business was also leaving behind, in the wealth hierarchy, other categories that had traditionally appeared among the (moderately) rich: not only shopkeepers and craftsmen working on their own account, but also civil servants and members of the liberal professions.[12] Again for Paris, it is possible to estimate that high-ranking officers and other state employees made up 20.3 per cent of the richest 5 per cent of residents in 1820 but just 7.1 per cent in 1911, and the drop is even more dramatic when the analysis is restricted to the richest 1 per cent (from 20.3% to 3.4%).[13] A similar tendency was followed by members of the liberal professions (at least looking at the top 5%), as can be seen in Figure 7.2 which also shows the substantial rise in the prevalence of entrepreneurs, great merchants and financiers (*négociants*) from the mid-nineteenth century and the inverted-U path followed by owners (*propriétaires*), which include the nobles. Interestingly, a broadly similar path has been reported for another great city of continental Europe, Milan. There, among those having a fortune of at least 1 million lire, professionals made up 8.6 per cent in 1862–70, declining to 6.7 per cent by 1891–1900. In the same period, the prevalence of nobles among Milanese millionaires dropped from 54.3 per cent to just 15.6 per cent, largely to the advantage of entrepreneurs and financiers who, in the favourable economic context of the Second Industrial Revolution in which north-western Italy fully participated, grew from 31.4 per cent to 58.9 per cent. Note that, by 1891–1900, in Milan entrepreneurs and financiers owned 60.8 per cent of the value of all assets belonging to patrimonies above 1 million lire, and nobles just 14.5 per cent.[14]

The Composition of the Richest from the Nineteenth Century to the Interwar Period

For at least some parts of the West, from the nineteenth century we can also provide some state-level estimates of the prevalence of different kinds of rich individuals. This is particularly the case for Britain where, as shown by Table 7.1, it is possible to get a glimpse of the origin of the wealth of a significant portion of the rich for several decades. The figures refer to those who left, upon their death, a fortune of at least 100,000 pounds (10 to 15 million in 2020 U.S. dollars, depending on the exact year considered). This represents only a small fraction of those who could be considered rich based on the broader definition used in this book. Nevertheless the figures do not include only the super-rich of the time but a significantly larger group (between the top 0.01% and 0.001%). The evaluations cover only the 'unsettled personalty', which means that they exclude lands and those assets which were set up as unalienable trusts. This obviously leads to a systematic under-evaluation of the nobility and especially of those holding landed titles. However, as the figures in Table 7.1 refer only to those who were above a fixed level of affluence, the degree to which excluding the aforementioned components of wealth distorts the results is unclear, especially considering the high prevalence of those whose main identified source of income was land. These made up 22 per cent of the total throughout the whole period 1808–39 but with a tendency towards monotonic decline decade by decade: from 24.5 per cent in 1808–19 down to just 19.7 per cent in 1830–9. The decline continued thereafter, and by 1906 the landed rich were just 12.3 per cent of the total. The vast majority were nobles and, indeed, many among them held an inherited title (peerage or baronetcy) as suggested by the reported figures for 1808–39. However, not all those holding a title had inherited their fortunes as at least some businessmen had been 'created' nobles (peers, baronets or knights), although they remained few in number: '[In 1808–39] it was still unusual for a business wealthholder to obtain a title, especially a peerage, with only a handful of newly created peerages coming to active businessmen, as opposed to landowners and senior military figures. This situation would continue until the 1860s or 1870s'.[15]

As noted by historian William D. Rubinstein, in the early nineteenth century the landed aristocracy continued to be the main component of the

TABLE 7.1. The Composition of the Very Rich in Britain, 1808–1906 (%)

Origin of Wealth	Year of Death					
	1808–19	1820–9	1830–9	1808–39 (tot)	1860–1	1906
Land	24.5	22.8	19.6	21.9	17.8	12.3
Industry and commerce*	42.6	43.8	37.3	40.9	54.2	67.3
Finance**	16.2	12.7	16.8	15.2	17.8	12.6
Profession	16.7	20.7	26.3	21.9	10.3	7.8
TOT	100.0	100.0	100.0	100.0	100.0	100.0
With title (inherited)	9.8	7.6	8.0	8.3	n.a.	n.a.
With title (created)	11.8	5.1	8.9	8.3	n.a.	n.a.
TOT	21.6	12.7	16.8	16.6		
Women	6.5	7.5	7.0	7.0	9.0	6.6

Notes: The table includes all those who died during the period leaving a fortune of at least 100,000 pounds in 'unsettled personalty'. Only in 1906 do the valuations include 'unsettled realty' (land) as well. (*) Also including the food, drink and tobacco sector and the publishing sector. (**) 'Finance' includes banking, merchant banking, insurance, stockbroking and the 'other finance' sectors.

British wealth structure.[16] Fortunes made or inherited in industry or finance were still being built. Indeed, the wealthiest Briton to die in 1808–39 was George Leveson-Gower, the first Duke of Sutherland, who had been Britain's ambassador to France during the Revolution. His fortune, which included the Bridgewater Canal in north-western England, was probably worth around 7 million pounds, including both personalty and land (about 871 million in 2020 U.S. dollars).[17] And yet, the signs of a progressive decline in the prevalence of the landed rich are clear. In the first decades of the nineteenth century they were slowly replaced not so much by those whose fortunes came from industry and commerce (oscillating around 40% of the total) but by financiers and professionals. For our purposes, the relatively high prevalence of financiers among the rich (15.2% on average in 1808–39) supports the view that this is the period when this specific path to wealth began to become more important, at least in Europe, relative to both that based on nobility (and closely connected to the transmission of landed wealth) and that based on entrepreneurship and innovation.

The more limited information which is available for the second half of the nineteenth century and the early twentieth suggests that, in this period, entrepreneurship in Britain was again on the rise as a path towards wealth: 54.2 per cent of bequeathed fortunes are associated with it in 1860–1 and even 67.2 per cent in 1906, mostly to the detriment of fortunes built on land and on liberal professions (a development precisely matching that reported for France and Italy in the previous section). As the figures refer to wealth left at death and given that wealth itself results from accumulated savings on incomes, the situation as observed in 1906 reflects changes in the British economy which occurred in earlier decades, and the same is obviously true for the figures related to the earlier period.[18] Finally, throughout the period the prevalence of women oscillated in the relatively tight band of 6.5–9 per cent, and most of them were widows or spinsters. For example, in 1906 the wealthiest woman was Ada Lewis-Hill, the widow of the financier and philanthropist Samuel Lewis who left a patrimony of 1,168,000 pounds (about 165 million in 2020 U.S. dollars). The second-wealthiest woman to die that year was Lucy Cohen, the sister-in-law of Mayer Rothschild.[19]

The case of Britain at the turn of the twentieth century can be fruitfully compared to that of Germany. For Prussia in 1908, an analysis of the richest hundred individuals suggests that industrialists and entrepreneurs had become prevalent at the top of the wealth distribution (55%, with merchants making up 10%). Bankers and financiers were a sizeable minority (22%), nearly as numerous as the old landowning elite (23%). Almost all landowners were also nobles, but so were almost half of the entrepreneurs, as the German bourgeoisie had been very active in buying titles from the mid-nineteenth century, as seen in chapter 3. So the relatively high prevalence of nobles of old or new blood should not hide the crucial fact that, by the eve of World War I, in Germany new money had largely replaced old money among the richest.[20] Concerning the relative prevalence of industrialists over financiers, a broader study of all German millionaires involved in industry, commerce or services reports, again for 1908, that 49.8 per cent of them came from industry (12.4% from heavy industry alone: a German specialty from the time of the Second Industrial Revolution), 15.8 per cent from commerce or transportation and 27.3 per cent from banking.[21] Considering that these estimates do not include landowners, they are basically aligned with those for the richest Prussians discussed above.

As a final comparison, it is possible to consider the case of the United States thanks to a database covering the richest Americans of the nineteenth and early twentieth centuries. Table 7.2 organizes the available information so as to make it comparable to Table 7.1, with two important caveats. First, the definition of who is included in the table is less rigid (as it is not based on systematic tax assessments but on a variety of sources) and, generally speaking, it covers a smaller proportion of the rich: probably between the top 0.001 per cent and 0.0001 per cent. Second, the data are organized by birth cohort, not by year of death. Hence, they tend to reflect the composition of the rich active in the decades *following* the period reported in the table, which is basically the opposite problem to that posed by the British data. To these can be added information coming from a list of millionaires published by the *New-York Tribune* in 1892. This list covers a considerably larger part of the rich (the top 0.03% of all households) and offers a picture of their composition in that precise year. As the list provides information about each person in a descriptive way, we rely upon the classification by 'primary source of wealth' made by economic historian Hugh Rockoff.[22]

The reported figures yield some relevant conclusions. First, they suggest that in the United States, as in the United Kingdom and elsewhere, in the first part of the nineteenth century land remained an important source of wealth at 14.8 per cent. Presumably, this figure reported for the cohort born before 1830 would seem low if we compared it with cohorts born during the eighteenth century. Indeed, a list of the richest individuals (by net worth) in the Thirteen Colonies in 1774 shows an overwhelming prevalence of planters and of 'esquires, gentlemen and officials' who frequently, especially in the south, were also large landholders.[23] The tendency of a further decline in landed wealth for cohorts born after 1830 is also clear. Importantly, when looking at a larger component of the rich, the prevalence of land- and estate-based fortunes increases: from the 6.7 per cent typical of the super-rich born in 1830–65, to 13.1 per cent in the 1892 list of 'mere' millionaires (when those super-rich were aged thirty to sixty). It also becomes possible to distinguish a small contingent of professionals and civil servants: 2.1 per cent of the total in 1892. The relative importance of finance as a path to wealth oscillated over time, with perhaps some signs of growth for the most recent cohorts. A deeper analysis of the information in the 1892 rich list reveals that, beyond the 11 per cent of millionaires for which it was the main source of wealth, finance was an additional source for about one-third of the others.[24] Finally, the high prevalence of industry and commerce for the cohorts born in 1830–99 matches the rise of the United States as an industrial power:

> Before the Civil War, land, trade and banking accounted for most vast accumulations of wealth. Beginning in the 1820s, manufacturing, especially textiles, and rail became a major source of great fortune. During the genera-

TABLE 7.2. The Composition of the Richest Americans, Nineteenth to Early Twentieth Century (%)

Origin of Wealth	Cohort of Birth				Year (Rich List)
	Pre-1830	1830–65	1866–99	1900–30*	1892**
Land and other real estate	14.8	6.7	1.8	5.5	13.1
Industry and commerce	63.0	76.2	85.0	67.3	72.1
Finance	18.5	14.3	9.7	16.4	11.0
Profession	n.a.	n.a.	n.a.	n.a.	2.1
Other	3.7	2.9	3.5	10.9	1.7
TOT	100.0	100.0	100.0	100.0	100.0
First-generation wealth	55.6	53.3	38.1	27.3	n.a.
Women	0.0	1.9	5.3	14.5	9.9

Notes: (*) The original publication by Jaher reports the final period as open: '1900–'. However, he also claims that 'only one of the monied elite was born after 1930' (Jaher 1980, 252); hence a closed period (1900–30) is an excellent approximation and allows us to avoid unnecessary ambiguities. (**) The figures related to the 1892 rich list do not include those for whom only 'inheritance' is mentioned as the source of wealth (about one-fifth of the overall sample).

tion after the Civil War America became the leading industrial power, a development reflected in the primacy of manufacturing as a source of colossal personal affluence.[25]

The quantitative evidence presented for the United States, which we can tentatively assume to be representative of a more encompassing trend involving all rich Americans,[26] is also perfectly in line with the historical evidence discussed in earlier chapters. This is true even regarding the aristocratic (albeit non-noble) character progressively acquired by the American rich, a process detailed in chapter 3. As seen in Table 7.2, over half of the rich born in the pre-1830 cohort were self-made men, but the situation quickly changed for cohorts born after the Civil War. By the early twentieth century, only one-quarter of the richest Americans were self-made, and the proportion was much lower in New York and in the other main cities on the East Coast. New wealth had become old, a process which, by the turn of the twentieth century, was also taking place in other Western countries. For example, a recent study of British millionaires in 1928–9, while it reported a further drop in the prevalence and in the relative importance of the landed nobility among the richest—partly a consequence of wealth destruction caused by World War I, which affected the landed rich much more than the others—suggests that we should be careful in analysing the unprecedented abundance of businesspeople at the top of the wealth distribution. In 1928–9, just 9.4 per cent of living British millionaires had an income coming predominantly from land, 13.5 per cent were involved in finance, 3.4 per cent were professionals, and businesspeople were a very sizeable 73.7 per cent.[27] However, not all of these took an active role in 'their' businesses: up to a quarter of them were de facto living as rentiers.[28] This issue, which has also been reported for other parts of the West in the early twentieth century (for example, France on the eve of World War I[29]), leads us again to the crucial issue of inherited wealth.

A Thorny Issue: Inheritance

The evidence provided so far supports the view that, across history, new opportunities appear in waves, allowing many 'new' individuals to become rich. But new wealth soon becomes old, and the descendants of self-made men do not necessarily share the same attitudes, or even the same aspirations, as the dynasty founders. And sometimes, as was arguably the case in much of the West at the turn of the twentieth century, the build-up of recently aged wealth and the enrooting of powerful family dynasties choke the social elevator and make it relatively difficult to rise beyond a middling level, which also tends to have the nasty consequence of bringing to an end phases of high economic effervescence fuelled by innovation. Crucial to these dynamics is the process of inheritance. Many aspects have already been explored, but it is now time to focus on it in a somewhat more general way.

Since prehistoric times the degree of inheritability of wealth has played a key role in defining whether a society was more or less prone to experiencing (relatively) high economic inequality. For 'small-scale societies', which include all societies of hunter-gatherers (past and present) as well as early farmers from the time of the Agricultural Revolution of the Neolithic period, it has been argued that the actual level of economic inequality closely depends upon the kind of wealth typical of each society. So pastoral societies, and agricultural ones to an even greater degree, whose characteristic wealth is mostly of the material kind, end up experiencing much higher inequality than hunter-gatherers, whose wealth is mostly embodied or relational. But even if we focus on material wealth alone, they are more unequal: the Gini index of material wealth inequality drops from an average of 0.57 for agricultural societies to just 0.36 for hunter-gatherers.[30] A crucial factor explaining these differences between societies that invariably remain close to subsistence levels is the degree of inheritability of their characteristic wealth, with material wealth being intrinsically more inheritable than embodied and relational wealth and land and cattle being more amenable to intergenerational transmission than the simple (and perishable) household goods owned by hunter-gatherers. In agricultural and pastoral societies, wealth concentration is further favoured by the presence of increasing returns to scale for herds of livestock, irrigated land and so on.[31]

The high inheritability of wealth also allows for an increase in wealth concentration over time, as the inheritance system plays a fundamental role in reproducing and deepening inequality across generations not only for small-scale societies but for *any* human society. For modern societies, this point has recently been emphasized by economist Thomas Piketty.[32] In his analysis, the high inheritability of wealth is one of the conditions that make it likely that, without some sort of public intervention, the current tendency of inequality growth will continue inexorably in future decades. Importantly, inheritability today does not depend so much on the nature of wealth, which in any agricultural, industrial or even post-industrial society is quite easy to transfer across generations, but on the institutional framework and in particular on the way in which inheritances are taxed (if they are). We will return to this point in the third and final part of this book. For now, it will suffice to note that the centrality of inheritance in setting the stage for wealth accumulation over time is one of the key reasons why exploring what proportion of individual or household wealth is 'made' and what proportion is inherited is not only useful in general but is also relevant to many current debates.

Before turning to the modern age, for which some systematic estimates of the share of inherited wealth are available, it is useful to briefly recall some characteristic elements of the long preindustrial period. As argued in chapter 1, from Antiquity until the eve of the Industrial Revolution, the vast majority of wealth consisted of land and other real estate, and hence it was highly inheritable.[33] But also in this context, it was the inheritance systems which defined whether a given society was likely to experience steady wealth accumulation across generations. The basic distinction here is between partible and impartible inheritance systems. Under partible ones, all sons received the same share of the inheritance, with daughters usually getting an equivalent share upon marriage through the dowry.[34] Under impartible inheritance systems, one inheritor—usually the oldest son—received a much larger share. The power of impartible inheritance to allow for wealth accumulation across generations can be easily demonstrated by means of economic modelling. This highlights another important finding: the quicker the rate of growth of the population, the more difficult intergenerational wealth accumulation will be. Indeed, as originally argued by economist James Meade, in a system of *partible* inheritance wealth concentration will tend to increase if $s * r \geq n$, with s being the saving rate, r the return on capital and n the rate of population growth. But, as clarified by subsequent refinements of this basic model, if the inheritance system is *impartible* then intergenerational wealth accumulation can occur even if $s * r < n$. And the same can occur under other reasonable assumptions, for example that the rich save more than the poor.[35]

To sum up, in the long run intergenerational wealth accumulation can reasonably be expected to be favoured by high rates of return on capital, by high saving rates, by a higher propensity of the rich to save compared to the rest of the population and by the presence of an impartible inheritance system. It is hindered, on the other hand, by rapid population growth, by partible inheritance and by estate or inheritance taxes that make wealth less transmissible. In preindustrial Europe, there was a difference between areas where inheritance was partible as a general rule (for example, in the case of Italy and southern Europe more generally) and others where it was impartible. However, historians have amply demonstrated that *in practice* the situation was much more complicated, for two reasons. First, the geography of inheritance customs is not as clear-cut as had been suggested by some early studies. Second, and more importantly, even in areas where inheritance was partible as a general rule, rich families could circumvent it by having recourse to institutions that allowed it to become impartible for specific patrimonies.[36]

The main such institution was the *fideicommissum* (entail) in its various forms. The *fideicommissum* established that a well-defined set of family properties was to be transferred unaltered from one generation to the next, with no end, usually being passed on to the oldest son. In partible-inheritance areas, this and other institutions with similar aims spread very considerably from the late Middle Ages and especially after the Black Death of 1347–52. Indeed, this development was an answer to the mutated conditions generated by the return of plague to Europe and as such will be discussed in detail in chapter 11. Here, it is important to highlight the final result: by the beginning of the early modern period, the largest patrimonies were all protected against unwanted, inheritance-driven patrimonial fragmentation. This also satisfied the general desire to ensure the survival *of the family* across generations.[37] In practice, then, in areas of partible inheritance the rules applied to the rich were mostly impartible, which tended to allow for further patrimonial consolidation at the top and to make the social composition of the rich more stable over time. This is even more the case if we consider that for one important component of the rich, the nobility, primogeniture represented the default way of transmitting their feudal properties.

In continental Europe, institutions like the *fideicommissum* began to draw criticism in the eighteenth century, but it was only at the turn of the nineteenth century, due to the impulse of the Napoleonic Code, that the principle of partible inheritance became universally applied (the surviving *fideicommissa* were dissolved by law). As discussed in chapter 3, this development significantly hindered the perpetuation of old noble wealth (except in the United Kingdom, where primogeniture remained the default rule for much longer and still survives for the high nobility). So, inheritance systems are clearly a factor setting modern societies apart from preindustrial ones. Another is the presence of estate or inheritance taxes. These were virtually absent in preindustrial Europe but were progressively introduced in the West during the nineteenth and early twentieth centuries, before becoming the object of criticism and rate-cutting in recent decades. But beyond the institutional framework, other variables which can affect intergenerational wealth accumulation tend to fluctuate over time and so are more relevant to explaining shorter-term dynamics compared to the epochal changes mentioned above. There is one possible exception: the growth rate of the population, which in modern times, after peaking during the demographic transition that affected the West in the nineteenth century, in many countries has fallen to unprecedentedly low levels, often even negative before immigration as a consequence of fertility rates well below two children per woman. Low fertility rates act as a powerful factor concentrating wealth in fewer and fewer hands, precisely when the gaping holes opened in the labour force are being filled by propertyless immigrants from non-Western countries: a two-sided process that strongly favours the growth of wealth inequality.[38]

It is beyond the scope of this chapter to further explore the factors shaping the general distributive dynamics of recent decades *in theory*.[39] We will pursue, instead, an empirical approach, focusing on what the available evidence suggests *in practice* regarding the level of inherited wealth as a share of overall private wealth, generation after generation. Lacking specific studies about preindustrial times (when, however, the general historical literature discussed above and in earlier chapters strongly suggests that wealth accumulation by means of inheritance was substantial, continuous and systematic) we will focus on the last couple of centuries. The information currently available,

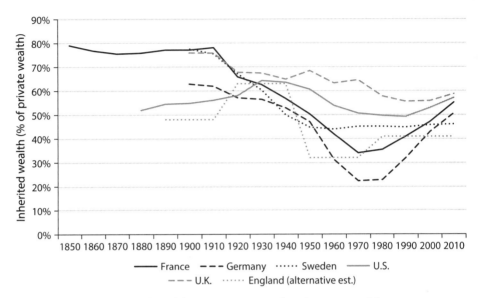

FIGURE 7.3. Inherited wealth as a proportion of total private wealth, 1850–2010.

which covers four European countries as well as the United States, is summarized in Figure 7.3.

The estimates suggest that up until World War I, in both Europe and the United States, most private wealth was inherited. In the United States in 1880, which is the first year for which we have information, the figure was 52 per cent: rather lower than the 76 per cent in France, but still very high and with a tendency towards further growth. By 1910, it was 56 per cent, not far from Germany (62%) but below the other European states, all in the tight range of 76–78 per cent. Thereafter, the relative position of Europe and the United States began to change:

> [In the United States t]he shocks caused by the 1930s and the Second World War led to a downturn, but much less pronounced than in Europe, so the US inheritance share became higher than in Europe by the mid-20th century. In recent decades, the inheritance share seems to have increased substantially in the U.S. However, there is significant uncertainty about the exact levels and trends, due in particular to the limitations of US estate tax data.[40]

Indeed, this inversion closely matches the inversion in the relative levels of wealth concentration reported in chapter 2, with the United States starting out as a relatively egalitarian country in the nineteenth century but becoming one of the most inegalitarian in the whole of the West from around the 1970s.[41]

The relative dynamics of the United States compared to Europe should not hide the most important detail: after the end of World War II, the share of inherited wealth as a portion of total private wealth tended to decline. In Europe as a whole, the minimum seems to have been reached by the 1970s, when in Germany inherited wealth was just 22 per cent of the total, although the most dramatic drop occurred in France, which reached a low of 34 per cent, less than half of the 77–78 per cent estimated for the beginning of the century. But across the West, the tendency inverted again from the 1980s or 1990s, and the prevalence of inherited wealth is currently on the rise as also shown by a few studies of other countries, like Italy.[42]

Estimates of the kind reported in Figure 7.3, which are a revised and expanded version of those originally proposed by Piketty in his influential book *Capital in the Twenty-First Century*,[43] have been considered too high by some scholars. For the United States, this kind of criticism has been made by economic historian Richard Sutch, who also proposed an estimate for Gilded Age America of 22.5–24 per cent circa 1870: less than half Piketty's estimate for 1880, although based on a sample of very rich individuals only (the top 0.06% of the overall population).[44] For Britain, economic historians Gregory Clark and Neil Cummins, based on an entirely different estimation approach, argued that in England the share of inherited wealth peaked at 63 per cent in 1920–49 and then declined to 32 per cent in 1950–79.[45] For this period, the figures are somewhat lower than those discussed earlier: compare the series 'U.K.' and 'England (alternative estimates)' in Figure 7.3. Interestingly, the alternative estimates for England show a trend closer to that reported for other European countries, like France and Germany: a large drop, followed by a tendency towards the increasing importance of inherited wealth, which rose to 41 per cent by 1980–2012 (unfortunately the format of the data does not allow us to disentangle decade-specific dynamics). Consequently, even if we accept that these alternative estimates might be closer to the mark, they do not alter the fact that inherited wealth in England/Britain is a very substantial part of the total and that the recent tendencies of further growth might be worrying. Additionally, Clark and Cummings argue for marked differences across society, as 'For the descendants of the wealthy, on average, all their wealth at death does indeed derive from inheritance'.[46]

Notwithstanding recent efforts, there is a clear need for more research on the prevalence of inherited wealth across time. As a matter of fact, from the

1930s until today many authors have argued that, in their respective countries, inheritances were a growing source of individual wealth. Although many among these studies failed to provide strong evidence to support their (usually very pessimistic) conclusions, they do signal a widespread concern.[47] In recent times, and with much stronger scientific backing, concerns of this kind have been highlighted by Thomas Piketty, who has argued that there is a risk of returning to a 'rentier society', that is, one in which 'rent' from inherited wealth would determine the income of a large part of the upper strata of society.[48] For Piketty this represents an existential risk for democracy and other Western institutions, a point which will be discussed in the next chapter. Interestingly, in Piketty's view it is Europe, and not America, which can be expected to experience the evils of 'patrimonial capitalism' sooner, basically because of its slower demographic growth rather than due to some sort of enrooted cultural difference.[49] And yet, during the nineteenth and the early twentieth centuries many believed that American and European culture and society differed radically regarding their approaches to wealth accumulation and bequests. Consider for example Elizabeth Bisland, an American journalist and author, who in 1897 stated:

> In America it is the custom—very nearly the universal custom—for the parents to spend upon the luxuries and pleasures of the family life the whole income. . . . They do not consider it obligatory to leave anything to their children at death. They have used all they could accumulate during their own lifetime—let their children do the same. The results of the system are crystallized in the American saying: 'There are but three generations from shirt sleeves to shirt sleeves.' The man who acquires wealth spends what he makes. . . . To a Frenchman such an existence would seem as uncertain and disturbing as is generally supposed to be that of a person who has built upon the crust of a volcano.[50]

Along similar lines, one could wonder whether a millennium-old tradition of landed aristocracy might have shaped European cultural norms in such a way as to make the pursuit of wealth accumulation for the purpose of dynasty-building more socially acceptable than in North America. Of this, however, there is currently no proof. What is more, if the data shown in Figure 7.3 are not entirely off the mark, then the history of the twentieth and twenty-first centuries does cast doubts upon whether this kind of cultural difference between the two sides of the Atlantic still exists (if it has ever existed at all), as from the 1950s inherited wealth has been more prevalent in the United States than in any European state for which we have systematic estimates, except for (and somewhat controversially) the United Kingdom.

As a conclusion to this section on inheritance, it is worth considering that the damage done to the correct functioning of institutions is only one of the (possible) pernicious consequences of an excessively high prevalence of inherited wealth. Another is the 'Carnegie effect', so-called because it relates to a conjecture put forward by Andrew Carnegie in his article 'The Advantages of Poverty' (1891). According to him, conspicuous inheritances are almost a curse on younger generations, as they deaden their talent and their willingness to work hard.[51] This view, for which there is at least some empirical support,[52] can lead to a range of possible conclusions: that those who accumulated considerable wealth should not die rich but should donate most of their wealth to serve worthy aims (this was Carnegie's own view), *or* that the hereditary transmission of wealth should be contained by means of estate taxes. In the early twentieth century this was, for example, the opinion of Winston Churchill, who in 1924 argued that death duties were '[a] corrective against the development of a race of idle rich.'[53] Importantly, Churchill's final aim was to *protect* capitalism in his country, de-escalating class conflict and fostering social harmony.[54] This is, clearly, a controversial and politically charged topic, to which we shall return in the third and final part of this book as it pertains to the role of the rich in society. For now, it will suffice to recall that, in the West, the tendencies regarding the taxation of inheritances from the 1940s until today seem to match quite closely, albeit in reverse, those shown in Figure 7.3; as discussed in chapter 2, the top rates of inheritance taxation, after peaking during World War II and in the immediate post-war decades, have been steadily declining in most Western countries since the 1980s, and this seems to be at least partly responsible for the U-shaped path followed, in the last seventy to eighty years or so, by the prevalence of inherited wealth as a portion of total personal wealth.

Wealth in the Early Twenty-First Century: Where Are We Heading?

The current tendency towards an increase in the prevalence of inherited wealth across the West is surely a cause for some concern. But there are others. As shall be remembered from chapter 5, many fear that the progressive financialization of the economy could promote a further increase in both income and wealth inequality, because the ownership of financial assets tends to be highly concentrated. These assets are increasingly being passed on by means of inheritance, so the two concerns are in fact closely connected. Today, financial assets tend to be the main component of the inheritance of the richest (while real estate remains prevalent if we consider the overall population). Take for example the case of Italy: there, in 2016, 90 per cent of the wealth of decedents belonging to the top 0.01 per cent was composed of financial assets and privately held business assets and only 10 per cent was composed of real estate (lands and buildings). The prevalence of financial and business assets declines quickly as we include more of the rich: in 2016, it was just over 15 per cent for the richest 1 per cent, three-quarters of whose wealth was composed of real estate.[55]

Not only are highly inheritable financial assets a growing component of the patrimonies of the rich, but finance has become a more important path towards wealth than ever before. In earlier sections of this chapter, we have discussed the onset of this process. During the nineteenth century, the share of very rich individuals who had made their fortune in finance, while no longer negligible, remained a minority. It is since the 1980s that the relative importance of finance as a means of personal enrichment has grown further, fuelled by financial deregulation which, among other things, allowed for substantial increases in the wages paid by this sector. As will be remembered from chapter 5, in Europe in 2010 employees of the financial sector already accounted for almost one-fifth of those receiving the highest 1 per cent of gross wages, and presumably this share was higher in the United States (see below). Increasingly, then, new wealth made in finance has added up to inherited wealth with financial origins. Unfortunately, we lack the information needed to explore this process across society. Again, we have to focus on the richest of all in order to detect tendencies that might have a broader significance. Table 7.3 reports information from a number of rich lists for the West as a whole and for selected countries for which information about a larger percentile of the rich is available. In fact, the figures for the West capture a tiny proportion of the overall population: the dollar-billionaires or the top 0.001 per cent to 0.0001 per cent of the wealth distribution. The figures for the United Kingdom, which relate to the richest 1,000 residents, are a somewhat larger share (the top 0.0015%). For Germany, the figures cover the top 0.0006 per cent in 2011 but just the top 0.0001 per cent in 2020.[56]

The figures in Table 7.3 suggest some relevant conclusions. First, the prevalence among the super-rich of those whose wealth originates from real estate seems to have declined further compared to the turn of the twentieth century

TABLE 7.3. The Composition of Western Billionaires and of the British and German Super-Rich, 2001–21 (%)

	West*					United Kingdom**	Germany***	
	2001	2011	2019	2020	2021	2020	2011	2020
Real estate	5.0	6.5	7.5	6.7	6.3	13.0	2.9	0.0
Industry, commerce and non-financial services	75.8	72.8	73.9	73.6	73.7	69.1	91.4	96.8
Finance	19.1	20.7	18.6	19.8	20.0	17.9	5.6	3.2
TOT	100.0	100.0	100.0	100.0	100.0	100.0	100.0	100.0
Inherited wealth	n.a.	n.a.	34.7	33.9	32.7	n.a.	n.a.	n.a.
Women	7.7	9.2	13.5	13.3	13.7	12.2	13.6	16.4

Notes: (*) Estimates for the West refer to billionaires only (net wealth ≥1 billion U.S. dollars in the year of reference, with no adjustments for inflation). (**) Estimates for the United Kingdom refer to the richest 1,000 individuals in each year (minimum entry in 2020: 120 million pounds, or 154 million U.S. dollars). (***) Estimates for Germany refer to those with estimated wealth above 900 million euros in 2020, or 1,027 million in 2020 U.S. dollars, and 200 million euros in 2011, or 321 million in 2020 U.S. dollars.

and is now in the range of 5–7.5 per cent across the West: about half that reported for the rich who died in Britain in 1906 or for the United States rich list of 1892 (Tables 7.1 and 7.2). This is the continuation of a pluri-secular path of decline, although the figures could also be read differently, that is, as proof of the persistence of 'aristocratic' wealth. This is particularly clear in the case of the United Kingdom where the combination of high inequality in land ownership and the increases in land values which have occurred since the late twentieth century have boosted the fortunes of many among the nobles. In 2020, 13 per cent of the thousand richest Britons held a fortune grounded in real estate, and of these, over one-quarter were nobles.[57] The case of the United Kingdom contrasts with that of Germany, where fortunes built on real estate are rare. Everywhere, liberal professions have disappeared from the top positions in the wealth ranking, which seems to reflect the growing distance between the super-rich and the other affluent strata of society. In contrast, finance has grown further, consolidating at a level of about 20 per cent: possibly slightly lower today than it was at the very beginning of the twenty-first century, as a consequence of the financial crisis of 2007–8 and the Great Recession that ensued. But if the tendencies reported for the period 2019–21 persist, early-century levels will be reached again (and very possibly beaten) soon enough. In this context, Germany stands out for the low prevalence of financial fortunes and the overwhelming dominance of those built on industry, commerce and non-financial services.

The table also includes some information about inherited wealth, which characterizes about one-third of Western billionaires in recent years. This is sizeable, but not nearly as worrying as the figures concerning the share of inherited wealth as a portion of total private wealth discussed in the earlier section, although obviously the data are not directly comparable.[58] It might be that the very top of the wealth distribution sees an over-representation of individuals who have been able to profit from the new opportunities of the computer and information age. In 2021, the richest five Westerners were Jeff Bezos (Amazon), Elon Musk (Tesla and Space X), Bernard Arnault (LVMH), Bill Gates (Microsoft) and Mark Zuckerberg (Facebook, renamed Meta in October 2021). Of these, only Arnault is reported by *Forbes* as having inherited (and subsequently increased) his wealth, which originates from the relatively traditional sector of fashion and retail. Of the 73.7 per cent of the super-rich of 2021 whose wealth originates from industry, commerce and non-financial services, almost one-fifth are reported to have made their fortune in the information technologies sector. This being said, *Forbes*, which is the source for much of the information in Table 7.3, reports self-made *billionaires*, but many among them came from already-wealthy families, as is, for example, the case for Bill Gates.[59] Additionally, a study of the richest 400 Americans in 1982–2013 has argued that, notwithstanding the undeniable growth of self-made wealth at the very top of the distribution, inherited fortunes are much less volatile and tend to remain listed for longer, a finding which probably also applies to the West in general.[60]

To conclude on a positive note, consider the growing prevalence of women. While they remain a minority (13%–14% in recent years), this is a more sizeable minority than at any earlier point in Western history; indeed, it is almost double that reported for 2001. And yet, this evidence can also be read somewhat less optimistically: in 2021, most Western female billionaires (84.2%) had inherited their wealth, but they accounted for only around one-third of all billionaire inheritors. This might betray a double gender-based discrimination: in the economic system at large, which might hinder the rise of women, and in society, with sons possibly being chosen over daughters as the main inheritors of the family fortune.[61]

Lists of the super-rich might well provide an excessively optimistic picture of the relative openness of the hierarchy of wealth. One reason is that many of the current self-made billionaires 'made' their fortunes decades ago, and the very nature of their businesses, as they have developed over time, risks stifling competition and suffocating the aspirations of younger cohorts of would-be innovators. We have evidence of this in the steady increase in the average age of Western billionaires: from 61.9 years in 2001, to 63.3 in 2011, finally peaking at 65.4 in 2020.[62] Importantly, this trend is greater than the parallel increase in life expectancy by a large margin, so it truly reflects the relative ageing of billionaires as a group. If their wealth is simply to be passed on to descendants, the view that large fortunes are the reward for one's abilities, or 'merit', will become difficult to sustain. The situation might end up mirroring that which many Western countries experienced at the turn of the twentieth century, when a long cycle of innovation, the massive creation of new wealth and sustained upward mobility ended.

Without evidence for the rich as a whole, or at least for a significantly larger top percentile of the wealth distribution, any analysis is bound to remain highly speculative. Unfortunately, such evidence is currently very scarce. For the United States, a study of the demographics of the richest 1 per cent (by net worth) based on the Survey of Consumer Finances (SCF) has provided information about their occupations, but unfortunately it does not go beyond 1992.[63] At that date, the occupations of 35.8 per cent of the employed among the richest percentile of household heads (the employed being about 85% of the full sample) were in finance, insurance or real estate, as opposed to just 13.8 per cent in the general population. Already at that time, the growth in the prevalence of financial occupations among the richest was drawing attention, as the comparable figure for 1983 was just 21.9 per cent. Interestingly, in the same timespan the proportion of those employed in business and services (professional or personal) was found to be in decline: from 25.9 per cent to 22.5 per cent. Again in 1992, other interesting features of the richest 1 per cent of Americans were the high prevalence of the self-employed (68.9% versus 17.2% in the general population) and of those declaring to have received inheritances (48.8% versus 20.6% in the general population. Note that inheritances received by the one-percenters were more than eight times larger than in the general population).[64]

In the absence of other detailed studies, we have to take the case of the United States in 1992 as indicative of the possible distortions that come from only looking at the super-rich. For example, occupations in finance might be underrepresented among billionaires compared to the top 1 per cent, and probably even more compared to the top 5 per cent.[65] While admittedly this is just a tentative hypothesis, it does find support in the relatively abundant studies that have reported a growing presence of people employed in the financial sector among those earning the largest incomes.[66] Income studies also suggest that liberal professions, while they no longer allow individuals to make it to the very top, continue to be a viable path towards wealthy status. Again in the United States, in 2005 those practising a medical profession made up 14.2 per cent of those earning the highest 1 per cent of total incomes, with lawyers at 7.7 per cent and professors or scientists at 1.8 per cent. However, when focusing on the top 0.1 per cent only, these percentages diminish by about two-thirds for doctors, one-third for professors and scientists and one-quarter for lawyers. This tendency is probably monotonic across all rich strata: moving upwards, this would lead to the total disappearance of professionals (which matches our earlier observations exactly), but moving downwards their prevalence would instead grow. The implication is that professionals are probably a larger share of the top 5 per cent (in both income and wealth) than of the top 1 per cent.

Interestingly, this is the opposite of what seems to happen for those rich active in the arts, media and sports sector, who made up 1.7 per cent of the top 1 per cent in 2005 but increase to a sizeable 2.8 per cent when just the top 0.1 per cent are considered.[67] This component of the rich seems to have been growing during the last few decades: by 21 per cent between 1979 and 2005 in the United States if we look at the top 1 per cent, but by 40 per cent if we focus on the top 0.1 per cent. In the United Kingdom in 2020, among the richest 1,000 individuals we find about 25 singers and musicians (led, in the wealth ranking, by Paul McCartney and Rihanna) as well as a scattering of writers and artists, like the neo-pop artist and collector Damien Hirst and Harry Potter's creator, J. K. Rowling. This being said, wealthy singers, artists, actors and athletes remain a small niche among the Western rich, although a very visible one due to their media exposure.

As a conclusion to this brief survey of research on the composition of the rich today, we might be surprised by how little we know about them. While there is no lack of studies of the super-rich, presumably because of the availability of regularly updated rich lists and because of the celebrity status of some specific individuals, for the rich as a whole—the top 5 per cent or even just the top 1 per cent—usually all we know about is their (often just presumed) share of the overall wealth. While this is important information, it is insufficient to get a better understanding of the characteristics of the rich as a distinctive (albeit an internally variegated) social group. This is all the more surprising if one considers that many current concerns would require such understanding in order to address them properly. Paradoxically, the overall picture becomes clearer if we observe it from a greater distance, that is, if we look at secular dynamics. This is a matter not only of tendencies (although the secular tendencies that we have described so far do seem to be adequately and consistently supported by the available evidence, notwithstanding its limitations), but also of perceptions. Modern concerns about a return to a society of rentiers are not that different from those expressed by the classical economists in the early nineteenth century, precisely because they were observing a society in which rentiers were highly prevalent. And concerns about wealth accumulation through finance—that is, by means of money used to make money—have preoccupied Western societies since the Middle Ages and even earlier. More generally, the very place that the rich occupy, or *should* properly occupy, in society appears to have always been a sore point for the West and a source of considerable social unease. It is to these aspects, and to the surprising elements of continuity which can be spotted across history, that we will now turn.

PART III

The Rich in Society

8

Why Wealth Concentration
Can Be a Social Problem

FROM THOMAS AQUINAS TO PIKETTY

The super-rich [*superabundantes*] are so unequal and exceed and overcome the
others regarding their political power so much that it is reasonable to think
that they are among the others as God is among men. . . . The cities which are
governed democratically, should relegate these people, i.e. they should send
them into exile or banish them, as such cities try and pursue equality of all.

—NICOLE ORESME 1370–74,
TRANSLATING AND ADAPTING ARISTOTLE'S *POLITICS*

People with inherited wealth need save only a portion of their income from
capital to see that capital grow more quickly than the economy as a whole.
Under such conditions . . . the concentration of capital will attain extremely
high levels—levels potentially incompatible with the meritocratic values and
principles of social justice fundamental to modern democratic societies.

—THOMAS PIKETTY 2014, 34

THE TWO PASSAGES ABOVE, from authors who are over six centuries apart
in time, perfectly introduce the topic of the third and final part of this book:
the position that the rich occupy in society and the social role that they play.
Throughout history, this role has never been quite clear, which has given rise
to considerable social wariness of the rich and especially the super-rich. This
chapter focuses on such wariness, as it was (and is) reflected in a scholarly
discourse which, while it surely pertains to high culture, nevertheless always

connects to the deeper feelings of society at large. In the following chapters, specific roles played by the rich in society—first as benefactors and patrons of the arts, then as political actors—will be explored, finally concluding with an analysis of their behaviour in times of deep crisis.

The two passages, by medieval philosopher Nicole Oresme and modern economist Thomas Piketty, clearly address the same concern: that the very presence of super-rich individuals within a society can have a disruptive effect on the inner workings of the society itself and of its institutions. This is even accounting for the fact that the two authors obviously had deeply different views about the meaning of the word 'democracy'. To avoid the risks of anti-historical comparisons, the chapter begins by exploring the medieval mistrust of great accumulators of wealth, a mistrust that was both instinctive and well-grounded in theology and general philosophical reflections about society. As will be seen, the situation began to change from the late Middle Ages, a development which was not without connection to growing disparities in wealth and in overall access to resources (including political and cultural resources) between human beings. But an instinctive distrust of the rich survived in Western societies, resurfacing in modern times, especially when, from the late nineteenth century, wealth inequality reached unprecedented heights. The relationship between inequality levels and the perception of the rich is as crucial to our understanding of past societies as it is to our understanding of society today. On this point, history has some warnings to give about our present and future, which are highlighted in the concluding section of the chapter.

The Medieval Distrust of the Rich and the Super-Rich

During the Middle Ages, Western societies were troubled by the very existence of the rich. Indeed, it would not be too far-fetched to state that they did not know precisely what to do with them. Certain aspects of this general mistrust have already been highlighted. In chapters 4 and 6, it has been recalled that a rich man was almost by definition a sinner, condemned by greed (a capital sin) to eternal damnation. As St Thomas Aquinas, the foremost medieval Scholastic philosopher and theologian, explained in the thirteenth century, greed (or avarice) was a sin against God as it led to the pursuit of 'temporal things' and the forsaking of all 'things eternal'. Avarice consisted in two excesses: an excess in *retaining* things (leading to hardheartedness and a lack of humanity and mercy) and an excess in *taking* things (leading to violence, deceit, fraud and treachery).[1] Of course, feudal society had no quarrel with the wealth of the nobility, whose high status and superior access to resources was believed to correspond to God's plans. It was the wealth of some among the commoners that created a problem, especially when, from the eleventh century, the Commercial Revolution began to offer unprecedented opportunities for building 'entrepreneurial' fortunes. As effectively stated by economic historian Robert Lopez, 'In the theoretical structure of feudal society there scarcely was room for a middle class between the exalted religious and lay lords and the lowly but irreplaceable laborers. Paupers were more acceptable than merchants: they would inherit the Kingdom of Heaven and help the almsgiving rich to earn entrance.'[2] Indeed, Scholastic theologians of the thirteenth and fourteenth centuries were basically unanimous in believing that merchant activity was particularly harmful to the soul; Thomas Aquinas even advised rulers to try to prevent their citizens from getting involved in large-scale trade.[3]

Given this cultural and social context, medieval merchants were under considerable psychological pressure, the more intense the more successful they were. Some repented spectacularly and came to be venerated as saints—remember the cases of St Francis and St Godric—but most others sought ways to get around the problem. They tried to open a path to heaven for themselves, presumably after a lengthy stay in purgatory (in Alighieri's *Divine Comedy*, the repenting greedy are found in the fifth terrace of purgatory, together with the profligate, which replicates a symmetry also found in hell, as seen in chapter 6). This led them to leave substantial bequests to charities and to religious institutions, to provide for regular prayers of intercession in their own favour and to give alms to the poor who, as noted by Lopez, found a clear social positioning precisely in their usefulness to the souls of the sinful rich. Examples of this behaviour abound, like Francesco di Marco Datini, the famous merchant from Prato, or Cosimo de' Medici, whose cases have already been introduced. In his old age, Cosimo grew particularly worried about the salvation of his soul, as on it weighed an even worse sin: not only was he inordinately rich, but he had also made much of his wealth by means of finance and, as will be recalled from chapter 5, medieval societies suspected that making money by means of money was potentially usurious and hence sinful.

In medieval societies, not only were the rich considered (and often considered themselves to be) sinners, but it was also feared that their very presence could destabilize society. As argued by Thomas Aquinas, excesses in taking could lead to acts of open violence and to all sorts of social and economic misconduct. These were more difficult to prevent, or even just to punish, the greater the distance between the wealthiest members of a community and the rest. This is precisely what Nicole Oresme pointed out, about a century after Aquinas, when, translating and adapting Aristotle's *Politics* to serve the practical needs of his time (at the request of the King of France, Charles V, of whom Oresme was a trusted counsellor[4]), he claimed that the super-rich 'overcome the others regarding their political power so much that it is reasonable to think that they are among the others as God is among men'.[5] And how will these 'gods' be punished, if they have acquired the means to control the community *politically*? The risk, which Oresme elucidates in his commentary (*glossae*) on Aristotle, was that their presence would prove fatally harmful to society, fostering rebellion. This fear was probably well-motivated, as the recent literature about urban revolts in medieval Europe has shown that political motivations were even more important than economic motivations in leading to the open, and usually violent, rebellion of 'the people' (the *popolo* in the Italian communes, the *peuple* in Oresme's native France) against the establishment.[6]

Social revolt could not be considered in any way desirable by a medieval theologian and philosopher like Oresme, especially given his first-hand experience of events of this kind, which greatly troubled France in the years immediately following the capture of King Jean II by the English at the Battle of Poitiers in 1356 (the main example was the *Grande Jacquerie* of 1358). Consequently, when discussing the 'democratic' form of government (by which Oresme means a government of the popular multitude, pursuing its own interest; therefore, not the ideal government as it does not actually pursue the 'common good'[7]), he states that in a society (a city) governed democratically, the super-rich[8] should be expelled. This idea was already present in Aristotle's original work, which discussed the practice of ostracism followed by Athens and other democracies of the Classical Age.[9] However, in writing his commentary, Oresme surely had in mind what had been common practice for the 'popular' governments of many medieval communes, which often had come into power by expelling the pre-existing political (and wealth) elite. As an alternative, they had totally forbidden families from the old elite to take up public office, precisely because this would have led to an excessive concentration of power; this occurred in Florence with the introduction of the *Ordinamenti di Giustizia* ('Regulations about Justice') of 1293, which forbade the *magnati* ('magnates') from holding the most important public positions. The *magnati* were members of the great and overbearing families that had dominated

Florentine politics in earlier decades and were distinguished mostly by their enormous wealth, usually accumulated in long-range trade, and only rarely by ancient nobility.[10] Anti-magnate laws were introduced in many other Italian cities around the same period (for example, in Bologna in 1282), but these developments were the local manifestation of an unease with the growing political power of the wealth elite that was felt across a much broader European area: basically, wherever communal governments had been captured by wealth oligarchies. For example, the so-called 'Flemish Revolution' of 1302, which started in Bruges and quickly spread to many other important cities of Flanders and northern France, can be understood as 'an attempt to revive the original communal ideology, which . . . had in practice been replaced by the oligarchic rule of a "patrician" class of merchants and urban landowners.'[11] This point will be discussed further in chapter 10.

As Oresme explains in a lengthy comment partially reproduced below, the practice of expelling the super-rich and the other *superabundantes* had to be considered dangerous. There was one alternative, which he clearly considered greatly preferable and which Aristotle had not considered: preventing the conditions which would have made expulsions desirable, which basically entailed preventing anybody from accumulating excessive wealth.

> [S]uch super-wealth can be the cause of harm and rebellion. Consequently, all laws that provide a remedy to this are right and effective. Additionally, they serve the common good, as it is not good for the community that the properties of all citizens are equal, nor that they are very unequally distributed. . . . It would be just a law establishing that a man can not have properties above a certain quantity, due to inheritance or otherwise.[12]

Oresme, then, considered it proper to place a legal cap on the maximum wealth that could be owned by any single member of a given community. Indeed, for him it was entirely justifiable, in pursuit of the common good, even to limit the size of inheritances. The wealth exceeding the maximum admissible bequest should be 'given to one or more other members of the same lineage, or confiscated, or distributed in another way based on a good law.'[13] In other words, Oresme was clearly arguing for the advisability of some sort of fiscal redistribution of wealth in order to preserve the social order.

Thomas Aquinas and Nicole Oresme can be taken as representative of a widespread mistrust of the super-rich (or, more properly, of the 'excessively wealthy' and the other *superabundantes*) as social players. While this mistrust is clearly rooted in a much older scholarly tradition—the whole Scholastic school of philosophy had Aristotle, the great Greek philosopher of the fourth century BCE, as its main point of reference—it is also deeply influenced by Christian ideas,[14] as well as by the new social problems that had arisen since at the least the eleventh century with the opening phase of the Commercial Revolution. For example, it would be impossible to understand the obsession with usury of Scholastic thinkers, Thomas Aquinas included, without placing it in the context of the phase of fervent financial innovation born of the need to service the booming long-distance trade.

And yet, we might wonder whether a scholarly discourse which clearly belongs to high culture reflects the broader cultural context of the West at that time. There is little doubt that the answer to the question is on the whole positive. Regarding the perception of the super-rich as potentially damaging to the correct functioning of political and government institutions, this is evidenced by the viscerally anti-magnate stance of many European polities. And regarding the perception of the rich as sinners, there is abundant proof that the rich themselves believed that their behaviour was sinful. To this, it is possible to add the appeal that radically anti-wealth heresies, like the Waldensians active in France and Italy from the late twelfth century, had, not only to the poor themselves, but even more to the artisans who composed the middling strata of medieval urban societies, which is indicative of a cultural context altogether adverse to the pursuit of material wealth.[15] After all, as noted by economic historian Amintore Fanfani almost a century ago (before becoming a prominent politician of post-war Italy), although the Scholastic doctrines were elaborated and discussed in specific social environments, everybody heard their echo. This was also because there was no alternative—the only theory about material goods had been built with the superior interests of the spirit in mind, something in which Thomas Aquinas played a key role.[16] But from the very end of the Middle Ages the situation began to change: the needs of the material world led to substantial changes in the way that some key features of the economy and society were conceptualized. It is in this context that the rich and the super-rich were finally assigned a social role.

Finding a Role for the Rich: From Sinners to Elect

When considering medieval treatises that discuss the place of the rich in society, it is apparent that from the fifteenth century a significant change was underway, which further strengthened during the sixteenth. The rich, and even the super-rich, who had previously been depicted by theologians and philosophers as socially troublesome sinners at best, began to be presented as important contributors to society, with specific moral virtues. Firstly, this process entailed explaining why the building of large private fortunes might be of some utility for society at large and, related to this, demonstrating that greed—without which such fortunes would never have emerged—also had a positive side. More precisely, the propensity to accumulate came to be redefined as potentially useful to the community, while a distinction continued to be made between those who made good or bad use of the accumulated resources.[17] As an example of this redefinition of the nature of greed and of the social function of the 'virtuous' greedy, let us consider an excerpt from the dialogue *De Avaritia* ('On Avarice') by the Tuscan humanist Poggio Bracciolini:

> You want to expel the greedy from the cities, as if they were guilty of the worst crimes. . . . I believe instead that their presence should be promoted, as a valid support for the people. In fact, they have abundant means to aid the sick, the weak, to benefit many in their needs, bringing help to private individuals and to the state. Consequently, as among the populations and in the cities which have good traditions it is customary to institute public granaries to distribute wheat in public donations, in the same way it would be very useful to place there many greedy individuals, in order for them to constitute a kind of private barn of money able to be of assistance to everybody. . . . In fact, if ever the city needs help, shall we make recourse to the poor labourers and to those who despise wealth, or to the rich, that is to the greedy—as it is rarely possible to grow rich without greed? Of whom is it better that the city is full? Of the rich, who with their means provide for themselves and for others, or of the poor who do not have enough to assist others, and not even themselves?[18]

In Bracciolini's dialogue these views are expressed by Antonio Loschi, papal secretary and humanist, and are contrasted with others which closely follow those typical of the earlier Scholastic literature discussed in the previous section in condemning the greedy and in calling for their removal from society. The rhetorical structure of the dialogue surely leads to each position being made somewhat extreme, but, as noted decades ago by economic historian David Herlihy, 'we can hardly doubt that the sentiments expressed [by Antonio] are Poggio's own'.[19] Bracciolini, then, is making a strong case for the virtues of wealth accumulation, as this is necessary for building private deposits of financial resources ('barns of money', every bit as necessary to the public wellbeing as granaries filled with wheat) into which the community can tap in case of need. Here, importantly, Bracciolini is not referring to the regular alms and charitable support provided by the rich to the poor and the sick, but to the occurrence of times of dire need, such as famines or wars, because it is precisely in these exceptional times that having access to exceptional resources comes to be of crucial importance. As effectively noted by Giacomo Todeschini, a historian of ideas, in the new scholarly and textual tradition to which Bracciolini belongs, 'The greedy [*avari*] come to be represented as *those who save for the city*, as ... money constitutes the nervous system of the city, that which keeps it alive and active.'[20]

The nervous system of the city, which is the metaphor employed by Bracciolini to describe why a prosperous community needs to have an abundance of money, is an example of the organic metaphors which, during the fifteenth century, became common when discussing the very nature of money. For example, at around the same time that Bracciolini composed his *De Avaritia*, the Franciscan theologian and saint Bernardino of Siena described money as the 'natural warmth' of the city. Its correct circulation was needed to prevent social disease in the same way as the natural warmth had to be correctly distributed in the human body to prevent dangerous and potentially deadly ailments. Importantly, for Bernardino, in both the city and the body problems arose from the excessive concentration of warmth/money. A century and a half later another Tuscan, Bernando Davanzati, would provide, in a highly influential treaty, a well-known and more elaborate variant of the metaphor, describing money as 'the second blood', that is, the blood of the state. But what is significant here is that, by the fifteenth century, a consensus had spread about the need to secure an abundance of money within the perimeter of a given community. In order to achieve this, accumulation (hence, greed) was a requirement. This, however, could lead to excess (Bernardino of Siena pointed out the harm done by excessive wealth inequality, while Bracciolini condemned those who accumulated wealth without caring for its public utility), and few were naïve enough to believe that all of the greedy would perform a positive social role.[21]

It was, then, the use of one's fortune which distinguished the virtuous greedy from the sinful miser, who accumulated wealth as an objective per se, pursued without any consideration for the broader society. In contrast, the virtuous greedy, beyond saving in the interest of the community, also invested part of their wealth in worthy endeavours and particularly in 'magnificent houses, nice villas, temples, hospitals ... without which the cities would lack

their main and prettiest ornaments'.[22] This additional social role played by
the rich—who in building splendid edifices, including their own palaces,
made the whole city splendid to everybody's advantage—is also clearly explained, at the end of the fifteenth century, by the Neapolitan humanist
Giovanni Pontano:

> In our age Cosimo the Florentine imitated the ancient magnificence both
> in building churches and villas, and in founding libraries; not only did he
> imitate, but, I would say, he was the first to revive the custom of *changing
> private wealth into public benefit* and into an ornament of the fatherland.
> Not a few men, although less advantaged than he, now seek to follow this
> custom.[23]

Pontano's text is interesting not only because it illustrates the social role of the
(virtuous) rich, which consists in investing in the physical improvement of
the city, converting 'private wealth' into 'public benefit', but also because it
refers to a specific situation: that of Florence exactly when the Medici were
strengthening their grip on the Republic. This prompts us to ask why, compared to the overall negative view of the rich typically provided by earlier authors, we observe such a significant shift beginning in the fifteenth century.
After the post-Black Death pause, from the turn of the fifteenth century wealth
inequality began to grow again in Tuscany, and this process was perhaps particularly strong and apparent in Florence.[24] A tipping point had been reached
and, as argued for usury in chapter 5, theology (and scholarship more generally) adapted to the realities of a new social and economic situation.

Many among the most prominent theologians of the time were acutely
aware of this new situation, given that they themselves issued from rich merchant families, as was the case for Bernardino of Siena. While in earlier times
scholarly reflection reacted to the novelty posed by the emergence of super-
rich individuals nurtured by the Commercial Revolution by pointing to their
potentially destabilizing impact on the social and political order, by the fifteenth century it became clear that a new order had emerged from which the
rich could no longer be excluded. The case of the Medici family, from Cosimo
to his successors who would, first, empty the Florentine republican institutions of any real meaning, and then change the form of government into a
hereditary principality, is exemplary of this more general process. It is in this
context that theologians and preachers like St Antonino Pierozzi, archbishop
of Florence from 1446 and very close to Cosimo de' Medici, developed a 'public theology of magnificence' which promoted a specific social function for

the rich.[25] On the one hand, this was inculcated through sermons in the general population, but on the other hand it was aimed (as were at least some of the 'lay' treatises on the rich, like for example Pontano's) at inducing the super-rich to use their enormous resources in ways which could be of some benefit to society at large.

It might seem that fifteenth- and sixteenth-century scholars praising the virtuous rich were too optimistic, and quite possibly, they were. But the fact remains that, in the late Middle Ages as today, whoever has the fortune to live in, or to visit, places like Florence and Venice or their counterparts in the Low Countries and in other parts of Europe continues to enjoy exceptional urban beauty, which would never have appeared without the super-rich of the Renaissance. So, at least to some degree, the theoretical function of the rich as those who invested in making the city magnificent for everybody's benefit did correspond to reality. The same can be said for their other function: that of saving for the benefit of the community. Cosimo de' Medici is, again, a perfect example of such behaviour as, in 1434, after returning from exile, he rescued Florence from financial catastrophe and was hailed as benefactor of the people (see chapter 5). Of course, we are again faced with considerable ambiguity, as the rich in their function as barns of money were not acting without self-interest, be it political (his generous help propelled Cosimo to the status of de facto ruler of his country) or economic. In fact, while late medieval and early modern polities of all kinds greatly benefited from the presence of super-rich families able and willing to provide their governments with substantial resources (remember that the main players in international finance played a crucial role as lenders to ruling princes), those resources were usually loaned and did not come cheap. And yet, in times of severe crises, for example famines, acts of great generosity on the part of the wealthy were not uncommon and contributed not only to alleviating the conditions of the poorest and weakest strata, but also to maintaining the social peace. The same can be said for other situations of dire need like sieges. An example is the siege of Florence in 1529–30 by the troops of Emperor Charles V, when the defence, according to an early sixteenth-century author, Donato Giannotti (interestingly, a fervent republican), would never have been so effective without the crucial financial contribution of its many rich residents.[26] The role played by the rich in times of crisis will be discussed further in chapter 11.

But how did the rich come to be depicted and, in time, actually perceived as not only useful but virtuous? This process developed in full during the fifteenth century, together with the re-elaboration of the role played by the rich, but has even earlier roots as at least from the fourteenth century merchants appear to have been proud of their own moral qualities. Indeed, a merchant without morality could not be a 'real' merchant as he would not have been considered worthy of trust (*fides*). In a sort of foreword to a treatise on commercial practices written around 1330, Francesco Pegolotti (a merchant and banker of the Bardi Company) discusses 'What a just and authentic merchant should have within himself' (*Quello che dee avere in sé il vero e diritto mercante*). It is a long list, which includes righteousness (*dirittura*), trustworthiness, good manners, honourable behaviour, caution, friendliness, regular religious practice and frequent alms-giving and the avoidance of usury and gambling. Scholars of the fifteenth century, from Bernardino of Siena to Leon Battista Alberti (the famous architect, philosopher and humanist from Genoa), systematically reinforced the view that the successful merchant possessed virtues of the kind indicated by Pegolotti a century before. At the same time, they indicated the causes of decline and bankruptcy in both moral and economic failings.[27]

There is little doubt that, by the fifteenth century, many members of the merchant class had internalized these views and perceived themselves not as sinners but as virtuous individuals. This change in perception and self-perception, grounded as it was in the aforementioned changes in social, political and economic structures and in the distribution of economic resources, was not without a dark side, as has also been perceptively argued by Todeschini:

> When we consider the economic European situation in the second half of the fifteenth century from the point of view of the enormously growing poverty of the working and lower middle class, we can easily understand that the cultivated self-representation produced by the merchants' class was also the expression of a social process to achieve cultural and economic exclusivity. The idealized and heroic or religious representation of the businessman's mind and body silently hinted at the rising cultural insignificance and the low price and value of work, body, and mind of the outcasts or 'exploited people'.[28]

The process of cultural change set in motion by the emergence of great fortunes in the late Middle Ages continued in early modern times. Indeed, the religious (self)representation of the businessman reached new heights with the Protestant Reformation. According to a famous interpretation by Max Weber (1930 [1904]), the Reformation, whose starting point is usually placed in 1517 when the German theologian and reformer Martin Luther advanced his 'Ninety-Five Theses', engendered a new economic ethic which fostered the emergence of the 'spirit of capitalism'. For Weber, modern capitalism consisted of an unprecedented union between rationality and the pursuit of the accumulation of wealth. While this was a characteristic of the Reformation as a whole, he also argued that the followers of the French theologian John Calvin were particularly encouraged to pursue economic success. This was because Calvin's doctrine of predestination (according to which salvation can be achieved by grace only; hence some are predestined to be saved and others to be damned) led believers to seek material success as a sort of proof that they belonged to the elect.

Weber's views about the Reformation have been the object of considerable criticism. Some of his early critics, in particular, argued that he was overstating the novelties it brought about in economic ethics and actual behaviour. In England, historian Richard H. Tawney suggested that there is indeed a connection between the Reformation and capitalism, but that it is the reverse of what Weber suggested: Protestants adopted the (pre-existing) ethics of capitalism favouring profit-making and the accumulation of wealth.[29] In Italy, Fanfani also argued that the birth of modern capitalism preceded the Reformation. For him, the spirit of capitalism was already operating in fifteenth-century Italy and consisted in a tendency to believe that wealth could be increased indefinitely without having to be redistributed by means of donations to the poor or patronage (as, he argued, had been the case before the Black Death).[30] A few decades later, the French historian Fernand Braudel was very direct in his own rejection of Weber's interpretation: 'All historians have opposed this tenuous theory, although they have not managed to get rid of it once and for all. Yet it is clearly false. The northern countries took over the place that earlier had so long and so brilliantly been occupied by the old capitalist centers of the Mediterranean'. The matter, though, is far from settled as Weber's views remain very influential in the social sciences.[31] Additionally, it is possible that Weber might have been wrong about the mechanism leading to quicker growth in Protestant areas (the supposedly new Protestant ethic) but right about the correlation between religious change and economic development, which might also have resulted from unintended consequences of the Reformation like changes in the legal and institutional framework, in economic policy, in literacy and so on.[32]

Based on our discussion so far, Weber's first critics, from Tawney to Fanfani, had a strong point when they argued for the importance of considering the continuity between the 'Protestant' ethic and the new behaviours that had spread in earlier centuries, beginning with the economic elite of merchants and bankers active in the most advanced areas of Europe. And yet, it is also true that Weber spotted a further, important stage in a centuries-long process of cultural change. While in the mind of many cultivated rich merchants and bankers of the fifteenth century the suspicion must have remained that at least some of their economic activities were, to a certain extent, sinful,[33] from the sixteenth century their Calvinist equivalents perceived their own economic success in an entirely different way. If personal enrichment was truly proof of divine favour, it could not be intrinsically sinful. While making good use of one's wealth remained important (to further strengthen both personal and *social* certainties about salvation, as being accepted among the elite of the righteous was key to feeling reassured about being destined for salvation), building a fortune acquired a religious character unto itself, independently of its final use. This is what Weber called *Beruf*, 'the calling', which for him was a true novelty of the Reformation and which characterized all of it, not only its Calvinist component.[34] Freed from even the suspicion of sin, the early modern rich of Protestant Europe also felt less committed to redistributing part of their wealth; as shown by a recent study, the prevalence and intensity of poverty increased in Protestant parts of Germany relative to those that had remained Catholic.[35] After all, salvation by grace had also freed the Protestant rich from the need to secure the prayers of the poor to obtain some spiritual benefit. Medieval sinners had finally become early modern elect, and their place in society was no longer in question.[36]

Red Threads in History

The self-perception and self-representation of the economic elite as virtuous, which we have seen emerging from the Middle Ages in the most economically advanced parts of Europe and which the Protestant Reformation contributed to strengthening by endowing hard work in a worldly context with a religious character, continued to spread throughout the early modern period. While most scholars have focused on changes in the associated work ethic, which arguably had a positive impact on economic development as had been originally argued by Weber, it is quite clear that a change had occurred in what was considered to be virtuous behaviour. Indeed, the 'bourgeois virtues' that economic historian Deirdre McCloskey finds at work across much of the West from the seventeenth or eighteenth century can be taken as a synthetic description of what had been achieved after centuries of cultural *change*. At the same time, they are an example of the existence of important cultural *continuities* over time as, for McCloskey, those same virtues continue to operate in the modern bourgeoise.[37]

Here, continuities over time of this kind will be referred to as 'red threads in history' which directly connect the past to the present, sometimes in surprising ways. The very idea that such continuities exist implies that it is possible to make an intellectual jump across the ages in an attempt to illuminate aspects of our society or at least of societies relatively close to ours chronologically, of which we could not easily become aware without some knowledge of a quite distant past. In particular, the focus will be on the social functions attributed to the rich and on the persistence of negative views about their very presence in society. Regarding the first point, the idea that their 'magnificence' (*magnificentia*, which literally means 'doing great deeds') offers to the rich opportunities for positive public action persisted through time, although in more recent periods this is often read, or presented, as 'munificence' (*munificentia*), that is, as generosity. For late medieval and early modern scholars, it was clear that the rich and especially the super-rich could be of public benefit through a specific kind of large-scale spending, which showed, at the same time, their economic *and moral* greatness. In this, they were following a tradition which can be traced back to the Greek philosophers Plato and Aristotle. Indeed, for Plato in *The Republic*, magnificence was one of the key virtues that should be possessed by the philosopher-king.[38] Consequently, it was understood that magnificence was a quality shown by individuals who also had an ambition to rule, or at least to lead, their societies.

If magnificence as a category of the super-rich's behaviour becomes confused with munificence, the aspect of society's dependence on the rich, together with their claim to have a right to rule, implicit in their socially useful spending, becomes lost. This is not to say that each and every act of generosity on the part of the rich is driven, consciously or unconsciously, by self-interest and by a desire to exert a degree of control over society, but that those acts that do have this motivation have become more difficult to distinguish in modern societies, compared to earlier epochs. When, in the 1440s, Cosimo founded the Medici Library at the Dominican Convent of San Marco, his fellow citizens were well aware that he was doing it in his role as de facto ruler of Florence, although the library itself was most definitely for public benefit. Today, many billionaires donate generously and are invariably praised for their munificence, but how much influence on society (and on politics) do they gain in this way?

This is a relevant and complex question, which will be explored in detail in the next chapter.

Regarding a second historical function of the rich, that of saving for the collective interest of society, it is again quite clear that, for the public, tapping into the private resources of the rich remained an option across the epochs. In the early modern period, this could acquire a compulsory character, as with the forced loans regularly imposed by the Spanish crown during the sixteenth and seventeenth centuries on rich merchants, including in the form of the capture, or *secuestro*, of private cargoes of American gold and silver. Forced loans were meant to fund the military needs of the kingdom and (later) to try to contain its financial difficulties. While many economic historians have argued that this practice made property rights insecure and was a sign of political absolutism, it was surely not exclusive to the Spanish. In about the same period, the Kingdom of France, that of England and others made use of forced loans, usually in times of dire need of resources for funding war efforts. Strikingly, forced loans were also imposed upon the rich by merchant republics, like the Dutch Republic in northern Europe or Venice and Genoa in the south. Indeed, the Republic of Venice, which throughout the Middle Ages was a hotspot of innovation in public finance, had imposed forced loans from as early as the twelfth century. The fact that merchant republics, whose governments were by definition protective of the interests of the merchant class, made systematic use of forced loans should give us pause when judging these procedures as the mere expression of an arbitrary, extortionist and 'absolutist' power. Close observation of what is usually considered the worst-case scenario (the Kingdom of Spain) should give us further pause, as the size and the terms of forced loans were usually negotiated with representatives of the merchants and the loans were repaid in full, with substantial interest.[39]

Rich merchants and financiers of the early modern period, the supposed 'victims' of forced loans, were well aware that in many circumstances they were contributing to the public good. After all, war has always been recognized as one of the more reasonable motivations for allowing central state authorities to request resources from their subjects. During World War I and World War II, Western powers systematically tried to increase their access to financial resources by launching public loans, like the 'liberty bonds' issued in the United States in 1917–18 to contribute to funding the Allied war effort. While these were not technically forced loans (although the introduction of forced loans was more or less openly threatened when 'voluntary' schemes were at risk of failure[40]), governments were rather active in trying to induce private individuals to subscribe them and welcomed any opportunity to increase the social pressure on those reluctant to contribute. Of course, the rich were expected to contribute more to this collective financial effort and, in this case, not to their own advantage. The war loans of the twentieth century paid little interest which, especially after World War I, tended to become negative in real terms due to post-war hyper-inflation. The invested capital was basically 'expropriated by inflation' in countries like Britain, France and Germany, as argued by Piketty who saw in this process one of the mechanisms leading to the war-related reduction in wealth inequality.[41]

It might appear that the recourse to strongly incentivized but ultimately voluntary war funding schemes by twentieth-century governments marked a positive difference compared with the earlier forced loans. But if we look at this from the point of view of states' ability to extract resources from their subjects, the conclusion must be the opposite: preindustrial governments used (negotiated) forced loans because they could not raise the tax burden above certain levels. During the two World Wars, across the West we find instead very substantial increases in taxation of both income and wealth, with a strongly progressive character which clearly placed the burden mostly on the shoulders of the rich. From this perspective, progressive taxation comes to represent the main way in which, in the modern world, the rich fulfil the specific function that they have had since medieval times of saving in the interest of the public. For example, the idea that in times of crisis they should contribute considerably more than the general population was explicit in the fiscal package introduced in the United States as part of Roosevelt's New Deal.[42] Recently, from the time of the financial crisis of 2007–8 and the ensuing Great Recession to the COVID-19 crisis which began in 2020 (still ongoing at the time of writing), calls for increasing taxation on the wealthiest members of society have resonated again in the West. And yet, the rich seem to be exceedingly reluctant to accede to these requests. Whatever one thinks about taxation and the proper size and functions of governments, from a historical point of view it must be recognized that in trying to avoid this kind of contribution in exceptional times, the rich are basically rejecting a role which has served to justify the very existence of substantial wealth inequalities, fuelling resentment and leaving their place in society uncertain. This important point will be developed further in the final section of this chapter, while more generally the (always somewhat tense) relationship of the rich with taxation will be discussed in chapter 10.

It is also important to consider those instances when the rich helped the collectivity with their private resources voluntarily, without even the kind of public pressure that was behind war loans and similar initiatives. The case of Cosimo de' Medici, who with his private resources saved Florence from financial collapse, is again the perfect example. But we might wonder until when, in history, we can find examples of individuals having the will and the means to save their country's finances basically on their own. Tentatively, for large countries, the endpoint can be placed at the turn of the twentieth century when, especially in the United States, some individuals had amassed fortunes large enough to allow them to perform this function, not merely at a local but also at a national level, even in the context of a modern industrial economy.

To the best of my knowledge, the last example is that of John Pierpont Morgan during the financial crisis of 1907. On that occasion, in the face of financial panic and bank runs, Morgan acted as a 'banker of last resort', in the effective definition of business historian Vincent P. Carosso.[43] True, Morgan was not alone in his swift action to save companies from bankruptcy and to restore the solvability of the financial system, but he led the rescue party of financiers who rose to the challenge, which included prominent individuals like George F. Baker and James Stillman. Such a team might not have come together without his personal and strong-willed involvement. A witness, the German-born banker and businessman Jacob H. Schiff, noted in a private letter that 'Probably no one could have got the banks to act together, and to join hands . . . as he did, in his autocratic way';[44] this 'autocratic way' included locking fellow bankers in his library until they had negotiated a solution to the crisis. Basically, this means that J. P. Morgan was able to save his country from bankruptcy thanks not only to his enormous financial resources, but also to the huge influence that he could exert on the American financial system as a whole. His crucial role in bringing the crisis to an end before greater harm was done was clearly recognized at the time; like Cosimo de' Medici about five centuries earlier, he was hailed as a saviour of his country. In June 1908, Yale University conferred on J. P. Morgan the degree of Doctor of Laws *honoris causa*, and on that occasion, a business newspaper wrote:

> [I]n the financial and industrial world . . . he ranks easily as the most commanding figure of the times, and that fact is recognized everywhere. . . . When disturbance has come and carrying corporations have found themselves in trouble, or when the Government itself has needed assistance, he has been the man to see how to make the best of circumstances and gradually lead to a restoration. . . . An instance of this which is still fresh in memory . . . was his action in checking disaster last October. . . . Mr. Morgan

has certainly exhibited, for mankind, the productive and beneficent uses of capital, and in a degree displayed by few if any of his contemporaries.[45]

The fact that, by 'checking disaster', J. P. Morgan had also served his own interests and those of the financial community does not alter the fact that his actions had been of great benefit to the public, especially considering that, at that time, the United States had no central banking system of the kind already in place in other countries, like Britain. And yet, the very same exhibition of economic power and vast influence that allowed Morgan to carry out his role as banker of last resort also reaped considerable criticism, fuelling suspicion of the 'money trust' that supposedly controlled U.S. finance (see chapter 5). As seen in the next section, this is just one of the many paradoxes that characterize the way in which the rich and their actions are perceived.

Since the 1907 crisis, it has been increasingly more difficult for the very rich to act as 'savers of last resort', and arguably they have grown increasingly less willing to do so, relying instead on public institutions (and taxpayers' money) to save the financial system. As will be discussed further in chapter 11, this might help to explain the resentment towards the rich which is currently quite widespread across the West. However, the waning of one of the key traditional functions of the Western rich should not hide the fact that a deeper subterranean current of thought continues to exist, basically adverse to them, which resurfaces in specific moments and places but never disappears entirely. This undercurrent connects medieval scholars directly to modern thinkers.

Distrust of the rich is clearly visible in the works of nineteenth-century German philosopher and economist Karl Marx. He saw in the original accumulation of wealth (also called the 'primitive' accumulation) which took place at the close of the Middle Ages a crucial step in the process leading workers to become ever more economically and politically oppressed, to the ultimate advantage of the bourgeois class. Interestingly, when discussing pre-capitalistic economies, Marx made a stark distinction between 'merchant's capital' and 'usurer's capital', by which he meant all 'interest-bearing capital'. Usury is attributed a role in wealth concentration which is purely 'parasitic', as it did not alter the mode of production but just made the living conditions of most of the population increasingly more pitiable. Under the capitalistic mode of production, interest-bearing capital adapts to the new conditions and interest represents its share of the surplus, but it does not change in nature, and its usurious character tends to show itself whenever the conditions allow.[46] With all due differences, Marx's judgement of finance was every bit as negative as that of the most severe theologians of the Middle Ages. His modern followers have expanded the criticism to the ongoing financialization of Western economies.[47]

At the turn of the twentieth century, a deep distaste for financial capitalism was shared by some influential, non-Marxist thinkers. The American economist Thorstein Veblen is an excellent example. Writing at the very end of the nineteenth century, he made a distinction between 'industry' and 'business', the latter being the realm of ruthless speculators (Veblen explicitly mentions J. P. Morgan as an example). Again, the connection with an earlier line of thought, with its roots in medieval theology and philosophy, is clear as Veblen was essentially condemning the practice of making money out of money. This criticism, however, was not made purely on a matter of principle, but was connected to the actual behaviour of the 'businessmen' of Gilded Age America, who according to him did not possess the virtues of the industrialists and because of this were detrimental to society. Importantly, Veblen also offered a moral condemnation of other categories of the rich, particularly of those who belonged to the 'leisure class'.[48] In doing this, he was providing a particularly effective criticism of those 'idle rich' who at about the same time were also coming under attack in Europe, where it was thought that they were particularly abundant among the nobility, especially that with ancient feudal origins. Take the case of England, where in the early twentieth century even conservative politicians like Winston Churchill were quite ready to take action against the idle rich, allegedly to stimulate enterprise, favour the creation of 'new' wealth and thus produce, as Churchill stated in 1925, 'the appeasement of class bitterness, the promotion of a spirit of co-operation, the stabilisation of our national life.'[49]

At about the same time, others were concerned with the social (and political) consequences of the growth of economic inequality per se. Consider for example Irving Fisher, who in his presidential address to the American Economic Association in 1919 expressed the concern that some novel features of American society, and particularly unprecedented wealth inequality, an abundance of inherited fortunes and new fortunes built through an excessive concentration of profits and sheer luck, were 'inconsistent with democratic ideals and democratic progress.'[50] A few years later, similar concerns were shared by the Roosevelt administration, which tried to contain inequality by introducing strongly progressive fiscal policies. More recently, fears that excessive disparities, especially in wealth, could prove incompatible with the correct functioning of democratic institutions have been expressed by French economist Thomas Piketty. In the passage reproduced at the opening of this chapter, he claims that an excessive concentration of capital is in direct contrast to the 'meritocratic values' and the 'principles of social justice' that, for him, are 'fundamental to modern democratic societies'.[51]

This supposed incompatibility between extreme wealth concentration and the correct functioning of democratic institutions calls for a more in-depth discussion of the role played by the rich in political systems, a topic covered in chapter 10. For now, it is important to highlight again a red thread in history, as medieval scholars like Nicole Oresme, based on an even older Aristotelian tradition, were already expressing concerns about the incompatibility of the presence of super-rich individuals and the correct functioning of 'democratic' institutions. In the social, political and cultural context of the Middle Ages, outright expulsion of the super-rich from the community was considered a viable and just solution to the problem. In a modern Western society, this would obviously be considered contrary to basic individual freedoms and rightly so. But for our societies, the problem remains of identifying the proper space within which the rich should contain their political influence and the proper ways to guarantee equal access to public institutions for everybody—to preserve the freedoms of all.

On Inequality and the Perception of the Rich

In our analysis of why wealth concentration can be a social problem, we have yet to directly address the issue of whether the very *perception* of inequality as a problem depends upon high inequality levels and, then, on the specific features acquired by a given society and not on a more general and somewhat a priori social-cultural distaste for inequality. It should be clear by now that the perception of wealth accumulation as something positive or negative changes across the centuries (although some basic instincts and views, like for example a mistrust of finance, remain a constant feature of Western culture). To this, we should add that the actual meaning of a condition of inequality is grounded in the deeper cultural context specific to any given society. Indeed, a recent study of medieval and early modern treatises has shown that, before the eighteenth century, the word 'inequality' (in all its Latin and vernacular versions) was not used to indicate differences between human beings and did not have an economic meaning.[52] This is indicative of societies which perceived themselves as structurally unequal and where, then, some sort of inequality was taken for granted; hence it remained 'unperceived'.

As noted in chapter 4, in medieval Europe the presence of a nobility with vastly greater access to economic resources compared to the average commoner was not usually perceived or conceptualized as problematic. It was, instead, the rise of *some* commoners over the others that seemed at odds with the way in which a society divided into hierarchically ordered components should function, especially when some of those commoners became so rich as to equal or even to overcome the nobility, in ways which threatened the established political order.

Related to this, we need to understand that for societies formally divided into orders or 'estates' (which was the norm in the West until the French Revolution of 1789), concepts like, for example, justice worked differently. In fact, while Old Regime societies were intrinsically hierarchical, they also perceived themselves as 'just'. However, this was according to their own criterion of justice, which was not one of 'fairness' (a concept that implies equality of some sort: for example, equality of opportunities as argued by American philosopher John Rawls[53]) but of *aequitas* ('equity'). *Aequitas* corresponds to a principle of distributive justice according to which everyone must receive what is due to them based on their condition or status, which does not imply that everybody will be treated in the same way.[54]

Today as in the past, a society which believes that it is suffering unjust conditions will tend to revolt, but it is telling that preindustrial societies rarely rebelled for purely economic reasons.[55] This confirms that such societies were culturally better-suited to tolerate relatively high levels of economic inequality. What they struggled to accept, at least originally, was the emergence of high wealth inequality within sectors of society whose members were not expected—were not 'entitled'—to rise so high. It is from this point of view that it is possible to argue that the relatively high levels of wealth inequality (and particularly the growing wealth share of the rich) that seem to have characterized Europe in the period preceding the 1347–52 Black Death triggered the anti-rich reaction that can be detected in scholarly discourse, which probably reflected widespread feelings. As seen in chapter 2, the Black Death led to a rare phase of reduced inequality. In a sense, this provided a window of opportunity to find a solution of sorts to a social-cultural problem that was bound to reappear, and indeed, when from the fifteenth century wealth inequality resumed its growth, the increasing prevalence of rich and even super-rich individuals had found a stronger justification. Changes in economic structures, then, prompted cultural change, but in a self-reinforcing mechanism 'cultural change also *allowed* for further structural changes, for example by providing a different and less negative concept of greed, and attributing to the super-rich an "acceptable" role to play within the community.[56]

Across Europe, throughout the early modern period, wealth inequality tended to increase continuously, with few exceptions well defined both geographically and chronologically, and the rich tended to become ever richer. Their claim to a rightful and increasingly prominent place in society was now basically unchallenged, and, as seen earlier, they even came to perceive and to present to others their propensity to accumulate as virtuous. But arguably, even in the context of a society relatively accepting of social-economic disparities of this kind, a threshold can be reached above which wealth inequality becomes so high that it begins to be seen as a problem. This is what might have happened in Europe from the eighteenth century, at least if we read in this way the slow spread of a discourse about the factors leading to inequality between human beings. In this process, the publication in 1754 of the treatise by the French philosopher Jean-Jacques Rousseau, *Le discours sur l'origine et les fondements de l'inégalité parmi les hommes*, seems to have been a threshold event.[57]

While clearly Rousseau's work can be placed in a specific tradition of philosophical reflection, notably that of early modern 'natural law',[58] it is significant that it appeared precisely when it did, especially considering that Rousseau composed his treatise in answer to a challenge launched by the Academy of Dijon, to debate 'What is the origin of inequality among men, and if it is authorized by the natural law'. In the mid-nineteenth century, then, a French research institution considered that question worthy of further research, which seems indicative of its perceived social, as well as scholarly, relevance.[59] Although this is not something that can be demonstrated with any kind of hard evidence, it seems reasonable to assume that, towards the end of the early modern period, the causes of inequality between human beings—both political *and* economic[60]—excited the interest of philosophers like Rousseau because actual inequality had become so high that it was difficult to tolerate.

Along the same lines, it is also possible (and equally contentious) to interpret the onset of the French Revolution, a few decades later, as numbering economic inequality among its (co-)causes, whilst acknowledging that its call for 'equality' was, primarily, a call for equal political rights. Without entering the complex debate about the origins of the French Revolution, it is interesting to note that studies of today's societies have established that there is a positive correlation between high economic inequality and the tendency for social instability, possibly leading to open revolt. This is also the result of the spread of notions of equality and justice that involve the economic sphere (if only in terms of requiring a 'just' society to ensure equality of opportunities) and is something that we should keep in mind when considering that in many parts of the West, wealth inequality, although still below the historical maximum reached on the eve of World War I, is now close to the highest levels documented for the last hundred years or so.[61]

As argued above, a society will tend to become more aware and more critical of inequality when economic disparities become larger. But we must also consider that our historical evidence suggests that, all other things being equal, performing specific functions that could reasonably be considered to be in the interest of the collectivity helped to attenuate the perception of high inequality levels in general and of the presence within the community of exceedingly rich individuals in particular. This is precisely what happened in the fifteenth century, paving the way for a further rise in economic (and political) power of many a European wealth dynasty. The functions that the rich claimed for themselves during the fifteenth century continued to be fulfilled until the end of the nineteenth, but at the turn of the twentieth century, the function of saving in the interest of the collectivity not only became increasingly difficult in practice, given the unprecedented size of modern economies, but was resented by the public as it revealed a capacity to influence the overall functioning of states and societies that seemed at odds with democratic institutions. During the 1907 crisis, J. P. Morgan was both applauded as a hero for having prevented the worst and criticized because he had the kind of hold over the national finances necessary to do so. The whole situation appears even more paradoxical if we understand that the extreme concentration of wealth in very few hands was a requirement for continuing to allow a rich person to perform this function in the modern era.

From this point of view, one might expect the rich to have encountered less criticism during the most recent financial crisis, that of 2007–8, precisely because that crisis was contained by 'public' institutional action and not, or only marginally, by private individual initiative. And yet, when considering for example the large-scale protests of the Occupy Wall Street movement, the opposite seems to have happened. From a long-term perspective, this is not surprising given that the crisis revealed that the super-rich, and especially those who had built their fortunes in finance, were no longer socially useful 'barns of money', which, once again, raised an issue about their legitimate existence. The situation was only made worse by the fact that *finance per se*, as a path towards wealth, has always been troubling to Western societies. The actions (and inactions) of the rich during a number of recent crises will be discussed further in chapter 11. But to anticipate one of this book's key conclusions, from the point of view of society at large, it appears that whatever they do, the rich are always in the wrong. If there is a solution to this social conundrum, Western civilization has yet to find it. While this is clear in the case of financial crises, arguably the rich encounter a similar paradox when they get themselves involved (or not) in politics. Before focusing on that, though, it is important to delve deeper into another traditional function of the rich, one which seems to have better stood the test of time: that of contributing to society by means of their magnificence, or of their generosity, including as patrons, benefactors and donors.

9

Patrons, Benefactors, Donors

ACROSS HISTORY, many among the rich have chosen to give back to society substantial portions of their accumulated fortunes. Already in Antiquity affluent individuals played an important role as patrons of the arts and sciences, a role which they have never abandoned. Equally clear is the continuity in their activity as benefactors, providing help to the weakest strata of society (the poor and destitute, the sick) and founding charities and care institutions, some of which have been functioning for centuries. In this way, the rich and the super-rich supplemented what was, until the modern age, a very deficient and in some historical contexts almost non-existent system of public welfare. In Western societies, with the development of the welfare state, the rich even began to move some of their charitable activities to other parts of the world, today especially to Africa. In recent times, organized movements encouraging the very affluent to donate have appeared, notably the 'Giving Pledge' initiative started by the Gates family and Warren Buffett in 2010. One of the objectives of these movements is to prevent the enrooting of economic inequalities that do not reflect individual merit.

Of all the different consequences that the presence of rich and especially of super-rich individuals can have for society, the spread of patronage and charity might seem to be the most uncontroversially positive. And yet, in this case too there are many ambiguities. As seen in the previous chapter, in medieval and early modern times the magnificence of the rich, which came to be understood as one of the main justifications for their very presence within society, also had clear political implications. It might be that the way in which preindustrial societies conceptualized magnificence as a characteristic of the prominent provides insight into today's societies as well, considering that the very nature of giving has not radically changed. Beyond continuities, however, new concerns about the activities of rich donors have emerged. In the United States and in countries with similar tax systems, many worry that donations might be used as a form of tax avoidance. This chapter ends by assessing this issue and by discussing the thorny question of whether spontaneous private giving is socially preferable to the taxation of patrimonies and inheritance and subsequent redistribution by public institutions.

Maecenatism and Patronage between Public Good and Personal Interest: From Antiquity to Early Modern Times

When thinking about maecenatism from a historical perspective, it seems unavoidable to begin with Antiquity: the very word comes from Maecenas, the Roman patron of the arts *par excellence* of Augustus' times. Perhaps more apposite, societies of the Classical Age seem to have conceptualized the public involvement of the rich, including by means of their conspicuous spending on patronage activities of various kinds, in a particularly clear way—so much so that arguably, when looking at our society in the mirror of Antiquity, we see features that we might not otherwise have noticed. This is maybe most clear when considering Greek society and culture. As an example, let us focus on a particularly explicit text, from Xenophon's *Oeconomicus* ('The Economist'), a Socratic dialogue that discusses the nature of wealth and good practices in household management. Socrates argues, addressing the rich Athenian businessman and landowner Critoboulos, that notwithstanding appearances Critoboulos is poorer than him, for these reasons:

> Why, first and foremost, I see you are called upon to offer many costly sacrifices, failing which, I take it, neither gods nor men would tolerate you; and, in the next place, you are bound to welcome numerous foreigners as guests, and to entertain them handsomely; thirdly, you must feast your fellow-citizens and ply them with all sorts of kindness, or else be cut adrift from your supporters. Furthermore, I perceive that even at present the state enjoins upon you various large contributions, such as the rearing of studs, the training of choruses, the superintendence of gymnastic schools, or consular duties, as patron of resident aliens, and so forth; while in the event of war you will, I am aware, have further obligations laid upon you in the shape of pay to carry on the trierarchy, ship money, and war taxes so onerous, you will find difficulty in supporting them. Remissness in respect of any of these charges will be visited upon you by the good citizens of Athens no less strictly than if they caught you stealing their own property.[1]

The point made by Xenophon, and expressed by Socrates in the dialogue, is clear: Athenian society expected a lot from its wealthiest citizens, including in terms of the patronage of choruses, schools and temples. Financial contributions expected from the rich covered numerous other areas and increased manyfold during crises such as wars when, among additional financial requests, they might be asked to outfit and maintain a trireme (trierarchy). The very acceptance of the rich within society depended on their willingness to contribute in many ways to the public good; otherwise 'neither gods nor men' would tolerate them. In the context of the Athenian democracy of Socrates' times (fifth century BCE), social repudiation might have had dramatic consequences, easily leading to exile or even a death sentence. This was also because a stingy rich man would have been 'cut adrift from [his] supporters'.[2]

As will be remembered from the previous chapter, in a preindustrial context the position of the rich, and especially of the super-rich, in society was far from implicitly assured. From this perspective, Xenophon's views resonate with the difficulties faced by the rich in becoming socially acceptable during the Middle Ages, although the social-cultural context was an entirely different one, and the medieval perception of the rich was deeply permeated by Christian theology. Another aspect that must be highlighted is that the 'giving' practices of wealthy Greeks were intrinsically political in nature. What has been reported for Athens also applies to other Greek city-states, as liturgies (which made the wealthy who accepted them responsible for certain public expenditures, like the *choregia* which required them to provide a chorus in a dramatic festival or the *gymnasiarchia* that made them responsible for a team competing in an athletic festival) and 'voluntary' contributions (*epidosis*) to raise funds were widely used. Notable *epidosis* included large-scale building projects; the new stadium built in circa 330 BCE outside Athens to host the four-yearly Panathenaic Games was funded in this way. While undoubtedly some wealthy individuals might have felt oppressed by such social obligations, with which they had to comply to avoid losing status among their peers but which might lead to financial ruin, in general this system of voluntary and semi-voluntary contributions was also instrumental in assuring that the economic elite kept its control over the political system. After all, as seen in chapter 8, according to the great disciple of Socrates, Plato, magnificence (*megaloprépeia*) was one of the characteristic virtues of the philosopher-king. Xenophon (also a disciple of Socrates) highlights the economic meaning of magnificence, which consists in achieving great things by means of conspicuous spending for the public good.[3]

If, in the Athenian democracy, the rich were motivated to engage in public patronage not only by the prospect of political power but also by the potential threat to their personal security when they failed to meet social expectations, in the much more stable, and socially conservative, political regime of the Roman Republic the connection between the willingness to sustain substantial expenditures for the public and one's political ambitions was even clearer. Cicero, the famous politician and orator, in the *De Officiis* ('On Duties') recommends that a wealthy man should be cautious in giving as he could quickly exhaust his resources, but at the same time, he argues that when appropriate, the rich should show an adequate degree of generosity (*liberalitas*), especially if they want to pursue a political career which could be fatally damaged by even a suspicion of miserliness. The example of Mamercus, a very wealthy man who refused the aedileship (a public charge which would have subjected him to the expectation of paying for public festivals and games) and, as a consequence, was defeated when running for the consulship, is contrasted with that of Publius Crassus (the son of the triumvir Marcus Licinius Crassus), a young politician whom Cicero held in high esteem. During his aedileship, Crassus had given splendid games and thus had managed to increase his support and to expand his political clout—for the public good, as (according to Cicero) he was a virtuous man.[4] While Cicero justified spending on organizing games, banquets, gladiatorial shows and similar frivolities, if this was demanded by the people and if it was useful to advance the career of an honest politician, he believed that other forms of giving for the public benefit, especially major infrastructure works like walls, docks, harbours or aqueducts, were much worthier of praise. Public improvements of this kind would, as he wrote, 'win us greater gratitude with posterity.'[5]

With the end of the Republic and the establishment of the Roman Principate by Augustus, whose reign began in 27 BCE, an ability and a willingness to do (and to pay for) great deeds, that is, to show magnificence, continued to be important for building a public career in the imperial system. A good example is that of Herodes Atticus (101–77 CE), a senator of the Antonine period and scion of an immensely wealthy Athenian family who rose to consular status. During his career, he distinguished himself as the patron of many public works (theatres, baths, aqueducts and so on) in Italy and in Greece, including a radical renovation of the Panathenaic Stadium in Athens, rebuilt in marble and expanded to a capacity of 50,000 seats. A distinguished philosopher and a famous orator himself, Herodes Atticus was a patron of the arts and letters. Indeed, this form of patronage might have become stronger and more widespread in imperial compared to republican times. What is certain is that the onset of the Empire coincided with the period of activity of Maecenas (68 BCE–8 BCE), a companion of Augustus and possibly the greatest patron of literature in Western history: his circle included poets like Virgil, Horace and Propertius and the historian Livy. A descendant of the Cilnii, a princely Etruscan family from Arretium (nowadays Arezzo in Tuscany), he had inherited substantial wealth but was also well-known as a capable administrator. According to many, he acted, in agreement with Augustus, as a sort of unofficial imperial minister of culture, in charge of producing propaganda in support of the new political regime. This view, however, has also been challenged, as there is no evidence that Maecenas explicitly required anything from the artists in his circle, whom he treated more as friends (*amici*) than as clients. Indeed, they might have been attracted to him because they shared similar views, including regarding politics. This said, the fact remains that the rise of the Principate was accompanied by widespread support from artists of various kinds, and many among them gravitated to Maecenas; the Roman concept of *amicitia* also involved an exchange of services; and Maecenas, notwithstanding some hypothesized disagreements with Augustus, always remained close to him, to the point of nominating the prince as his universal heir.[6]

In many ways, public patronage during Roman times was seen as a model in medieval Europe, including when, during the Renaissance, the ancient concept of magnificence was recalled and adapted to provide a justification of sorts for the presence in society, and even for the new political aspirations, of an economic elite increasingly distant from their fellow citizens on account of their wealth accumulated in trade, industry and finance. As seen in chapter 8, it was transparent in late medieval times that the magnificence of the rich, from which the collectivity could benefit greatly, was nonetheless a feature characteristic of those who also harboured the ambition to politically lead that collectivity. A perfect example is Cosimo the Elder who, according to the Italian writer of the late fifteenth century Giovanni Pontano, stood out for having been the first in his age to show magnificence on a scale comparable to the Romans, building marvellous palaces and churches and founding libraries, and at the same time, and partly because of his magnificence, becoming the de facto ruler of Florence.[7]

Beyond the desire to acquire social acceptance and to build up political support, the late medieval rich had another strong motivation to donate: the accrual of spiritual benefits. Affluence in itself was considered potentially sinful, and the ways in which it had been accumulated entailed many additional spiritual risks, surely in the case of finance but also, at least according to theologians like St Thomas Aquinas, in that of large-scale trade.[8] This led to substantial charity and the patronage of religious institutions in old age, as well as to generous bequests for the same purposes. Cosimo the Elder is, again, an excellent example,[9] as is Francesco di Marco Datini who, as will be remembered, bequeathed the bulk of his patrimony to charity and even provided for the establishment of the first specialized orphanage for abandoned children in Western history, the *Spedale degli Innocenti* of Florence. Its construction, which began in 1419, was based on plans by the famous architect Filippo Brunelleschi. The *Spedale degli Innocenti* is one of the earliest examples of Renaissance architecture and is also a good example of the frequent intertwining of charity and patronage of the arts.

Charity and the patronage of religious institutions did not only answer a spiritual need. Insofar as being charitable corresponded to the behaviour expected from the 'good merchant', giving was instrumental in creating the conditions for acquiring status and for being admitted into the social, political *and economic* elite. Consequently, this kind of charity and patronage can *also* be conceptualized as an investment aimed at generating future returns (without negating the advantages to the poor and other beneficiaries).[10] A good example is that of Donato Ferrario, a Milanese merchant active in the early fifteenth century. Originally from the rural village of Pantigliate, in Milan he was a *homo novus* (a 'new man') and, as such, his social and economic ascent was not without difficulties. He was, however, successful, and his social promotion was completed and made clear and visible to the community by the establishment in 1429 of a pious foundation, the *Scuola della Divinità di Tutti i Santi* (School of Divinity of All Saints), whose statutory objective was to distribute alms to the city's poor. Ferrario himself had laid down the charity statute, and indeed, he did not relinquish the administration of the endowment and particularly of the real estate. Not only did he have a dominant position on the management board composed of well-respected men (all chosen by him), but he also established that even after his death the prior and two members of the board had to be selected from within the Ferrario family.

As argued by Todeschini, by founding his *Scuola* Ferrario was demonstrating a willingness 'to transform his wealth in a public wealth', following a model that had at its root the way in which religious institutions, such as churches or monasteries, 'owned' their patrimonies: not as personal property of the clergy, but (at least in principle) as the collective property of all Christians that was simply administered by the clergy.[11] And yet, by maintaining a substantial degree of (hereditary) control over the foundation, Ferrario also maintained an ability to leverage his 'public' wealth to obtain private gains, be they status, political power or additional business opportunities. The fact that, from 1435, the Duke of Milan, Filippo Maria Visconti, exempted the *Scuola* from paying tax upon the goods meant to be distributed to the poor can undoubtedly be seen (as most scholars do) as recognition of the good deeds done by the foundation. At the same time, though, it might have increased the economic appeal, for Ferrario and his lineage, of safely moving more wealth to the foundation's coffers, which Ferrario did by including an additional bequest in his will.[12]

Across Europe, pious foundations established by rich merchants multiplied during the fifteenth and sixteenth centuries and in many instances adopted institutional arrangements similar to those described above for the *Scuola della Divinità di Tutti i Santi*, namely by allowing the founder and his or her descendants to maintain some sort of control over the endowment. Practices of this kind continued to be used in the following centuries, and indeed, they are still used today. Although many among the donors were certainly motivated by the best intentions, the fact remains that control over foundations was a valuable resource in itself and still is. As modern-day sociologists argue, control over foundations of various kinds is a crucial component of the institutional power of the elite which, according to them, dominates America.[13]

While fifteenth-century charity and religious patronage perpetuated a tradition of giving that can be traced back to at least the twelfth century, it changed its colours, reflecting deeper social and cultural change.[14] According to Cohn, 'The late Renaissance . . . assumed . . . an entirely different posture on ecclesiastical charities . . . with testators resting their futures less with the soul and more with the preservation of landed estates and family names.'[15] As part of this process, the indiscriminate redistribution of substantial portions of one's wealth to the poor (which, in wills, took the shape of formulaic demands to sell off estates), a practice which had been frequent in earlier periods, from the second half of the fifteenth century had almost vanished. Instead, religious bequests became increasingly more specific, conditional and basically self-interested, as with the foundation of family chapels in well-known churches. This practice, which in many places, for example the city of Siena in Tuscany, seems to have been extremely rare until the early fifteenth century, by the turn of the sixteenth had become common for wealthy families. In this way, they tried to accumulate honours to ensure the continued prestige of their lineage. This development seems to have gone hand in hand with the increasing self-confidence and political power of the rich who, by then, had finally found a clear place in society, a place which, as seen in chapter 8 and in explicit ideological connection with the celebrated tradition of Antiquity discussed above, was defined by their magnificence and by their very financial resources, upon which the community could rely (at least in principle) in times of crisis.

Without doubt, their activities as patrons and benefactors served the private interests of the medieval and early modern rich. Nonetheless, it cannot be denied that the fruits of their magnificence have often truly benefited many through the ages. This is clearly the case with charitable institutions—the *Casa del Ceppo dei poveri*, another charity founded by Francesco Datini in 1410 to assist the poor in the city of Prato, has remained in operation until today—but also of more 'private' endeavours. We could not enjoy, in the way that we can today, sailing along the Canal Grande of Venice or walking the streets of the booming capital cities of early modern Europe, like Madrid in Spain, Paris in France or Turin in Italy, without benefiting aesthetically from the efforts of the preindustrial rich to display their magnificence while competing to increase the splendour of their urban palaces. So in a sense it is true, as fifteenth-century authors like Bracciolini or Pontano argued, that by building their palaces, their fountains and their gardens the rich were making the city splendid for the (incidental) benefit of the collectivity.[16]

At its best, preindustrial patronage also allowed the enlightened rich to apply their entrepreneurial attitude and propensity for innovation to alleviate the emerging plights of their times, in a period when public welfare was very limited and social spending did not absorb more than a semi-symbolic share of public budgets. In the case of the Republic of Venice, for example, social expenditure of any kind accounted for no more than 0.5 per cent of the yearly budget of the central state from the sixteenth until the mid-eighteenth century.[17] At the aggregate level, private charity and patronage did not do much to alter these serious constraints on social spending: according to a recent estimate, 'direct bequests' for poor relief broadly meant were of the order of 0.2 per cent of GDP in England circa 1500, to which we can add some 'guesstimates' for central-northern Italy (0.1% of GDP circa 1430, 0.2% circa 1640) and the western Netherlands (0.1% circa 1530, 0.3% circa 1760).[18] And yet, there is no denying that, locally, some of the institutions set up by rich donors made a difference for many among the poor.

The aforementioned *Casa del Ceppo dei poveri* funded by Francesco Datini is a good example. Another is the so-called *Fuggerei* (literally, 'the place of Fugger'), a social housing complex established by Jacob Fugger 'The Rich' in

1521 in the German city of Augsburg. At a time when the poorest strata of urban populations often lived in overcrowded, unhealthy and unsafe houses, in filthy quarters which were the focus of epidemics of terrible infectious diseases, Fugger created a social settlement on an unprecedented scale, able to house more than 500 people divided into 52 houses (each hosting a couple of family units: one per floor) which, while simple, were built to a high standard of construction. The settlement itself was similar to a city within a city, surrounded by a wall (both to increase safety and to impose discipline on the residents, who were subject to a curfew and the risk of a fine) and equipped with a hospital for the sick.

Fugger set some rules for the residents of the complex. Firstly, they were not housed for free but paid a heavily subsidized rent of one guilder per year (one-quarter of the market rent), corresponding to about eighteen to nineteen daily wages for an unskilled worker.[19] Additionally, beggars were not allowed in, and the residents could not accept alms from other institutions. Finally, all residents had to say prayers for Jacob Fugger, his mother and his nephews. The latter condition was not unusual at the time, and surely Fugger the Catholic had reason to believe that he might need spiritual help to enter Heaven. The first two conditions, however, betray a specific ideology of Fugger the Rich: one which valued thrift and 'merit' (without a job, tenants could not have afforded to pay even the *Fuggerei*'s subsidized rent) and at the same time considered extreme poverty the consequence of some sort of moral failure. As similar views continue to be shared by some of the rich, it would be unfair to criticize Fugger for being, essentially, a man of his time (in many parts of sixteenth-century Europe, laws and regulations were spreading which established clear distinctions between the 'worthy' and the 'unworthy' poor). It is maybe more proper to praise his vision instead. It is true that by building his social houses Jacob Fugger's aim was to portray himself as a good and virtuous merchant, generous and charitable, and thus silence his enemies who described him as a rapacious profiteer and usurer. And yet, he could easily have donated to the poor through more traditional institutions, even ones he had founded himself. Instead, he set out to create something new, addressing a growing social issue with a solution that others, across the centuries, came to imitate. Well-endowed by the founder (the original deposit amounted to 10,000 guilders, or 2.75 tonnes of silver), the *Fuggerei* continues to operate to this day, as a residence for needy elderly people, and is considered to be the oldest surviving social settlement in Europe. And to this day, one of Fugger's descendants continues to preside over the foundation.[20]

Benefactors and Philanthropists of the Industrial Age

The rich continued to donate throughout the early modern period, although probably with less intensity than during the Middle Ages. It has been argued that in the parts of Europe which joined the Reformation, patronage and philanthropy, especially of the religious kind, declined with the waning of the idea that good deeds could provide spiritual benefits, such as a shorter time spent in Purgatory. This was the case in England, while for the Protestant areas of Germany there is evidence of a decline in private giving for the benefit of the needy, leading to a higher prevalence of poverty.[21] The matter, however, remains markedly under-studied. What is more, differences between European regions grounded in religious divides should not make us lose sight of a general development across the West: as the social position of the rich became more assured, their participation in the ruling elite unchallenged (or almost) and their presence within the community unquestioned, they also felt less and less obliged to give part of their wealth back to society. In other words, when the very existence of the rich no longer needed to be justified by their willingness to convert private wealth into public benefit, their donations came to be increasingly characterized and perceived as shows of generosity pure and simple. As will be remembered from chapter 8, this corresponds to the crucial shift from the idea of magnificence to that of munificence. While magnificence entails a sense of responsibility on the part of the rich towards society coupled with the claim to have the standing (economic and moral) to rule, munificence refers to free acts of generosity, with nothing owed by the rich and nothing required in exchange. While this distinction appears to be clear, there is reason to wonder whether in reality modern patronage and philanthropy continue to *also* be used to claim a public role and influence, including political influence, just as during the Classical Age and medieval times, but in a much less transparent way.

Before discussing this issue further, let us consider some general characteristics of the benefactors and philanthropists of the Industrial Age. A first point to make is that 'philanthropy', in its current meaning and notwithstanding the Greek origins of the word (which literally means 'love of mankind'), is a concept that emerged during the late eighteenth century and developed fully only from the nineteenth century. The foundation of the *Société Philanthropique* in Paris in 1780 is of particular import, as in its 1787 manifesto it declared that philanthropy was a civic duty, not a religious necessity. In 1788 Robert Young, inspired by the Parisian example, founded the Philanthropic Society of

London which focused on helping young criminals or the sons of convicted felons to stay on the path towards an honest life.[22] Philanthropy was closely related to earlier patronage, charity and magnificence, but it also had new features. Some point to its more systematic character compared to preindustrial charity, but this is questionable: as we have seen, medieval and early modern charity and patronage could be organized in highly systematic and 'entrepreneurial' ways, even making recourse to institutional arrangements, like foundations ruled by the donors and their descendants, which indeed look quite 'modern'. The real divide lies in the motivation of the donor: if he or she expects something in return, even simple influence or an increase in status, he or she could qualify as a benefactor (due to the 'good' done to others) but not as a philanthropist. As argued by Harvey, Maclean and Suddaby, 'philanthropists invest their own resources in causes they believe will benefit others and that yield no direct benefit to themselves or their families. . . . These acts of generosity bring satisfactions and rewards, which, though intangible and experienced subjectively, enrich the lives of philanthropists'.[23] More generally, the word philanthropy involves a 'normative dimension of benevolence' which was introduced, in modern English, by Samuel Johnson in his *Dictionary of the English Language* of 1755 and which continues to be perceived to this day.[24] Indeed, especially in modern American elite culture, there is a widespread belief that, for those who enjoy a privileged position, philanthropy is an obligation.[25]

The fact that *in theory* philanthropists do not expect any material (or spiritual) benefit from their benevolent actions does not mean that *in practice* they do not receive anything, by design or otherwise. This brings us back to the opening of this section and to the consideration that, compared to preindustrial times, *all* modern patronage and charity tend to be presented and perceived as generosity. This is, surely, the view that transpires from Carnegie's *Gospel of Wealth* (1889). Carnegie himself is the best example of nineteenth-century American entrepreneurial philanthropy, as throughout his life he donated over 350 million dollars (10.2 billion dollars 2020). Over one-third of this sum went to the Carnegie Corporation of New York, established in 1911 to support higher education and research. The rest was used to found libraries and to establish a long list of benevolent institutions with various purposes across the United States and the British Empire, for example the Carnegie Trust for the Universities of Scotland and the Carnegie Institute of Technology, which constitutes the original nucleus of today's Carnegie Mellon University in Pittsburgh.[26] While the scale of his giving was exceptional—Carnegie donated most of his fortune—he was certainly not the only, or the first, rich or super-rich entrepreneur of the Industrial Age to give on a large scale. In earlier chapters, we have encountered other socially conscious entrepreneurs, like Wedgwood in England and Solvay in Belgium. Both were particularly concerned with the living conditions and general welfare of their workers so that, like Jacob Fugger centuries before them, they invested heavily in social housing, creating model villages close to their factories. Solvay's achievements in this regard are particularly impressive as, given the multinational character of his company, 'Solvay villages' are found across the West, for example in Syracuse (United States), in Lieres (Spain) and in Rosignano Marittimo (Italy). In their time, they stood out for guaranteeing to all residents minimum conditions which they could only have dreamed of in another setting, as well as a variety of services (in 1902, the Syracuse village also became the beneficiary of a Carnegie Library).

Additional examples of industrial-age philanthropy and patronage abound, as the practice was quite widespread. Looking for example at higher education, while the United States clearly stands out for the large number of privately funded universities, these were far from unknown in Europe.[27] In England in 1879 Thomas Holloway, a pharmaceutical entrepreneur who made a fortune producing and aggressively marketing his patented 'Holloway's Universal Family Ointment' as a (supposed) remedy for a long series of ailments, founded Royal Holloway College near London to educate young women. This was a controversial endeavour for the period (reportedly, Thomas had been inspired to take this step by his deceased wife, Jane Pearce Driver, and the college was founded in her memory), but also another example of how private patronage at its best can break new ground and provide guidance for future public investment. In Italy in 1902, Ferdinando Bocconi, a wealthy merchant of relatively modest origins (he had initiated his career as a street peddler of fabrics) whose key innovation was to introduce, first to Milan (in 1877) and then to other Italian cities, a new model of mass distribution of ready-made suits and clothes based on large department stores in the new Parisian and London fashion founded Bocconi University. The institution was named after Ferdinando's son, Luigi, who had died in the Italian colonial defeat of Adua in 1896, and was aimed at promoting higher education in business and trade. In this case too, private patronage was ahead of its time, as Bocconi University was the first in Italy to provide a formal degree in these subjects.[28]

During the nineteenth and early twentieth centuries, as the Industrial Revolution progressed, the need to provide better education both to the masses and the elite was acutely felt by many entrepreneurial philanthropists. At the same time, the rich continued to donate to more traditional sectors, such as hospitals and institutions for caring for the poor, orphans and the elderly (before founding his college, Thomas Holloway had established a model sanatorium to treat the mentally ill in a pleasant location in Surrey). And the public could also become the ultimate beneficiary of at least some of their conspicuous consumption habits, to use Veblen's definition. Many art collections today displayed in museums originate from this period. Again, this is particularly apparent in the case of the United States, due to the exceptionally large fortunes that blossomed in late nineteenth-century America. J. P. Morgan was a particularly passionate collector, relying upon a network of agents in European cities like Antwerp, Paris, Rome and Vienna to acquire drawings, paintings, illuminated manuscripts and other works of art which he displayed mostly in his house in London and his private library in New York. The latter became a museum in 1924, established by J. P. Morgan's son as a memorial for his father. Another important part of the original collection belongs today to the Metropolitan Museum of Art, again in New York, which J. P. Morgan contributed to founding in 1870, had been a trustee of and finally presided over from 1904 until his death in 1913.[29]

For all their ability to improve the conditions of the needy and more generally to provide the public with various benefits, nineteenth- and early twentieth-century donors and philanthropists did not escape criticism, which became stronger the larger the scale of their patronage. Thorstein Veblen was particularly harsh towards them, arguing that activities such as collecting art or becoming involved in charity tended to acquire a competitive character and that the ultimate aim of the patrons was to demonstrate their pecuniary success: 'The initial motive of furthering the facility of life in these [lower] classes comes gradually to be an ostensible motive only.'[30] Even when building asylums or hospitals, the funds set apart for this purpose tended to be diverted towards what Veblen called 'honorific waste', meaning that the structures were built according to the aesthetic principles of the leisure class, with excessive expenditure and without much consideration for their eventual effectiveness. While undoubtedly Veblen's views were quite extreme in this regard, many modern commentators have agreed that the large-scale patronage and giving of the time cannot be understood simply as generosity. Some have passed judgements as severe as Veblen's, arguing for example that philanthropy, as it was practised by robber barons, amounted to 'reputation laundering on a massive scale.'[31] Many others have provided substantial, but more circumscribed criticism, highlighting the paternalistic, and ultimately the authoritarian, way in which wealthy donors ran their campaigns for social reform and managed their foundations.[32] Even Carnegie has been accused of egotism, although there is also clear evidence that his focus on the establishment of educational institutions was grounded in his childhood experience, when his access to books was constrained by his family's poverty and by the lack of free libraries in his native Scotland.[33]

Historian Frederic C. Jaher, in a comparative study of the behaviour of the nineteenth-century urban elites of New York and Boston, was more lenient towards the rich, noticing that their patronage had a positive impact upon society:

> The historical function of urban aristocracies has not been to reproduce great minds but to support them. Patronage is the real test of cultural quality in the patriciate. Boston's great cultural and intellectual institutions, The North American Review, the Boston Museum of Fine Arts, the Boston Symphony Orchestra, and Harvard University, were Brahmin-founded or -financed or -directed.[34]

At the same time, however, Jaher argued that overall, these activities absorbed only a small part of the social time and expenditure of the wealth elite, especially in New York where, during the nineteenth century, cultural institutions, creative artists and patrons were scarcer than in Boston. Indeed, an exploration of the 1882–3 social season in Manhattan revealed 849 events (marriages excluded) mentioned by the *Tribune*; of these, only 4 per cent had been organized for charitable purposes, and just about 12 per cent had some sort of cultural content. These percentages would grow a little by the 1900 season, to about 8 per cent and 13 per cent respectively, but they remained minimal. Additionally, most members of the Four Hundred's social milieu, and especially the most worldly, were keener on building family dynasties than on bequeathing their fortunes to worthy endeavours. William B. Astor, heir to one of the main merchant families of Manhattan and husband of the well-known socialite Caroline Schermerhorn Astor, bequeathed just 0.3 per cent of his fortune to public service organizations. William H. Vanderbilt, the railroad entrepreneur and husband to another of the main socialites of the time, Alva Erskine Smith Vanderbilt, bequeathed to various philanthropic institutions just 0.75 per cent of his patrimony. These rates appear to have been typical of New York's Four Hundred.[35]

This evidence for nineteenth-century America reminds us of two important facts. First, exceptional cases like that of Carnegie should not make us forget that, for the vast majority of the rich and the very rich, substantial patronage and giving was very far from their main objective (a point which has also been made for other parts of the West, like Britain[36]). Indeed, Carnegie's behaviour, had it been widespread, would have been incompatible with the observed reality of the enrooting of many wealthy dynasties, a development which has been discussed in previous chapters. Second, direct involvement in institutions for the public good—whether cultural, charitable or other—which led to essentially *controlling* them, often in a hereditary or almost-hereditary way, was crucial to building institutional power and influence, as argued by many sociologists (see the earlier section). This kind of institutional power could, and still can, also lead to a further expansion of economic power, in a virtuous circle of which the 'generous' donors are in fact the main beneficiaries: 'Philanthropy at scale brings with it the right to call the shots in the domains of the cultural, social, and political as well as the economic and, as such, is seen by critics as profoundly undemocratic.'[37]

Beyond the possible economic benefits of patronage, there are also potential political benefits that risk altering the way in which Western political systems work, and this is why modern patronage and philanthropy could be characterized as 'undemocratic', leading to considerable concern today as is discussed further in the next section. For now, it seems proper to conclude the discussion of Industrial Age patronage by recalling a final episode, in which the suspicion of political interests in large-scale charity became the object of intense public debate. In 1906 John D. Rockefeller, the great oil magnate, endowed the newly established Rockefeller Foundation with the enormous sum of 50 million dollars (about 1.5 billion 2020 dollars). This was meant to be a sort of perpetual charitable trust with a general purpose: the statutory objectives were so broad as to basically allow the trustees to pursue any mission that they might deem worthy. The original handpicked trustees were Rockefeller's own son and son-in-law and Frederick T. Gates, a former Baptist minister who had been acting as Rockefeller's 'charity advisor' from as early as 1891, so in practice, directly *and* indirectly, John D. Rockefeller would have retained full control over the foundation and its resources.

Rockefeller, however, was faced with a problem. Given the encompassing and, indeed, the global ambition of the foundation, he aspired to avoid being hindered by the regulations applied by state legislatures. So, following Gates' advice, he sought a charter (formal permission to incorporate, without which the foundation would have been unable to operate) directly from the U.S. Congress. This was unprecedented, as was the sheer size of the foundation and its lack of a specific focus beyond the general (and laudable) aim of trying to address the roots of social problems, as opposed to simply alleviating their consequences. Rockefeller's plans immediately met with strong political opposition in Washington. No small part of this came from prejudice and distaste for Rockefeller and the supposedly ruthless ways in which he had amassed his wealth. More interesting are the objections made to the very idea of a general-purpose foundation on such a scale. For example, Senator Frank Walsh, who chaired the Industrial Relations Commission, explicitly stated that 'the huge philanthropic trusts, known as foundations, appear to be a menace to the welfare of society.'[38] Many witnesses called to testify in front of the Commission expressed concerns about whether institutions of this kind were compatible with a democratic society, because in their basically free and substantially unaccountable action, foundations could tip the political balance in whichever direction they wanted, promoting their desired policies and undermining the very notion of political equality.

After years of lobbying and rewriting the statute in order to ensure some public scrutiny of the foundation's activities and to contain its size (its assets were never to exceed a cap of 100 million dollars or about 3 billion in 2020 dollars) and duration (the foundation was to spend all of its principal within 50 years of incorporation), in 1913 Rockefeller managed to get the bill approved by the House of Representatives—but not by the Senate. He had then to accept a defeat, of sorts: in the same year he turned to the New York state legislature and persuaded it to approve the bill in its original form, removing all the amendments that had been introduced to protect the public from the foundation's feared political interference. According to political scientist Rob Reich, with hindsight, it might be that the U.S. Senate had made a serious mistake:

> Had the U.S. Senate passed the House bill to approve the Rockefeller Foundation, it would have created a legal template for the institutional design of foundations with limits on size and time and provisions for clear public oversight. The balance between plutocratic voice and democratic voice in the operation of American foundations would have been struck much differently.[39]

While this issue is particularly relevant to the United States, where foundations of this kind have become exceptionally prevalent, similar concerns are ubiquitous across the West today, in part because, according to their critics, foundations have become instrumental to the tax avoidance strategies of the richest citizens, leading to a significant downsizing of the resources available to democratic governments.[40]

A Modern Dilemma: To Donate or to Pay Tax?

There is today a growing concern that for at least some among the rich and super-rich, giving is simply a means of eluding taxation, exploiting privileged fiscal treatment while maintaining de facto control over the assets that they have 'donated'. It would surely be wrong to believe that this is the sole motivation of patrons, and indeed, historical experience strongly supports the view that large-scale patronage can exist even without fiscal incentives. While it might be that some private economic advantages were obtained from patronage even in medieval and early modern times (remember the fiscal exemptions granted to some charities by the fourteenth-century Dukes of Milan), by the nineteenth century the situation remained deeply different from that of at least some modern-day Western countries. The best researched case is, again, that of the United States, where, notwithstanding the very substantial scale of patronage and giving, at the turn of the twentieth century neither private individuals nor corporations enjoyed any fiscal incentive to donate. Indeed, at that time, inheritance taxes were more punishing towards bequests in favour of 'strangers in blood' (which included charities and other institutions) than to one's relations.[41] Only from 1917 did it become possible for American citizens to deduct donations from their taxable income. After that, the relative intensity of donations has tended to show an inverse correlation with the top marginal rate of income tax, which suggests that at a certain point eluding taxation did become an important motivation for many donors (who consequently, based on the definition introduced previously, could no longer be properly classified as 'philanthropists').[42] Although the long-term tendencies in donation are less well-known for European countries, today the overall structure of fiscal incentives is fairly similar across Western countries, as revealed by a recent study by the OECD, and so are the concerns about the potential for unscrupulous tax avoidance or even for tax evasion.[43]

There are many reasons to be critical of the practice of using donations to elude taxation. First, in all instances when the donor retains, in practice, control over the assets or otherwise gains some substantial economic and/or political benefit from his or her patronage, giving becomes indistinguishable from the acquisition of tax-free goods and services, and any claim to having shown generosity and virtue becomes pure hypocrisy. Second, the unpaid taxes lead, at least in principle, to the reduced ability of the public to provide services and other benefits to society as a whole, which seems to run contrary to what is supposed to be the ultimate aim of philanthropy (improving the wellbeing of other human beings). Both of these aspects require further discussion.

Regarding the first point, the direct involvement of the donors and their families in foundations, donor-advised funds and other beneficiary institutions is clearly a complex and very controversial topic.[44] On the one hand, it seems natural that a donor who believes they have substantial coordination and management skills might wish to also contribute some of his or her effort and time as a means of maximizing the social returns from the gift. The Hungarian-born financier George Soros has been particularly explicit in highlighting his own value to the Open Society Foundations network that he set up around the world in the 1990s:

> What will be missing when I am gone is the entrepreneurial and innovative spirit that has characterized the Open Society Foundations. . . . I was able to move fast and take big risks. The governing board that will succeed me will not be able to follow my example; it will be weighed down by fiduciary responsibilities. Some of its members will try to be faithful to the founder's intentions; others will be risk averse; but the founder is anything but risk averse.[45]

On the other hand, however, retaining some sort of control over the donated assets exposes the donor to substantial criticism. First, and especially in those cases when a specific provision is made to ensure the continued presence of family members on the managing boards of charities and other institutions after the death or retirement of the original donor, there are no guarantees that future generations will possess any of the (real or supposed) qualities of the founder. Second, this practice arouses considerable suspicion about the real motivation and the ultimate aim of the donors themselves: a problem already encountered by John D. Rockefeller at the turn of the twentieth century (see the earlier section). But even when a donor's motivations are entirely sincere and no economic or political advantage is expected in return, his or her involvement with the management of the donated assets can be seen as the manifestation of an arrogant and paternalistic attitude. This charge has been levied repeatedly against foundations, including some of those endowed with more resources like the Bill and Melinda Gates Foundation.[46] But there is more: beyond being paternalistic, the involvement of the donor can ultimately be understood as the expression of an un-democratic attitude. Many donors may not trust any-body else, and especially not governments, to decide what to do with the re-sources that they are willing to set aside for philanthropic ends.[47] This also leads them to resist any attempt to subject the activities of foundations to public scrutiny. So, foundations end up being unaccountable and opaque in-stitutions, which however can exert an important influence on society and also benefit from public support in the form of fiscal advantages (usually the ex-emption of their income from taxation or preferential VAT treatment[48]). This is one key reason why, according to political scientist Rob Reich, they consti-tute 'institutional oddities' in democratic societies and require substantial reform, for example towards greater transparency, in order to make them 'sup-portive of rather than injurious to democracy'.[49]

The anti-government stance of many a rich donor, especially but not exclu-sively in the United States,[50] and the perception that money donated is freely 'given' while tax money is forcefully 'taken away',[51] leads us back to the second troubling feature of giving in order to avoid taxation: the practice tends to starve public institutions of resources that they might otherwise use to reach democratically identified objectives. To this, it could be objected that if private patronage and charity can provide the same benefits to the public, and pos-sibly with greater effectiveness and a more efficient use of resources, there is no reason to fear. And yet, throughout history, we have many examples that show that societies whose members grow increasingly reliant upon the good-will of the rich also tend to become economically and socially sclerotic. This is not because their individual members become addicted to receiving free support but because large strata of society come to be structurally deprived of the means and the general conditions that might have allowed them to im-prove their status. A good example is that of the Republic of Venice where, from the fifteenth to the eighteenth centuries, wealth became increasingly more concentrated and society became ever more polarized between a few extremely affluent individuals and families and a large body of relatively poor ones, with a tendency towards the waning of the middling groups. As will be seen in chapter 10, this was largely the outcome of a regressive fiscal system kept in place for centuries by the ruling elite. And yet, as the Republic remained politically very stable throughout the period, it is clear that an increasing part of the resources accumulated at the top had to trickle down somehow, just to keep the poorest strata above the level of subsistence.[52]

Given that public welfare expenditure was extremely limited at the time (see the opening section of this chapter), systematic donations by the rich surely played a crucial role. This happened, for example, through the system of private confraternities called *Scuole*, and there is some evidence that the amount of resources that they spent to benefit the poorest strata increased significantly from at least the mid-sixteenth century.[53] However,

> [e]ven if private charity helped to reduce the imbalances generated by the fiscal system . . . , surely it stopped a long way from providing real equality of opportunities to the poorest strata of society. Additionally, this kind of private redistribution tended to make the poor dependent on the rich, a fact which made social structures more resilient, but not, as it seems, in the sense of helping to achieve in time a better and more open society for all.[54]

Had the rich been less generous, Venetian society would probably have quickly grown socially and politically unstable. This is paradoxical because arguably, especially from the turn of the eighteenth century, the continued stability, while it allowed the old patrician families to maintain their grip on state government with the placid support of the lower strata, was instrumental in locking the Republic into a path clearly orientated towards becoming a social and economic backwater because it prevented new, and potentially more dynamic, economic forces from having a stronger influence on policy-making. This path of decline might have been avoided, at least in part (there is no denying that the Republic was facing many difficulties), had social tensions triggered a period of greater political openness and even just moderate economic reforms.

Once again, looking at ourselves in the mirror of preindustrial societies leads to some troubling questions. In general, it seems clear that a society whose public institutions are unable to ensure decent conditions for all of its citizens and relies instead on private contributions is also a society which is subjecting itself to the goodwill of its wealthiest components. Such goodwill cannot be presumed to be everlasting, nor to come without a cost. Consequently, to answer our original question, taxation seems preferable to giving as a means to ensure social welfare. For modern Western societies, this is also advisable for strengthening democracy. As noted by sociologist Elisabeth Clemens, from the beginning of the great American democracy, 'Because the receiving, if not the giving, of gifts carried the risk of dependence and indebtedness, managing the coexistence of civic benevolence and democratic governance has been no simple task. . . . Giving may generate power relationships that are at odds with liberal democratic commitments to equality and individual self-sufficiency.'[55] This being said, a democratic society can obviously be expected to set taxation at whatever level the voters and their representatives see fit. In this context, one could say that the only thing that should be asked from the rich is not to violate the law and to pay their apportioned taxes, because fiscal incentives have themselves been introduced by the citizens' elected representatives. And yet, if we go back again to the concept of magnificence, it would be utterly naïve to presume that the rich, including by means of their patronage, do not influence the political process in a range of different ways, as seen in the next chapter.[56]

To conclude our discussion of modern-day patronage and giving, it seems necessary to briefly discuss the Giving Pledge, created in 2010 by Bill and Melinda Gates and Warren Buffett, which is arguably the most significant novelty in large-scale philanthropy of the early twenty-first century. The signatories of the pledge (a group originally composed only of super-rich Americans but which by now has acquired an international character) commit to divest the majority of their wealth for philanthropic aims, either during their lifetimes or in their wills. This is declared to be for moral reasons—as Bill Gates put it simply in 2021, 'I've always believed that if you're in a position to help somebody, you should do it'[57]—which places the Giving Pledge squarely within an American philanthropic and cultural tradition that has in Andrew Carnegie a major point of reference. As each 'pledger' pursues their philanthropic objectives independently from the others, any criticism regarding possible self-interest or benefit gained from giving should be judged on an individual basis. But at the same time, pledgers as a collectivity incur the aforementioned criticism of starving the public of resources, mostly by avoiding taxation on inheritance. Interestingly, Bill Gates has also been one of the relatively few American superrich to speak in defence of the taxation of inheritances, a position that he has in common with his father. So, to some degree, the erosion of the tax base of fiscal levies on inheritances can be considered an unintentional side-effect of the Giving Pledge. But there is also a darker side. [58]

Although in recent decades the tendency across Western countries has been to slash estate and inheritance taxes, for large patrimonies they remain substantial. For example, in the United States in 2021 the rate of the 'federal estate tax' was set at 40 per cent for patrimonies above 11.7 million dollars; below that threshold nothing was due. The same rate applied to the British inheritance tax, although with a much lower bar for exemption (325,000 pounds or about 450,000 dollars). Obviously, this situation risks creating a strong incentive to 'donate' up to the threshold, possibly in a way which allows the giver to maintain de facto control over the assets, for example with the establishment of a new trust, donor-advised fund or foundation. Looked at from this angle, the claim that in recent years giving has reached unprecedented heights should be considered with at least a modicum of suspicion that it may also have reached unprecedented heights in insincerity. From a long-term perspective, this situation is more than a little paradoxical. At a time when the enormous wealth accumulated in the hands of the few would allow for truly exceptional magnificence, the rich shy away from the social functions that they have been required to serve from the late Middle Ages: they are no longer willing to contribute with their resources to the needs of the collectivity (unless they get to decide exactly how those resources will be used and if they can conceptualize this as their own and 'free' choice), not even in times of crisis, and they hide their actual magnificence, and its ensuing political influence, behind the screen of a neutral and antiseptic 'philanthropy'. These are important reasons why the presence and the role of the rich in society have become, once again, the object of discussion, as will be seen in the following chapters.

10

The Super-Rich and Politics

IN RECENT YEARS, many Western countries have seen billionaires, like Silvio Berlusconi in Italy or Donald Trump in the United States, become heads of government. But the involvement of the super-rich in high politics is hardly a novelty in human history. Some striking cases, like the Medici in late medieval Florence, have already been mentioned. However, the political activity of super-rich individuals is, today, highly controversial and begs important questions: how do the super-rich come to exert political power? And has the process changed over time? While some of the topics covered by this chapter relate to the rich more generally, the focus will mostly be on the wealthiest of all, as it is specifically their political activity which can throw institutions and society off balance.

After an introduction concerning the long preindustrial period, with a focus on early republics, particular attention will be paid to modern times, as it is only from the late eighteenth century, when the 'Age of Revolutions' began, that the principle of equality of rights (including of political rights) has become a cornerstone of Western societies. For a period, during the twentieth century, politics seemed to grow less dependent on wealth. This period, however, may have come to an end. This is due, at least in part, to the historically unprecedented size of some patrimonies, as well as to the opportunities offered by new technologies to transform wealth into the power to influence voters. Connected to this, worries are spreading that extreme wealth concentration could lead to a de facto change in the very nature of Western democracies.

While a major concern of this chapter is to illustrate how great wealth can lead to the acquisition of political power, the opposite path will also be explored, as throughout history many politicians have used their institutional leverage and their influence to enrich themselves or have at least been strongly suspected of doing so. The issue of corruption, a common concern whenever wealth and politics become intertwined, leads us to return to the discussion of taxation, as the rich could be tempted to apply their political influence to shape fiscal systems to serve their private interests. Once again, the analysis of some apparently remote historical settings offers useful lessons for contemporary dilemmas and highlights some possible dangers that might otherwise go unnoticed.

Wealth as a Path to Politics in Early Republics

Whether examining Antiquity or the early modern period, the historical record points to an uncomfortable reality: in most settings some extremely wealthy individuals were recognized as having the right to rule because of their noble status, as was typical of feudal regimes, or through some other mechanism of inheritance of political pre-eminence. Indeed, the hold on political power is one of the characterizing features of the nobility as a specific path towards wealth. For the long preindustrial period, then, it is to exceptional and relatively open political systems that we should turn, from the Athenian democracy to the medieval communes and the early modern patrician republics. These were exceptions in their time; nevertheless their study can illuminate aspects of general relevance, not least because early republics represented an important model for the first 'modern' parliamentary regimes.

The Athenian democracy developed around the sixth century BCE and lasted until 322 BCE, when the Macedonians established an oligarchic government in the city. Especially after the reforms introduced by Cleisthenes (one of the most celebrated statesmen of all Antiquity) in 508 BCE to break the power of the old tribes, the Athenians enjoyed substantial political equality. This was exercised through institutions such as the Council of Five Hundred or *Boule* (recruited through a system of ten newly formed tribes, each providing fifty councillors), which were exceptionally open for their time.[1] The potential contrast between political equality and substantial economic inequality was considerably attenuated by the system of liturgies, which led to the wealthiest individuals charging themselves with expensive tasks required by the collectivity and, in this way, also led to the redistribution of a sizeable amount of resources from the top to the bottom of society. As seen in chapter 9, this system not only allowed the very rich to accumulate honours and to expand their social, economic *and* political influence, but at some level it justified their very presence within society and protected them from the anger of the masses, so much so that in Xenophon's opinion it wasn't at all a given that the wealthi-

est Athenians occupied a particularly enviable position. Many political ora-
tions reiterate the view that the only justification for great personal wealth was
to make oneself useful to the collectivity.[2]

Even during its golden age, though, the political system of Athens was fragile in more than one way, as it could be tipped against the rich or in their favour, a point most clearly formulated by Aristotle. In the *Politics* (Book 3, Part
13), he argued that if in a community there existed individuals with a dramatic
pre-eminence of virtues or political capacity compared to all others, including
because of their extreme wealth, they would essentially be placed above the
law or they could even become 'the' law. The other components of society
could complain, as (in Antisthenes' fable) the hares did at the council of the
beasts when they claimed equality for all, but the answer would inevitably be
the one given by the lions at said council: 'You speak well, hares, but where
are your teeth and claws?'[3] Based on reflections of this kind, Aristotle came to
justify the practice of ostracism (banishment), applied by Athens and by some
other ancient democracies, as necessary for the preservation of social order
and of a kind of political justice in such a setting.[4] This view was shared by
medieval commentators on Aristotle, like Nicole Oresme, who even more
clearly identified in the super-rich (*superabundantes*) of their time the category
which risked leading to the collapse of 'democratic' political systems and
which consequently had to be expelled from the city. Indeed, the practice of
banishing individuals—almost invariably very wealthy—who seemed to be
trying to accumulate overbearing political influence, or were just accused of
aspiring to acquire control over the state, was widespread in the European
communes of the Middle Ages.[5]

Expulsion and exile were the fate suffered by Cosimo de' Medici in 1433. At
that time, he was one of the richest men in Europe and nobody could have
missed that his wealth was vastly greater than that of the average citizen of
Florence. He had also been accruing political influence for many years, having
steered away from the policy of his father, Giovanni di Bicci, who had actively
avoided involvement in politics. Supposedly a champion of the 'new men' of
Florence who, emboldened by their wealth, were claiming a greater share of
political power, Cosimo proved exceedingly effective in making use of inter-
factional disputes (all the more abundant, given the high level of factiousness
of Florentine politics) to serve his own interests, his family's and those of the
immediate clients of the Medici. In a well-known interpretation, Cosimo's
action (or 'robust action', as it has been labelled), especially after his return
from exile in 1434, was extremely successful precisely because it did not appear

to pursue any specific goal. But Cosimo was focused on the long game, his vast resources allowed him to play on all the tables at once, and in the brutal political environment of fifteenth-century Florence, where violence could erupt suddenly, this kind of 'flexible opportunism' may have allowed him to achieve a degree of control over the state that otherwise would have been impossible.[6] Whatever Cosimo's actual political objectives, which were surely extremely ambitious if they are to be judged by the magnificence that underpinned them, he was instrumental in establishing the conditions for three centuries of Medici domination over the Florentine State. His grandson Lorenzo 'The Magnificent' ruled Florence in 1469–92, and although he held no formal title of nobility, he was considered one of the most exemplary princes of Europe. By his time, the political and diplomatic reach of the Medici had begun to surpass their economic influence, which indeed was shrinking due to the increasing difficulties of the Medici Bank and the failure or the closure of many branches from London to Bruges.

Lorenzo was probably too distracted by politics to effectively manage the traditional family businesses: a flaw that seems to have characterized others among the Medici, including Cosimo in his old age. Additionally, between Cosimo's death and Lorenzo's ascent to power, political considerations might have compromised the attempts by Piero (Lorenzo's father) to reorganize the family affairs by financial retrenchment: 'the calling in of loans was to run afoul of political imperatives', especially when such loans had been made to ruling princes, and 'in an emergency, it was well-nigh impossible to turn down requests without losing favor and influence.'[7] The other side of the coin is that difficulties in business probably led the Medici to focus on their social and political ascent, strengthening their grip on the state. Lorenzo played a key role in emptying what was left of the republican institutions in Florence of any real meaning. His enemies called him a tyrant and celebrated his would-be assassins, members of the Pazzi family, as idealistic freedom-fighters, which they were not. The Pazzis' plot of 1478 failed, but it cost the life of Lorenzo's younger brother Giuliano. Interestingly, the city rose in support of the Medici against a group of horsemen led by Jacopo de' Pazzi, who had been trying to rally the Florentines to the rebels' cause with the cry of 'People and freedom!' (*popolo e libertà*).[8] In the aftermath of all this violence, it was easy for Lorenzo to introduce reforms that would radically alter the institutional framework to better serve the interests of his family, in particular by introducing the Council of the Seventy, whose members were for the most part tied to the Medici and to which the older Florentine assemblies were now subordinated. As noted about thirty years after these events by the Florentine historian and statesman Francesco Guicciardini, '[The day of the conspiracy] Lorenzo was recognized the master [*padrone*] of the city; . . . he so thoroughly took control of the state, that he thereafter remained, freely and completely, the arbiter and almost the lord [*signore*] of the city, and the great but insecure power that he had enjoyed until that day, became extremely great and secure.'[9]

Before the rise of the Medici, Florence had been a relatively open polity, like many other medieval communes in Tuscany and elsewhere. True, the great families (*magnati*) had enjoyed phases of strong control over institutions and government, but so had the lower strata, often in political alternation with the *magnati* (see chapter 8). Other polities, including some of the most resilient republics in history like Venice, had a more markedly aristocratic, or more properly, a 'patrician', character. An early antecedent of such an arrangement (and indeed, its main model) was the Republic of Rome, where a relatively homogeneous and interconnected aristocracy, whose main component was the senatorial families, concentrated both political power and wealth. Originally, access to public office was strictly their perquisite, but, as many such offices required the holder to spend significant amounts of their own money, in practice they were controlled by the richest among the rich. From the fifth century BCE, plebeians (that is, the non-patrician citizens of Rome) obtained the right to elect their own officials, the tribunes of the plebs, and progressively also obtained access to other public offices. In practice, however, a new 'plebeian aristocracy' developed, and its defining feature was, even more markedly than with the patricians, great wealth.[10]

For outsiders, while great wealth was a necessary condition for entering the Roman aristocracy, it was not sufficient. Political support from, and personal connections to, influential aristocratic families were also needed. The general contours of this model of exclusion-inclusion are similar to those of the late medieval and early modern patrician republics and even of the last to appear, in the late sixteenth century: the Dutch Republic. There, the requisite of wealth for entering the urban patriciates was combined with substantial revenues from office to create conditions particularly favourable to the concentration of wealth and political power in the same hands. As clarified by Jan de Vries and Ad van der Woude,

[A]s the central government itself became more complex, adding new commissions, councils, and colleges, it called more often on the patrician families to fill the new positions. These positions often required prolonged absences from one's home city. . . . [I]n the peculiarly decentralized context of the Republic's constitution, [this led] to the creation of urban patriciates that found (and sought) their chief work in the field of governance. Entry to the patriciate tended more and more to require the abandonment of active involvement in private economic life. Consequently, one could not seriously consider such work, let alone be considered an eligible candidate, without possessing substantial real property and/or financial wealth. Such assets came to form the economic foundation for patrician families, but this foundation was renewed and strengthened by the handsome salaries attached to many of the offices.[11]

This interpretation of Dutch political and economic developments has recently been re-instated by economic historian Bas van Bavel. In his view, it was the early rise of flexible markets for land, labour and capital in the Low Countries that, from the fifteenth century, undermined the role (also political) traditionally played by associations of independent producers and allowed a well-to-do minority to start upon a path of accumulating political and economic resources, ultimately leading to social polarization and institutional sclerosis and helping to bring the Dutch Golden Age to an end.[12] A similar path might have been followed by the Republic of Venice in early modern times, although the first thing that must be highlighted is the exceptional resilience of this polity, whose key 'republican' institution, the *Maggior Consiglio*, was established in 1130 (then called the *Consilium Sapientium*) and maintained its constitutional prerogatives until 1797, when it voted for its own dissolution in the face of the invasion of the French revolutionary army led by Napoleon. The patrician character of the Republic of Venice, as well as the financially onerous conditions required to join the patriciate in early modern times, have already been discussed in chapter 3. It is worth adding that traditionally, in Venice, the political ambitions of each patrician, defined in terms of the offices that he could legitimately aspire to, depended upon three factors: the antiquity of his family (when had it joined the patriciate?); his connections, including by kinship; and his wealth. By the mid-eighteenth century, however, only one thing mattered: wealth.[13] As a proof of this, Lodovico Manin, the last Doge of Venice, was, at the moment of his election in 1789, the richest man in the Republic. Many old-blood patricians considered him a parvenu, as his forebears had only bought their place in the *Maggior Consiglio* in 1651. Indeed, Manin was the first (and the last, given the circumstances) Doge to be elected from among the 'new' patricians. Although he was not without qualities as a businessman and as an administrator, his ascent to power was seen by his contemporaries, and has been seen by many modern scholars, as a sign of the final decadence of the once-proud Republic.[14] But in truth, the time of the patrician republics had come to an end, and in other parts of Europe political change was brewing: in France, surely, but also in England, which is usually considered to have been a forerunner of the modern parliamentary systems.

Wealth as a Path to Politics in Modern Parliamentary Democracies

According to historian Frederic C. Lane, it is precisely in its last years that the Republic of Venice reached the 'apex of oligarchy', meaning a kind of government controlled by a restricted political elite, itself increasingly dominated by the richest individuals.[15] As such, the Republic was viewed with suspicion by the French revolutionary government, which portrayed itself as a champion of political equality (*égalité*) regardless of one's ancestry and wealth, and this contributed to the decision to put an end to its long history. More generally, many scholars have highlighted the importance of the development of relatively open political institutions in leading to the economic (and military) success of north-western Europe against all its potential competitors. According to a recent interpretation, parliaments were a southern European innovation dating back to the Middle Ages and specifically to the time of the Spanish *reconquista* against the Moorish kingdoms during the twelfth and thirteenth centuries, when the Spanish sovereigns introduced them to establish political bonds with their new subjects. Later, these institutions would spread to other European areas, finding particularly fertile ground in the north, especially in England, the northern Low Countries and Sweden. In this view, political innovation allowed for an increase in the fiscal capacity of states and ultimately fostered economic growth.[16] An older tradition in economic history has focused on England, stressing the importance of the 'Glorious Revolution' of 1688 in guaranteeing specific 'freedoms' across the country, including the freedom to elect members of parliament without interference by the sovereign and the freedom from taxes not agreed upon by the parliament. The latter, in particular, was crucial in protecting property rights in the country, favouring economic development in many ways (stimulus to entrepreneurship, reduced cost of private and public borrowing and so on).[17]

If we move from a general concept of the (difficult to measure) 'openness' of a political system to a more substantial consideration of what the institutional and political changes which started to spread in the eighteenth century meant for the rich, we have to recognize that a crucial development was common to both England and the traditional, and maybe antiquated, patrician republics. The rich, who during the Middle Ages had suffered many attempts to keep them at the margins of political life or to exclude them altogether from government—an attitude which was also common in feudal political systems, where anti-parvenu policies and behaviours survived well into early modern times (see chapter 3)—were now becoming the key political actors. Indeed, in the early phases of the development of modern parliamentary institutions, the rich were the only commoners who were allowed to participate in political life and were also the only ones who might aspire to certain offices. Relatively open early modern political systems might have been intrinsically more receptive to the requests of the economic elite. In such an institutional context, great merchants and other key economic players were able to promote policies that allowed them to fully exploit new opportunities (beginning with those related to the Atlantic trade), to further enrich themselves and to establish the conditions for strengthening their political influence, 'opening' the system further to their own interests in a self-reinforcing mechanism.[18]

Later, the grip on politics acquired by the rich became clearly visible in the European 'proto-democratic' states, which restricted the benefit of full political rights to wealthy males only. This was the general situation in nineteenth-century Europe, clearly shown by regulations about suffrage which usually limited it to those who had wealth or income above a certain threshold or who paid a certain amount of taxes. The exceptions were marginal: only Greece introduced, after the 1843 revolution, universal suffrage for all males over twenty-five years of age. Apart from that, even in France after the 1789 Revolution the payment of a minimum amount of tax was a requirement for voting. Although the threshold was relatively low, the French 'First Republic' never introduced universal suffrage (the constitution drafted in 1793 would have done so but never came into effect). During the nineteenth century, however, the requests to expand suffrage multiplied and the electoral base expanded accordingly. For example, in the United Kingdom three subsequent reforms, in 1832, 1867 and 1884, progressively expanded the franchise, allowing for a dramatic opening of the political system: voters were about 5.7 per cent of all adult males in 1831, rising to 14.3 per cent immediately after the 1832 reform, 27.8 per cent after 1867 and almost 60 per cent after 1884.[19] And yet, the contemporary political elite's motivation to introduce the reform might have been quite selfish: as the British prime minister Charles Grey (the second Earl Grey) stated in 1831 in support of the so-called 'Great Reform Act':

> [M]y object would be to propose . . . such a reform as would . . . satisfy the public expectation, without endangering . . . by sudden change and violent disturbance, the settled institutions of the country. . . . The principle of my reform is, to prevent the necessity for revolution. . . . The principle on which I mean to act is neither more or less than that of reforming to preserve and not to overthrow.[20]

The idea that, throughout much of the West, nineteenth-century political reforms were introduced by elites to prevent a violent upturning of the social order remains widespread among scholars. Others, however, highlight the successful initiatives by the lower classes and the political parties that organized their action and tried to further expand the franchise, until universal suffrage was achieved, first only for males and later (well into the twentieth century) including women.[21] Whatever the reason, it is clear that by the early twentieth century the situation had dramatically changed and that the grip of the rich on politics had become much weaker than it had been for a long time. As is often the case in Western history, changes in military practices played a role as well. In an age of mass conscription it seemed impossible to deny the right to vote to those who were asked to risk their lives for their country. So in Sweden, immediately after the introduction of a law establishing universal conscription for men, in 1901, the Social Democratic Party began campaigning for universal suffrage, with the rallying cry of 'one man, one gun, one vote'. Male universal suffrage was introduced shortly thereafter in 1909.[22]

When we think of modern Western democracies as places where everybody has the right to vote and anybody can be elected to parliament and achieve high office in government, we have in mind a political system that did not exist before the twentieth century. In early nineteenth-century Europe, parliaments and governments were firmly in the hands of the wealth elite, plus what was left of the traditional political elite which usually issued from the nobility. Even the last decades of the century were just a period of transition. Together, the World Wars, the fight against Italian and German fascism and the political and ideological challenge posed by the Soviet Union in the immediate postwar decades shaped a historical context uniquely favourable to the establishment of exceptionally open and egalitarian political systems across most of the West. True, rich men continued to find their way into parliaments and governments with relative ease, but the path of wealth was far from being the only one to political success.

Recognizing the historical exceptionality of Western democracies, however, also leads to worries about their future. The principle of equality of political rights, both active and passive (voting *for*, or being voted *into*, a public office), can easily conceal a reality in which election to office is in practice the prerogative of a restricted elite wielding economic (and *therefore*, in the modern world, political) power and in which the vote of large strata of the population can be influenced by those who hold privileged access to economic resources, either because they are super-rich themselves or because they are backed by super-rich donors. In recent decades across the West such concerns have been expressed not only by many social scientists, but also by many politicians, usually but not exclusively left-leaning, and by a significant part of civil society.[23]

Whatever one thinks of the involvement of super-rich individuals in politics, in the decades following World War II in most Western countries it had become relatively difficult for them to rise to the highest positions of executive power. Only from the 1990s do we have striking examples to the contrary, and those examples have intensified in more recent years.[24] It is useful to discuss some notable cases, steering clear of any consideration of the inner motivations of those super-rich who decided to run for high office, but at the same time, considering whether their exceptional hold over economic assets and other valuable resources might have placed them on an entirely different footing compared to the average citizen. It seems proper to start the analysis with Silvio Berlusconi, prime minister in four distinct Italian governments, who is not only an early example of the aforementioned tendency, but is also a perfect example of a super-rich politician who had privileged access to the media and has been accused of using it to influence the electorate.

Born into a middle-class family in Milan (his father was a bank employee who later rose to a managerial position), Berlusconi began his entrepreneurial career as a building contractor. He undertook his first project in 1961, aged twenty-five, immediately after graduating in law. In the following years his ambitions grew, and he developed a very innovative project for 1960s Italy: building large-scale residential complexes on the outskirts of Milan to serve the needs of the middle class, embracing some of the ideas of the 'new towns' urbanistic movement that had been spreading in the United Kingdom, in France and elsewhere. This project culminated in the building of the 'Milano 2' complex in 1972–9, which had some striking characteristics, such as total walkability (through a system of walkways and bridges, pedestrians could

reach any point of the complex without ever meeting traffic), an abundance
of green areas and the local provision of all key services. Importantly, residents
also had access to what was, then, cutting-edge technology: cable television.
For this purpose Berlusconi developed, through his holding Fininvest, a new
company (Telemilano) which originally only served Milano 2 but later reached
the whole of Lombardy. This was the first step in Berlusconi's very successful
career as a media mogul. In 1980, in a very aggressive move against the monopoly of RAI, Italy's public television company, Berlusconi launched the first
private national TV channel in the country, Canale 5. The move was highly
successful and took all of its Italian competitors by surprise; these were usually
established publishers, such as Rizzoli and Mondadori, that had recently set
up their own private channels. Berlusconi eventually acquired all of their TV
assets, which allowed him to diversify his offering in Italy by adding two new
channels broadcasting nationwide, Italia 1 and Rete 4. The reaction of the old
public monopolist, RAI, was forceful: in 1984, invoking the Italian postal and
telecommunications code which Berlusconi had blatantly tried to get around,
it obtained a partial shutdown of the signal and started legal proceedings
against Fininvest. That was a defining moment in Berlusconi's entrepreneurial
career, as he decided to tap into his strong political connections to solve the
problem: thanks to the personal intervention of Bettino Craxi, the leader of
the Socialist Party (of which Berlusconi was a generous supporter) and then
the Italian prime minister, all prosecutions were dropped and ad-hoc legislation was introduced to prevent future problems for Fininvest. In the opinion
of the business historian Franco Amatori, these facts contributed to shaping
Berlusconi's future behaviour:

> In conducting his activities, Berlusconi was always forced to deal with the
> public sector in its role as regulator of economic activity. The challenges of
> building Milano 2 were highly complex. . . . Even more difficult were the
> problems entailed in building three national television networks. Berlus-
> coni overcame the roadblocks by acting as if antitrust laws had never
> been—and never would be—enacted in Italy. Bolstered by political sup-
> port, he secured legislation that sanctioned the duopoly between his three
> networks and those of RAI, the Italian state television. This was a demand-
> ing battle for Berlusconi that clarified for him the importance of interfacing
> with the state.[25]

While he was kickstarting his media empire, Berlusconi diversified into
another, and related, sector: advertising. A new company, Publitalia '80, was

created to provide ads for Fininvest's new TV channels. The company, which again adopted an innovative business model by producing more engaging and well-targeted commercials than was usually the case in Italy at that time, immediately proved successful, starting to churn out large profits. In early 1994, on the eve of the official start of his political career, Berlusconi had already acquired super-rich status (according to *Forbes*, in 2001 his patrimony amounted to 10.3 billion dollars). Not only did Berlusconi command vast resources, they were the 'right' ones, that is, those which could potentially allow him to maximize his electoral influence. Beyond the three national TV channels (of the six then existing in Italy), Berlusconi had a strong grip on the publishing sector as in 1990 he had acquired a majority stake of Mondadori and of a range of lesser publishers, which allowed him to control important news outlets such as *Il Giornale*, a newspaper. He owned a major football team, AC Milan, which under his presidency had gone from success to success, consolidating Berlusconi's reputation as a high-achiever. Finally, he had Publitalia '80 at his service. The advertising company played a key role in the launch of Berlusconi's brand-new political party, Forza Italia, 'whose candidates [in the 1994 political election] had been selected and groomed, more or less in secret, by Publitalia 80.'[26]

Although Berlusconi's campaign was undoubtedly boosted by his media empire, it is also true that he was filling a political hole that had opened up at the end of the Italian 'First Republic', when the traditional party system was overwhelmed by a vast corruption scandal, the so-called *Tangentopoli* ('City of Bribes'). His centrist political platform (which in time would veer more clearly towards the centre-right) and the mistrust of many voters for the Italian left, which some considered to have remained too close to the political and ideological tradition of the old Communist Party, are key in explaining his success. In May 1994, Berlusconi was sworn in as prime minister. Although his first government was short-lived, killed by coalition infighting (Forza Italia had only won about one-fifth of the votes: a lot in the highly fragmented Italian political circumstances of the time but not nearly enough to form a government without allies), under Berlusconi's charismatic leadership the centre-right won two other general political elections, in 2001 and 2008. Notwithstanding the repeated scandals to do with accusations concerning economic crimes or related to his personal and markedly un-monastic life, and notwithstanding widespread criticism for the continued use of his companies and personal resources to support his political activities, for many decades Berlusconi was a key figure in Italian politics; Franco Amatori aptly describes him as 'an entrepreneur who took on the state'. His personal fortune continued to grow during the years of his active political involvement, reaching a peak in 2005 when, according to *Forbes*, his patrimony reached 12.1 billion U.S. dollars, making him the twenty-fifth richest man in the world (his fortune had somewhat reduced, to 7.6 billion, by 2021).[27]

When judging the political activity of somebody like Silvio Berlusconi, who repeatedly won free elections in his own country in a period when Italians' satisfaction with their political system was relatively high, exceptional care is needed to avoid being unduly influenced by personal preferences.[28] What seems unquestionable, however, is that Berlusconi's rise to power is a textbook case of political ascent facilitated by extreme wealth. In more recent years, other super-rich political leaders have emerged, typically coming from the entrepreneurial world, which allowed them to claim to have the right skill-set for governing public institutions with the same effectiveness that (as is invariably the argument) they had shown in their private companies.

The better-known case is surely that of Donald Trump, president of the United States during 2017–21. The scion of a rich family from New York—the dynasty founder, Frederick Trump, was a German immigrant who made a fortune during the Klondike Gold Rush of 1896–9 running a restaurant and hotel (with, allegedly, additional services) that catered to miners—Donald Trump was clearly not born into rags. And yet, throughout his career, he has consistently presented himself as a self-made man, tapping into the American cultural myth that, for the hard-working and capable, extreme wealth is achievable despite their initial conditions. That myth, as seen in chapter 4, was already false during the Gilded Age and is decidedly false today, in view of the strong evidence of relatively low social-economic mobility in the United States (lower, in fact, than in many other Western countries).[29]

Like Berlusconi, Trump has become a highly divisive politician, making it all the more difficult to judge his achievements as an entrepreneur in a balanced way. Based on the wealth that he has accumulated (estimated by *Forbes* at 1.7 billion U.S. dollars in 2001, peaking at 4.6 billion on the eve of the 2016 presidential campaign and later declining to 2.4 billion by 2021), it seems clear that, overall, he has been a very successful businessman. Not only did he continue his family's activities as a developer of real estate, but he also built a valuable brand: from the 1980s, the Trump name has been licensed to many economic activities not directly owned by the Trump Organization, his holding company. In this process, a crucial role was played by the publication of a blockbuster book, *The Art of the Deal*,[30] and by the co-production and hosting of the highly successful reality TV series *The Apprentice* during 2004–15. With these means, Trump made himself known to even broader strata of American society and carefully crafted his reputation as a shrewd and tough negotiator, willing and able to make difficult decisions—all characteristics that, whether he truly possessed them or not, he claimed could be very useful to a U.S. president. This helped him to build the political platform which led to a narrow and hard-fought electoral victory (he lost the popular vote) against Hillary Clinton in the 2016 presidential election.[31]

Like Silvio Berlusconi, Donald Trump is a successful entrepreneur who 'took on the state'. And like Berlusconi, he has been accused of various economic and political crimes, as well as of questionable personal behaviour. But from our perspective what needs to be stressed is that, without any reasonable doubt, Trump's vast wealth and involvement with the media favoured his political rise. To this, one could counter that, in the end, personal wealth does not matter as much as the overall funds that are provided by the supporters of a political campaign (especially perhaps in the American political system). This leads to a related issue: that of politicians who, while not super-rich themselves, nevertheless are backed by super-rich individuals or in some way enjoy the support of the richest strata. As seen above, before becoming a politician himself, Berlusconi supported the socialist leader Bettino Craxi, a circumstance which allegedly allowed him to push legislation favourable to his businesses. The plutocratic support enjoyed by some politicians is a general concern in Western countries. It is strongly felt, for example, in France where both Nicolas Sarkozy, *Président de la République* during 2007–12, and Emmanuel Macron, whose first mandate started in 2017, have been accused of being backed by, and of being compliant with the wishes of, very rich entrepreneurs and financiers. Macron, in particular, benefited during his 2017 campaign from the endorsement of Bernard Arnault, chairman and chief executive of the LVMH luxury industry holding, the richest Frenchman and one of the wealthiest people in the world (third in the absolute global ranking in 2021, according to *Forbes'* estimate of a net patrimony of 150 billion U.S. dollars). Macron seems to have also profited from the support of the media controlled by Arnault, which include many important French newspapers such as *Les Echos*. This is what led some of Macron's critics to label him *Le président des ultra-riches* (while Sarkozy would have been, more modestly, *Le président des riches*).[32]

Other examples could be given,[33] but the nature of the problem is clear already. Whether they run for public office themselves or they back some politician or political party, the super-rich can exert exceptional influence over the election process and, more generally, over politics and government. In this sense, they truly are to be considered gods among men or, in a democratic context, gods among voters. This being said, it is a fundamental rule of modern democracies that everybody has a right to be elected to public office, a right of which the rich and even the super-rich could not, and should not, be deprived as this would compromise the very foundations of those same political systems that we wish to preserve. What was (more or less) proper in classical Athens or in medieval Florence is not acceptable today. And we might also wonder whether it would be ethically proper for a super-rich individual *not* to try to steer fellow voters away from individuals or parties that he or she might genuinely think could cause great harm to the public should they win an election. This is not to imply that the super-rich *should* get involved in politics instead, as, historically, it seems quite clear that when they compete for high public office, there is no practical way of ensuring that, with their overwhelming access to resources, they will not end up wrecking the political system, intentionally or not. From such a perspective, democracies appear to be particularly fragile. This is a complex issue which has to do more generally with the kind of constraints that the rich should spontaneously impose upon their own actions within society, a delicate point which will be discussed further in the conclusion of this book. All of this, of course, is assuming that the super-rich who become involved, directly or indirectly, in politics are well-meaning and genuinely convinced they are serving the public interest, because if such involvement is motivated by self-interest and is aimed at maximizing personal economic benefits, it is to be condemned unequivocally, as argued in the next section.

Politics as a Path to Wealth

By now, it should be clear that across history the wealthy have always had privileged access to political power. According to a certain cultural and political tradition, this might even appear to be desirable: as stated by Aristotle, those best fit for political activity are those with time to spare, 'since leisure is necessary both for the development of virtue and the performance of political duties', which in his view made artisans, traders and farmers all politically unfit.[34] For Aristotle, the perfect politician was a man of property, a view which corresponds perfectly to the wealth-based limitations on suffrage typical of many Western countries during the nineteenth century, discussed in the earlier section, and which resurfaced regularly in eighteenth- and nineteenth-century debates about how best to organize a political system. For example, among the founding fathers of the United States the position that political power should rest mostly in the hands of the wealthy, to ensure social order and security across society, was championed by Alexander Hamilton, the closest advisor to the first president of the United States, George Washington.[35] Of course, neither Aristotle nor Hamilton, who had fairly humble origins, were thinking of the 'super'-rich as particularly fit for government. The idea was simply that possessing some personal wealth helps one to maintain independence in the face of political pressure and to truly pursue the public good. After all, the view that, in the land-abundant United States of the nineteenth century, a relatively even distribution of wealth allowed for a particularly effective democratic system was held by many political theorists of the time, including Alexis de Tocqueville. Also for this reason, establishing the conditions for preventing an excessive concentration of wealth was a major preoccupation of the leaders of the American Revolution.[36]

Interestingly, many among them, for example Thomas Jefferson (who also became the third president of the United States), were fearful that excessive wealth inequality could be *produced* by the political system. This was based on what historian James L. Huston aptly defined as a 'political economy of aristocracy':

> For Americans, aristocracy became at least by the 1780s the natural enemy of republicanism, a perception that in the nineteenth century grew into a popular mania. Republicanism was founded on political equality; aristocracy was based on favoritism, hierarchy, and special privilege. . . . For Americans traveling to Europe in the last half of the eighteenth century, the most salient aspect of European society was its horrid maldistribution of wealth. . . . Americans then connected the two aspects of European society and posited a causal relationship. Aristocracy, the social system of hierarchy and special advantages for the few, ruled the society of Europe; Europe had a maldistribution of wealth that favored the aristocracy. Therefore, the social system of aristocracy produced inequality and maldistribution of wealth. . . . It was control of politics that enabled aristocrats to steal the fruits of labor, to enrich themselves and pauperize the multitudes. By the time of the writing of the Constitution, literate Americans had clearly voiced the idea that a maldistribution of wealth was almost entirely a political act.[37]

To prevent the emergence of wealth inequality (and, we could say, the establishment of a wealth aristocracy), Jefferson and other like-minded American political thinkers argued for a small government: low taxes, a small bureaucracy and economic laissez-faire would starve the political system of the very resources needed to achieve this kind of inegalitarian redistribution. As seen in chapter 3, in the long run this project failed, as from the last decades of the nineteenth century a strong wealth aristocracy did appear in the United States. Again according to Huston, between 1880 and 1920 the rise of big business led to a widespread 'mental readjustment', with wealth inequality no longer seen as the result of politics and government, but as the product of unchecked capitalism.[38] For the purposes of this book, though, it is important to discuss further the idea that politics can constitute a specific path towards wealth, especially for republican and democratic regimes, as for premodern monarchies and empires the situation seems uncontroversial. After all, a 3,000-year-old poem, the 'Babylonian Theodicy', stated that 'The king is the one at whose side wealth walks', meaning that those who have easy access to political power (embodied by the king) also enjoy exceptional opportunities to grow rich.[39] This is not, however, how a modern system built on the principle of substantial equality among citizens, including political equality, is supposed to work. It would be naïve to think that corruption could be kept entirely out of *any* political system. Nevertheless, it would be useful to know the historical conditions and institutional framework in which becoming involved in politics (including by becoming involved with professional *politicians*) led more easily to personal enrichment, given that, in large part, such enrichment must have been the result of corruption or of the improper (and unlawful) management of public resources.[40]

Unfortunately, due to its nature, political corruption is difficult to measure with accuracy for any society, past or present, and this is why it is currently impossible to provide a comparison of this kind. What we have is substantial cumulated evidence that, in order to become very rich, let alone super-rich, political connections can be extremely useful. In the previous section, the case of Silvio Berlusconi, who exploited the political protection provided by the Italian prime minister, Bettino Craxi, to establish his television empire, has been discussed. More generally, some comparative studies of the biographies of scores of super-rich entrepreneurs suggest that political connections, if not strictly a necessity, are nevertheless a recurring feature in paths of enrichment in the West during the twentieth century and beyond.[41] These connections rarely come for free, but to the super-rich, they can appear to be relatively *bon marché*. What is more, it is easy to come up with excuses for indulging in corruption. As the American railroad magnate Collis Potter Huntington argued in

1877, 'If you have to pay money [to a politician] to have the right thing done, it is only just and fair to do it. . . . If a [politician] has the power to do great evil and won't do right things unless he is bribed to do it, I think . . . it is a man's duty to go up and bribe.'[42] Of course, the premise here is that the wealthy industrialist has better judgement than the elected politician concerning what is 'right'. This is not to say that some politicians weren't taking bribes quite willingly, as stated, with more than a bit of venom, by another super-rich American of the Gilded Age, William H. Vanderbilt, in 1882: 'When I want to buy up any politician, I always find the anti-monopolist the most purchasable—they don't come so high.'[43] Vanderbilt was referring to the regulations put in place to counter monopolies in the railroads sector. In the New York legislature (Vanderbilt owned the New York Central Railroad company), for the determined super-rich such regulations were exceedingly easy to elude or get rid of altogether, in part thanks to a bipartisan group of representatives, the so-called Black Horse Cavalry, that was ready to push through legislation favouring specific companies for 5,000–10,000 dollars a vote (131,000–262,000 in 2020 U.S. dollars). In other instances, the same unscrupulous politicians blackmailed companies, threatening them with the introduction of ad-hoc legislation.[44]

Similar examples—of super-rich individuals bribing politicians or of politicians taking or soliciting bribes and becoming rich in this way—are, unfortunately, abundant across Western societies past and present. What should be highlighted is that in recent decades concerns of this kind have spread, at least in some sectors of civil society, along with the growing concentration of economic resources in the hands of the few. In the same way that the appearance of personal fortunes of unprecedented size fuels the concern that more super-rich individuals might decide to personally run for top public office (with all the risks that this entails, as seen in the previous section), the fear that professional politicians are becoming increasingly accessible to the will of the wealth elite has also spread.[45] According to a study, globally the size of 'politically connected' billionaires' wealth doubled from the 1980s to the 1990s and was at least 11 per cent of billionaires' wealth in total in 1996, but the actual figure might have been much higher.[46] In Europe, the conditions prevailing in many ex-communist countries have attracted particular attention, and a considerable amount of research has been conducted on the political connections of the so-called oligarchs who, after the fall of the Berlin Wall in 1989, quickly gained control of previously state-owned enterprises. As the Russian oil magnate Vladimir Yevtushenkov commented with striking clarity in 2014, when he stood accused of money-laundering, 'The size of your business should be matched by the size of your political influence. If your political influence is smaller than your business, it will be taken away from you. If your political influence is bigger than your business, then you are a politician.'[47]

Yevtushenkov was referring to the specific context of Russia; nevertheless his words are another example of how the super-rich can come to rationalize the (mercenary) acquisition of political influence. In order to get things done, goes this line of reasoning, one needs political support to overcome the resistances of the 'system', be they of the juridical-institutional or social-economic kind. The argument is flawed for many reasons, including the fact that by exploiting the political system in this way one simply makes it worse, which could also have negative economic consequences for the community.[48] An entrepreneur, in Schumpeter's definition introduced in chapter 4, is some-body who is able to overcome resistance to innovation, but Schumpeter did not count corruption among the entrepreneur's tools nor, when debating the importance of entrepreneurial 'creative destruction', was he referring to the wrecking of democratic institutions, that is, of precisely those institutions that are needed to ensure an even playing field in which (in theory) everybody has an opportunity to be successful and grow rich. So, an entrepreneur who fails to overcome resistance by playing according to the rules and tries instead to get round the obstacles by buying political support might succeed in becoming rich but fails at being a good entrepreneur. Consequently, he or she surely does not deserve the heroic and sometimes romantic characterization that today's Western societies seem to be quite ready to confer upon any 'self-made' super-rich individual.[49]

The example of the eastern European oligarchs should also make us wary of another claim that is sometimes made by the Western super-rich who be-come politicians, that is, that because they are enormously wealthy already they will not use their newly acquired political power to become even richer and will also be immune to the temptation of stealing from the public (a temp-tation which supposedly besieges the politician of more modest means). In-stead, in certain conditions, entering the political arena might be perceived as an easy way to solve one's financial or industrial difficulties or to overcome barriers preventing further enrichment. As seen in the previous section, Silvio Berlusconi increased his patrimony very significantly in the period during which he was in office, and there have been persistent rumours that his deci-sion to enter politics was made to save Fininvest, his holding company, from bankruptcy. And yet in 2000 he declared, 'Most people know that if the richest man in Italy wants to govern the country, it is not because he wants to get wealthier, but because he wants the complete confidence, the affection, the love and the respect of the people.'[50] We should be cautious in passing quick judgement, as Berlusconi has never been convicted for episodes related to Fininvest's financial difficulties or for activities related to his office. But while we should be open-minded about the motivations of the super-rich who decide to enter politics, we should also keep our eyes wide open concerning the multiple ways in which the political influence of the very affluent might allow them to tweak the system in their favour, including by nudging the institutional framework in certain directions, for example, by pushing for a pro-rich fiscal system.

Politics and Taxation

[A]s the wind moves sand from one place to another, so the wealth of
Florence passes from the powerless to the powerful citizens, under the name
of taxes, with the favour of war.[51]

In this way the fifteenth-century Florentine chronicler Giovanni Cavalcanti accused his city of implementing a fiscal system geared to benefit the most (politically) powerful citizens. Undoubtedly, he was partly moved by personal anger, as his *Istorie Fiorentine* ('Florentine Histories') were composed in jail, where Cavalcanti had ended up for failing to pay his allotted part of the extraordinary taxes levied to fund war against Milan. Nevertheless, historians agree that, overall, the fiscal system of Renaissance Florence was 'flagrantly regressive by any modern standard',[52] meaning that it systematically favoured the richest part of the population and especially (as Cavalcanti pointedly indicated) those members of the wealth elite who were also the most politically powerful. While the distributive impact of preindustrial taxation has only rarely been the object of specific studies, it seems assured that from the late Middle Ages and throughout the early modern period, across the West, fiscal systems were invariably regressive. The reasons for this include the fiscal privileges granted to part of the population (basically, the nobles), the relatively higher fiscal pressure imposed upon rural dwellers by the domineering urban elites and the high prevalence of indirect taxation on consumption, which always tends to place at a disadvantage those who have to spend all of their income to achieve the minimum standard for social acceptability or even just to survive. Taking into account these and other sources of fiscal regressivity, a recent study of the Republic of Venice has estimated that, circa 1550, the total effective fiscal rate (that is, the percentage of income used to pay taxes to the central state) was 3.9–4.4 per cent for the richest 5 per cent of the population but increased monotonically going down the social ladder, reaching 5.4–6 per cent for the poorest 10 per cent. This made for a significant difference, especially considering that the estimate refers to ordinary (yearly) taxation. In the following centuries, the distance between the rates weighing on the extremes of the income distribution would increase proportionally to increases in per-capita fiscal pressure: by 1750, the richest 5 per cent were subjected to a total effective fiscal rate of 6.6–7.6 per cent, while the poorest 10 per cent paid 9.3–10.3 per cent.[53]

As seen in chapter 2, increases in (regressive) per-capita taxation probably contributed greatly to the ever-higher concentration of wealth which characterized early modern Europe. This process has been described both for areas of the continent whose economy was flourishing, like the Dutch Republic, and for those which were stagnating, including the Republic of Venice itself from the mid-seventeenth century. As per Cavalcanti's words, war did indeed favour the process: the rising cost of waging war or simply of defending one's territory justified raising more taxes, thus increasing the ability of fiscal systems to promote the further concentration of economic resources.[54] The way in which these resources were used, which beyond military expenditures included the service of the public debt (itself cumulated mostly to hurriedly raise funds for war), tended to increase inequality even further. Potentially inequality-reducing, 'social' expenditure was minimal: between 0.1 per cent and 0.5 per cent of the yearly budget of the Republic of Venice throughout the seventeenth century, while military expenditure and service of the public debt were usually in the range of 40–60 per cent and 15–40 per cent respectively.[55]

If we focus on the political side of this process, there are two additional aspects to highlight. First, we may wonder how a system which appears to have systematically punished the weakest strata could prove compatible with relatively stable societies. To answer this question one must understand that preindustrial European societies perceived themselves as structurally unequal, which allowed some differences in treatment to go unnoticed or almost unnoticed.[56] What was deemed just, in such a cultural context, was that the rich paid greater absolute amounts of tax than the poor, which they did due to their much higher fiscal capacity (in the Republic of Venice circa 1550, the richest 5% paid 47%–49% of all taxes, increasing to 58%–59% by 1750), and the fact that what they paid was less than proportional to their share of the pie could be, if not properly forgiven, at least forgotten or hushed up.[57] Additionally, there is a difference between the formal ownership of economic resources and actual access to them: as the richest concentrated more and more resources in their hands, they also had to give back an increasing amount of them, through charity, in order to avoid mass suffering and starvation (and consequently, rioting and anti-rich violence) at the bottom of the wealth pyramid. Finally, in times of dire crisis the rich were expected to contribute with their private resources to public needs: for the rich to properly fulfil their function of public 'barns of money', in the phrasing of another Tuscan of the fifteenth century, Poggio Bracciolini, those barns needed to be replenished when the harvest was abundant. From this perspective, a regressive fiscal system was functional to a specific form of social and political organization.[58]

And yet, we should not come to believe that such a fiscal system was meant to serve the best interests of the collectivity. It would be more proper to say that it was compatible with the correct functioning and survival across time of polities characterized by a highly uneven distribution of resources, economic *and* political, polities that however guaranteed to everybody (most of the time) access to basic necessities as a necessary condition for achieving social and political stability. The second point that must be highlighted is that the regressive fiscal systems found across preindustrial Europe, in all their local variants, were *intended* to systematically advantage the political elite which had shaped them across the centuries, and this political elite increasingly tended to overlap with the wealth elite. This was maybe more apparent in patrician 'republics' like Venice or the Dutch Republic. Yet, as will be remembered from the first sections of this chapter, across the West the rich progressively strengthened their grip on politics along with the spread of parliamentary institutions, continuing well into the nineteenth century, when proto-democracies appeared in which wealth was a typical condition for being accorded full political rights. So, in a sense, the American revolutionary leaders and politicians were not far off the mark when they argued that Europe's high levels of economic inequality were the product of politics and government: they certainly were *also* the product of a specific political and institutional framework, but this was *because* this framework had been shaped, across the centuries, by wealthy elites.

As seen in the previous section, by the end of the nineteenth century American politicians had changed their views about the origins of economic inequality. Although a penchant for small government persisted in American politics compared to other parts of the West and certainly compared to much of continental Europe, few today would argue that higher taxation is always instrumental in achieving higher inequality. On the contrary: as we have grown used to fiscal systems which are, or are supposed to be, progressive, we tend to forget that progressive fiscal systems are a relative novelty in human history. As has been discussed in chapter 2, in the West the shift from overall regressive to overall progressive fiscal systems took place between the late nineteenth and the early twentieth century. At the same time, social spending increased and the functions performed by the government expanded, finally leading to the emergence of the first welfare states.[59] As will be remembered, this process was also accompanied by the progressive extension of the franchise, which was not by chance if we consider the role played by the World Wars. As argued by political scientist David Stavasage, 'In a context of mass mobilization for war it was possible for the political left to create new fairness-based arguments for steeply progressive taxation. If labor was to be conscripted, then the same should be true of capital.'[60] Of course, the situation could be quite different across political regimes, and ideology certainly could help achieve mass mobilization while pursuing pro-rich policies, as appears to have been the case for the totalitarian regimes that emerged in Germany and Italy during the interwar period.[61] Nonetheless, it is in the years immediately following World War II, in the context of the restoration of democracy almost everywhere in the West, that we find the most progressive personal income taxes and the highest rates of inheritance taxation in history. As late as 1975 in some countries (including Italy, the United States and the United Kingdom) the top rate on earned income was 70 per cent or higher. Arguably, this was also a period in the history of Western democracies during which wealth had a relatively limited influence on politics.[62]

The history of the taxation of top incomes has already been sketched in chapter 2, and in general, the significance of the shift in politics and in fiscal policies which began in the late 1970s, a shift which seems to have helped to trigger a phase of relatively quick accumulation of wealth in the hands of the richest that continues to this day, has already been mentioned many times in this book. For the purposes of this chapter, it is necessary to focus on a narrower question: to what extent have the rich themselves contributed to steering politics in such a direction? This amounts to asking about the extent to which the fiscal systems found across the West today have been shaped by the wealthiest, presumably to serve their own interests. There is little doubt that the fiscal reforms of the last decades have been advantageous to the earners of the largest incomes and the owners of the greatest patrimonies. In fact, the usual argument in defence of those reforms is not that they have desirable distributive consequences but that they allow for quicker economic growth to the ultimate benefit of all. There are reasons to doubt that this is true,[63] but even if we accepted the argument we would still have to consider whether this period has been one during which the rich have actively strengthened their grip on the political system, which per se (that is, independently of its presumed consequences for economic growth) could not be deemed desirable as it is at odds with the ideal of political equality characteristic of a modern democracy.

The kind of tax reform that we are focusing on, which typically includes simplifications of personal income tax (with sizeable reductions of the top rates) and large cuts to, or even the abolishment of, inheritance tax, has been a staple of right-wing political platforms, at least from the 1980s when it was promoted by Ronald Reagan in the United States and Margaret Thatcher in the United Kingdom.[64] In Italy, policies of this kind have been championed by the centre-right coalition beginning with Silvio Berlusconi's successful campaign of 1994, when he proposed the replacement of a relatively progressive personal income tax with a flat tax set at about 30 per cent. When in office, Berlusconi settled for a much more modest fiscal reform, which did however reduce the progressive character of taxation in Italy (note that the flat tax remains to this day a recurrent proposal of Italian centre-right parties, although as of 2022 the declared aim is a considerably lower rate of 23% or even 15% in the most extreme version of the proposal). In the United States, Donald Trump's tax reform of 2017 also modified the structure of personal income tax in ways which especially favoured those earning the largest incomes and greatly extended the exemption threshold for the estate tax, from 5.6 to 11.2 million dollars (these and other innovations were introduced as temporary— but, in principle, renewable—measures valid until 2025, apparently in order to avoid the Democrats' filibuster).[65]

When a super-rich head of state or government champions pro-rich tax reform, suspicions about his or her motivations are unavoidable. But in most cases, the affluent try to influence politics in a much less direct way than running for office themselves. They can fund political campaigns, think tanks, action groups or protest movements against specific policies or even resort to illicit practices like bribing politicians (see the previous section). The way in which such influence-building activities take place varies across the West, depending on specific political and social systems, and furthermore, the political influence of big money can be found to support opposing political platforms. Like everybody else, the choices and preferences of the rich are shaped by their personal beliefs and ideologies, so it is not a given that they will push for policies aimed at making them even richer, just as we find many people of modest means supporting political coalitions with more or less explicitly pro-rich electoral platforms.

A study of Germany during 2005–14 has confirmed that the political views of the rich are heterogeneous at an individual level but has also confirmed that on average they are more right-wing compared to the general population (especially regarding economic policies) and that this tendency becomes stronger when moving up the wealth ladder. Importantly, the same study has shown that wealth tends to shape individual political attitudes much more than income.[66] In general, the historical evidence that the richest of all have leaned towards right and centre-right political positions is quite strong. For example, in the United States it has been estimated that of the richest Americans born during the nineteenth century or at the turn of the twentieth, 73 per cent were Republicans and just 24 per cent were Democrats. This helps to explain why, during the 1980s, Republican campaigns vastly outraised Democratic ones (by a two to one margin in congressional elections), although by the early twenty-first century the gap had basically closed.[67] But even when donations to opposite political camps offset each other, the working of the political system is altered in troubling ways, as the opinion of the common voter cannot be expected to weigh as much as that of the most generous donors.[68]

Given the complexity of the issue and its frankly opaque nature, the best that we can currently do is to judge how political systems have worked in recent years by considering the outcome, which has definitely been the spread of pro-rich fiscal reforms. Admittedly, in part these new policies spread by the imitation of charismatic innovators (Reagan and Thatcher, originally) in the context of an ideological (and, to a degree, scientific) shift away from certain practices, like for example the micro-management of tax brackets or the implementation of very high top tax rates. This process, which has *also* involved the political left, has more than a few connections to the spread of innovations in financial regulations described in chapter 5.[69] And yet, aside from this, it seems highly probable that recent fiscal reforms are also shaped by a stronger influence exerted by wealth on politics, which goes hand in hand with the growing interconnectedness of political and economic power discussed previously.

A final question, then, might be why many among the rich are so opposed to the idea of paying substantial taxes. The answer might seem obvious were it not for the fact that relatively few among the rich and maybe especially the super-rich would describe their lack of enthusiasm for taxation as the consequence of greed pure and simple. There is, instead, widespread distrust of state and government and scepticism about the ability of public institutions to solve major social problems. This is why even the more socially conscious among the super-rich might be tempted to pump more of their wealth into philanthropic endeavours, subtracting it from taxation (see chapter 9). After all, as affirmed by many of the super-rich, they already pay much greater absolute amounts of taxes than anybody else. Such an argument could have come straight from the mouth of a seventeenth-century Venetian patrician, were it not for the fact that a patrician would not have felt compelled to provide *any* justification for his privileged fiscal treatment. The same line of reasoning might bring a modern super-rich individual to conclude that, in the face of a government perceived as both rapacious and inept (bizarrely, all the more rapacious and inept as it is not the direct expression of the wealth elite, which would be the case in a proper patrician republic), tax evasion or elusion is somehow morally acceptable. This attitude might help to explain why recent estimates of the 'hidden wealth' of the very affluent suggest massive fiscal evasion. In Britain, for example, from the late nineteenth century until 2016 wealthy dynasties may have hidden over one-third of their total wealth.[70]

Fiscal evasion is to be condemned unequivocally. For our purposes, however, highlighting the (possible) moral faults of the rich is not nearly as relevant as noticing that, in trying to resist taxation, including by promoting changes to the fiscal system, they are in fact undermining their social position. As should be clear by this point in the book, in Western culture the rich originally found a place in society precisely because they *allowed* the public to benefit from their private resources, not primarily because of their charity or philanthropy but because they were ready to pay tax when the collectivity urgently needed to access additional resources. This was typically the case during major crises such as wars, famines and severe epidemics. From this perspective, it is easy to understand why, during the COVID-19 emergency, criticism of the super-rich—perceived as profiteers and hence as being part of the problem and *not of* the solution—mounted. The point is further demonstrated by a growing awareness among the super-rich themselves: a group of them mobilized during the pandemic and launched the international 'In Tax We Trust' campaign, with the declared objective of restoring trust in democratic institutions (which might otherwise come to be perceived as doing the bidding of the wealth elite) and in the rich themselves as a useful and productive component of society. And, as the movement clarifies in its manifesto, '[T]he bedrock of a strong democracy is a fair tax system. A *fair* tax system.'[71] The behaviour of the super-rich during COVID-19 and other recent crises is explored further in the next chapter.

11

The Rich in Times of Crisis from the Black Death to COVID-19

MAJOR CRISES AFFECT all social-economic strata. Their impact, however, can be very uneven across society. The rich, like everybody else, have much to lose during certain crises; after all, nobody was really safe during the Black Death. And yet, in other instances, for example during severe famines, their overall access to resources shielded them from the worst consequences and even allowed some among them to considerably increase their wealth. The charge of profiteering has repeatedly been levied against the rich during the crises of the past, and it continues to echo to this day. It was surely heard many times during the most recent pandemic, that caused by COVID-19. We might wonder, however, whether these suspicions are justified or whether they spread and affect the way in which the rich as a whole are perceived because of the misbehaviour, or of the simple good fortune, of a small minority among them. This chapter focuses on the rich in times of crisis, considering both the situations in which they tend to be victims and those in which they are relatively well placed to profit from the opportunities that even the most terrible crises have to offer. As will be argued, some specific kinds of crisis, like famines or even wars, tend to be relatively favourable to the rich, while others, like major financial crises, affect them severely. And yet, there are differences both at the individual level (even if we restrict the observation to the rich only, all crises create both winners and losers) and between specific historical crises of a given kind. The Black Death surely affected the rich more severely than COVID-19, not only in absolute terms, which is obvious given the vastly different mortality rates of the two pandemics, but also in relative terms, that is, in comparison to the rest of society. Similarly, the Great Depression which began in 1929 seems to have had more enduring negative effects for the fortunes of the rich than the Great Recession of 2008–9 and the sovereign debt crisis that followed it, and we might wonder whether, in recent decades, the rich have improved not only their relative position in terms of the share of the overall wealth, but also their relative resilience to adversity. This also calls into question the social role that the rich are expected to play during crises, based on a cultural tradition that, as has been seen in previous chapters, has ancient origins—a role that they may have grown increasingly reluctant to play precisely because they (or at least those at the very top of the wealth hierarchy) are now better sheltered from the negative effects of crises of any kind.

The Rich and the Black Death: Boom or Bust?

Among the most severe preindustrial crises, the Black Death of 1347–52 is definitely the one for which we have the strongest evidence of substantial 'egalitarian' effects. As will be remembered from chapter 2, the Black Death led to a long-lasting decline in wealth inequality across Europe, including in the more prosperous and most economically advanced areas like central-northern Italy. In the cities of Piedmont, Tuscany and southern France, the observed decline in the wealth share of the richest 5 per cent went from a minimum of 8–10 percentage points to a maximum of 20–5, and that of the richest 1 per cent ranged from about 5 percentage points to 14–18. In rural Tuscan villages the decline was of comparable size, as for example the richest 5 per cent lost their grip on almost 9 percentage points of the overall wealth in Santa Maria Impruneta and 16 in Poggibonsi. In Germany as a whole, between 1350 and 1400 the wealth share of the richest 5 per cent declined by more than 4 percentage points and that of the richest 1 per cent by almost 3; the decline would surely be more sizeable were we able to compare it with the situation preceding the crisis. The decline in the wealth share of the richest percentiles of the population was accompanied by an even more marked decline in the prevalence of the rich (defined as those having wealth above ten times the median), by between one-third and two-thirds depending on the area.[1]

Wealth lost by the richest strata trickled down the social ladder reaching even the poor, whose relative position became, for a period, the best in centuries and remained relatively good for a fairly long time. This was also due to the scarcity of the labour force (the pandemic had eliminated about half of the population of Europe and the Mediterranean) which gave workers an edge in negotiating larger salaries and better overall working conditions. In England, for example, after the pandemic the households unable to afford a 'respectability basket' of consumption goods declined from about 40 per cent typical of the previous decades to less than 20 per cent by 1381, which clearly made poverty more manageable as a social problem. Recent research has confirmed this 'poor-friendly' scenario from another angle, that of social-economic mobility. Rising in the wealth hierarchy was probably easier in the aftermath of the Black Death than in any other phase of the Middle Ages and of the early modern period. In Tuscany, which is currently the only part of the world where an attempt at measuring this process has been completed, the prevalence of households which managed to dramatically improve their position (measured as movements between quintiles of the wealth distribution) increased by 30–40 per cent in the years immediately following the pandemic. Social-economic mobility began to decline slowly from the mid-1360s, but the mobility boost of the Black Death was still visible two generations after the event. In other parts of Italy and Europe it might have lasted longer, maybe in parallel with the longer-lasting levelling impact on wealth inequality which has been observed, for example, in north-western Italy (Sabaudian State/Piedmont) and in Germany.[2]

There is little doubt that, overall, the Black Death was the rare catastrophe in Western history which tended to be relatively advantageous for those among the survivors who had relatively humble origins. Although the traditional view that the pandemic triggered a 'Golden Age of labour' is maybe an exaggeration, few scholars would deny that 'improved living conditions for the lower ranks of wage earners was a memorable characteristic of the late medieval economy' and that this was a consequence of the Black Death.[3] Being forced to offer better economic conditions to labourers obliged the economic elite to share more of the bounty of the post-pandemic years, when resources that had become very scarce were suddenly exceptionally abundant, allowing for significant increases in the product per capita. The elites in power tried to fight back, as shown by the many decrees *contra laboratores* ('against the labourers') which were quickly introduced by urban governments, in Italy and elsewhere, to try to contain the supposed 'greed' of the lower classes, especially in the rural areas. Such decrees, however, in the circumstances characterizing the post–Black Death period soon became untenable and were repealed, and a similar fate was suffered by royal ordinances in France and Aragon. The economic elites, then, tended to suffer a decline in their share of the overall income and also of overall wealth, both because the price of land and other real estate had declined at exactly the same time as higher real wages were allowing more members of the lower classes to acquire property, and because the pandemic-induced mass mortality led to the fragmentation of many patrimonies. These were divided more or less evenly among the children of the deceased, in accordance with the unmitigated partible inheritance systems that characterized much of Europe at that time (see also the next section). Part of the inherited properties were then sold on the market, further driving down the prices of real estate and fuelling a continued equalization of the wealth distribution.[4]

Large-scale, sudden patrimonial fragmentation caused by mass mortality is one reason why at least part of the old wealth elite saw its relative position compromised. Others, including some among those who had been more economically dynamic and successful in the pre-pandemic period, suffered because their economic activities were wrecked by the Black Death. This was surely the case for some extremely rich merchant families that had built their fortunes during the Commercial Revolution of the previous centuries. First, rich merchants tended to be at greater-than-average risk of dying of the plague itself, for the very simple reason that the infection spread along the main commercial routes. Although we have no exact estimates of the individual risk of death by status or by occupation during the Black Death, we do have some evidence that the plague affected the main commercial cities more severely.[5] So, we can reasonably presume that rich merchants and their families were particularly at risk simply because they resided in the wrong places; indeed, they themselves might have often been the carriers of the infection to previously unaffected areas. Second, and for the same reasons, their economic interests, which were concentrated in the main commercial nodes, could quickly and easily be disrupted by the pandemic. Third, in the post-apocalyptic decades the population had collapsed to historically very low levels, where it remained for a century or so mostly because plague had become a recurrent scourge of Europe and the broader Mediterranean area, compromising the potential for prompt demographic recovery. Across Europe, this situation changed the economic opportunities and the conditions of trade dramatically, to the point of leading, at least in areas like Spain, where the population was not very abundant even before the pandemic, to the overall collapse of the trade network. In the context of large-scale commercial, economic and financial reorganization, the incumbents always have something to lose. Take the case of Florence: there, the Black Death compromised the fortunes of the banking sector, already badly shaken by the bankruptcies suffered by the Bardi and the Peruzzi firms a few years earlier (see chapter 5). To some degree, this was a simple matter of scale: in a continent deprived of half of its population, the size of certain traditional trades, for example the grain trade, contracted, which also led to a diminished need for large-scale financing. Sometimes, though, the damage to economic activities was proportionally greater than the demographic damage: the Florentine textile sector suffered a terrible blow, with the production of cloth falling from over 75,000 pieces a year in 1338 to less than 25,000 a year by 1378. Similar catastrophic drops in production have also been reported for other European cities, for example Marseille in France and Ypres in Belgium. They weren't painless for the local rich in the short run. What is more, the reduced scale of operations tended to lead to reduced opportunities for the accumulation of vast fortunes in the following decades.[6]

If the merchants, and more generally the entrepreneurial elites, might have been affected relatively severely by the Black Death, other components of the rich were not spared either. Although some city-country differential in overall mortality rates seems to fit the available evidence, a striking feature of the Black Death (one which it has in common with the last great European plagues of the seventeenth century, at least in the south of the continent) was that it proved able to spread effectively in the rural areas, deeply affecting the country-based nobility. For example, in England, as argued by Scheidel,

> [T]he nobility faced crisis as the value of the agricultural products of their estates dropped and the wages of those who made them rose. . . . [T]he elite captured less of the surplus and others received more for about a century and a half. . . . Members of the gentry suffered downward mobility, whereas great lords managed to maintain their standing on reduced income. The plague contributed to a dramatic contraction of the nobility: over two generations, three quarters of noble families were left without heirs, causing old families to disappear even as new ones emerged. Elite ranks shrank in size and fortune.[7]

The impact of the pandemic upon different categories of the rich, then, was asymmetrical (with consequences that remain to be explored in detail). Perhaps more importantly, even if we restrict the analysis to entrepreneurs and financiers, it is clear that the Black Death created both losers and winners. The exceptionally high social-economic mobility which characterized the second half of the fourteenth century made way for people and family dynasties to tumble down from the top positions in the wealth hierarchy, only to be replaced by 'new-wealth' individuals keen to found entrepreneurial dynasties of their own. In earlier chapters, some examples have already been discussed, like that of the merchant from Prato (Tuscany), Francesco di Marco Datini, who was made an orphan by the Black Death, inherited some capital because of this, moved to Avignon in France and set out to quite aggressively exploit the opportunities of post-pandemic Europe, turning a personal tragedy into an opportunity for rapid enrichment. In Florence, a 'huge tidal wave' of new lineages entering the local economic and political elite has been described;[8] as will be remembered, it is precisely in this context that the Medici family was able to rise. A similar flourishing of post-plague opportunities for enrichment in emerging sectors has been described for many other European areas. In England, for example, the soaring price of wine caused by the pandemic's disruption of traditional trades as well as by growing demand in a context of higher per-capita incomes, and maybe of perturbed psychological conditions among a population scarred by the Black Death, led to excellent commercial opportunities from which both English and French traders from Bordeaux and Gascony profited greatly throughout the 1350s. From about the same period, exports of woollen cloth from England began to grow quickly, reaching unprecedented heights and replacing part of the Italian and Flemish production, at least in the market for lower-quality textiles. At the same time, the increased production of cloth in England generated new commercial opportunities for others, prominent among them the Genoese merchants who provided the English textile entrepreneurs with growing quantities of dyes and alum from their mines in Asia Minor.[9]

This mixture of individual difficulties and successes is mirrored by a long-running debate about the economic consequences of the Black Death: were they positive or negative overall? A potential confusion arises depending on the time frame that we consider. In the short run (during the plague itself, which usually lasted less than two years, and presumably for a few years immediately following the crisis[10]) the economic effects were clearly and deeply negative. This is the period when many among the old rich suffered considerably and lost their grip on a substantial part of their economic resources. It is in the decades immediately following the pandemic that we find signs of recovery and that the picture, regarding individual paths, becomes more complex with at least some established lineages managing to improve their fortunes and with the emergence of many new-wealth families. Although most scholars today would agree that the long-term economic consequences of the Black Death were positive overall, nobody would deny that the situation is different if we look at the pandemic and immediate post-pandemic years and that, at an individual level, the crisis created both winners and losers. If we focus on the short run, which is proper for the purposes of this chapter, we can reaffirm what was stated at the beginning of this section: the Black Death was damaging to the economic interests and to the relative position of the rich. The pandemic taught the economic elites a hard lesson, which they learned well, becoming progressively better prepared to face shocks of such a kind, as seen in the following section.[11]

The Crises of Early Modern Times: Plagues and Famines

The Black Death of the fourteenth century was an exceptional crisis in many respects: the sheer magnitude of the overall mortality, surely, but also its ability to give rise to a less unequal society, to the relative disadvantage of the richest strata. After this pandemic, the plague affected Europe recurrently, but never were similar egalitarian effects encountered again. Although our knowledge of these later epidemics remains imperfect, there is currently no evidence that they caused any substantial rebalancing in the distribution of income and wealth, neither looking at real wages nor at the long-term reconstructions of wealth and income inequality that have recently become available. In many cases, this could have been due to the fact that post-Black Death plagues were less severe and maybe also due to their tendency, at least from the late fifteenth century on, to mostly affect cities, sparing the countryside. But not even in the seventeenth century, when most of southern and central Europe was stricken by the worst plagues since the Black Death, with regional mortality rates sometimes reaching 35–40 per cent, do we find any substantial and long-lasting sign of equalization (the partial exception being Germany, due to the simultaneous unfolding of the Thirty Years' War; see the next section). If we consider the implications for the rich, we must conclude that in early modern times they were much better able than their fourteenth-century peers to weather the storm and protect their patrimonies from misfortune.[12]

We have strong evidence that the early modern rich were, in fact, actively trying to protect their *patrimonies* as a means to protect their *family* (the lineage) from the negative consequences of epidemic shocks, in a context in which individual survival during a major plague remained highly uncertain even for economic and political elites, as confirmed by recent, in-depth micro-demographic studies.[13] As will be remembered from chapter 6, this cultural tradition is reflected in the juridic motto *familia, id est substantia*: the family *is* the patrimony. Hence, by ensuring that the bulk of the patrimony was preserved, undivided, across the generations, the objective of ensuring the continued survival of the lineage was also achieved. After all, even before the Black

Death, Dante Alighieri in the *Divine Comedy* had placed together in hell (in the seventh circle) suicides and those who had squandered their family fortunes, suggesting a close connection between harming the body and harming the patrimony.

It is, then, within a specific cultural context, and as meeting the social-economic challenges posed by a biological environment which had been radically changed by the return of plague to Europe in 1347, that we must understand the reported tendency of the spread of institutions which derogated from the general rule of partible inheritance. The nature of these institutions, like the *fideicommissum* (entail), has already been discussed.[14] Here it seems important to provide some additional details about the timing of their appearance. Although these institutions were already known in some parts of Europe before the Black Death (in Italy, for example, the *fideicommissum* had been used by noble families in Rome since the early fourteenth century), archival records suggest that they became commonplace, including outside of the nobility, only in the centuries following the pandemic; by the sixteenth century their use was quite generalized. In those areas, especially in southern Europe, where medieval law had been more clearly favourable to partible, 'egalitarian' inheritance, this process also involved substantial changes in jurisprudence. In Tuscany, the *fideicommissum* was already amply used in Florence in the second half of the fifteenth century, while in Siena its spread seems to have lagged behind by a few decades. Allowing for some local variation, a similar timing seems to characterize the rest of central-northern Italy as well. The same is true for other practices, like for example the *in solido* ('collective') inheritance reported for Piedmont and even more clearly the *fraterna* (undivided property among brothers) customs of the Venetian merchant families and the associated 'restricted marriage' system.[15]

Practices and institutions of this kind, which are to be encountered in a variety of forms across Europe (think of the Spanish *mayorazgo*, analogous to the *fideicommissum*, regulated in detail by Castilian law from 1505 but already existing before that date), all served similar purposes: to protect the lineage across generations by avoiding the dispersion of the family resources. Consequently, when the southern European economies began to suffer from northern competition (especially from the seventeenth century on), they continued to be used and spread even further, which does not conflict with the view that their original diffusion was the direct consequence of the plague becoming endemic in Europe in the decades following the Black Death. In terms of building resilience (in favour of the elites) to this kind of environmental challenge, these institutions appear to have been effective: a growing body of evidence suggests that they played a crucial role in preventing plague-induced equalization in early modern Europe, and they could achieve this precisely because they protected the largest patrimonies from undesired fragmentation in times of mass mortality.[16]

So when the last great plagues affected seventeenth-century Europe, the rich were ready, and they appear to have been able to preserve their social-economic status much better than during the fourteenth century, when the Black Death had taken them by surprise. This, however, also had the unfortunate side-effect of preventing mortality crises from levelling the playing field and maybe from liberating fresh social-economic energies. For the simple fact that the incumbent wealth elite was better able to maintain its strong grip on an overwhelming share of the economic (and social and political) resources meant that the opportunities open to other parts of society to move up the social ladder were drastically curtailed, which is being confirmed by much ongoing research.[17] More generally, the rich of early modern times seem to have been able to prosper relatively well in times of crisis. This is particularly apparent during famines.

Unlike plagues, when the rich suffered an increase in their individual risk of death on a scale comparable to the poor (although not necessarily reaching exactly the same level), during a famine uneven access to economic resources led to huge variations in individual experiences of the crisis. First of all, during a famine (defined, in a strict sense, as an event leading to mortality markedly exceeding the 'normal' levels, due to starvation or to the spread of hunger-induced diseases[18]) those who died tended to come from the lower strata. It seems almost a truism to state that a rich man does not die of starvation, although he could still die of a local epidemic (such as typhus) triggered by the famine or of hunger-induced violence. Second, during this kind of crisis many among the rich found themselves in an advantageous position not only because of their general financial means, but also because of their vast food reserves. Especially in cities, keeping private food reserves required the availability of storage space suitable for the preservation of grain and other foodstuffs, so that only a small number of families could do it. In the case of northern Italy, in Pavia at the end of the sixteenth century, sixty families privately stored 40 per cent of all the grain physically available within the city, while in Ivrea in 1613 less than 11 per cent of all resident households stored any kind of food reserves (grain, pulses or wine). Owning food reserves stored at home, be that an urban mansion or a rural villa, and/or owning substantial landholdings in the surrounding areas allowed the richest strata not only to weather the crisis, but also to exert social-economic leverage from which unscrupulous individuals could profit in many ways.[19]

To see how a rich man could profit from a famine at the expense of the peasants and small owners, we can look at a literary description from the mid-sixteenth century, provided by the short story writer from Lombardy Giovan Francesco Straparola. Here is how he describes the activities of his character Andrigetto di Valsabbia, a rich citizen of Como, during a famine:

> Andrigetto, then, being extremely wealthy, and having much wheat and other kinds of grain, supplied by his farms, dispensed all his revenue to poor peasants and to other miserable persons, neither did he wish to sell that to merchants or others for money. And he did this not because he had at heart to succour the poor, but so that he could take from them some lands, and enlarge his farms and revenues; and he always tried to choose places that brought him profit, and little by little he took possession of everything. It happened that in those parts there came a great penury and it was such that men, and women and children were in many places found dead of hunger. For this all, the neighbouring peasants, both from the lowlands and the mountains, turned to Andrigetto; and some gave him a meadow, some a wood, and some a field of ploughed land, and in return, received as much wheat or other grain as they might need. Such was the number of people who came from all parts to the house of Andrigetto, that it seemed like a Jubilee.[20]

The behaviour of Andrigetto, a fictional character, corresponds perfectly to what has been repeatedly reported by historians based on the available evidence. Great landowners who systematically exploited the opportunities offered by famines to expand their holdings were a common feature of early modern Europe. The French historian Emmanuel Le Roy Ladurie, in his classic book on the peasantry of the Languedoc from the fifteenth to the early eighteenth century, described this as a kind of 'natural selection' which tended to favour the greatest landowners, leading to the progressive concentration of land in fewer and fewer hands.[21] Other historians have employed the concept of 'proletarianization', referring to a process through which an increasing proportion of the European population lost control of the means of production and had to sell its labour to survive. Proletarianization tended to come in waves, precisely because it was connected to population pressure and was triggered by large-scale crises, most prominent among them continent-wide famines such as the particularly terrible ones in the 1590s and the 1690s.[22] Contemporaries (like Straparola) generally declared their abhorrence of this kind of profiteering, although to some degree this was simply virtue-signalling. In rural areas, little could be done to protect the famine-stricken peasantry from those who were prepared to dispossess them (and perhaps face a modicum of social scorn from their peers). In the cities, on the other hand, strict regulations existed against profiteering and the hoarding of food reserves in times of crisis, and serious attempts were made to enforce them. In fact, urban governments across continental Europe were keen to try and contain the worst effects of famines, because while the population was ready to accept severe scarcity and even starvation when the conditions seemed to justify it (famines were considered a fact of life, just like the unreliability of harvests), what could *not* be tolerated was the inaction of institutions when there was still an opportunity to mitigate the crisis or when there was the suspicion that some (bakers or grain merchants, for example) were hoarding food reserves or were exacting unreasonable prices. In such a situation, the threat of popular violence was entirely credible, and the ruling elites were acutely aware of this.[23]

Fear of bread revolts helps to explain why, during many famines and especially in cities, the rich were often quite ready to help to finance public relief initiatives. This behaviour, which has clear antecedents in the Classical Age (in Athens, the 'voluntary' contributions by the rich called *epidosis* played an important role in funding public relief during food crises[24]), was well-grounded in Christian theology and in a juridical tradition that was shaped by it: as many Scholastic theologians, including Thomas Aquinas, had stated, 'in cases of extreme necessity, everything is common property.'[25] In a pre-industrial, agrarian society, no condition of more extreme necessity could be conceived than a severe famine, which caused terrible and very prolonged suffering among the masses. Consequently, the fact that the rich contributed to alleviating the plight of the people in various ways was not only appreciated, but was expected by society. After all, when better than during a crisis, when the grain barns were empty, for the rich to fulfil their role as 'barns of money', providing the community with the financial means (as donations or even just as loans) to buy and distribute what foodstuffs could be found, even importing them from countries far away? Sometimes, 'private' and 'public' actions (and resources) became difficult to distinguish, which is particularly the case for patrician republics. An instructive case is that of the Republic of Genoa during the famine of 1590–3, when public institutions (ruled by the local wealthy patricians) organized the collective action of the city's main merchant families (also belonging to, or closely connected with, the patriciate), relying upon their contacts, networks and ships to open new trade routes to bring grain from the Baltic.[26] Thanks to these efforts, from December 1592, well before the end of the crisis in other Italian regions, Genoa and its domains were well provided with grain; on 18 January 1593 alone, 130 ships laden with grain entered the city port. The fact that it then became possible to export the surplus to other areas, with huge profits for the Genoese merchants, is not surprising and does not alter the fact that the primary objective of the initiative had genuinely been, for all the parties involved, to help the local population.[27]

It might seem paradoxical that, of all preindustrial crises, famines are those which offered the affluent the easiest opportunities for further enrichment, and at the same time they are those during which the rich seem to have been the most ready (or probably, in many cases, simply resigned) to contribute to mitigating the crisis with their personal resources. This might also appear to be at odds with a strand of the literature on famines, which has focused on inefficient or unfair distribution (potentially also because of profiteering) as the cause of famine. However, when analysed closely, the vast majority of the great preindustrial famines appear to have taken place in phases of high demographic pressure on resources and to have been triggered by sequences of meteorological events that caused a substantial drop in agrarian produce for several years in a row, so that food reserves had also become depleted and could not be used to make up for harvest failures. It is in a context such as this that many among the rich were able to shine, fully performing their traditional social function of using their private resources to supplement public budgets that were inadequate to face the crisis. By the early nineteenth century, however, famines had become a rarity in the West. Situations of acute scarcity are not unknown in the last two centuries, but they appear to have been 'man-made', usually triggered by another kind of crisis: war.[28]

The Rich during Wars and the Wars of the Rich

Repeatedly, across history, it has been argued that wars have mostly been fought by the common people and the poor to serve the interests, and to protect the property, of the powerful and the rich. Today this view is held by much of the political left across the West, with some connections to the Marxist school of thought, which sees modern wars as the direct consequence of the inner workings of the global capitalist system.[29] As such, they intrinsically correspond to the interests of the capitalists and, generally speaking, of the rich. However, if, instead of focusing on general theories of war, we look at the historical evidence regarding how *in practice* the rich fared in wartime, the situation appears to be rather more complex. While there are no doubts that, as with famines, all wars offer excellent opportunities for enrichment to some, they also pose clear threats to many among the rich: of the direct despoliation of their fortunes or of the simple destruction of their financial and real assets.

To provide a balanced discussion of the position of the rich during wars, we have to recognize that their affluence alone made them a target of invading armies keen on looting. In medieval and early modern times, this was particularly clear in conquered cities, especially during a sack, that is, that specific span of time during which conquering soldiers were permitted to steal and harm the local population almost indiscriminately, both as a reward for their victory and as punishment for a city which had refused to surrender. City sacks were ubiquitous in preindustrial wars, and while they lasted great merchants, bankers and other members of the wealth elite became the most desirable prey. Although they did not necessarily experience a higher risk of losing their lives compared to the general population, because they could usually negotiate (at great expenditure) for more humane treatment, they had little hope of being left unmolested. As Niccolò Machiavelli pointed out in his treatise *The Art of War*, 'the unarmed rich man is the reward of a poor soldier.'[30] Shortly after Machiavelli made this statement, in 1527, the point was demonstrated by the sack of Rome, the centre of Catholicism, at the hands of the German Lutheran Landsknechts. The overall value of the spoils was staggering (another Florentine, the historian Francesco Guicciardini, estimated it at over 1 million ducats), but it was overshadowed by the size of the ransoms and of the 'settlements' (*composizioni*) which affluent families paid for their houses or palaces to be spared the pillage.[31]

In time, the ways of waging war changed, as did the treatment reserved for the conquered population, but the practice of putting to the sack cities that had failed to surrender was formally forbidden under international law only in 1899. Indeed, sacks were frequent during the Napoleonic Wars, with some relatively well-known cases (like the sack of Badajoz in 1812) being perpetrated by the British Army during the 'Peninsular War' in French-occupied Spain.[32] But apart from the sacks, something that remained a constant even after 1899 is that the affluent were a favoured target for conquering armies. Sometimes, specific groups became the object of exceptionally thorough despoliation, as was most definitely the case for affluent Jews during World War II. Across German-occupied Europe, all their properties were confiscated in a highly systematic and bureaucratized way which was specifically aimed at protecting the legal title to each item of property, hence ensuring that the Reich would be able to dispose of it at a later stage: 'after the deportations, the Nazis used legal artifice to make it appear that they were merely collecting, on behalf of the state, ownerless property left behind.'[33] A clearly unplanned consequence of this legalistic approach was that in the post-war period it facilitated the restitution of properties to survivors.[34]

While during World War II the property of the Jews was specifically targeted as part of a more general plan of persecution and, finally, of extermination, in less extreme situations what put the rich at risk was the high visibility of their wealth, some crucial components of which (think of urban mansions) could not be hidden. During the Russian war of aggression against Ukraine of 2022, ongoing at the time of writing, across the West the properties of Russian oligarchs and of their relatives were sequestered and their assets frozen. The objective was to stifle the willingness of the invaders to continue the war, and the focus on the oligarchs was justified by the argument that, as a body, they could be considered a constituent part of the Russian political regime. There was, however, also a practical reason for targeting the oligarchs: they had substantial and highly visible assets abroad (it is difficult to hide a six-level, 140-metre-long yacht, like the *Scheherazade*, sequestered by the Italian police in a Tuscan harbour in March 2022 and possibly the property of the president of the Russian Federation himself, Vladimir Putin). Consequently, they were targeted because their very wealth made them a relatively *easy* target.

During a war, then, the rich and especially the super-rich are the most coveted prey, but at the same time, they are the apex predator, as they tend to be those best placed, due to their control of war-related sectors of the economy, their financial resources and their access to information and political connections, to profit from those opportunities that any war generates. It is, indeed, this specific situation, and the high visibility that those rich who gain from the conflict tend to acquire during wartime, that has favoured the spread, in Western culture and across history, of the perception of the rich as war profiteers *tout court*. While undoubtedly this judgement is correct for some unscrupulous individuals, in other cases those who prospered during wars simply enjoyed a positional advantage (for example because their enterprises could enter the market for army supplies, including of a non-military kind), while many others, instead of profiting, suffered from the conflict, for the reasons discussed above or otherwise. This ambivalence is apparent in an adage quite popular among modern investors, attributed to Nathan Rothschild (but probably apocryphal): 'Buy when there's blood in the streets, even if the blood is your own'; Rothschild would have pronounced it in the aftermath of the Battle of Waterloo (1815).

In medieval and early modern times, great merchants played a crucial role in keeping armies well equipped and provisioned. They acted as big contractors, organizing the activity of a plethora of artisans and workers to satisfy bulk orders from governments and military authorities. They were, in fact, the only ones who had the ready capital, the knowledge and the connections to satisfy the military needs which tended to balloon during war emergencies. A well-known case is that of the Republic of Venice. During the War of Cyprus of 1570–3 against the Ottoman Empire, single orders of rows for the fleet were on the scale of about 10,000 each, a scale which was vastly larger than what could be assured by any single producer at that time. The contractors who took on the order had to organize the provisioning of wood from various areas, including from beyond the borders of the Republic; the roughing of the oars; and finally, their timely delivery to the Arsenal of Venice. All this, obviously, was for a nice profit and was repeated for the tens of thousands of arquebuses and the thousands of swords and corslets for the infantry provisioned from the iron-working provinces of Bergamo and Brescia and for all the other needs of the army and the fleet (foodstuffs of various kinds, ropes and sails, munitions and so on).[35] The physical needs of the military, however, were less pressing than its financial needs, as nothing could be provisioned when money was lacking. During the most important and longest wars even countries that were in the habit of keeping sizeable 'war chests' in peacetime, again like the Republic of Venice, needed the services of great international bankers, who were happy to help—again, for a profit, which was also compensation for the significant risks incurred by those who lent to princes in arms. This aspect has already been discussed in chapter 5, where some cases were mentioned, like that of the Bardi and Peruzzi families during the Hundred Years' War or that of Anton Fugger during the wars of the Holy Roman Emperor, Charles V, against the Protestants.

A related business was that of raising armies themselves; in this case, members of the nobility were those who profited most. In politically fragmented Italy, the system of the *condotte* (consolidated military contracts) was considered by nobles an 'honourable means of acquiring riches, far more suitable and efficacious than risky commerce.'[36] The Montefeltro are a good example of a family whose revenues crucially depended upon the *condotte*. In the mid-fifteenth century Federico of Montefeltro, Duke of Urbino, as

Captain-General of the Italian League received an enormous personal stipend of 45,000 gold ducats in times of war, out of a total *condotta* of 120,000 ducats that he had to use to provide 600 men-at-arms and as many foot soldiers. The stipend was reduced to 25,000 gold ducats in peacetime out of a *condotta* of 65,000. In early modern times, the Italian Wars of 1494–1559 offered many opportunities for enrichment to lucky *condottieri* and their states, like for example Vespasiano Gonzaga, Duke of Sabbioneta, who from 1554 on used his substantial personal revenues to rebuild his seat into a typical 'ideal city' of the Renaissance. After the Italian Wars, in the service of the Spanish Empire, he was given commissions across Europe which brought him great wealth and honour: in 1558 he was nominated *Grande de España*, and later he was awarded the Golden Fleece.[37]

The best early modern example of great personal enrichment achieved in the business of raising armies is possibly that of Albrecht von Wallenstein. From an impoverished family of the lower Bohemian nobility, Wallenstein was raised bilingual and received a good education. His perfect command of the German language helped him to enter the service of the Holy Roman Emperor in his wars against the Ottomans (1604–6). Originally a Protestant, in 1606 he converted to Catholicism, which further helped his rise in the service of the emperor. Over time, and especially with the onset of the Thirty Years' War in 1618, Wallenstein distinguished himself as an excellent military commander. His growing renown gave him easy access to credit, which he used to raise progressively larger military units for the emperor. The large profits which he made in the process were used to buy lands, including many estates which had previously belonged to dispossessed Protestant nobles of Bohemia. At the culmination of his career, Wallenstein was able to recruit and equip entire armies through a complex system of subcontracting and financing; in 1632, when he was commissioned to fight an invading Swedish army, he managed to raise and equip 120,000 men. Over time, the emperor had become so financially indebted to Wallenstein that in 1628 he had to repay him with the Duchy of Mecklenburg and award him the status of prince, notwithstanding his Bohemian origins; by then, Wallenstein was probably one of the richest men in the whole Empire.[38]

From the late Middle Ages and throughout the early modern period, the cost of war and defence grew constantly, due both to substantial increases in the efficient size of armies and to ever more expensive military equipment.[39] The opportunities for personal enrichment during wars grew at about the same speed and continued to do so when the West began to industrialize, as most industrial sectors had some military relevance. This is obvious in the case of new sectors, like those of explosives, automotives and aeroplanes, but it is also true for some traditional ones, like the textile sector (think of the provisioning of uniforms to vast masses of soldiers).

It is in this context that we must place the large number of fortunes made during a number of large-scale modern wars and particularly World War I. According to an estimate, in the United States there were about 7,500 millionaires in 1914, but their numbers had increased five-fold, to almost 39,000, by the 1920s, a change which has been directly connected to huge war profits. For Europe, some studies have reported that many merchants and industrialists greatly increased their fortunes during World War I, for example linen manufacturers and shipbuilders in Ireland, although they also faced difficulties in the interwar period, especially after 1922.[40]

An example of large-scale enrichment during World War I and the interwar period is that of Marcel Bloch and Henry Potez, both graduates from an aviation polytechnic school in Toulouse, France.[41] At the start of the war, they were drafted and assigned the task of evaluating the alternative propeller designs proposed to the French air force by the various aeroplane manufacturers operating in the country. At the end of their service, in 1916, they decided to set up their own small factory making propellers but quickly became more ambitious. In 1917 they founded the Société d'Études Aéronautiques Bloch-Lévy (SEA) to produce, under licence from the company Blériot, the SPAD VII fighter. At the same time, 'inspired' by the SPAD, they started to design their own two-seat fighter, which was ready towards the end of 1918. The apparent misfortune of arriving late for the war (the armistice was signed on 11 November, on the very day of the presentation of the prototype) had, instead, protected SEA and its founders from investing in large-scale production on the eve of collapsing military demand, a fate which befell many French aviation companies, in the context of an excessively fragmented sector. Bloch temporarily abandoned the aviation industry to focus on real estate, while Potez remained at the head of SEA, managing to thrive in the interwar period by securing contracts for designing new planes. Only a few were actually manufactured, but the Potez-15, introduced in 1923, enjoyed commercial success and was sold to both the French and Polish air forces.

With the advance payment for the new aircraft Potez financed the building of a large new factory in Méaulte, Somme. The town had been razed during World War I, and additional funds from war reparations were available for those willing to establish new activities there. The new factory allowed SEA to become a serious competitor to even the largest French producers, like Bréguet. When, in 1929, Bloch returned to the aviation scene, he used his connections with politicians and military officials (his brother was fourth in the absolute wartime hierarchy of the French Army) to secure substantial contracts for SEA and for the other companies that he and/or Potez controlled. The same contacts also helped them to acquire, with favourable conditions, bankrupt or near-bankrupt competitors, profiting from a crisis in the sector in the early 1930s. The icing on the cake, however, was the government's drive towards the nationalization of the war industry, which both Bloch and Potez advocated as a means to increase national companies' ability to innovate (the idea was that inventors had to be protected from corporate directives motivated by profit alone). They might have been sincere, but it did not prevent them from receiving huge indemnities (in cash) for their nationalized companies and substantial inventors' royalties, while retaining the ownership of the commercial contracts signed by their old companies and even direct managerial control over them after nationalization, due to their appointment as associate directors.

The confusion that all of this contributed to creating in the French aviation industry is one reason why, in the years immediately preceding World War II, relatively few of the most advanced planes could be delivered to the French Army and what could be delivered was often faulty. This helps to explain the ineffectiveness of French aviation against the German Luftwaffe. While there is no doubt that both Potez and Bloch had started their rise to affluence by fully exploiting the opportunities offered by World War I (and those which the end of the conflict had created in the 1920s), it would be wrong to claim that they were not also negatively affected by war. Bloch in particular, who was a Jew, was placed under house arrest by the collaborationist Vichy government and in 1943 was deported to the Buchenwald concentration camp. He survived; upon returning home, he recovered what was left of his property (some of which he had successfully hidden from the Nazis by using dummy companies), changed his surname to Dassault (his brother's battle name during the Resistance) and resumed his industrial activities. At the time of his death, in 1986, he was the wealthiest man in France.[42]

Bloch's case is yet another stark reminder of the ambivalent situation experienced by the rich during wars. Another aspect to consider is that the most devastating conflicts were able to cause levelling on such a scale that (whatever the individual experiences) the rich as a body lost their grip on a substantial share of the overall wealth. This, however, was not primarily the consequence of redistribution (as in the case of the spoliation of the rich during the sack of cities), but of the simple destruction of wealth. To illustrate the point, consider a hypothetical situation in which the only kind of wealth existing is urban real estate, unevenly distributed among citizens. If the city is razed to the ground by carpet bombing (as was the case for many European cities during World War II), the wealth distribution will automatically become much more even, but in a context in which everybody loses something (with the exception of the entirely destitute) and nobody gains anything. This said, it is difficult to find examples of wars destructive enough to cause large-scale levelling in Western history.

For preindustrial times, the only case for which we have substantial evidence so far is the Thirty Years' War in Germany in 1618–48, which was concomitant with the 1627–9 plague, probably the worst epidemic affecting the area after the Black Death. Across Germany, between 1600 and 1650 the richest 5 per cent lost their grip on about 3 per cent of the total wealth (2% if only the richest 1% are considered), which is substantial if one considers that, in 1600, the poorest 50 per cent collectively owned less than 8 per cent of the total wealth. While it is difficult to disentangle the impact of the war from that of the epidemic, an attempt has been made using some northern Italian areas, and particularly the Sabaudian State (which was part of the Holy Roman Empire and affected by the same plague as Germany, but not affected, or only marginally affected, by the Thirty Years' War), as a control group for a counterfactual analysis. This analysis provided strong support for the view that most of the reduction in inequality observed in seventeenth-century Germany was war-induced. This conclusion, which has been obtained based on community-level data, is also supported by the available reconstructions of top wealth shares at the regional/state level; as can be seen in Figure 11.1, until circa 1600 wealth inequality across Germany and the Sabaudian State followed almost exactly the same path, including the reduction in inequality after the Black Death, but from the onset of the Thirty Years' War in 1618 their destinies clearly appear to diverge.[43]

As the levelling power of war is directly correlated with the ability of warfare to lead to the substantial destruction of material wealth, it is clear why recent literature has focused on the two World Wars as possible examples. Undoubtedly, World War II stands out as the most materially destructive conflict in human history; however, if we add the destruction of financial capital to the picture, World War I was clearly also a 'great equalizer'. This point, which was made by economist Thomas Piketty and then strongly reaffirmed by

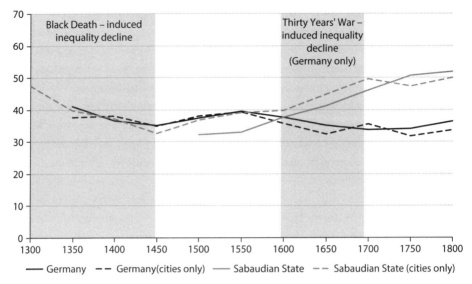

FIGURE 11.1. Wealth share of the richest 5 per cent of households in Germany and the Sabaudian State (north-western Italy), 1300–1800.

historian Walter Scheidel a few years later, has recently been the object of attempts at more precise estimation.[44] In particular, economic historian Neil Cummins has argued that, in Britain, World War I wiped out 59 per cent of the wealth of the Victorian elite (defined as the richest 1,500 dynasties of the 1892–1920 period) versus a global loss of 38 per cent, and World War II another 26 per cent versus a global loss of 16 per cent.[45] If this seems extreme, consider that in France the value of the largest 0.01 per cent estates declined by about 75 per cent between 1914 and the mid-1920s and by another two-thirds during World War II.[46]

World War I, then, seems to have been even more adverse to the affluent than World War II, as confirmed by the evidence available for other Western countries, such as Germany.[47] This finding, however, needs to be qualified. First of all, the lower proportional damage to the patrimony of the wealthy during World War II compared to World War I is partly due to the fact that, in the 1930s, they were proportionally much less rich than they had been in 1914: their fortunes had just started to recover after the damage suffered during the previous conflict and the 1920s. Second, World War I was particularly harmful to certain specific components of the rich and particularly to what was left of the old landed nobility and other great landowners, for example in the United

Kingdom,[48] while, as seen above, many industrialists and merchants profited from the war. This is what Piketty referred to as a 'crisis of the rentiers', based on evidence for France and a range of other countries.

But how could the war destroy financial capital? Partly, this came from the loss of foreign investments, for example because of expropriation in Russia after the 1917 revolution. More important, however, was the impact of war-related hyper-inflation: the gold standard was suspended and Western governments resorted to printing money as a means to manage their public debts, which increased manyfold during the war. Inflation became a particularly serious problem in Germany (where in 1913–50 the average yearly inflation was 17%) and France (13%).[49] This also led to a sort of expropriation through inflation, a phenomenon which tended to disproportionately affect those who owned more financial capital and/or relied upon rents fixed in nominal values to fund their costly consumption habits. Indeed, if we assume some rigidity in the consumption habits of the economic elites (especially for those who used their 'conspicuous consumption' to signal status: see discussion in chapter 6), it is easy to see how the combination of fixed rents, inflexible consumption and high inflation might have led to a substantial decline in the patrimony of many among the rich.[50]

The very concept of 'expropriation through inflation', which is usually conceptualized as a process of destruction of private wealth, at the same time hints at a rebalancing between private and public wealth. From this point of view, it reminds us that the story of the declining affluence of the wealth elite in the first half of the twentieth century is not solely one of the destruction of wealth, but also of the redistribution of what was left of it. In part, this redistribution was from some components of the rich (the landed, the rentiers) to others (the merchants, the industrialists), as detailed above. But in part, it was directed from the top to the bottom of society and was obtained mostly by means of quickly growing inheritance taxes and the more progressive and more intense taxation of top incomes, a process which has already been discussed in earlier parts of this book.[51] Here, it seems important to recall a final aspect. From the Classical Age on, Western societies have expected the rich to contribute heavily, using their own private wealth, to the funding of wars. In historical settings, like those prevailing in late medieval and early modern times, when these contributions took the form of loans (spontaneous or 'forced'), this could also lead to excellent, although sometimes very risky, opportunities for enrichment. By the twentieth century, the situation had not changed much, as the rich were still expected to invest in war loans. Often, they were quite ready to do so, either because of patriotism or because of the mounting social and governmental pressure to contribute to the war effort, only to end up losing their capital to hyper-inflation and, in that way, facilitating the reduction of the public debt: something which may, or may not, have been of some comfort to them in the face of heavy private financial losses.[52]

The Rich during Financial Crises

During the World Wars and the interwar period, many among the rich suffered a large drop in the value of their financial assets due to war-induced hyper-inflation. This is just one example of how the volatility of asset prices can lead to sharp oscillations in the wealth of the richest, both in absolute and in relative terms. Indeed, of all the many components of wealth, financial assets tend to be among the ones distributed most unevenly. This is why, among crises of various kinds, those of a financial nature stand out as affecting the rich severely. Some large-scale financial crises have already been described in chapter 5, from the bank crisis of Florence in the 1340s to the 'panic' of 1907 and the crisis of 2007–8 which triggered the Great Recession. Here, the focus will not be primarily on the causes and overall consequences of financial crises, but specifically on the way in which they affected the rich. For this purpose, it seems particularly relevant to compare the distributive effects of the crisis of the 1930s with those of the Great Recession for two reasons: first, because in the heat of the Great Recession, and also based on evidence from the 1930s, many have argued that a particularly high inequality of income and wealth might have acted as a co-cause of the crisis itself, and second, because the long-term consequences for the rich of the two crises seem to have been deeply different.

Regarding the first point, already in 2010 a report by the U.S. Congress Joint Economic Committee argued that the peaks in income inequality reached in 1929 and in 2007 might have had a destabilizing effect on the economy as a whole, leading to the Great Depression and the Great Recession respectively.[53] This argument, which was made primarily looking at income inequality, could be replicated for wealth inequality, at least for the United States where the tendency towards growing wealth inequality from the 1980s has been stronger. Admittedly, if we look at the wealth share of the richest Americans—say, the top 0.1 per cent—based on recent estimates in 2007 it remained much lower than it had been in 1929 (16.8% versus 24.8%), and the same is true if we expand the analysis to the richest 1 per cent or 5 per cent (34.1% and 56.2% respectively in 2007, versus 50.6% and 74.1% in 1929). However, in both cases the levels of wealth concentration were very high compared to previous years and resulted from a long phase of accumulation. Notably, in the United States the tendency towards inequality reduction triggered by World War I (see the preceding section) had inverted from 1920, and by 1929 wealth inequality had temporarily gone back to pre-war levels.[54] A tendency towards growing wealth inequality during the 1920s has also been reported for Germany, although the recovery of pre-war inequality levels was not nearly as complete as in the United States.[55] No similar pattern has been reported for any other Western country (with the partial exceptions of Switzerland and Finland), so the case of the United States appears exceptional; however, for some countries, this might also be due to the unavailability of frequent (yearly) observations, with the result that oscillations within the interwar period disappear and we can glimpse only the general trend, everywhere orientated towards wealth inequality decline from the onset of World War I to the aftermath of World War II.[56] The exceptionality of the United States is further confirmed by looking at the situation in 2007 (compare chapter 2, Table 2.1).

Even if the situation in the United States is not representative of the West as a whole, both the 1929 and the 2007 crises *began* in that country, later spreading abroad. Consequently, exploring the possible causal connection between high American inequality and the onset of global financial crises remains relevant. The underlying mechanism remains under debate. For the 2007–8 crisis, the 2010 U.S. Congress Report suggested that stagnant incomes for all but the wealthiest might have played a role, increasing borrowing to sustain consumption and contributing to the generation of an 'unsustainable credit bubble' in a context of financial deregulation and exceptionally greedy behaviour. Subsequent research has made this argument more precise, clarifying the reasons for income stagnation across most of society in the decades preceding the crisis and explaining how the middle class and the lower social strata might have opted to become indebted in the face of stagnant incomes due to the desire to maintain their consumption levels (including for the purpose of status-signalling) or even to imitate the consumption habits of the most affluent, which were becoming increasingly more extravagant and 'visible', hence better able to influence the preferences of the rest of society. In other words, the middle class might have tried to maintain its status relative to the upper class by boosting consumption beyond an economically sustainable level, a behaviour which would have been encouraged by excessively easy access to credit.[57]

From this perspective, then, the rich as a body might come to be considered responsible for the crisis both unwittingly, due to their higher consumption levels than those of the rest of society, and because of their intentional economic activity (especially that of bankers and traders) and, ultimately, their greed. The continuities with earlier criticism of excesses in consumption and of greed, as well as with a general mistrust of finance, from the Middle Ages to the late Gilded Age, are, once again, clear.[58] This is further confirmed by looking at how many contemporaries tended to blame the richest components of society for having caused the 1929 crisis and the ensuing Great Depression. On the one hand, the argument was simply that the economic and financial elite had grown wealthier at the expense of all others and that this ultimately led to the ruin of the country. This argument was mostly a visceral and instinctive one, but some made more specific critiques, pointing for example at the fact that, by 1929, the purchasing power of the lower strata had become insufficient to maintain their consumption levels (with substantial analogies with the interpretations of the 2007 crisis discussed above).[59] On the other hand, the super-rich who had emerged from the Gilded Age and who supposedly constituted a 'money trust' in control of U.S. finance came to be considered directly responsible for the economic catastrophe and for having exposed the national economy to financial risks—again, because of their greed and maybe even due to their power-seeking attitude.[60] Together, these varied views and sentiments tended to portray the rich as culpable for the crisis, which further justified breaking down their economic (and, potentially, political) power by means of strict antitrust and financial regulations and making them contribute to alleviating the economic plight of the general population by means of unprecedently high top rates of personal income tax. When Franklin D. Roosevelt became the U.S. president in 1933, he increased the top rate to 63 per cent, and even 79 per cent from 1937. The top rates of inheritance tax were also increased substantially. In this, the United States was participating in a broader tendency, which involved most of the West and characterized the period of the World Wars, towards fiscal reform aimed at substantial redistribution (see the earlier section), but the exact timing of the reforms was dependent upon specific events, including the 1929 financial crisis.

If the 1929 crisis 'damaged' the rich because it fostered more progressive taxation and stricter economic regulations which made it more difficult to build great fortunes (especially in finance) and to establish wealth dynasties, it also affected them in a more immediate and direct way, by undermining the value of their financial assets. The stock-market crash of October 1929 caught many rich Americans flat-footed. The crash came at the end of a phase of rapid expansion of financial markets, which the war loans of 1917–18 (the 'liberty bonds') had helped to promote as they had been purposefully made very easy to buy and to trade, which contributed to turning many U.S. citizens into investors. From early 1928, in the face of stagnant house prices and a saturated bond market with declining real yields, investors began to focus on the stock market. By the end of the year, the Dow Jones Industrial Average (DJIA) index had grown by about 60 per cent. High stock prices induced corporations to offer more shares to finance themselves, leading to further exuberance and very substantial increases in valuations throughout most of 1929, until, in late October, a sudden sell-off of shares in the automobile industry led to a general fall in the prices of stock traded on Wall Street. On 24 October, 'Black Thursday', panic set in, and for a couple of months any attempt at recovery was followed by a new collapse in stock prices. By 13 November, the DJIA had lost 48 per cent of its value, but the onset of economic depression was associated with further declines: by July 1932, the DJIA had lost 89.2 per cent of its value compared to the 1929 peak. While no other Western country experienced such an extreme stock-market collapse, nevertheless global stock markets were already closely connected and losses were often huge, for example in France where between 1929 and 1932 stock prices fell by 56 per cent.[61]

The consequences of the 1929 stock-market collapse for the rich were substantial. Many great fortunes, especially those which were mostly composed of securities, took a severe blow. A relatively well-known and somewhat spectacular case is that of the economist Irving Fisher who, as will be remembered from chapter 8, in the years following World War I had been particularly vocal in warning about the possible negative consequences of high wealth concentration for American democratic institutions. During the 1920s, Fisher made a fortune by producing and commercializing his invention (an index card filing system) and by investing heavily in the stock market. The turning point was in 1925, when he sold his Index Visible Company for 660,000 dollars (almost 10 million in 2020 U.S. dollars) plus preferred stocks and bonds in the buying company, Kardex Rand. He reinvested these proceeds in a range of small and medium-sized companies focusing on innovatory products, at exactly the right moment to profit fully from the aforementioned expansion of the stock market. By 1928 his net worth was around 10 million dollars (151 million in 2020 U.S. dollars), and he operated mostly as a speculator. Famously, on the eve of the 1929 crisis (16 October), Fisher authoritatively declared that stock prices had reached 'what looks like a permanently high plateau'.[62] For months after the crash, he remained convinced that a quick recovery would follow, a conviction which ultimately led him to bankruptcy and ruined his academic reputation (today largely restored, due to his major contributions to economic theory). In the years of collapsing stock prices, Fisher's case was far from isolated. At a macro level, this is shown by the quick decline in the wealth share of the richest, which was mostly due to damage suffered at the very top of the distribution (in the United States, the wealth share of the richest 0.01% declined by 2.7 percentage points, from 10.2% in 1929 to 7.5% in 1932; if we expand the analysis to the top 1%, the overall decline increases, but not by much, amounting to 3.6 percentage points of the overall wealth).[63]

At the time of the 1929 crisis and the Great Depression of the 1930s there were also those who prospered, including those who bought stock at very low prices after the minimum had finally been reached in July 1932. However, there is no doubt that this specific crisis was exceptionally harmful to the rich (in relative terms and without forgetting the vast sufferings that the Great Depression caused to the poorest and weakest strata). From this point of view, the experience of the 2007–8 crisis and the Great Recession was entirely different. Admittedly, in the initial phases of this more recent crisis there were also signs that the fortunes of the richest had been damaged relatively badly. To some degree, however, this was more an expectation (based on the evidence from earlier episodes, especially 1929) than an actual estimation. When proper estimates became available, they offered little evidence that the Great Recession had caused a general decline in the fortunes of the rich. Looking at the top 1 per cent, between 2007 and 2009 their wealth share had declined only fractionally (for example, by 0.9 percentage points in France and the United States and 0.7 in the United Kingdom; a more substantial decline of 2.6 percentage points is found for Spain) or not at all, including, possibly, in the United States where an alternative estimate even suggests an increase of 1.3 percentage points. Additionally, this decline in wealth inequality was very short-lived, including in European countries which were badly affected by the sovereign debt crisis that peaked in 2010–11: in Italy, one of the main victims of that crisis, the wealth share of the top 1 per cent in 2012 was 1.5 percentage points higher than it had been in 2007 (18.6% compared to 17.1%).[64] The deep difference in the fortunes of the rich after the 1929 and the 2007–8 crises can also be perceived graphically (Figure 11.2).

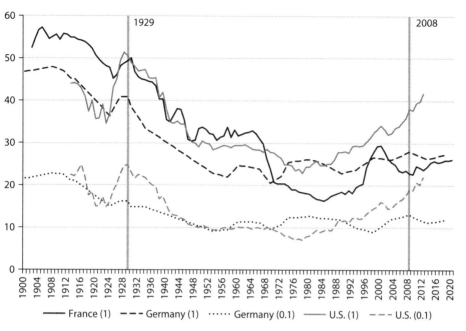

FIGURE 11.2. Wealth share of the richest 1 per cent and 0.1 per cent of households in France, Germany and the United States, 1900–2020.

During the Great Recession, then, the rich were exceptionally successful in protecting their patrimonies, at least in relative terms (the kind of information captured by wealth shares), which is the most relevant information when considering their general position in society. The reasons for this remain debated and probably will continue to be the object of academic discussion for many years to come.[65] Something which clearly differentiated the Great Recession from the Great Depression, across the West, was the kind of policy interventions that it triggered, which were much less intrusive with regard to economic activity[66] and, contextually, much less 'punishing' towards the rich and impactful upon their behaviours and their incomes, especially when the financial sector is considered. As a matter of fact, shortly after the initial crisis, an impression spread of a general return to the old vices, leading to the Occupy Wall Street protests of 2011.[67] Another factor which surely helped to inflame the protests, which spread to other countries albeit with varying intensity, was the perception that the 'one-percenters' were quite unwilling to contribute, by means of higher or more progressive taxation or otherwise, to alleviating the collective economic difficulties. Shortly after the end of the Great Recession, the same concern arose again during the COVID-19 pandemic and the related sudden economic recession. This may be the sign of an emerging twenty-first century regularity, as discussed in the following.

The Rich and COVID-19

During the Great Recession of 2008–9 (which in some countries led to the sovereign debt crisis and lasted until 2013), to many the rich appeared aloof and insensitive to the sufferings of the rest of society. Often blamed for having caused the crisis with their greedy behaviour, the 'one-percenters' seemed to collectively refuse to play their traditional role of contributing from their private resources to help to contain the damage. The same widespread criticism was rekindled by the economic recession caused by the COVID-19 pandemic and by the public health policies implemented to contain it. In this case, apart from some serial conspiracy theorists, few would accuse the rich of having 'caused' the crisis (although in some countries, criticism was levelled at pre-crisis policies, for example those leading to the privatization of many public health services, a development which may have mostly benefited the affluent while reducing overall societal resilience to pandemic threats[68]). Another kind of critique, however, is in perfect continuity with those levied against the rich during the Great Recession: that of having failed to help in (paying for) finding a solution.

As has already been discussed in depth, the expectation that, during a major crisis, the rich contribute their own resources to alleviate its effects is deeply enrooted in Western culture, and is something which has not been erased by the ideological shift towards lower and less progressive taxation since the 1980s. And yet, in the context of today's fiscal systems, which are the direct consequence of this ideological shift, and given the prevailing fault-lines of political confrontation across the West, it has perhaps become more difficult than it has ever been to induce the rich to fulfil their expected role. Although great care is necessary when addressing this issue, the fact remains that across the West there are extremely limited examples of crisis-related fiscal reform aimed at tapping into the private resources of the rich for the public benefit. True, proposals for increasing the top rates of personal income tax or for taxing wealth, either permanently or by means of one-off or temporary measures, have entered the political debate in many countries. But so far, discussion has not been followed by action: based on a recent survey, during the first year of the COVID-19 crisis only a handful of Western countries introduced modest increases in the top rates of personal income tax or of wealth taxes. The best example is probably Spain, where the top rate of tax on net wealth was increased significantly, to 3.5 per cent (from 2.5%), for patrimonies over 10.7 million euros (12.2 million U.S. dollars). In other countries, for example, the Netherlands, a selection of small tweaks was applied, usually to personal income tax, in order to increase fairness and, at the same time, increase state revenues.[69]

Overall, the fiscal reforms that were introduced in Western countries during the pandemic appear to do little to make the rich contribute more. Admittedly, this seems to fit a strategy of temporary tax reductions and other ad-hoc measures aimed at mitigating the economic impact of COVID-19. These reductions and measures were generally funded by increasing the public debt, which begs the question of who will repay it. Given the relatively low progressivity of many Western fiscal systems today, if no impactful fiscal reforms are introduced in the coming years the bill for the COVID-19 crisis will weigh on the shoulders of the rich to an extremely low degree relative to historical crises. In many countries, ongoing debates about increasing taxation for the most affluent might change that. For example, in the United States in 2022 the Biden administration proposed a 'billionaire minimum income tax' of 20 per cent on the total income (including unrealized gains) of those with a net worth above 100 million dollars, roughly the richest 0.01 per cent (according to a governmental estimate, currently U.S. billionaires pay an average rate of only 8.2% on their total incomes). Although this measure was quite mild compared to those introduced by Roosevelt in the 1930s, it did not make it through Congress, partly because of the technical difficulties of assessing increases in unrealized gains, but mostly because of political opposition to it (President Biden relaunched the proposal for a billionaire minimum income tax in early 2023, but at the time of writing it does not seem likely that it will be approved). So far, similar opposition has stopped more traditional reforms also proposed by Biden, such as a relatively modest increase (from 37% to 39.6%) in the top rate of personal income tax.

While tax reform is particularly divisive in the United States given its highly polarized politics, currently there is no reason to expect that other Western countries will be much more successful in their attempts to make the wealthy contribute more. Paradoxically, a political consensus on this objective has failed to coalesce notwithstanding the growing public outrage at the perceived benefits that the crisis brought to the rich (a sentiment further exacerbated by the fact that the infection appeared to spread less, and kill less, among the rich, who could protect themselves better, than among the poor, who often needed to continue working in relatively unsafe conditions to avoid losing their jobs).[70] At most, such outrage has helped to thwart plans for tax reform which went in the *opposite* direction; consider the proposals voiced, in the United Kingdom, by the short-lived Truss government in September 2022, which included ditching the top rate of income tax, set at 45 per cent.

As is often the case, the perception of the crisis as favourable to the rich is based on some particularly visible success stories, like that of the Swiss entrepreneur Guillaume Pousaz who during the COVID-19 pandemic became one of the richest men in the world thanks to the booming stock-market value of his online payment services company, Checkout.com,[71] or of the French entrepreneur Stéphane Bancel, the CEO and co-owner of Moderna, a pharmaceutical and biotechnology company which acquired global renown by being one of the very first to develop and get a vaccine approved for COVID-19 (Bancel entered *Forbes'* list of billionaires in 2021, with a net worth of more than 4 billion dollars). Without doubt, however, the billionaire who the general public most commonly associates with great success during COVID-19 is the American Jeff Bezos, founder of Amazon, who in 2020, when he was already the richest man in the world, saw his patrimony balloon together with the market value of his company. Admittedly, it is not Bezos' fault that he was active in one of the few sectors of the economy which could profit considerably from an unexpected event.[72] However, his behaviour also appeared to many to be rapacious and unfair towards Amazon's employees: they experienced relatively ungenerous work conditions from before the pandemic; they were, allegedly, systematically bullied into not complaining publicly; and during the crisis they not only seemed not to benefit from their company's good fortune but also were exposed instead to a significant risk of infection. Amazon tried to avert damage to its public image, for example, by introducing temporary wage increases for the pandemic period, but apparently with only partial success, probably in part because in the meantime its founder had become the preferred target of a campaign aimed at building awareness about the motivations for taxing the rich more. According to an estimate by Oxfam which resonated globally, and which here is taken simply as indicative of the cultural and social climate of the moment, 'In September 2020, Jeff Bezos, then the richest man on Earth, could have personally paid each of Amazon's 876,000 employees a one-off $105,000 bonus with the wealth he accumulated between March and August 2020 alone, and still be as wealthy as he was at the beginning of the pandemic.'[73]

Whatever Bezos' personal opinions regarding how much the rich should be taxed (in 2021, he and his company expressed mild support for at least some of the tax reforms planned by the Biden administration), it must be noted that, across the West, at least some of the rich have distanced themselves from the taxation-reluctant, embracing the view that it is their responsibility to contribute more. A direct expression of this is the 'In Tax We Trust' campaign, whose political significance was discussed in the previous chapter. And yet, the over one hundred signatories of the open letter written by this group in advance of the 2022 World Economic Forum in Davos do not include any of the very richest people in the world. Admittedly, some among the super-rich had already argued that taxation on the most affluent should be stepped up, and this opinion was expressed well before the COVID-19 pandemic (Warren Buffett and Bill Gates are good examples). Others significantly increased their contribution to society during 2020–2, although usually through their foundations or by other means of giving; for example, the Bill and Melinda Gates Foundation contributed several billion dollars to fighting COVID-19 globally.[74]

As seen in chapter 9, however, giving is not the same as subjecting oneself to taxation, first and foremost because it does not allow the public to decide, through representative and democratic institutions, how the resources will be used. While this is an issue of general import when pondering the impact that extreme wealth concentration can have for a Western democracy, it should be clear by now that the nature of the issue changes deeply during a major crisis. If, in Western history, crises gave the rich the opportunity to demonstrate their social usefulness by agreeing to convert part of their private resources into a public benefit, this did not happen during the COVID-19 pandemic, just as it didn't during the previous Great Recession, generating the risk that the rich, and especially the super-rich, will be collectively considered, at best, free riders and, at worst, profiteers. It may be too early to argue that this is the beginning of a twenty-first-century pattern. However, it is definitely *not* too early to warn that if there truly is an enrooted cultural norm requiring the rich of the West to contribute more during crises, then the high frequency of crises of various kinds, which is an unfortunate characteristic of the century so far, might quickly make the position of the 'aloof rich' socially untenable. It is not usually the historian's task to make normative statements, but it is the historian's duty to highlight what the past has to offer for addressing the concerns of the present. This leads to a few concluding remarks.

Concluding Remarks

BY THE END OF OUR STUDY of the rich, one question remains open: what exactly should they do to fit into society without raising concerns among other social groups? Because it should be clear by now that in the cultural tradition of the West, and despite the fascination that they elicit today, the rich (and especially the super-rich) *are not* considered the best that society can offer. Far from it: they have historically struggled to find a recognized social role and have been the object of intense suspicion, if not outright criticism and scorn. Returning to a metaphor used in the introduction, they are like the pearl in the oyster: shiny indeed, and produced by the living body of the oyster, but at the same time somewhat extraneous to the organism.

If the nature of the problem is clear, the solution, unfortunately, is not. *Whatever they do*, the rich attract criticism, and the super-rich all the more readily and vehemently. If they consume in too conspicuous a way, they appear showy and arouse social envy, but if they stop consuming and begin saving more, they only increase their distance in terms of affluence from all others (and also favour the emergence of dynasties of wealth, making any argument about having 'merited' one's privileged social-economic status increasingly unconvincing). If they prove unwilling to donate and to be charitable towards the weak and the destitute, they are considered miserly and callous, but if they set about giving back large parts of their patrimonies by means of foundations, donor-advised funds and similar, they are suspected of trying to dodge taxation. If they get involved in politics, fear grows that they will exert oversized influence on voters or on political system, but if they steer clear of politics entirely, they risk appearing aloof and uninterested in the concerns of the common people. And so on.

Rarely does history invite clear-cut judgements on human behaviour, as it leads rather to an appreciation of its multifaceted nature and its variation across time and space. There are, however, patterns to highlight and perhaps some lessons to learn because, when it is considered as a whole, the historical experience of the West allows us to see our current concerns from a different perspective. By seeing our societies reflected in the mirror of history, we grasp better what is at stake and what we really risk in these troubled times.

A first point which is strongly supported by all the historical evidence discussed throughout the book is that the position of the rich in Western societies *is intrinsically fragile*. When applied to the current situation, this conclusion appears counter-intuitive, given the high level of command of economic (and social, cultural and political) resources which has been achieved by the rich in recent decades and, more specifically, given the exceptional resilience that they have demonstrated during the string of crises which has plagued the twenty-first century so far. This is, however, an unavoidable conclusion if we consider the broader historical picture, and there are even some signs that an awareness of the delicate position of the rich is growing. This awareness can be observed not so much in anti-rich protest movements like Occupy Wall Street, as in the collective action of the rich themselves coalescing into initiatives such as the 'In Tax We Trust' campaign.

'It's taxes or pitchforks. Let's listen to history and choose wisely', was the conclusion of an open letter which the group of very rich people powering the campaign addressed to participants of the Davos meeting in May 2022.[1] Considered from our long-term perspective, the point appears well-made for two reasons. First, because repeatedly and systematically across history, when the rich have been perceived to be insensitive to the plight of the masses, and especially when they have appeared to be profiteering from such plights (or have simply been suspected of doing so), society has become unstable, leading to riots, open revolts, sometimes even revolution and frequently to acts of outright violence against the rich. This is not to say that these societal responses and behaviour were ethically justified, and sometimes they did not correspond to real misdeeds or even to indifference on the part of the rich, but in cases such as these, *perception* is king.

Second, taxes, which in Western history, and perhaps even more so in recent epochs compared to preindustrial times, are the proper way (institutionally *and* culturally) for the rich to contribute to society. Not giving, but taxes. Generosity (even assuming that all giving is disinterested, which seems a bold assumption) is not sufficient; what is required is to appear to be willing to allow society, through its political and representative institutions, to decide how the resources collected will be used. The matter here is partly again one of perception (showing solidarity and willingness to contribute) and partly of substance, as decisions about society should be shared across society. Many among the rich, and especially among the super-rich, object to the idea that parliaments and governments could do a better job than they themselves could in setting societal objectives and in using 'their' resources to provide solutions—but this is only human as most of us, not only the rich, believe we know best how to use our own money. And how many of us like paying taxes, really?

Like all human beings, the rich and the super-rich are perfectly capable of making mistakes. In this case, the error is in focusing on the way in which the resources transferred to the public are used, while the crucial issue is fulfilling the main social function which, from the late Middle Ages on, has been attributed to the wealthy of the West: acting as private reserves of money into which the public can tap when there is an urgent and motivated need, which is especially the case, as seen in the concluding chapter, in times of dire crisis. Unfortunately, and against all the expectations with which we entered the twenty-first century, major crises have become so frequent as to appear almost the norm; consider the seamless way in which we moved from the COVID-19 pandemic to the Russia–Ukraine war in Europe.

It is here that our long-term perspective leads to worries, as it is precisely at a time when wealth concentration is historically high, crises are very frequent and the rich have become, perhaps, better able than they have ever been to escape them (even financial ones) practically unscathed, that they appear to be exceptionally reluctant to fulfil their traditional role. Across the West, the rich have not been called upon to help to pay the bill for *any* of the most recent crises, including when (as is the case for the Great Recession triggered by the 2007–8 financial crisis) they could be credibly accused of having contributed to triggering the crisis itself. This, at a time when, at least in some institutional settings (like, arguably, the American one), the principle of progressivity in taxation has become somewhat compromised.

This unwillingness to help, while it is not laudable, in principle could be overcome by public institutions; after all, historically, the rich have fulfilled their role as much through the acceptance of a duty towards their country and fellow citizens as through forced contributions and loans (and from the twentieth century, strongly progressive taxation of incomes and inheritances). The fact that this is not happening, all across the West, not even in the form of temporary fiscal measures, leads us to wonder whether today's rich, who concentrate in their hands a historically exceptional amount of economic resources, aren't also using these resources to achieve exceptional control over the political system or just to steer voters away from certain positions. Are they systematically mobilizing political resources to protect themselves from any attempt at selective tax increases? Are they finally acting as gods among men, wrecking democratic institutions and creating a scenario which some had already imagined in the Middle Ages? If so, they had better brush up on their classical mythology, as in the Western tradition, gods can also fall, except when they do, the impact is cataclysmic and everybody suffers.

Perhaps a time of recurring crises is the best time for wisdom, and here, considering our common history might help to overcome rigid and somewhat ideological visions that appear to be deeply enrooted but are in fact relatively recent. We are clearly set upon a path which presents dangers for the preservation of some of the defining characteristics of modern Western societies. Recognizing these dangers is the first and unavoidable step in finding a solution, possibly one shared by the whole of society and in the best interests of all.

Sources for Tables and Figures in the Main Text

TO AVOID CLUTTERING the main text, this appendix details the data sources for the figures and tables and provides some additional information.

Chapter 2

Table 2.1: for all countries, the 2020 estimates come from the *Global Wealth Databook* (GWD) 2021. Regarding other dates: for Denmark, the Netherlands, Norway and Switzerland, see Roine and Waldenström 2015. For France, see *World Inequality Database* (WID), consulted in May 2022. For Germany, see Albers, Bartels and Schularick 2022, as well as GWD 2017 (only for 2002) and new elaborations based on Alfani, Gierok and Schaff 2022 (only for 1800). For Italy, new elaboration for 1800 (see notes to Figure 2.3) and Brandolini et al. 2004. For Finland and Sweden, see Roine and Waldenström 2015 and (for 1800, 1850 and 1900) Bengtsson et al. 2019. For the United Kingdom, see Lindert 1986 for 1875, WID for 1900, 1950 and 2000 and GWD 2017 (for top 5% in 2000 only). For Canada, see Davies and Di Matteo 2018, Di Matteo 2018 and additional material kindly provided by Livio Di Matteo (the estimate for 1902 refers to the Ontario area only); some new elaborations are also included. For the United States, see WID, GWD 2017 (for top 5% in 2001 only), Sutch 2016 (for 1870 only) and the 'From the Black Death (and Earlier) to the American Revolution' section in chapter 2 for the estimate for 1774.

Figure 2.1: new information from the EINITE database for the Florentine State, the Kingdom of Naples and the Republic of Venice. For the

Sabaudian State, see Alfani 2015 and new information from the
EINITE database. For Germany, new elaborations based on Alfani,
Gierok and Schaff 2022. For England, see Lindert 1986 for the period
1650–1800 and Alfani and García Montero 2022 for 1300–1500.

Figure 2.2: for France, see WID, consulted in May 2022. For Sweden, see
Bengtsson et al. (2018) for 1800–1900, Roine and Waldenström (2015)
for 1908–94 and WID thereafter. For the United States, the estimate
for 1774 is discussed in the 'From the Black Death (and Earlier) to the
American Revolution' section in chapter 2, and see Sutch (2016) for
1870 and WID from 1913.

Figure 2.3: for Denmark and Norway, see Roine and Waldenström 2015.
For the United States, see Saez and Zucman 2016.

Figure 2.4: new estimates for Italy 1300–1800, Brandolini et al. 2004 and
GWD for 1990–2020. For Europe, see Piketty 2014. For the United
States, see Lindert 2000, Sutch 2016 and WID, consulted in May 2022.
For the United Kingdom, see Lindert 2000, Alfani and García Mon-
tero 2022 and WID.

Figure 2.5: new information from the EINITE database for the Florentine
State, the Kingdom of Naples and the Republic of Venice. For the
Sabaudian State, see Alfani 2015 and new information from the
EINITE database. For Germany, new elaborations based on Alfani,
Gierok and Schaff 2022.

Chapter 6

Table 6.1: new estimates based on information from Mira 1940, Lane 1944,
Woolf 1963, Goldthwaite 1968, Gullino 1984, Malanima 1977, Ferrari
2012, Biagioli 2000 and Alfani and Di Tullio 2019.

Chapter 7

Table 7.1: own elaboration based on data from Rubinstein 2011, 2018.

Table 7.2: new elaborations based on data from Jaher 1980 and, for 1892,
Rockoff 2012 with some integrations from Ratner 1953, reclassified to
maximize comparability with Table 7.1.

Table 7.3: estimates for the West refer to billionaires only (net wealth
≥ 1 billion U.S. dollars in the year of reference, with no adjustments for
inflation), as recorded in the *Forbes* Billionaires Database. Estimates
for the United Kingdom refer to the richest 1,000 individuals in each

year (minimum entry in 2020: 120 million pounds or 154 million U.S. dollars), as recorded in the *Sunday Times Rich List*. Estimates for Germany refer to those with estimated wealth above 900 million euros in 2020 or 1,027 million U.S. dollars, and 200 million euros in 2011 or 321 million 2020 U.S. dollars (with two exceptions, at 100 and 150 million euros respectively), as recorded in the *Manager Magazin*.

Figure 7.1: State Archive of Verona, *Antico Archivio del Comune— Campioni d'estimo*, folders 249, 250, 261, 271, 273.

Figure 7.2: new elaborations based on data from Daumard 1973, 214–19.

Figure 7.3: Alvaredo, Garbinti and Piketty 2017 for France, Germany, Sweden, the United States and the United Kingdom. Clark and Cummins 2015b for England (alternative estimate).

Chapter 11

Figure 11.1: for Germany, new elaborations based on Alfani, Gierok and Schaff 2022; for the Sabaudian State, see Alfani 2015 and new information from the EINITE database.

Figure 11.2: WID for France (consulted in May 2022); Albers, Bartels and Schularick 2022 for Germany; Saez and Zucman 2016 for the United States.

NOTES

Introduction

1. A few years ago, in a period when my research focused on reconstructing long-term trends in economic inequality, Peter Lindert and Jeff Williamson asked me to contribute to an edited issue of the journal *Cliometrica* dedicated to historical inequality (Williamson and Lindert 2017). A little earlier, I had become aware of a new and potentially useful method for exploring 'richness': a sort of combination of the prevalence of the rich and of the relative intensity of their wealth. So, the idea of contributing with an article on the rich, applying this new method of analysis to the data that I had been collecting and which in part remained unpublished, came quite naturally to my mind. At the time, I took for granted that it would be relatively easy to contextualize these dry numbers, as I presumed that there must be a sizeable literature on the rich in Europe. But I soon realized that, on the contrary, very few scholarly works specifically dedicated to the history of the rich existed, especially for preindustrial times. This led me to dig deeper into my own archival sources, trying to provide an adequate contextualization for my quantitative data. This improved the article considerably (Alfani 2017a), but it also generated in me a deep curiosity for all the aspects of the history of the rich that I could not explore in a short article, and definitely not based on the limited amount of information that I had available at the time. This scientific curiosity led me to begin a much more systematic and deeper enquiry, which finally resulted in this book.

2. For a rare example of a comparative, scholarly study of the rich (dynasties), see Landes 2006. Most comparative books on the rich tend to take a more popular approach and have been published by journalists or writers; when they are well-researched, they can also be useful. Early examples of the genre are Lundberg 1937, 1973; a good recent case is Kampfner 2014.

3. On the analytical choices made by the Italian Marxist school of economic history due to their class categorization, and the criticism that they have attracted, see Alfani 2014; similarly, for Germany, see Sreenivasan 2013.

4. The criticism of class-based studies focused on the long run does not imply that the sociological concept of class cannot be profitably applied, maybe to more circumscribed periods. For examples of recent studies which usefully apply the concept of class to today's societies, see Savage 2015; Friedman and Laurison 2019. Also note that, at least in the Weberian sociological tradition, the notion of 'class' can be distinguished from that of 'status' and 'party'. From this perspective, the class to which an individual belongs is determined by his or her position in the market, which tends to define his or her life chances, and in this way it will also tend to influence

his or her position in the wealth hierarchy (see Goldthorpe 2007 for modern applications of Weber-inspired definitions of class).

5. Even before Piketty, the importance of wealth distribution in modern societies had already been recognized by some scholars. In particular, it was central to the research agenda of economist Tony Atkinson and of the scholars associated with him: see, e.g., Atkinson 1974, 1980; Alvaredo et al. 2013.

6. See Alfani 2021 for a survey of studies of preindustrial inequality; for surveys concerning inequality from the nineteenth century on, see Roine and Waldenström 2015; Alfani 2019; for the United States, see also Lindert and Williamson 2016. Good examples of recent studies which shine a spotlight on long-term tendencies in inequality include Milanović 2016 and Scheidel 2017. Most of the information that has recently become available about preindustrial inequality has been produced by a project funded by the European Research Council (ERC), *EINITE— Economic Inequality across Italy and Europe, 1300–1800* (www.dondena.unibocconi.it/EINITE).

7. See Medeiros and Ferreira de Souza 2015 for a useful survey of studies about the rich in today's societies. For the nineteenth and early twentieth centuries, see, e.g., the various country-specific studies collected in Rubinstein 1980.

8. Sorokin 1925, 627.

9. Regarding the rich in the United States, see, e.g., Jaher 1980; Wolff 2000, 2017, 436–91; Rockoff 2012; Korom, Lutter and Beckert 2017; Sutch 2017. On the rich in the United Kingdom, see Rubinstein 2006, 2018; Scott 2021. As examples of comparative studies of today's rich across the West and globally, see Freund 2016; Tsigos and Daly 2020. See chapter 7 for additional international references. For a critical discussion of the social and cultural differences between the United States and Europe regarding the perception of the rich, see McCall 2013.

1. What Is Wealth, and How Much Is Needed to Be Rich?

1. In anthropologist Frederick H. Damon's definition (1980, 284), the *kula* are 'wealth of a socially determined and socially produced form'. About the *kula* trade, see also the classic study by Malinowski 1922 (with the equally classic comment/criticism of Mauss 1967 [1925]) as well as Hage, Harari and Brent 1986 and Damon 2002.

2. Borgerhoff Mulder et al. 2009; Bowles, Smith and Borgerhoff Mulder 2010. For a definition of small-scale society see Benedict 2004.

3. On this point, see Roine and Waldenström 2015, 514; Soltow 1989, 179–81. According to Soltow, where slaves were highly prevalent, as in the United States before the Civil War, they could represent a large share of the total national wealth: about 12.5% ca. 1800 and 19% ca. 1860. For further discussion of whether human capital should or should not be included in a definition of wealth, see Davies and Shorrocks 2000.

4. Roine and Waldenström 2015, 514–17.

5. Elaborations based on data from Herlihy 1977, 5–7. On the 1427 *catasto*, see Herlihy and Klapisch-Zuber 1985; about wealth distribution in medieval and early modern Tuscany, see Alfani and Ammannati 2017. About Florence as a major financial hub of medieval Europe, see chapter 5.

6. Note that a correlation of 1 would imply exactly the same distribution of lands and movable wealth and that relative measures—such as, e.g., the wealth share of the richest 5% or

1%—would be the same if calculated on each of the two distributions separately or on the joint distribution. On England, see Alfani and García Montero 2022, appendix H; on Florence, this is a new elaboration based on a dataset kindly provided by Peter Lindert. See Herlihy and Klapisch-Zuber 1985 for the original data-collection effort (note that for Florence, the correlation is that between real estate and overall invested capital, including shares of the public debt).

7. For Paris, Daumard 1980, 108; for Milan, Licini 2020, 91.

8. *Global Wealth Databook* 2021, 135.

9. Milanović 2020.

10. As estimated by Milanović (2011, 42 and 44), with his annual income Crassus could command the work of 32,000 Romans; Slim that of 440,000 Mexicans.

11. For a discussion of objective standards of wealth, see Heilbroner 2008. About wealth comparisons based on the command of labour, see Milanović 2011, 2020.

12. While, as stated, directly comparing the wealth of the rich of different epochs is not a specific objective of this book, sometimes it is useful to give at least an impression of how wealth expressed in past measures—say, pounds from 1830—compares to current monetary measures (2020 U.S. dollars have been selected as the standard reference). The conversion of past values into current ones, however, could be made following many different approaches, and no single solution appears preferable from each and every point of view. For the purposes of this book, a simple solution has been selected, which is also the one prevalent in the literature: converting monetary values based on the Consumer Price Index (CPI). On principle, this allows the comparison of the actual purchasing power of different monetary amounts, accounting for inflation. This kind of conversion, however, will not be attempted for historical periods preceding the late eighteenth century. Of course, all conversions of past monetary values into current ones have to be considered approximate and purely indicative, the more so the longer the time period which has to be crossed. Practically, the conversions have been made using the tools provided by the Measuring Worth project (www.MeasuringWorth.com, consulted in November 2022).

13. As clarified by Wade (2014, 118), before the onset of the Great Recession most economists tended to consider inequality as 'an inevitable outcome of the market as a coordinating mechanism, and a necessary outcome for the market to function as an incentive mechanism'—in other words, as a sort of necessary evil. For further discussion of this point (and for a criticism of the interpretation of economic inequality as a relatively 'benign' phenomenon), see, apart from Wade, Piketty 2014; Lindert and Williamson 2016; Alfani 2021.

14. Except for perfectly or almost perfectly egalitarian societies in which, in the presence of many individuals with exactly the same wealth, it could be impossible to establish exactly who belongs to the top percentiles.

15. As rightly pointed out by Marcelo Medeiros and Pedro Ferreira de Souza (2015, 871), in today's societies 'the rich are mostly "working rich" when lower affluence lines are used but predominantly capitalists and rentiers when these lines are raised'; on this issue see also Piketty 2014.

16. See chapter 2 for a survey of the studies that have focused on the wealth share of the rich, and chapter 7 for some quantifications about the composition of the rich across time.

17. Formally: $R^{HC}(x) = \dfrac{1}{n}\sum_{i=1}^{n} 1_{x_i > \rho} = \dfrac{r}{n}$ with $1_{x_i > \rho} = 1$ for $x_i > \rho$ and $1_{x_i > \rho} = 0$ elsewhere, n being the number of individuals or households, r the number of rich individuals or households

and ρ the richness line. The way in which ρ is defined distinguishes among different indexes of the prevalence of the rich. See Peichl, Schaefer and Scheicher 2010; Alfani 2017a.

18. Robeyns et al. 2021 for the Netherlands; Arndt 2020, 143, for Germany. More generally, on the difficulties related to the establishing of absolute richness lines, see Medeiros and Ferreira de Souza 2014, 10–11. Interestingly, for England, a 2003 survey conducted by the BBC found that a quarter of the respondents considered 100,000 pounds in 'ready cash' sufficient to be rich, but 12% argued that more than 1 million pounds was needed or more than 2 million in 2020 U.S. dollars (Lansley 2006, 4–6).

19. For a general discussion of the setting of the richness line for contemporary societies, see Medeiros 2006; Peichl, Schaefer and Scheicher 2010; Medeiros and Ferreira de Souza 2014. For the setting of a wealth-based richness line for preindustrial societies, see Alfani 2017a; Alfani and Di Tullio 2019, 72–6 (these publications also offer a systematic comparison of results coming from setting the richness line at different levels).

20. 'Consegna delli beni stabili feudali mollini forni censi esercitij trafighi capitali officij bestiami et vituaglie fatti dalli Cittadini et habitanti nella Citta d'Ivrea'. City Archive of Ivrea, Category 14 (*censimento*), n. 1750.

21. 'Sabaudian State' (or 'Savoyard State') is a collective term used to identify the territories ruled by the House of Savoy. Technically, this was a composite state, which in early modern times included the Duchy of Savoy, the Duchy of Piedmont, the Duchy of Aosta and other minor domains. In this book, the term will usually be employed to refer to the part of the state today belonging to Italy, and especially to the administrative region of Piedmont.

22. About the 1613 Piedmontese census and its use, see Alfani and Caracausi 2009; Alfani 2010a, 2017a.

23. About the fiscal system of the Sabaudian State in early modern times, see Stumpo 1979; Alfani 2013a. About the general development of European fiscal systems in early modern times, see Yun-Casalilla and O'Brien 2012.

24. The main changes usually date back to the late Middle Ages, when in some localities we observe a process of simplifying the property tax records with a growing focus on real estate as the only basis of direct taxation—the case of Tuscany after 1427 is a good example.

25. For examples of the use of these sources to study wealth distribution and inequality, see, for Italy, Alfani 2015; 2017; Alfani and Di Tullio 2019; for Catalonia, García-Montero 2015; Alfani 2017a; for Germany, Alfani, Gierok and Schaff 2022 (the sources available for Germany are somewhat more varied, but overall they are analogous to those available for southern Europe); for a general overview, including examples for southern France, Alfani 2021.

26. For studies of income inequality in the Low Countries based on the rental value of houses, see van Zanden 1995; Soltow and van Zanden 1998; Ryckbosch 2016; Alfani and Ryckbosch 2016. The latter also includes some information about wealth inequality.

27. See the 'Defining Wealth across the Ages' section in this chapter for further discussion of this point.

28. See Alfani and García Montero 2022 for a study of English wealth inequality based on the lay subsidies and Tudor subsidies; see Hoyle 1994, Dyer 1996 and Schofield 2004 for additional information about the English medieval and early modern fiscal system.

29. Lindert 1986; 2000; for a more recent use of English probates to reconstruct household wealth (from ca. 1500), see Clark and Cummins 2015a.

30. Jones 1980; Lindert 2000; Lindert and Williamson 2016.

31. Bengtsson et al. 2018, 2019.

32. Alfani and Schifano 2021, 107.

33. Technically, while the estate tax is paid by the 'estate' upon the death of an individual (in practice, it is paid by the executor out of the estate's funds), an inheritance tax is paid by each heir on the amount received. The kind of information which can be obtained concerning the patrimony of the decedents is entirely comparable, which is why the literature on wealth inequality tends to use the two definitions interchangeably (see, for example, Piketty 2014, 643–4). For an example of the use of inheritance tax data (instead of estate tax data), see Acciari and Morelli 2020.

34. Piketty, Postel-Vinay and Rosenthal 2006, 2014; Piketty 2014.

35. For an updated survey of the available information concerning wealth distribution during the nineteenth century (and to compare with the twentieth), see Alfani and Schifano 2021.

36. *World Inequality Database*, https://wid.world, last consulted in May 2022. Note that currently WID provides information about the personal net wealth of adults, but for most countries this comes from the equal split of household wealth, and consequently (in distributional terms) it can be roughly treated as household wealth, which is exactly the approach followed by the research team behind the *World Inequality Database*. In fact, their regular World Inequality Reports simply present the wealth-based metrics as built on 'household wealth' (see, e.g., Chancel et al. 2022).

37. Davies, Lluberas and Shorrocks 2010–21, *Global Wealth Databooks* of Credit Suisse, downloadable from https://www.credit-suisse.com/about-us/en/reports-research/global-wealth-report.html.

38. Regarding the sources used for measuring wealth inequality during the twentieth century, see Davies and Shorrocks 2000; Roine and Waldenström 2015; Alfani and Schifano 2021.

39. Davies and Shorrocks 2000, 629; Roine and Waldenström 2015, 513; for the superiority of households over individuals as the unit of measurement of wealth, see Lindert and Williamson 2016, 20, as well as the recommendations by the OECD 2013.

40. For additional discussion of the possible faults of preindustrial sources for studying wealth distribution, see Alfani 2021; for examples of preindustrial social control against fiscal misbehaviour, see Alfani 2015, 1064. For concerns about modern tax evasion and avoidance, see Roine and Waldenström 2015, 518–19; Alstadsæter, Johannesen and Zucman 2019.

41. Davies and Shorrocks 2000, 643.

42. For additional discussion of the rich lists as sources for studying wealth distribution, see Davies and Shorrocks 2000, 642–3; Medeiros and Ferreira de Souza 2014, 5–7; for recent examples of their use in social science research, see Rockoff 2012; Freund 2016; Korom, Lutter and Beckert 2017; Bonica and Rosenthal 2018.

2. Wealth Concentration and the Prevalence of the Rich across History

1. See the 'Defining Wealth across the Ages' section in chapter 1, on the components of wealth in small-scale societies. In general, on inequality in prehistory, see Borgerhoff Mulder et al. 2009; Bowles, Smith and Borgerhoff Mulder 2010; Kohler et al. 2017; Bogaard, Fochesato

and Bowles 2019; also see the 'A Thorny Issue: Inheritance' section in chapter 7 for some data and further discussion. On the impact on inequality of the appearance of the first city-states, see Diamond 1997 and Scheidel 2017, as well as the early intuitions by Lenski 1966.

2. Milanović 2011, 42; Scheidel 2017, 71–5; Lavan and Weisweiler 2022, 228–33.

3. We have some tentative estimates of income (not wealth) inequality. At the apogee of the Roman Empire, around 150 CE, the Gini inequality index may have been slightly above 0.4 (the point estimate is 0.413) in the empire as a whole (Milanović 2019, 12, based on Scheidel and Friesen 2009; also see Scheidel 2017, 78). Previously, in 14 CE, the Gini index has been estimated to vary in the 0.364–0.394 range (Milanović, Lindert and Williamson 2007, 77). Inequality declined steeply in later periods, to around 0.1 by the year 600 or 700, associated with the empire's decline and fall (Milanović 2019, 8–10). On Roman inequality, see also the synthesis in Alfani 2021, 7–8.

4. New estimates based on the datasets introduced in Alfani 2015 and Alfani and Ammannati 2017 for the Sabaudian State and the Florentine State; for Italy today, see *Global Wealth Databook* 2021, 136.

5. The estimate of Black Death mortality is from Alfani and Murphy 2017, 316; the same article also offers an overview of the long-term impact of the pandemic (on this topic, see also Jedwab, Johnson and Koyama 2022 and the additional literature cited in the 'The Rich and the Black Death: Boom or Bust?' section in chapter 11).

6. See the 'The Rich and the Black Death: Boom or Bust?' section in chapter 11 for a more detailed discussion of the underlying mechanism. For Toulouse, I provide new estimates based on the dataset introduced in Alfani 2021; on income inequality in the Low Countries, see Ryckbosch 2016; on the impact of the Black Death on real wages, see Pamuk 2007; Campbell 2010; Fochesato 2018. On the general distributive consequences of major plagues, see Alfani 2022.

7. Note that, for England, a slightly higher wealth inequality ca. 1500 compared to ca. 1300 cannot be taken as evidence of monotonic inequality growth between the two dates, as, based on the overall evidence available, it is virtually a certainty that, there as well, inequality decreased after the Black Death and recovered thereafter. On this issue, see Alfani and García Montero 2022.

8. An increase in the share of the top 5% is found, for example, in the French city of Vence in Provence, where it equalled 22.6% in 1550, 26.3% in 1679 and 28.2% in 1777. In the rural village of Cornillon in Languedoc, the richest 5% owned 32.7% of all wealth in 1442, 36.7% in 1642 and 44.1% in 1691. Moving westwards, we have some information about the region of Catalonia in Spain. Here, in the town of Cervera, the richest 5% owned 25.3% of all wealth around 1400, 33.4% in 1500 and slightly less in 1600 (32.5%). By 1700 they had recovered a bit (32.8%); thereafter their share grew considerably, peaking at 37.4% by 1800. In the small city of Reus, the richest 5% owned 25.4% of all wealth around 1450, 31.5% in 1550 and 31.6% in 1650 (new information from the EINITE database). In the region of Valencia, immediately south of Catalonia, we have information for the city of Castellón. Here, the share of the top 5% was 23.6% in 1398, 20.3% in 1464, 20.8% in 1497 and 25.9% in 1499 (Furió 2017). An overall tendency for wealth inequality to grow has also been reported for the province of Madrid in central Spain from 1500 to 1800 (Santiago-Caballero and Fernández 2013).

9. Lindert 1986, 2000; Alfani and García Montero 2022.

10. New elaborations based on the dataset introduced by Alfani, Gierok and Schaff 2022.

11. See chapter 4 for examples of personal enrichment in England in early modern and early industrial times. On current estimates of per-capita GDP, see the Maddison Project Database (2020) as well as Fouquet and Broadberry 2015. Regarding the concept of 'inequality extraction ration', see Milanović, Williamson and Lindert 2011, and on its application to preindustrial societies, see Alfani and Ryckbosch 2016 and Alfani 2021.

12. In the rural areas of Flanders and Brabant, in 1570 the richest 1% and 5% owned, respectively, 13.7% and 34.4% of all land. Land became more concentrated in the following centuries, probably continuing a pre-existing trend, if we can generalize the case of the rural areas around the city of Kortrijk, where the share of the top 1% grew from 6.1% in 1383 to 11.1% in 1570, while that of the top 5% rose from 28.2% to 37.9%. See Alfani and Ryckbosch 2016, appendix D, and new information from the EINITE database.

13. For Sweden, see Bengtsson et al. 2018, 780; for Finland, see Bengtsson et al. 2019, 237. For Scotland, see Soltow 1990, 46.

14. Wealth defined as net worth. Lindert (2000, 188) provides the figure for the top 1% as well as one for the top 10% (59%). These figures include both free and slave households. The figure for the top 5% has been obtained by interpolating these estimates with others related to property incomes. The latter have been kindly provided by Peter Lindert, to whom I am also grateful for advice on how to use them to produce estimates of net worth. The assumption used for estimating the net worth of the top 5% is that, in America in 1774, the rates of return across all assets owned by the top 10% were the same.

15. Data from the same sources reported for Table 2.1. For France, see also Piketty, Postel-Vinay and Rosenthal 2006, 2014; Piketty 2014.

16. On wealth concentration in North America see also, for the United States, Lindert and Williamson 2016, 121–2; for Canada, Di Matteo 2018. On broad comparisons between countries and world areas, see also the recent synthesis in Alfani and Schifano 2021 (with data about Gini indexes and the wealth share of the top 10% in 1820–2010).

17. Regarding inequality reduction in the period from World War I to World War II, see Piketty 2014, 182–5, as well as the in-depth discussion in chapter 11, especially the sections 'The Rich during Wars and the Wars of the Rich' and 'The Rich during Financial Crises'.

18. Alvaredo et al. 2013, 5–6.

19. Data for the United States are from Saez and Zucman 2016; for Denmark, Norway and Sweden from Roine and Waldenström 2015; for Spain, Alvaredo and Saez 2010, 543. See also chapter 11, Figure 11.2, for the trend in the wealth share of the richest 0.1% in Germany.

20. *Global Wealth Databook* 2021, 136.

21. Piketty 2014; see also, for the trend of the wealth share of the top 10%, Alfani 2021.

22. See Alfani 2019, 2021 for a more thorough discussion.

23. Piketty 2014, 184. See the 'The Rich during Wars and the Wars of the Rich' section in chapter 11 for further discussion of the distributive impact of the World Wars and other major wars. On progressive/regressive fiscal systems in their historical manifestations, see Atkinson 2004; Piketty 2014; and (for preindustrial times) Alfani and Di Tullio 2019.

24. This had been argued by Herlihy (1967, 1968), whose pioneering studies on the distributive impact of the Black Death remained for many decades the only ones available. Reversing the conventional wisdom entailed demonstrating that Herlihy's conclusions were based on faulty data for Tuscany (see discussion in Alfani and Ammannati 2017 and Alfani 2021, 17–18).

The first study to report post-Black Death inequality decline (for the Sabaudian State in north-western Italy) and to discuss the discrepancy with Herlihy's conclusions is Alfani 2015.

25. Scheidel 2017; see also critical discussion in Alfani 2021.

26. See further discussion in chapter 11. For a more optimistic interpretation of the role that could be played by preindustrial institutions, see van Bavel 2022.

27. Milanović 2016; see also critical discussion in Alfani 2021.

28. On the applicability of Kuznets' hypothesis to wealth, see Lindert 1991, 215–19; 2014; Alfani 2021; on criticism of Kuznets' conclusions, see Lindert 2000; Alfani 2021; Alfani and Schifano 2021.

29. Van Zanden 1995; Soltow and van Zanden 1998. More recently, van Bavel (2016) made a similar argument. For him, in the Dutch Republic in early modern times income and wealth inequality increased due to the development of market economies and the related increases in the efficient scale of trade and production, growing opportunities for financial dealing and speculation and growing investment opportunities. See the 'A New World of Opportunities' section in chapter 4 for a discussion of opportunities for personal enrichment during the Dutch 'Golden Age'.

30. Alfani 2010a, 2015; Alfani and Ryckbosch 2016; Alfani and Ammannati 2017; Alfani and Di Tullio 2019.

31. On the redistributive effects of increasing taxation in preindustrial times, see Alfani 2015, 2021; Alfani and Ryckbosch 2016; Alfani and Di Tullio 2019. On the rise of the fiscal state as a historical process, see Yun-Casalilla and O'Brien 2012.

32. See chapter 10 for additional discussion.

33. In the United States, the top rate peaked at 94% in 1944–5. In the same period, it reached 97.5% in the United Kingdom. Atkinson 2004; Alvaredo et al. 2013.

34. For an overall discussion of changes in the degree of progressivity of fiscal systems, see Atkinson 2004; Atkinson et al. 2011; Alvaredo et al. 2013; Lindert 2021a, chapter 10. See Messere, de Kam and Heady 2003, 23, for the reported top rates in personal income tax and Piketty 2014, 644, for top rates in estate/inheritance tax. On the way in which changes in the top rates of personal income tax might have affected wage negotiation, see Alvaredo et al. 2013.

35. Lindert and Williamson 2016. For an overview of different concurrent explanations of wealth and income inequality growth after 1980, see Roine and Waldenström 2015.

36. See the 'Who Can Be Considered "Rich"?' section in chapter 1 for additional technical discussion, as well as Alfani 2017a.

37. Estimating the prevalence of the rich in preindustrial England is impossible for technical reasons; as will be remembered from the 'From the Black Death (and Earlier) to the American Revolution' section in chapter 2, the English data for the period 1650–1800 come from social tables, which do not allow the production of the kind of detailed distribution needed for this purpose.

38. On the impact of the Thirty Years' War on the prevalence of poverty in Germany, see Alfani 2020a; Alfani, Ammannati and Ryckbosch 2022; Alfani, Gierok and Schaff 2022, 2023.

39. On this methodological choice, see Alfani 2017a.

40. On the relative economic and urbanization tendencies of the Italian pre-unification states, see Alfani and Percoco 2019; Alfani 2020b, 203–6.

41. Data from *Global Wealth Databook* 2012 and 2021.

3. On Aristocracy, New and Past

1. Our definition of nobility does not aim to reflect any specific historical system of classification but simply has the purpose of identifying with sufficient clarity a social group with characteristics that are relevant to our analysis. This is because definitions of nobility (both formal/juridical definitions *and* those which were used in practice) varied greatly across space and time. In general, 'Every European state had its own peculiarities. Most had a de facto or de iure division between a lesser, untitled nobility and an upper titled nobility of princes, dukes, counts or earls, marquises, barons and equivalents. In Britain this was represented by the peers, in France by the so-called *ducs et pairs*, in individual German states by the *Herrenstand* ("estate of lords") or *Hochadel* ("high nobility") as opposed to the *Ritterstand* ("the estate of knights") or the *Adel*, the ordinary, non-titled nobility. . . . Complex gradations, forming often bewildering sub-hierarchies, existed everywhere. . . . There was no lack of gray areas. Iberian *grandes* or *titulos* were generally wealthier and more powerful versions of *hidalgos* or *nobres*—but whether the former would really view many of the latter as the same social species is highly questionable' (Lukowski 2003, 3).

2. Weber 1978 [1956].

3. Dewald 1996; Mączak 2001; Lukowski 2003.

4. This is, again, in basic accordance with Weber 1978 [1956].

5. Weber 1978 [1956], 1064.

6. This point will be discussed further in the 'Nobility and Wealth: Some Further Reflections' section in chapter 3.

7. Beresford and Rubinstein 2007, 19–22, and elsewhere. For additional information about Alan Rufus, see Fleming 1991; Golding 2013; Kampfner 2014.

8. Mitchell 1973.

9. Bringmann 1998, 9–14.

10. Mączak 2001.

11. Mączak 2001, 738.

12. Duby 1973, 1978; Mączak 2001.

13. Tilly 1992, 184.

14. This point will be discussed in detail in the 'The Rich during Wars and the Wars of the Rich' section in chapter 11.

15. On the self-understanding of preindustrial societies as unequal, see the 'On Inequality and the Perception of the Rich' section in chapter 8 for further discussion, as well as Levi 2003; Alfani and Frigeni 2016.

16. Weber 1978 [1956], 248.

17. Mousnier 1974, 107–8, 130–5; Dewald 1996; Mączak 2001.

18. For more information about the Crozat dynasty, see Ménard 2017.

19. Lane 1973, 112–14, 252–3. Note that each and every patrician of Venice could also use the title of *nobiluomo* or 'nobleman' (Cozzi 1995, 168).

20. Knapton 1995, 480; Alfani and Di Tullio 2019, 82.

21. Lane 1973, 430; Sabbadini 1995, 15–16, 20–2. According to Lane, 100,000 Venetian ducats at the time were 'socially comparable' to 10 million in 1970 U.S. dollars or about 67 million in 2020 U.S. dollars.

22. Mocarelli 2009, 118.

23. See Alfani 2013a for the Sabaudian State; see Endres 1993, 90, for Prussia.

24. Lukowski 2003, 22.

25. Bayard 1988, 439.

26. Lukowski 2003.

27. Veblen 2007 [1899].

28. Weber 1978 [1956], 692.

29. Piketty, Postel-Vinay and Rosenthal 2006, 244–6.

30. Article I, Section 9, Clause 8, and Section 10, Clause 1.

31. Romaniuk and Wasylciw 2014, 111.

32. Rubinstein 2006, 312.

33. The relative prevalence of nobles among the British rich will be explored in chapter 7.

34. Goody 1983.

35. Barker 2004.

36. At the time of writing, only for succession to the crown has the male-preference primogeniture rule been replaced by an absolute primogeniture rule in Britain.

37. This was for example the case after the substantial increase in death duties which occurred from the 1920s to the 1940s, although their ultimate impact on the transmission of inherited wealth remains somewhat unclear (Hardbury 1962, 1980; Cannadine 1999, 95–8; Atkinson 2018).

38. On the British nobility of the nineteenth and twentieth centuries, see Becket 1986; Cannadine 1999; Friedman and Reeves 2020. On marriages between British nobles and daughters of rich industrialists, see Rubinstein 2006, 250–1; Friedman and Reeves 2020, 331–2. On Boni de Castellane and Anna Gould's marriage, see Cannadine 1999, 25; Mension-Rigau 2008.

39. Lansely 2006, 101–5.

40. See Tocqueville 2017 [1835–40], and the insightful comment by Pakulski 2005, 155–7.

41. Jaher 1972, 35.

42. Jaher 1972, 34–5.

43. Jones 1980; Kilbride 2006.

44. Burt 1999 [1963].

45. Jaher 1972, 57.

46. Jaher 1973, 263–6.

47. Dewald 1996, 40–7.

48. Callahan 1972; Dewald 1996, 20; Lukowski 2003, 19–20.

49. Beyond the rather drastic measure of the revocation of nobility, in much of continental Europe, e.g., in France, nobility could be suspended and become dormant—a procedure known as *dérogeance* or 'derogation'—allowing an individual to pursue more profitable careers (for example in the merchant navy) and investments, but at the cost of the suspension of all privileges including fiscal ones. Wealth restored, that individual or his descendants could resume living nobly and apply for an end to the derogation of nobility (although some sort of bourgeois taint would usually continue to be perceived). Hence, the principle that nobility of blood cannot be lost was preserved, while the enjoyment of the privileges of nobility was conditional upon conduct proper for a noble (Mousnier 1974, 137–8).

50. Paci 1987, 30.

51. Mousnier 1974, 137, my translation.

52. Lane 1973, 264; Del Negro 1998, 18–19; Harivel 2019, 131.

53. Mousnier 1974, 137.

54. Dewald 1996, 93–4.

55. Temin and Voth 2013; Ventura and Voth 2019.

56. Alfani and Di Tullio 2019, 173; Pezzolo 2012, 279. Also note that, for the least risk-averse among nobles and at least in some settings, new investment opportunities appeared with the introduction of stock markets and public banks from the early seventeenth century (Venice was, again, a pioneer together with its northern rival, Amsterdam), as well as with the expansion of colonial empires and the development of opportunities to invest in the booming Atlantic trade (Dewald 1996, 95). This point is developed further in chapter 5.

57. Weber 1946, 188, and, for an application to today's society, see Doob 2013, 32–3.

58. Mörke 1996, 143.

59. Cited from Augustine 1994, 203.

60. Berghoff 1994, 183–6.

61. Augustine 1994, 239–42.

62. Berghoff 1994, 183.

63. Haseler 2000, xi.

64. See, e.g., the forecasts about the annual inheritance flow proposed by Piketty (2014, 504–10, 538–40) or, for current developments in Italy, Acciari and Morelli 2020. On worries about the emergence of a new global aristocracy, see also Rothkopf 2009.

65. According to Mills (1956, 11) the members of a power elite 'accept one another, understand one another, marry one another, tend to work and to think, if not together at least alike', and this is *without* them necessarily being aware of this behaviour. Mills' views have been widely influential and have been further developed and applied to American society today by other scholars, like, e.g., Dye (2002) and especially Domhoff (2007, 2010).

66. Reeves et al. 2017; Friedman and Laurison 2019, 148–9.

67. Khan 2012, 372. For the case of the United States, see also Khan 2011. Note that although the United States has a very strong tradition of public secondary schooling (somewhat damaged in recent years by a tendency towards resegregation: compare Irvin 2008, 156), at least in some parts of the country (especially the north-east) prep schools play an important role in the upbringing of the children of the very rich and apparently provide their pupils with a decisive advantage over public school applicants when seeking admission to Ivy League universities (Beeghley 2016, 196).

68. Independent School Council Census and Annual Report 2020; Independent School Council Census 2017. The figures for Eton come from the Independent Schools Inspectorate, *Regulatory Compliance Inspection Report*, Eton College, March 2019.

69. Reeves et al. 2017, 1161.

4. On Innovation and Technology

1. Schumpeter 1934, 1942.

2. On the interpretation of the Roman Empire as a setting relatively unfavourable to trade and entrepreneurial activities, see Lopez 1976, 6–10, and more recently Scheidel 2019.

3. Braudel 1992; for a recent take on this topic, see van Bavel 2016.

4. Weber 1978 [1956], 1099.

5. On the early phases of the Commercial Revolution, see Lopez 1976; Hunt and Murray 1999.

6. In the words of historian Robert Lopez, 'In the theoretical structure of feudal society there scarcely was room for a middle class between the exalted religious and lay lords and the lowly but irreplaceable laborers. Paupers were more acceptable than merchants: they would inherit the Kingdom of Heaven and help the almsgiving rich to earn entrance. Merchants were gold-hungry, said Rathier, the Belgian bishop of Verona; they were less useful than farmers who fed the entire population, said Aelfric, the English abbot of Eynsham; they did not know what honor means, said Ramon Muntaner, the Catalan soldier-adventurer' (Lopez 1971, 60).

7. Todeschini 2002; Levi 2003; Alfani and Frigeni 2016.

8. Here is how a monk who frequently visited Godric, Reginald of Durham, describes his ascent: 'Thus aspiring ever higher and higher, and yearning upward with his whole heart, at length his great labours and cares bore much fruit of worldly gain. For he laboured not only as a merchant but also as a shipman . . . to Denmark and Flanders and Scotland; in all which lands he found certain rare, and therefore more precious, wares, which he carried to other parts wherein he knew them to be least familiar, and coveted by the inhabitants beyond the price of gold itself; wherefore he exchanged these wares for others coveted by men of other lands; and thus he chaffered most freely and assiduously. Hence he made great profit in all his bargains, and gathered much wealth in the sweat of his brow; for he sold dear in one place the wares which he had bought elsewhere at a small price' (Reginald of Durham, *Life of St Godric*, quoted from Coulton 1918, 417–18).

9. On the case of Godric of Finchale, see Coulton 1918, 415–20; Pirenne 1927; Tudor 1981.

10. This system, which replaced earlier unitary companies that were often the collective endeavour of entire merchant families, was a 'network-star' ownership system in which a controlling partner who did not manage branches directly established legally separated part-nerships with branch managers in different industries or locations (Padgett and McLean 2006, 1465–7).

11. On Francesco di Marco Datini and his business activities, see Melis 1962; Luzzati 1987; Padgett and McLean 2006; Nanni 2010; Nigro 2010.

12. Cohn 1988.

13. Padgett 2010; Lindholm 2017; Alfani 2022; Alfani, Ammannati and Balbo 2022.

14. Lopez and Miskimin 1962, 423–5.

15. Franceschi 2020.

16. The impact of major crises, and especially of pandemics, on the rich and the would-be rich will be explored in detail in chapter 11.

17. See the case of the Mendes family in chapter 5.

18. See chapter 5 for further discussion. On the opening of the Atlantic trade routes and their historical significance, see Chaunu 1977; Braudel 1992; Findlay and O'Rourke 2009; Miller 2015; de Zwart and van Zanden 2018.

19. A global estimate for the seventeenth and eighteenth centuries places the mortality rate for Dutch seamen embarked on VOC trips to Asia at about 40% and that of Dutch soldiers at 70%. The mortality rate among other European personnel embarked on VOC ships was even

higher: about 58% and 81% for seamen and soldiers respectively. These figures include mortality during the outbound journey, the period of stay in Asia and the return journey. Lucassen 2004, 15–16.

20. Findlay and O'Rourke 2009, 179.

21. On Jan Pieterszoon Coen, see Findlay and O'Rourke 2009, 178–84; Kampfner 2014; Prak and van Zanden 2022.

22. De Zwart and van Zanden 2018, 268. Note that the question of how the early modern commercial and colonial expansion affected Europe's economy, and how it might potentially be connected to the onset of the Industrial Revolution, is a thorny and much-debated one— compare, e.g., the different views in O'Brien 1982; David and Huttenback 1987; Pomeranz 2000; Findlay and O'Rourke 2009; de Zwart and van Zanden 2018.

23. The estimate of the earnings of a VOC governor-general (which does not refer specifically to Jan Pieterszoon Coen) and that of the yearly dividend paid by the company come from Landes 1998, 145–6.

24. Lane 2015.

25. Andrews 1984, 154–5.

26. *Forbes*, 'Top-Earning Pirates', 2008. https://www.forbes.com/2008/09/18/top-earning -pirates-biz-logistics-cx_mw_0919piracy.html?sh=ee25d347263b. The companion article to the pirates list dubs high-seas piracy the 'investment banking of the colonial era'. This is surely an improper comparison; however it is indicative of an enduring cultural mistrust of financiers, as will be discussed in the next chapter.

27. Lane 2015.

28. This episode was followed by the founding in the same spot of a new city on a Dutch model, Batavia (today Jakarta), which was to become VOC's headquarters and indeed remained the capital of the Dutch East Indies until Indonesia's independence in 1949.

29. Findlay and O'Rourke 2009, 179–81; Kampfner 2014, 166–9, 173–4; on the controversies regarding Coen's figure, see Johnson 2014.

30. On the ascent of Francisco Pizarro and his family, see Varon Gabai and Jacobs 1987; Varon Gabai 1997; Kampfner 2014.

31. Cited from Lane 2015, 391.

32. Livi Bacci 2006.

33. Varon Gabai and Jacobs 1987, 662.

34. Findlay and O'Rourke 2009, 183.

35. Manning 1992, 119.

36. For some estimates of the revenues from the import of slaves from West Africa to Brazil, see Miller 1988, 476–81. Note that the actual profitability of the slave trade (in various epochs) is a rather contentious issue. For a brief survey of the debate, see Antunes and Ribeiro da Silva 2012, 3–5; Burnard and Riello 2020, 233–5.

37. In general, on the Atlantic slave trade, see Miller 1988; Eltis and Richardson 2010; Antunes and Ribeiro da Silva 2012; Richardson 2015; de Zwart and van Zanden 2018.

38. Andrews 1984; Pomeranz 2000. For a recent overview of the debate about the importance of slavery for European economic development, see Burnard and Riello 2020. For an attempt at providing a balanced interpretation of the nature and long-term effects of the early phase of economic globalization, see de Zwart and van Zanden 2018.

39. Hunt and Murray 1999, 188–9.

40. De Vries and van der Woude 1997, 249.

41. On the early modern Dutch fishing industry, see Prak 2005; de Vries and van der Woude 1997, especially 243–54.

42. Specifically, this was a water-powered throwing mill which allowed considerable amounts of labour to be saved, dramatically reduced the production cost of silkware and thus led to a dramatic expansion of its potential market (Lopez 1952, 76; Crippa 1990).

43. Van der Linden 2012, 293.

44. Van der Linden 2012, 294.

45. Technically this was the renewal of the Imperial Post Privilege (*kaiserliches Postregal*) from which the Tasso had benefited from the late sixteenth century, but now Emperor Matthias (Rudolph II's brother and successor) made it inheritable for Lamoral's descendants (Behringer 1990).

46. On the Tasso/Thurn und Taxis family, see Behringer 1990; Bottani 2012; Cavarzere 2019.

47. Landes 1969, 1.

48. On the debate on the nature of the Industrial Revolution and to cite but a few recent examples from a vast literature, see Allen 2009; Mokyr 2016; Wrigley 2016. On the Second Industrial Revolution, see also Landes 1969.

49. This view was strongly supported by Karl Marx and by Marxist economic historians, but also by other scholars who could not be easily linked to the political left, in a tradition that dates back to Adam Smith. The topic will be further discussed in chapter 6.

50. 'The proposition I put forward . . . is that the explosion of technological progress in the West was made possible by cultural changes. "Culture" affected technology both directly, by changing attitudes toward the natural world, and indirectly, by creating and nurturing institutions that stimulated and supported the accumulation and diffusion of "useful knowledge"' (Mokyr 2017, 7).

51. McCloskey 2006, 2016.

52. On Richard Arkwright, see Fitton 1989; Mason 2004; Beresford and Rubinstein 2007, 359.

53. On Josiah Wedgwood, see McKendrick 1960; Dolan 2004; Beresford and Rubinstein 2007, 372–3.

54. On Solvay, see Bolle 1963; Despy-Meyer and Devriese 1997; Bertrams et al. 2013.

55. On the German *Raubritter* (a historiographic category whose utility has been challenged in recent years), see Görner 1987.

56. Note that while many have highlighted the exploitative attitude of the 'robber barons' and their monopolistic ambitions, others, in a tradition that dates back to business historian Alfred Chandler (1959, 1977), have argued that their entrepreneurship played a positive role in establishing certain characteristic features of American industry and in particular the presence of great corporations able to exploit the vast integrated market created by the building of a national railroad network.

57. On the robber barons in general, see White 2011; Geisst 2012. On Andrew Carnegie, see Edge 2004; Livesay 2006; Harvey 2011.

58. On Gould 'the monopolist', see Geisst 2000; for a more positive judgement, see the classic Chandler 1977.

59. Klein 1978, 167.

60. Lindert and Williamson 2016, and Cashman 1993, 40, for the *New-York Tribune* enquiry. See chapter 3 for further discussion of Tocqueville's views.

61. Carnegie 1889, 3–6.

62. Remember the distinction between 'aristocracy' and 'nobility' which was introduced in the 'What's in a Noble? Some Initial Definitions' section in chapter 3.

63. Veblen 2007 [1899], 7.

64. Roughly from the late-sixteenth to the late-seventeenth century.

65. De Vries and van der Woude 1997, 586–96; Prak 2005, 126–7; Prak and van Zanden 2022, 184–6.

66. Prak 2005, 127–8.

67. Cattini and Romani 2005; Di Tullio 2014.

68. Alfani 2013b; Alfani and Di Tullio 2019; Alfani and Percoco 2019.

69. In Italy, these processes were further exacerbated by the fact that the famines of the sixteenth and early seventeenth centuries also contributed to the disappearance of many of the residual common properties. Local communities put them up for sale, and they were promptly bought by the same capital-rich individuals and families that were buying up small owners' lands. On these dynamics, see Alfani and Rao 2011; Alfani 2013c; Di Tullio 2014.

70. On the Wedgwood-Darwin dynasty, see Clift 2008.

71. Beresford and Rubinstein 2007, 359.

72. Fitton 1989.

73. On the Whitbread family, see Fulford 1967; Rapp 1974.

74. Daunton 1989; Rubinstein 1991; Nicholas 1999. We will return to some aspects of this debate in chapters 5 and 7.

75. Augustine 1994, 28

76. Amatori and Colli 1999; Colli 2003.

77. Zuckerberg co-founded Facebook (the company was renamed Meta in October 2021) with Chris Hughes, Andrew McCollum, Dustin Moskovitz and Eduardo Saverin (each of them a billionaire today), but he is the one who has retained control of the company to this day, also acting as chairman and CEO. For a brief synthesis of the rise of Silicon Valley enterprises, see Levy 2021, 637–47.

78. J. Bick, 'The Microsoft Millionaires Come of Age', *The New York Times*, 29 May 2005, https://www.nytimes.com/2005/05/29/business/yourmoney/the-microsoft-millionaires -come-of-age.html.

79. On Bill Gates and Microsoft, see Cringely 1996; Kampfner 2014. On the antitrust case generated by the Browser War with Netscape, see Geisst 2000, 317–19.

80. On Amazon's trial, see Press Release of the European Commission, 10 November 2020, https://ec.europa.eu/commission/presscorner/detail/en/ip_20_2077. On fines imposed on Google, see, e.g., Press Release of the European Commission, 20 March 2019, https://ec.europa .eu/commission/presscorner/detail/en/IP_19_1770.

81. Kampfner 2014, 353.

82. For a synthesis, see Alvaredo et al. 2013.

83. Growing within-company inequalities in remuneration have been the object of a large scientific literature, e.g., Bebchuk and Fried 2004; Mueller et al. 2017.

84. Freund 2016, 38, 41–2.

85. See chapter 7 for further details.

86. Harvey, Maclean and Suddaby 2019.

5. On Finance

1. Cited in Melis 1962, 213, my translation.

2. For example, in the New Testament, Luke 4:34–5: 'If you lend to those from whom you expect repayment, what credit is that to you? Even sinners lend to sinners, expecting to be repaid in full. But love your enemies, do good to them, and lend to them without expecting to get anything back. Then your reward will be great'.

3. Le Goff 1964, 1986.

4. Le Goff 1986, 18, my translation.

5. Le Goff 1986, 26–7.

6. Fourquin 1969, 259; 1981, 428–54.

7. Todeschini 2009; 2011, 150–3; 2019.

8. Todeschini 2002.

9. De Roover 1963, 11–14. Note that in medieval and early modern Europe bills of exchange became widely used as means to settle accounts in international trade because they didn't require the physical transfer of large quantities of money. As used in mercantile activity, the bill of exchange (*cambium*) simply consisted of a letter addressed by one merchant based in city A to his agent-banker in city B, ordering him to make a payment (in city B's currency) on behalf of another merchant. For its use in international banking, this simple but highly versatile instrument could be adapted in a variety of ways. For example, a second letter could be required (the *recambium*), by which the beneficiary in city B arranged for the restitution at a later date of the sum in city A. As seen, interest could be included in the price of the bill, hidden in the exchange rate applied to the currencies of city A and city B. However, 'the merchants argued—and most of the theologians accepted these views—that an exchange transaction was not a loan (*cambium non est mutuum*) but either a commutation of moneys (*permutatio*) or a buying and selling of foreign currency (*emptio venditio*). . . . [I]t was argued that *cambium* was not usurious, since there could be no usury where there was no loan' (De Roover 1963, 11). The boundary between licit and illicit activities, however, was not clear-cut. For example, when *cambium* and *recambium* bills were issued but no actual settlement took place in city B (the so-called 'dry exchange'), then the overall transaction was reproved by medieval theologians as a concealed loan (De Roover 1963, 132–4).

10. On the Peruzzi, Bardi and Acciaiuoli see Sapori 1926; Hunt 1994; Hunt and Murray 1999, 102–17.

11. Padgett and Ansell 1993, 1262.

12. Based on de Roover 1963, 30–1, 47, 55 and 69–70.

13. De Roover 1963, 213.

14. Machiavelli 2006 [1532], Book 4, Chapter 7.

15. In general, on the rise of the Medici family, see de Roover 1963; Kent 1975, 1978; Goldthwaite 1987; Padgett and Ansell 1993; Najemy 2006.

16. Braudel 1966; Miskimin 1977, 173; Häberlein 1998, 37–8, 157–8.

17. This kind of arrangement worked for both sides—nobles and financier-entrepreneurs—as the aristocratic owners of the mineral deposits usually lacked the means and the skills to develop

them, so they were happy to lease the rights of exploitation in exchange for high and regular incomes. While these were usually a fraction of the profits reaped by the entrepreneurs, the latter had to suffer constant requests for loans from the lords, which they could not easily refuse for fear of losing the mining rights and other concessions (Hunt and Murray 1999, 224–5).

18. The simple confiscation in Antwerp in 1557 of a shipment of American silver destined for the Fuggers caused them a loss of 570,000 Spanish ducats or about 952,000 florins (Häberlein 2006, 93).

19. On the Fugger family, see Häberlein 2012; Steinmetz 2015; Schneider 2016; Blendinger 2021. On the financial crises triggered by Philip II's default, see the classic account by Braudel (1966), which however has been deeply revised by recent studies, and particularly Álvarez-Nogal and Chamley 2014 and Drelichman and Voth 2014.

20. Álvarez-Nogal and Chamley 2014; Drelichman and Voth 2014; Neal 2015, 45–9.

21. Hunt and Murray 1999, 224.

22. Parker 1988; Rogers 1995.

23. Bonney 1999, 7–9, although the 'modernity' of the Roman Imperial fiscal system should not be exaggerated: compare Scheidel 2015, 233–42.

24. Pezzolo 1998, 54; Alfani and Di Tullio 2019, 34–6.

25. De Vries 1976, 202; Kindleberger 1984, 169.

26. Bonney 1999; Yun-Casalilla and O'Brien 2012.

27. Bayard 1988.

28. Collins 1988.

29. Miskimin 1977, 164.

30. City Archive of Ivrea, Category 14 (*censimento*), n. 1750.

31. Consider again the case of the Sabaudian State in 1613: in Susa, the second-richest individual was the local governor; in Ivrea, the richest of all was the *referendario* (an officer who received requests for justice or pleas to the duke); finally in Moncalieri, the richest was the superintendent (*maggiordomo*) of the duke and the second-richest was the prefect.

32. Quinn and Turner 2020. See chapter 11 for some additional discussion of financial crises.

33. VOC stands for *Vereenigde Oost-Indische compagnie* and WIC for *West-Indische compagnie*: respectively, East and West India Company.

34. Some of the societal characteristics of the VOC had their antecedents in earlier innovations, like the *partenrederij* which had developed in the fishing industry: see the 'New Opportunities in the Old World' section in chapter 4.

35. De Vries and van der Woude 1997, 384–8; Neal 2015, 55–8.

36. Chaudhury 1999 [1965], 31–3; Smith 2021, 70–5.

37. Roy 2012, 15. On investors in the EIC, see also Chaudhuri 1978, 1999 [1965]; Mays and Shea 2011. Note that one reason why shareholding of the EIC was much more restricted compared to the VOC was a higher minimum investment, which in 1609 was set at 100 pounds (Chaudhuri 1999 [1965], 33).

38. Dewald 1996, 95–6.

39. Neal 2015, 39; Alfani and Di Tullio 2019, 272–3. See also, on the owners of the public debt of the Republic of Venice and of other Italian preindustrial states, Pezzolo 1995.

40. De Vries and van der Woude 1997, 119.

41. For the older view about England, see Hobsbawm 1968. For the more recent position (sceptical about the idea of a special interest of noble landowners in canals) see Ward 1974; Jones 2010.

42. Bogart 2019, 861–3.

43. Historian Eric Jones has recently argued that many among those who had made a fortune in London or Bristol, or even industrialists from the north, transferred to the gentle countryside of the south, buying estates, as a step in their and their descendants' gentrification. As a consequence, 'Capital was withdrawn from commerce and applied to rustic futilities offering minimal social return' (Jones 2010, 159).

44. Winkel 1968.

45. On Court Jews, or court factors (*Hoffaktoren* in Germany, where they were particularly widespread), see Israel 1989, 123–44.

46. On the Rothschild family, see Davis 1983; Ferguson 1999, 2000; Landes 2006.

47. Veblen 2007 [1899], 150–1.

48. 'To the business man who aims at a differential gain arising out of interstitial adjustments or disturbances of the industrial system, it is not a material question whether his operations have an immediate furthering or hindering effect upon the system at large. The end is pecuniary gain, the means is disturbance of the industrial system . . . The outcome of this management of industrial affairs through pecuniary transactions . . . has been to dissociate the interests of those men who exercise the discretion from the interests of the community' (Veblen 1904, 28–9). The 'disturbances of the industrial system' from which, in Veblen's view, those belonging to the world of business obtained their profits led directly to societal damage, e.g., by leading to higher unemployment. Successful businessmen had interests diverging from those of the community at large; in a sense, they did not fit in, as, according to many across history, was the case for the super-rich more generally, as will be seen in chapter 8.

49. See for example Landes 2006.

50. Indeed, 'Wall Street finance before World War I was . . . several orders of magnitude more concentrated than it has been at any time since. This concentration of finance was a major political flashpoint' (De Long 1991, 207).

51. On the Morgan family, see Carosso 1987; Chernow 1990; Landes 2006. On the 1907 financial crisis, see Bruner and Carr 2007; Levy 2012, 268–72. On the pre-World War I American 'money trust', see de Long 1991; Geisst 2000.

52. De Luca 1996, 198–9.

53. On women's legal capacity to act in preindustrial and early industrial Europe, see Feci 2004, 2018; Pasciuta 2018.

54. Laurence, Malby and Rutterford 2009, 7–10; Robb 2017, 6–7.

55. Dermineur 2018; Lorenzini 2021.

56. On the notion of dark matter credit see Hoffman, Postel-Vinay and Rosenthal 2019.

57. For Milan, Lorenzini 2021, 7; for France, Hoffman, Postel-Vinay and Rosenthal 2000, 66–8; Dermineur 2014, 6–9.

58. Lorenzini 2021, 10.

59. Gracia Nasi is also known by her Christian name, Beatriz de Luna.

60. On Gracia Nasi and the Mendes family see Roth 1977; Muzzarelli 1991; Birnbaum 2003.

61. Acheson et al. 2021.

62. Carlos and Neal 2004, 217–18; Laurence 2009, 47; Robb 2017, 3–5.

63. Robb 2017, 13.

64. Robb 2017, 40–61, and elsewhere.

65. While this 'in practice' was a split, technically the Morgan bank chose to pursue commercial banking, handing over the investment banking activities to a newly founded institute, Morgan Stanley & Co, which was run by former employees of the Morgan bank (Geisst 2000, 135).

66. On the New Deal legislation and the Glass–Steagall Act, see Geisst 2000, 126–38; Neal and White 2012; Neal 2015; Eichengreen 2015.

67. Piketty 2014, 181–92.

68. Also known as the Gramm–Leach–Bliley Act.

69. On financial deregulation in Europe and the United States, see Barth, Brumbaugh and Wilcox 2000; Dermine 2002; Davies et al. 2010; Eichengreen 2015, 68–73; Duffie 2019; Goddard, Molyneux and Wilson 2019. Note that the arguments in favour of 'free banking' in the 1990s relied crucially upon the presumed capacity of the market to properly value bank assets. This made regulation unnecessary; removing it (many believed) would make the financial system more efficient without making it less resilient. These views prevailed against sceptical, or altogether worried, ones (see Dow 1996 for a synthesis).

70. Neal and White 2012; Eichengreen 2015, 70–7; Duffie 2019; Quinn and Turner 2020. Note that the housing bubble was also fuelled by hyper-lax mortgage lending policies which would not have been possible to such an extent without financial innovations (and in particular the introduction of mortgage-backed securities) and which arguably were themselves connected to deregulation in the financial sector.

71. Dermine 2002, 13.

72. Cournède, Denk and Hoeller 2015, 9–13.

73. Based on data from the OECD, *Value Added per Activity*, retrieved 28 January 2021, https://data.oecd.org/natincome/value-added-by-activity.htm.

74. For example, Battiston et al. 2018.

75. For a recent survey of this literature, see Hyde 2020. For the specific case of the United States, see Tomaskovic-Devey and Ken-Hou 2011.

76. Philippon and Reshef 2012.

77. Denk 2015, 8.

78. This process will be further detailed and measured in chapter 7.

79. Bivens and Mishel 2013; Denk 2015.

80. Alvaredo et al. 2013.

81. Some research has shown that in the United States the finance wage premium dropped only modestly during the crisis, thereafter quickly returning to pre-crisis levels (or almost), with only a minimal moderating impact of newly introduced regulations like the Dodd–Frank Wall Street Reform. See, e.g., Capuano, Lai and Schmererer 2014. On worries about the connection between executive compensation and risk-taking, see, e.g., Bolton, Mehran and Shapiro 2011.

82. According to an enquiry by the *Financial Times*, as of September 2018, worldwide, forty-seven people had been sent to jail for the role that they played in the financial crisis. Of all these convictions, twenty-five took place in Iceland and just one in the United States where the crisis had started. *Financial Times*, 'Who Went to Jail for Their Role in the Financial Crisis?', 20 September 2018.

83. Bernanke, Testimony before the Financial Crisis Inquiry Commission, Washington, DC, 2 September 2010, https://www.federalreserve.gov/newsevents/testimony/bernanke20100902a .htm. On the issue of too-big-to-fail banks see also Duffie 2019.

6. The Curse of Smaug: The Saving and Consumption Habits of the Rich

1. *Forbes*, 'The Forbes Fictional 15', various years. https://www.forbes.com/special-report /2013/fictional-15/index.html. On dragons in the Old Norse and Germanic tradition, see Evans 2005.

2. Weber 1946, 193.

3. Todeschini 2002, 107–11. See the 'Brilliant Sinners: Traders and Merchant-Entrepreneurs in the Middle Ages (and Before)' section in chapter 4, and chapter 8 for additional discussion.

4. See Muzzarelli 2002, 150–1, for the actual Bolognese provisions (in Latin); see Muzzarelli 2003, 2020, 2022 for a general comment.

5. Alfani and Gourdon 2009, 162–5.

6. Recent works have explored the economic consequences of this attempt at social disciplining: Ogilvie 2010; Desierto and Koyama 2023.

7. On Montpellier, see Bulst 2003, 131; on Faenza, Rimini and Parma, Muzzarelli 2003, 22.

8. Kampfner 2014, 359–60.

9. Mension-Rigau 2007, 363.

10. Veblen 2007 [1899], 52–3.

11. An example is the fancy-dress ball organized by the Vanderbilts in their New York house in 1883: 'A delightful surprise greeted the guests upon the second floor, as they reached the head of the grand stairway. Grouped around the clustered columns which ornament either side of the stately hall were tall palms overtopping a dense mass of ferns and ornamental grasses, while suspended between the capitals of the columns were strings of variegated Japanese lanterns. Entered through this hall is the gymnasium, a spacious apartment, where supper was served on numerous small tables. But it had not the appearance of an apartment last night; it was like a garden in a tropical forest. The walls were nowhere to be seen, but in their places an impenetrable thicket of fern and palm above palm, while from the branches of the palm hung a profusion of lovely orchids, displaying a rich variety of colour and an almost endless variation of fantastic forms' (*The New York Times*, 27 March 1883, cited from Kampfner 2014, 227). Most guests wore costumes inspired by the European aristocracies of olden times.

12. A particularly notable episode is the Great Buffalo Hunt that Jerome co-organized with other wealthy New Yorkers and General Philip Sheridan in 1871. They hired Buffalo Bill Cody to act as their hunting guide in the Western Plains. The expedition counted eighty-five mounted men, fifteen wagons and three ambulances. They were provided the best guns by the U.S. Army, as well as an armed escort. The participants made sure that they would have all comforts, including a travelling icehouse to keep their wine properly chilled. After having killed over forty bison and a large variety of other game, the merry party made its return to the east by means of a 'palace car' provided by the Kansas and Pacific Railroad. Sutch 2017, 56; J. Wheston Phippen, 'Kill Every Buffalo You Can! Every Buffalo Dead Is an Indian Gone!', *The Atlantic*, 13 May 2016, https://www.theatlantic.com/national/archive/2016/05/the-buffalo-killers/482349/.

13. Beeghley 2016, 195.

14. Friedman and Laurison 2019, 148.

15. See chapter 3 for further discussion. On highbrow culture consumption acting more as a 'fence' than a 'bridge' in network relations, see Lizardo 2006.

16. Based on Geloso and Lindert 2020, 421–4.

17. Sutch 2017, 55. And we should not forget the maintenance costs of palaces and mansions: the wealthiest New Yorkers of the 1890s spent 200,000–300,000 dollars (6–12 million in 2020 U.S. dollars) yearly to maintain their urban townhouses and an additional 100,000 dollars if they also kept a Newport mansion; much of these expenses came from paying scores of servants. In the summer season, super-wealthy socialites like Alva Vanderbilt spent several hundred thousand dollars to throw balls and parties in Newport (Jaher 1980, 198–9). These expenditures, however, relate to even smaller percentages of the rich population, surely no more than the richest 0.001%.

18. Estimates from Geloso and Lindert 2020, 424.

19. Gullino 1984, 4–5.

20. Gullino 1984, 5–6.

21. Quoted from Jungnickel and McCormmach 2016, 484. On Cavendish, see Partington 1962; Rubinstein 2006, 246–7; Jungnickel and McCormmach 2016, especially 481–7.

22. Cashman 1993, 41.

23. Carnegie 1889, 15.

24. Woolf 1963, 146–7.

25. Goldthwaite 1968, 114–5.

26. On the wealth of the Guicciardini, Capponi and other Florentine families, see Goldthwaite 1968.

27. Alfani and Di Tullio 2019.

28. De Vries and van der Woude 1997, 120.

29. This simple statistical exercise has been carried out by assuming a saving rate of 0% up to the fifteenth percentile (following Alfani and Di Tullio 2019) and of 20%–40% for the ninety-seventh percentile. Then, the exponential rate of growth in-between the fifteenth and ninety-seventh percentiles has been derived, and it has been used to project the saving rate up to the hundredth percentile.

30. Fesseau and Mattonetti 2013, 42–3. For the United States, and using a different approach, Saez and Zucman (2016, 564) estimated a saving rate of almost 40% for the richest 1% in 2010–12, while the bottom 90% would have saved nothing. The saving rate of the richest was reported to have grown in the previous decades, although it remained below the historical maximum of about 45% reached in the mid-1980s.

31. Quoted from Carrol 2000, 477.

32. Friedman 1957.

33. Dynan, Skinner and Zeldes 2004.

34. Part of this difference might also be due to the decade separating the periods covered by the two studies, as the saving rates of the American rich might have increased in-between.

35. Trump and Schwartz 1987, 48.

36. Carroll 1998, Abstract.

37. Cited from Carroll 2000, 478.

38. Jaher 1980, 259–60.

39. 'In fact, the *summum bonum* of this ethic, the earning of more and more money, combined with the strict avoidance of all spontaneous enjoyment of life . . . is thought of so purely as an end in itself, that from the point of view of the happiness of, or utility to, the single individual, it appears entirely transcendental and absolutely irrational. Man is dominated by the making of money, by acquisition as the ultimate purpose of his life. Economic acquisition is no longer subordinated to man as the means for the satisfaction of his material needs' (Weber 2005 [1930], 18).

40. Carnegie 1889, 19.

41. In general, on the psychological and social-economic motivations of the rich, see Jaher 1980; Carrol 2000; Sutch 2016. On philanthropy, see chapter 9.

42. For a brief discussion of the distributive implications of Modigliani's life-cycle model, see Carroll 2000 and Sutch 2016.

43. Carroll 2000.

44. On these juridical aspects, see Leverotti 2005, 164–5; Garlati 2011, 4–5; for the analysis of a specific case (the Republic of Venice), see Lanaro 2000, 2012.

45. The hoarders and the spenders are condemned to roll great weights forwards along two semi-circles that converge on the same point. When they clash, they shout at each other 'Why keepest?' and, 'Why squanderest thou?' Then they turn and push their weights until they clash again at the opposite point in the circle; all this repeated for eternity. Dante Alighieri, *Divine Comedy*, Chant 7.

46. Machiavelli 2006 [1532], book 7, chapter 1.

47. Klein 1978, 192, 167. It seems Gould was aware of this unfortunate situation. Here is how he himself described it: 'I have the disadvantage of not being sociable. Wall Street men are fond of company and sport. A man makes one hundred thousand dollars there and immediately buys a yacht, begins to drive fast horses, and becomes a sport generally. My tastes lie in a different direction. When business hours are over, I go home and spend the remainder of the day with my wife, my children, and my books. Every man has normal inclinations of his own. Mine are domestic. They are not calculated to make me particularly popular in Wall Street, and I cannot help that' (quoted from Klein 1978, 195).

48. Mandeville 1988 [1732], 428.

49. On Keynes' reading of Mandeville see Lagueux 1998.

50. For a recent synthesis of the positions of the classical economists on this topic, see Wrigley 2016, 22–7.

51. Even if capital was relatively abundant in a preindustrial setting, a greater quantity of it would still have led to higher GDP levels, although with diminishing returns, which is why the existence and the extent of net positive externalities (that is, positive consequences for society as a whole, able to compensate for possible negative consequences, e.g., in terms of social stability) of the private accumulation of capital *in the hands of the rich* and *above a certain level* can be questioned.

52. Allen 2009, 138–44.

7. Making It to the Top: An Overview

1. The elaborations on the Florentine *catasto* of 1427 are new, based on a dataset kindly provided by Peter Lindert. On this source and the original data collection effort, see Herlihy and Klapisch-Zuber 1985.

2. The estimates for Bergamo have been produced based on these sources: Public Library A. Mai of Bergamo, *Archivio Storico del Comune di Bergamo—Sezione antico regime, Estimi*, folder 1.2.16-XIII A and B (1555); State Archive of Bergamo, *Estimo Veneto*, folders 6 and 7 (1640) and folders 11–14 (1704). See Alfani and Di Tullio 2019 for more details.

3. For Verona, see Tagliaferri 1966; for Vicenza, see Scherman 2009; for an overview of the general situation in the Republic of Venice, see Alfani and Di Tullio 2019; for additional insights, see Pezzolo 2021. For the Sabaudian State in 1613, the situation can be described as follows: '[in Ivrea] among the rich [defined as those above the 1000% richness line] we find highly skilled professionals (lawyers and notaries; doctors and speziali, i.e. pharmacists) and high officials (the tax collector, the captain of the militia, etc.); merchants (especially of cloths and iron); and finally the "gentillhomini" or gentlemen, who belonged to the nobility. The richest household was that of a *referendario* of the Duke (an officer who received requests of justice or pleas to the Duke). . . . In Susa, where information about occupations is relatively sparse, we know at least that the richest household was that of an 'oste' (innkeeper)—although his very considerable wealth . . . came also from his secondary activities as leaser of the properties of the priory of Susa and probably most importantly, as tax collector (he had the sub-tender for the dacito, an indirect tax on the transit of goods through the Susa valley, for which he employed directly two agents). The second richest was another individual holding an important office: the governor of the city. . . . The other components of the local rich for whom an occupation is declared include notaries, merchants and owners of the local tanning activities. . . . In Turin, the capital of the State, the presence among the very richest (say, the top 0.1% of the distribution) of high officials of the ducal court and of nobles is . . . clear—and also clear is a marked difference in the extent of their wealth compared to that of the top rich of the secondary Sabaudian cities' (Alfani 2017a, 337).

4. Except for 1409, when 5.2% of all households were placed above the richness line.

5. The best information is that for the fifteenth century, when we can classify over 40% of those belonging to the richest 5%, which for the period is exceptionally good coverage. For the seventeenth century, coverage is still very good (about 35% in 1616 and 33% in 1635). The worst situation is that for 1515, when it was possible to classify only about one-quarter of the rich. Note that, in order to make the figures for different years directly comparable, they have been standardized taking as a reference the percentage of the rich for which the occupation was known in 1409.

6. See Munro 2010 for England; see Prak and van Zanden 2022 (especially Table 8.3, 186) for the Dutch Republic.

7. Alfani 2017a.

8. Mousnier 1974, 152.

9. Piketty, Postel-Vinay and Rosenthal 2006, 244–6.

10. As seen in chapter 3 (the section 'Becoming a Noble, from the Early Modern Period to Napoleon's Time and Beyond') the decline in the prevalence of nobles among the rich after 1847 is also connected to the 1848 revolution and the establishment of the Second Republic.

11. Piketty, Postel-Vinay and Rosenthal 2006, 255.

12. Daumard 1980, 103.

13. Note that the relatively high prevalence of civil servants of all kinds among the richest 5% is also due to the special status of Paris, the capital city of a highly centralized and bureaucratic state. Also note that, according to Daumard (1973, 197), the increase in the prevalence of

owners between 1820 and 1847 'is explained in large part by the transfer of noble fortunes from the group of high-ranking officers to that of owners [*propriétraires*], after the July Revolution [of 1830]', my translation.

14. Licini 2020, 79–81.

15. Rubinstein 2018, xxi. Also note that Lansley argues that the real decline of the British nobility started from the 1870s and has slowly continued to the present day. However, according to him, 'the decline of the aristocracy in terms of wealth is largely, though not exclusively, a story of the fall of the majority group of lesser aristocrats, the landed gentry with smaller estates, rather than the titled classes themselves' (Lansley 2006, 106); as seen in chapter 3, the 'landed gentry' are still very well-represented among the richest U.K. citizens.

16. Rubinstein 2018, xxi.

17. On Leveson-Gower, see Beresford and Rubinstein 2007, 45–6; Rubinstein 2022. Apart from him, among the eight individuals leaving over 1 million pounds we find some encountered in earlier chapters, in particular the banker Nathan Rothschild and the scientist Henry Cavendish.

18. This point is made for example by Rubinstein (2011, 53). Note that compared to his original work, in this book the data that he collected have been organized in a different way in order to produce Table 7.1. In particular, Rubinstein has tended to consider fortunes related to financial activities together with those built on commerce, because his aim was to demonstrate that 'the wealthy in Britain have disproportionately earned their fortunes in commerce and finance—that is, as merchants, bankers, shipowners, merchant bankers and stock and insurance agents and brokers, rather than in manufacturing or industry' (Rubinstein 2006, 80). This interpretation of British social and economic dynamics during the eighteenth and nineteenth centuries, however, has been much debated (see, e.g., Daunton 1989; Rubinstein 1991; Nicholas 1999; Thompson 2001). Here it is not possible to provide further details about this important debate, in part because it is not very relevant to our approach, which distinguishes finance from other entrepreneurial activities (mostly in industry *or* in commerce).

19. Rubinstein 2011, 28.

20. Albers and Bartels 2023.

21. Based on Augustine 1994, 28–30.

22. Rockoff 2012. Note that the information provided by Rockoff has been reorganized to maximize comparability with the other figures reported in Tables 7.1 and 7.2.

23. Of the ten richest individuals in the Colonies, all bar one (a physician) fall into these categories. Only when looking separately at different regions do we find other categories emerging, especially merchants in the north (Jones 1980, 171–6, 218–19)

24. According to Rockoff (2012, 245), 'It is clear that investments in finance and real estate were the major ways that capitalists of the Gilded Age expanded their fortunes after starting them in other sectors'.

25. Jaher 1980, 232, 237.

26. We have some, admittedly limited, confirmation of this for the mid-century period in Soltow's study of wealth inequality in the United States in 1850–70. Referring to those with wealth greater than 10,000 dollars (about 200,000–350,000 in 2020 U.S. dollars, depending on the exact year considered) in 1870, which covers the top 5%, he describes them as relatively old (forty-nine years of age on average), with relatively few foreign-born individuals and relatively

few farmers (but not by much) compared to the general population. Importantly, he also reports an increase in the prevalence of those labelled 'manufacturer' in 1870 compared to 1860 (Soltow 1975, 104–5), which seems to reflect structural changes in the American economy, as well as changes in the opportunities for enrichment open to the population. Additional confirmation comes from a sample representative of the richest 0.06% of Americans alive in 1870, which shows a large prevalence of entrepreneurs active in industry and commerce (68.8%), vastly exceeding finance (8.3%) and land (10.4%—note that this figure might be inflated due to the tentative inclusion in this category of California town-funders like Carlos Maria Weber and of gold-rushers like John Boggs). Women (almost all widows) constitute 10.4% of the sample (new estimates based on Sutch 2017).

27. The figures have been obtained from Scott (2021, table 3, 650) by applying the same classification of occupations used in our Table 7.1.

28. Scott 2021, 653.

29. Piketty, Postel-Vinay and Rosenthal 2006, 239.

30. Borgerhoff Mulder et al. 2009, Table S5.

31. On wealth concentration and its intergenerational transmission in small-scale societies, see Borgerhoff Mulder et al. 2009; Bowles, Smith and Borgerhoff Mulder 2010. See also chapter 1 for a definition of what constitutes 'wealth'.

32. Piketty 2014, 2015b.

33. This is allowing for some specific situations in which the formal ownership and/or inheritability of land was not perfectly established, especially in the early Middle Ages, i.e., in the centuries immediately following the fall of the Roman Empire and preceding the enrooting of the European feudal system with its landed, hereditary nobility (see the 'The Enrooting of the Feudal Nobility in Medieval Europe' section in chapter 3). On the consequences of the fall of the Roman Empire for accumulated wealth and its distribution see also Scheidel 2017.

34. The way in which the dowry system actually worked changed a bit across Europe. Some information is provided in the 'Women in Finance: An Overview' section in chapter 5. Beyond this, see Goody and Tambiah 1973; Botticini 1999; van Zanden et al. 2019.

35. Meade 1964. Technically, the condition of higher saving rates among the rich is usually modelled by a convex savings function (note that saving rates across society have been discussed in detail in chapter 6). For a synthesis of the literature on economic models of wealth accumulation across time, see Piketty 2000, 436–45; Roine and Waldenström 2015, 552–3. For some additional insights about the implications for our understanding of historical dynamics, see Alfani 2021.

36. On the geography of European inheritance customs, see Goody, Thirsk and Thompson 1978; Goy 1988.

37. On this point, see the 'The Rich, the Race and the Inheritance' section in chapter 6.

38. Imagine a society of lone children (that is, a society with a total fertility rate of one child per woman, which is not very different from the case of, say, Italy where in 2020 it was 1.3 children per woman). If everybody establishes a reproductive couple and has exactly one child, the population will halve in each generation, and each newborn will eventually inherit the wealth of two parents. If propertyless people immigrate to bolster the labour force of this demographically declining country, they will feed the wealth distribution 'from the bottom' (starting out at zero wealth) precisely when inheritance is making those at the top relatively wealthier.

Keeping these conditions constant, wealth inequality will increase continuously over time. Of course, this is a simplistic model which does not take into account many relevant variables which could condition the steady state, but the intuition concerning the impact of low fertility/declining population per se is clear.

39. Some of these factors have been discussed in the 'Why Does Wealth Concentration (Almost) Always Grow?' section in chapter 2.

40. Alvaredo, Garbinti and Piketty 2017, 240.

41. On the inversion in the relative positions of the United States and Europe, see also Alfani 2019; Alfani and Schifano 2021; and for income inequality, see Lindert and Williamson 2016, 118–21.

42. Acciari and Morelli 2020.

43. Piketty 2014.

44. Sutch 2017, 28.

45. Clark and Cummins 2015b.

46. Clark and Cummins 2015b, 532.

47. See, e.g., what the U.S. journalist and writer Ferdinand Lundberg wrote in the late 1960s: 'Nearly all the current large incomes, those exceeding $1 million, $500,000 or even $50,000 a year, are derived in fact from old property accumulations by inheritors—that is, by people who never did whatever one is required to do, approved or disapproved, creative or noncreative, in order to assemble a fortune. And, it would appear, no amount of dedicated entrepreneurial effort by newcomers can place them in the financial class of the inheritors' (Lundberg 1973, 132). He had been expressing similar views since the 1930s (Lundberg 1937).

48. Piketty 2014, 529–43.

49. Piketty 2014, 543.

50. Bisland 1897, 39–40, quoted from Sutch 2016, 26.

51. 'The parent who leaves his son enormous wealth generally deadens the talents and energies of the son, and tempts him to lead a less useful and less worthy life than he otherwise would' (Carnegie 1891, 56). On Carnegie, see chapter 4, and on his views, see chapters 6 and 9.

52. Holtz-Eakin, Joulfaian and Rosen 1993.

53. Cited from Daunton 1997, 1068.

54. 'Churchill's visions of co-operation and stabilisation depended upon a reduction in the taxation of active wealth at the expense of inherited wealth, a reduction in the tax burden on moderately well-to-do middle-class families, and the extension of pensions' (Daunton 1997, 1068).

55. Acciari and Morelli 2020, 21–2.

56. Note that for the United States, those listed in the well-known *Forbes* 400 database (https://www.forbes.com/forbes-400/) are a subset of the Americans included in the *Forbes* Billionaires Database. For example, in 2020, the minimum wealth required to be included in the *Forbes* 400 was 2.1 billion dollars.

57. See the 'The Survival of the Nobility in the Twentieth and Twenty-First Centuries and the Emergence of New Aristocracies' section in chapter 3 for examples and for further discussion of the case of the United Kingdom. Also note that at the turn of the twenty-first century, 'the top 40,000 millionaires amongst Britain's agricultural landowners (including the Queen's Crown Estates, the royal Duchies of Lancaster and Cornwall and the Dukes of Buccleuch, Atholl, West-

minster, Northumberland and so forth) own some 28 million acres while Britain's nearly 17 million homeowners own only one-tenth of this figure, or 2.8 million acres. It should be noted that the boom in Britain's land market is in no small measure due to this iniquity in land distribution which leaves the average homeowner with just 0.16 of an acre' (Irvin 2008, 41).

58. We are now considering billionaires who 'mostly' inherited, or made, their wealth. In the earlier section we focused on the share of inherited wealth across all large patrimonies.

59. On Bill Gates and other super-rich individuals who made their fortunes in the computer and information age, see the 'Achieving Great Wealth in the Age of Information: Opportunities for All?' section in chapter 4.

60. Korom, Lutter and Beckert 2017.

61. Freund (2016, 125–6) offers some examples of male-preference in bequests of the world billionaires. See also the 'The Survival of the Nobility in the Twentieth and Twenty-First Centuries and the Emergence of New Aristocracies' section in chapter 3 on the enduring discrimination against women in the inheritance of peerages in Britain.

62. The case of North American billionaires who made their fortune in the information technology sector during the 1990s, as reported by Tsigos and Daly (2020, 135), is highly indicative. In 1994, their mean age peaked at sixty. Then it decreased dramatically, to forty to forty-five in 1996–2001. From 2001, their mean age has been steadily increasing, contributing to fuelling the overall ageing process characterizing Western billionaires (in our estimate, in 2021 their mean age was back to 56.3).

63. To the best of my knowledge, no study based on later iterations of the SCF has provided this kind of information.

64. Wolff 2000, 79–87.

65. This would be the opposite situation to that reported in the 'The Composition of the Rich from the Late Middle Ages to the Nineteenth Century' section in chapter 7 for the Middle Ages and the beginning of the early modern period. The mutated situation would be explained by the rise of finance as a major path to affluence, a process which, as previously discussed, began in the nineteenth century (while in medieval times finance-based opportunities for enrichment were reserved for a small and highly specialized elite, leading to the concentration of the few financiers at the very top of the wealth pyramid; see chapter 5 for further discussion).

66. See the 'The Progressive Financialization of the Modern Economy' section in chapter 5 for a detailed discussion of this point.

67. Bakija, Cole and Heim 2012, 36–8.

8. Why Wealth Concentration Can Be a Social Problem: From Thomas Aquinas to Piketty

1. '[T]wo things belong to avarice, one of which is to be excessive in retaining things, and this part of avarice results in hardheartedness against mercy, or lack of humanity, namely, that avaricious persons harden their hearts so as not to dispense their possessions to help someone out of mercy. And the second thing belonging to avarice is to be excessive in taking things, and we can accordingly indeed first consider avarice as it belongs to an avaricious person's heart. And then avarice leads to restlessness, since avarice brings unnecessary anxieties and cares to human beings, "for money does not satisfy an avaricious person," as Eccl. 5:9 says. And second, we can

consider avarice in excessive taking as executed in deed, and then an avaricious person indeed sometimes uses force in taking things belonging to another, and so there are acts of violence. And sometimes an avaricious person uses deceit, which if done by words will be falsehood in the ordinary speech whereby one deceives another for gain, and which if done by words confirmed under oath will be perjury. And if one perpetrates deceit in deeds, then there will be fraud regarding things and treachery regarding persons' (Thomas Aquinas 2003 [1269–72], 730–1).

2. Lopez 1976, 60.

3. Fanfani 1931, 560.

4. Babbitt 1985.

5. Oresme 1370–74, 142, my translation. In this passage, Oresme closely follows Aristotle's original text, except for one thing: compared to Aristotle, who refers to the problems posed by the presence of individuals who have pre-eminence in virtues or political capacity in general, Oresme specifies in his translation that this is a matter of political power (*puissance politique*), and in his comments he seems to suggest that this excess of political power usually originates in an excess of wealth, as is further discussed in the following.

6. Cohn 2006; also see below.

7. Babbitt 1985, 82.

8. Oresme (1370–74, 142) refers more generally to the '*superhabundance de puissance*', that is, to the 'superabundance of power'. This can be obtained by means of either extremely great wealth or extremely great political power such as that held by local aristocracies (which usually also retained control over very substantial economic resources). Consequently, by translating *superhabundance* as super-wealthy status the focus is deliberately brought onto a specific aspect of Oresme's analysis, without, however, altering its general meaning, as shortly after, Oresme (144) explicitly refers to excessive wealth as the cause of *superhabundance* leading to 'harm and rebellion'. See also the additional passage reported in the main text.

9. 'And for this reason democratic states have instituted ostracism; equality is above all things their aim, and therefore they ostracized and banished from the city for a time those who seemed to predominate too much through their wealth, or the number of their friends, or through any other political influence' (Artistotle, *Politics*, book 3, part 13, transl. B. Jowett). The word 'ostracism' comes from *óstrakon*, the shell or potsherd used when voting to banish somebody.

10. Pampaloni 1971, 390.

11. Dumolyn and Haemers 2015, 163. Also in Germany attempts to limit the overbearing political power of rich patricians were frequent in the main trading cities during the fourteenth century, where they were spearheaded by the crafts. Although these movements were not quite as extreme as those found in Italy or in Flanders, the crafts managed to obtain seats in the city councils, for example in Nürnberg in 1370 and in Cologne in 1391–6, although sometimes this attempt failed, like in Lübeck in 1403–8 (Hergemöller 2012, 60–1, 101–2, 112).

12. Oresme 1370–4, 144, my translation.

13. Oresme 1370–4, 144, my translation.

14. As Jesus said: 'It is easier for a camel to go through the eye of a needle than for a rich man to enter the kingdom of God' (Matthew 19:24).

15. Fanfani 1931, 581.

16. 'Two worlds fidget in the Middle Ages: that of the spirit, that of the flesh; and only one has a theory able to organize everything. The only theory about [material] goods is built to

defend the superior interests of the spirit. The world of the flesh operates despite this theory, but does not build its own defense, does not have a theory that justifies it, and its actions remain illegitimate, as the only measure of what is legitimate are the principles elaborated by [Thomas] Aquinas' (Fanfani 1931, 581, my translation).

17. Todeschini 2002, 320–4.

18. Bracciolini 1428–9, 270, my translation.

19. Herlihy 1977, 165. Along the same lines, see Garin 1994, 54–5, as well as (with some nuances) Fubini 1990, 202–16; Todeschini 2002, 322–4.

20. Todeschini 2002, 320, my translation and italics.

21. On the organic metaphors of money in the late Middle Ages, see Todeschini 2002; Nederman 2004. On the distinction between good and bad uses of wealth in both Bracciolini and Pontano (see below), see Evangelisti 2016, 230–6.

22. Bracciolini 1428–9, 272, my translation.

23. Pontano 1493–8, quoted from Herlihy 1977, 14, my italics.

24. See chapter 2 on inequality trends after the Black Death.

25. Howard 2008.

26. 'The Republic, given the world that we live in, needs rich men, to make use of their riches in times of need; as it did in the past siege, during which if it had relied upon the resources of those, who wanted the houses and the estates [poderi] of the rich to be distributed randomly in the Consiglio, the city would not have achieved such a glorious defence' (Giannotti 1531, book 3, chapter 16, my translation).

27. Todeschini 2008, 28, 32–3.

28. Todeschini 2008, 38.

29. Tawney 1926.

30. Fanfani 1935.

31. Braudel 1977, 65–6. As rightly argued by Delacroix and Nielsen (2001), it is a simplified 'common interpretation' of Weber, without all the nuances of the original, which remains popular in the social sciences. Among economic historians, the matter remains debated (for a critical synthesis, see Hoffman 2006; Alfani 2012; Cantoni 2015; Kersting et al. 2020). For example, according to David Landes, 'it is fair to say that most historians today would look upon the Weber thesis as implausible and unacceptable: it had its moment and was gone. I do not agree. Not on the empirical level, where records show that Protestant merchants and manufacturers played a leading role in trade, banking and industry. . . . Nor on the theoretical. The heart of the matter lay indeed in the making of a new kind of man—rational, ordered, diligent, productive. These virtues, while not new, were hardly commonplace. Protestantism generalized them among its adherents, who judged one another by conformity to these standards' (Landes 1998, 177).

32. This view, which is in fact in line with Tawney's (1926) interpretation of the economic consequences of the Reformation, has recently found some empirical support (e.g., Becker and Woessman 2009; Dittmar and Meisenzahl 2020).

33. As their lifelong greed was definitely not motivated solely by end-of-life altruism, which is demonstrated by the rise of wealthy dynasties, as discussed at length in previous chapters.

34. '[In the Reformation] at least one thing was unquestionably new: the valuation of the fulfilment of duty in worldly affairs as the highest form which the moral activity of the individual

could assume. This it was which inevitably gave every-day worldly activity a religious significance, and which first created the conception of a calling in this sense' (Weber 1930 [1904], 40).

35. Schaff 2022.

36. Interestingly, this is the inverse situation compared to the poor, who had a clear role in
medieval Christian societies (see the first section of this chapter), but whose very presence was
increasingly resented in early modern ones. On these dynamics, which did not affect solely the
Protestant areas but Catholic ones as well, see Jütte 1994; Alfani 2020a.

37. McCloskey 2006. See Mokyr 2017 for a synthesis of the debate about the connection
between cultural change and economic development before and during the Industrial Revolution. Also note that, as argued by McCloskey (2006, 8–9), in the eighteenth century bourgeois
virtues had become integral to the ethical systems developed by some of the most influential
philosophers of the epoch: 'in eighteenth-century Europe certain theorists such as Montesquieu
and Voltaire and Hume and Smith had articulated a balanced ethical system for a society of
commerce, veritable "bourgeois virtues", fanciful and calculative together'.

38. This virtue, in classic Greek *megaloprépeia*, is discussed by Plato in the fifth and sixth
books of *The Republic*. Aristotle discusses it in the *Nicomachean Ethics*, pointing out that the
virtue of magnificence does not have to do with large-scale spending per se, but with the proper
way of doing it, which also requires an ability to recognize and to appreciate what is beautiful
(Maclaren 2003, 42–6).

39. On the negative economic interpretation of forced loans, see North and Thomas 1973.
For a more nuanced view, especially for Spain, see Yun-Casalilla and Comín Comín 2012; Grafe
and Irigoin 2013; Sardone 2019. On the early use of forced loans in Venice, see Luzzatto 1963;
Pezzolo 1996. On the Spanish kingdom as an 'absolutist' polity, see Acemoglu, Johnson and
Robinson 2005.

40. This was for example the case in Britain in 1917, when Andrew Bonar Law, the chancellor,
threatened financiers with the confiscation of bank and insurance company assets should the
capital raised not meet a minimum amount (Cohen 2019, 28). On the U.S. liberty bonds, see
Garbade 2012; Quinn and Turner 2020, 116–18.

41. Piketty 2014, 184.

42. Thorndike 2013; Levy 2021, 416–18.

43. Carosso 1987.

44. Quoted from Carosso 1987, 536.

45. *The Commercial & Financial Chronicle*, 27 June 1908, 1555–6.

46. Marx 1993 [1894], chapter 36.

47. On recent criticism of financialization from a Marxist perspective, see Chesnais 2016;
Manigat 2020.

48. See Veblen 2007 [1899]. For a detailed discussion of this aspect of Veblen's thought, see
the 'The Problem of Entrepreneurial Dynasties: From Merit to Privilege?' section in chapter 4,
and for his distaste of speculators see the 'Bankers of the Modern Era: Continuity and Change'
section in chapter 5.

49. Quoted from Gilbert 2000, 471.

50. Fisher 1919, 14.

51. Piketty 2014, 34.

52. Alfani and Frigeni 2016.

53. See in particular Rawls 1971.

54. About the distinction between *aequitas* and fairness, see Levi 2003; for an analysis of its implications, see Alfani and Frigeni 2016; Alfani and Di Tullio 2019. Note that the idea that equals should be treated equally, and un-equals unequally, originates from Artistotle's *Nicomachean Ethics*.

55. Cohn 2006.

56. Alfani and Frigeni 2016, 55.

57. Alfani and Frigeni 2016, 48 and 64–5.

58. Natural law is a philosophical theory according to which there exists a set of rules governing human behaviour which are universal and immutable and predate any historical manifestation of positive law. According to early modern natural law theorists, in the 'state of nature' which existed before societies appeared, all human beings were equal.

59. On the role played by Rousseau's *Discours* in changing the way in which inequality between human beings was conceptualized, see Alfani and Frigeni 2016.

60. Rousseau (2011 [1754]) is quite explicit in connecting political power to wealth and even singles out the rich as those who had the greatest interest in setting up an unequal political system capable of both keeping the peace across society and preserving the fortunes of a wealthy elite.

61. See chapter 2 for estimates of inequality levels. On the correlation between economic inequality and the propensity to revolt, see Alesina and Perotti 1996; MacCulloch 2003. On the 'economic' interpretation of the French Revolution, see Aftalion 1990; for other interpretations, see the brief synthesis in Alfani and Frigeni 2016, 55–6.

9. Patrons, Benefactors, Donors

1. Xenophon, *Oeconomicus*, II, 2–6.

2. 'The liturgical system . . . not only extracted necessary revenues from the rich, but also defused—through the redistribution of wealth from the élite to the masses—possible tensions between the different classes; tensions which might otherwise have been caused by the realism of political equality versus economic inequality in Athenian society' (Deene 2013, 74).

3. On the contributions expected from the rich in ancient Greek societies and their political implications, see Maclaren 2003; Oulhen 2004; Deene 2013; Fawcett 2016.

4. Cicero, *De Officiis*, book 2, 52–9.

5. Cicero, *De Officiis*, book 2, 60.

6. On Roman patronage of public works and of the arts, see Gold 1982; Parker 1991; Cecconi 2017. On Herodes Atticus, see also Bowie 2013; on Maecenas, see Graverini 1997.

7. The ways in which members of the Medici family made use of their enormous wealth to achieve political objectives will be explored further in chapter 10.

8. On St Thomas's concerns with trade, see the 'Brilliant Sinners: Traders and Merchant-Entrepreneurs in the Middle Ages (and Before)' section in chapter 4.

9. As will be remembered from the 'Usurers or Bankers? The Commerce of Money in Medieval and Early Modern Times' section in chapter 5.

10. This kind of self-interest can also be found in the patronage of municipal infrastructures (the building or repair of roads, bridges, etc.) which, according to a recent study (Casson and

Casson 2019), was particularly frequent among medieval English entrepreneurs and could directly generate more business opportunities, including for the donors.

11. Todeschini 2008, 33.

12. On Donato Ferrario, see Gazzini 2002; Todeschini 2008.

13. For example, Dye 2002; Domhoff 2010.

14. Todeschini 2008, 33.

15. Cohn 1988, 248.

16. For Poggio Bracciolini's and Giovanni Pontano's views, see the 'Finding a Role for the Rich: From Sinners to Elect' section in chapter 8. On late medieval and early modern magnificence, and patronage of the arts, in Italy see also Guerzoni 2006.

17. Alfani and Di Tullio 2019, 167.

18. Estimates from van Bavel and Rijpma 2016, 171. On the (slow) historical development of poor relief, see also Lindert 2021a, 25–47.

19. Calculation based on Pfister 2017, online appendix n. 4.

20. Tietz-Strödel 1982, 36–96; Steinmetz 2015, 166–71. On the concept of 'worthy' and 'unworthy' poor, see the synthesis in Alfani 2020a; Alfani, Ammannati and Ryckbosch 2022.

21. On England, see Burgess 1987; Kelly and Ó Gráda 2010, 343. On Germany, see Schaff 2022. Note that the increase in the prevalence of poverty in Germany might also come from a more discriminatory attitude towards different categories of the poor (Jütte 1994; Schaff 2022).

22. Cunningham 2016, 48.

23. Harvey, Maclean and Suddaby 2019, 443.

24. Phillips and Jung 2016, 7.

25. Ostrower 1995, 12–13. Note that Phillips and Jung (2016, 7) argue that, for a proper scholarly use in the social sciences, it would be better to provide a more encompassing definition of philanthropy, as 'the use of private resources—treasure, time and talent—for public purposes', without any reference to the motivation of the donors or to how they might benefit from such a use of their resources. This definition, while it undoubtedly covers more historical manifestations of giving and patronage, hides the shift in perception implicit in the modern *common* use of the word philanthropy; hence it is not useful for the purposes of this book.

26. Harvey et al. 2011.

27. On privately funded universities in nineteenth-century America, see Wren 1983.

28. On Thomas Holloway and Jane Pearce Driver, see Davis 1985–6; Corley 2004; Anderson 2005. On Ferdinando Bocconi, see Gobbini 1969; Resti 1990; Cattini, Decleva and De Maddalena 1992.

29. On J. P. Morgan as an art collector and a patron of the arts, see Chernow 1990.

30. Veblen 2007 [1899], 225–6.

31. Kampfner 2014, 220.

32. For example, Lansley 2006, 162.

33. Cashman 1993, 71.

34. Jaher 1972, 63.

35. Jaher 1972, 64–5 and elsewhere; 1980, 205–6. On Boston's Brahmin elite and New York's Four Hundred, see chapter 3 (the section 'The Survival of the Nobility in the Twentieth and Twenty-First Centuries and the Emergence of New Aristocracies').

36. Lansley 2006, 162.

37. Harvey, Maclean and Suddaby 2019, 46.

38. Cited from Reich 2018, 5.

39. Reich 2018, 139–40.

40. On the establishment of the Rockefeller Foundation, see Reich 2018 and Clemens 2020, 116–18; for the foundation's own perspective on this episode, see Abrahamson, Hurst and Shubinski 2013, 24–44.

41. Wren 1983, 340–2.

42. On the way in which the historical intensity of donations reflects changes in the fiscal system, see Duquette 2018, 2019.

43. OECD 2020.

44. Donor-advised funds (DAFs) are private philanthropical funds of a kind that have been expanding quickly over the last few years. Unlike foundations, they are not legal entities; they are simply 'giving accounts' set up within a non-profit sponsor organization. As such, they tend to be subjected to even fewer transparency rules than foundations, and for this reason, they are increasingly being criticized as a tool through which affluent people can easily escape taxation, in part because DAFs are free to delay the actual giving. On DAFs, see Andreoni 2018.

45. Soros 2011, 42.

46. McGoey 2015.

47. See, e.g., Ostrower 1995, 113–22.

48. OECD 2020, 129–30.

49. Reich 2018, 168.

50. As noted by sociologist Francie Ostrower (1995, 100), in the United States, 'Decisions about philanthropic bequests . . . occur against the backdrop of a tax structure that encourages donations, an ideological framework that discourages letting wealth pass to government, and a culturally defined set of attitudes concerning wealth, success, and inheritance'.

51. Ostrower 1995, 101.

52. Note that the situation described here for the Republic of Venice seems to have characterized other Italian early modern polities as well, for example the Florentine State. More generally, as revealed by the ongoing research of the project *SMITE—Social Mobility and Inequality across Italy and Europe, 1300–1800*, by the turn of the seventeenth century in much of southern Europe high and growing economic inequality went hand in hand with low and declining social mobility and with relative economic stagnation. But also in northern Europe, the growing concentration of economic (and political) resources contributed crucially to the end of the Dutch Golden Age, as argued by Van Bavel 2016, 195–200 (see chapter 10 for further discussion).

53. Pullan 1971, 128–9, with additional information about the multiplication of the confraternities system in early modern times from MacKenney 2019, 316–18 and elsewhere.

54. Alfani and Di Tullio 2019, 177.

55. Clemens 2020, 13.

56. Similar concerns have been expressed about corporate philanthropy, including through corporate foundations (i.e., foundations set up by corporations, not by specific rich individuals). According to an estimate, in the United States in 2014 about 6.3% of corporate charitable giving was politically motivated (Bertrand et al. 2020, 2069).

57. The Giving Pledge, Press Release, 14 December 2021, https://givingpledge.org /pressrelease?date=12.14.2021.

58. On the positions of Bill Gates and Bill H. Gates Sr. on the American estate tax, see Collins and Gates 2002; Zelinsky 2014.

10. The Super-Rich and Politics

1. The four old tribes were based exclusively on descent and, among other things, were used to determine who could be considered Athenian and eligible for military service. Cleisthenes replaced them with ten new tribes based exclusively on residence, without any consideration of descent or wealth. To foster further political cohesiveness, each tribe was regionally diverse in membership, being composed of 'demes' from the city of Athens and its suburbs, from coastal areas of Attica and from inland areas, at one-third each. Councillors of the *Boule* were paid for their service and were selected by ballot at the deme level among males of at least thirty years of age, each deme contributing in proportion to its population to each tribe's total of fifty councillors. According to an estimate, about a generation after the introduction of the new system one-third of all Athenians over thirty had served at least a year as a councillor. This ensured not only the very broad political participation of citizens, but also a wide distribution across the population of some practical knowledge of the inner workings of government. On Cleisthenes' reforms, and more generally on the Athenian political system, see Ober 2015, 162–6 and elsewhere.

2. On the way in which liturgies promoted social peace in the Athenian democracy, see Deene 2013. On the way in which the rich were portrayed in political speeches, see Seager 1973. See chapter 9 for Xenophon's views and for further discussion.

3. Aristotle does not specify the words used by the lions in Antisthenes' version of the fable, but we can infer them by analogy with Aesop's version (Antisthenes was a disciple of Socrates and is usually considered to have been the founder of the philosophical school of Cynicism).

4. Note that Aristotle was critical of democracy as in his view it could not be expected to ensure government by the most virtuous and to serve the interests of all.

5. See chapter 8 for a detailed discussion of Oresme's comments to Aristotle, as well as for historical details concerning the various attempts at limiting the power of the wealthiest put in place by the communes in Italy, the Low Countries, Germany and elsewhere.

6. Padgett and Ansell 1993, 1263–4.

7. De Roover 1963, 360.

8. To which, reportedly, the people counter-cried '*palle*' (Bullard 1994, 36).

9. Guicciardini 1988 [1508–9], IV, 126–7, my translation. For more details about the ascent to wealth (and then to great political power) of the Medici family, see chapter 5. On the magnificence of Cosimo de' Medici, see chapter 9. On the rule of Lorenzo de' Medici and the Pazzi conspiracy, see Bullard 1994; Rubinstein 1997; Najemy 2006.

10. See chapter 9 on personal expenditures for public offices in the Roman Republic, and Mitchell 1973, 32 and elsewhere, on the development of a 'plebeian aristocracy'.

11. De Vries and van der Woude 1997, 587.

12. Van Bavel 2016, 195–200.

13. Del Negro 1984, 333.

14. On Lodovico Manin, see Raines 2007. More generally, on the last years of the Republic, see Lane 1973, 423–36; Scarabello 1995. On Venice's final decadence and how it was viewed abroad and especially in England, see Fusaro 2015, 355–8 and elsewhere.

15. Lane 1973, 427–31.

16. Van Zanden, Buringh and Bosker 2012; on medieval parliaments, see also Marongiu 1968; on the early parliaments in Spain, see O'Callaghan 1969.

17. On the possible economic effects of the Glorious Revolution, see the classic article by North and Weingast (1989). More generally, on the consequences that relatively open political institutions might have had for long-term divergence between world areas, see Acemoglu, Johnson and Robinson 2005.

18. On this interpretation, see Acemoglu, Johnson and Robinson 2005.

19. See Przeworski 2009 for an overview of the progressive extension of the suffrage, with additional insights from Acemoglu and Robinson 2000, Piketty 2020 and Stavasage 2020. See Crook 1996 for elections in the French revolutionary governments. The data about the percentage of voters in the United Kingdom are taken from Piketty 2020, supplementary information to Figure 5.3, 178, downloadable from piketty.pse.ens.fr/ideology.

20. Quoted from Evans 1983, 212.

21. Przeworski 2009.

22. Stavasage 2020, 266.

23. Among social scientists worried about current tendencies, Thomas Piketty has been particularly influential. First, he highlighted how the development of extreme wealth inequalities leads to highly unequal access to public institutions, including political ones, and therefore changes the way in which they operate *in practice* (Piketty 2014). Later, he developed an encompassing critique of the current political and ideological situation across the West and beyond. For example, '[An] aspect of the [current] political regime is . . . in need of urgent attention: the financing of political campaigns and of political life more generally. In theory, universal suffrage is based on a simple principle: one woman (or man), one vote. In practice, financial and economic interests can exert an outsized influence on the political process, either directly by financing parties and campaigns or indirectly through the media, think tanks, or universities' (Piketty 2020, 1017).

24. The recent intensification in the prevalence of the richest among those holding top government positions is noticeable, e.g., when looking at American state governors. Interestingly, the trend seems to involve both Republican and Democratic governors (for examples, see *The Economist*, 'The Rise of Rich Governors', 21 October 2017). Also note that in the second half of the twentieth century the United States seemed to stand out, among Western countries, for being relatively more open to the involvement of very rich individuals in politics (many U.S. presidents, both Democratic and Republican, have come from very wealthy families, including John F. Kennedy, Lyndon B. Johnson and George H. W. Bush).

25. Amatori 2011, 176.

26. Donovan and Gilbert 2015, 396.

27. On Silvio Berlusconi, see Amatori 2011; Mazzoleni 2011; Donovan and Gilbert 2015; Friedman 2015. On his role in international politics, see Diodato and Niglia 2018.

28. Italians' satisfaction with their political system started to decline only with the 2011 economic and political crisis (Donovan and Gilbert 2015, 400–1). At the very least, from 1994 the political systems of the 'Second Republic' had ensured alternation between centre-right and centre-left governments, after forty years of the political predominance of the Christian Democratic Party (DC), and this novelty might have been appreciated by the average voter.

29. On social mobility rates in the United States compared to other Western countries, see Osberg and Smeeding 2006; OECD 2018.

30. Trump and Schwartz 1987.

31. On the Trump family dynasty, see Blair 2015. Note that in the U.S. presidential elections, the candidate who gets the largest number of votes (the 'popular vote') does not necessarily win. Victory goes to the candidate who gets the majority of the 538 'electoral votes' divided among the various states of the Union.

32. Pinçon-Charlot and Pinçon 2010, 2019.

33. Take, for example, Rishi Sunak, who became prime minister of the United Kingdom in October 2022 and has an estimated net worth, jointly with his wife Akshata Murty, of 730 million pounds (almost 850 million U.S. dollars). Interestingly, Sunak came to power immediately after the short-lived government led by Liz Truss (September–October 2022) had collapsed under widespread criticism of its proposed fiscal policies, which included a substantial cut in the top rate of personal income tax and other pro-rich reforms.

34. Aristotle, *Politics*, book 3, part 9.

35. Tugwell and Dorfman 1937, 224–5; Dorfman 1940, 98; West 1997, 121–6.

36. Huston 1993, 2017; for partially different views, see Mettler 2015, 567–8. On Tocqueville and other European views on nineteenth-century America, see Huston 2017, especially 54–73, 102–15; specifically on wealth distribution, see Tocqueville 2017 [1835–40], 57–8.

37. Huston 1993, 1083–4.

38. Huston 1993, 1105. Note that this might have contributed to preventing the establishment of a 'plutocracy' in the early twentieth-century United States: see Dawley 2005. In general, on the connection between wealth and political power in American history, see Phillips 2002; Gerstle and Fraser 2005.

39. Quoted from Scheidel 2017, 58. In Scheidel's own words (43), 'premodern states generated unprecedented opportunities for the accumulation and concentration of material resources in the hands of the few, both by providing a measure of protection for commercial activity and by opening up new sources of personal gain for those most closely associated with the exercise of political power. In the long run, political and material inequality evolved in tandem'.

40. In general, for modern societies of the last few decades there is a growing literature about how the influence exerted by the wealth elite on politics and on public policies can lead to further personal enrichment and contribute significantly to fostering the growth of economic inequality. For a synthesis, see Brady and Sosnaud 2010; Volscho and Kelly 2012; Medeiros and Ferreira de Souza 2015.

41. Villette and Vuillermot 2009, 140.

42. Quoted from McCloskey 2006, 493.

43. Quoted from Geisst 2000, 25–6.

44. On political corruption in the railroad sector and the Black Horse Cavalry, see Geisst 2000, 24–30; White 2011, 131–3.

45. For some empirical evidence supporting this view, e.g., in the case of the United States, see Bartels 2008; Volscho and Kelly 2012; for a global perspective, see Bagchi and Svejnar 2016.

46. The estimate refers to the cumulated fortunes of *Forbes*' billionaires who clearly profited from political connections as a percentage of total billionaires' wealth and is based on data from Bagchi and Svejnar 2015, 509.

47. Quoted from Freund 2016, 42–3. On eastern European oligarchs, see Guriev and Rachinsky 2005; Markus and Charnysh 2017; for a study of the political connections of the super-rich in a post-communist country which joined the EU (Poland), see Salach and Brzezinski 2020.

48. Bagchi and Svejnar (2016, 176) provide some quantitative evidence that the rise of 'politically connected' billionaires' wealth has a negative impact on economic growth.

49. For a polemical discussion of this attitude, see Villette and Vuillermot 2009, 1–6.

50. Interview with the *Financial Times*, 16 October 2000, quoted from Mazzoleni 2011, 37.

51. Giovanni Cavalcanti 1838 [1450 ca.], book I, 24, my translation.

52. Herlihy 1977, 11.

53. Alfani and Di Tullio 2019, 145–65.

54. See the 'Why Does Wealth Concentration (Almost) Always Grow?' section in chapter 2, for additional details about preindustrial regressive taxation. For an in-depth discussion, see Alfani and Di Tullio 2019 and Alfani 2021. Also note that only exceptionally, in a preindustrial context, did war cause sufficient damage to produce large-scale levelling (overcoming the effects of war-related regressive taxation); as seen in the 'The Rich during Wars and the Wars of the Rich' section in chapter 11, the only clear example of this kind that we currently have is the Thirty Years' War of 1618–48 in Germany. See also Alfani, Gierok and Schaff 2022 and in general, on the levelling potential of war, Scheidel 2017.

55. Alfani and Di Tullio 2019, 167. On the way in which service of the preindustrial public debt tended to favour the affluent and to increase inequality, see the 'On Investors, from Preindustrial to Industrial Times' section in chapter 5.

56. See the 'On Inequality and the Perception of the Rich' section in chapter 8 for further discussion of this point.

57. In the Republic of Venice, the richest 5% owned over 50% of all wealth ca. 1550, and close to 60% by 1750: Alfani and Di Tullio 2019, 157–62.

58. On Poggio Bracciolini's views, see the 'Finding a Role for the Rich: From Sinners to Elect' section in chapter 8; on the way in which private charity ensured social stability, see the 'A Modern Dilemma: To Donate or to Pay Tax?' section in chapter 9.

59. Based on recent estimates by Lindert (2021b, 79–80), ca. 1880 social spending (excluding spending in public education) remained well below 1% of GDP in Western countries, but it increased significantly in the following decades. By 1940, social spending was above 4% of GDP in at least some Western countries (including Italy, Sweden, the United Kingdom and the United States), then rose dramatically in the post-war years; by 1960, in all the democratic countries of western Europe it was above 10% of GDP, with a maximum in Germany (18%), while North American countries lagged behind (9% in Canada and just about 7% in the United States). On this topic, see also Lindert 2004.

60. Stavasage 2020, 274.

61. On the pro-rich fiscal policies introduced by the Fascist regime in Italy, see Gabbuti 2021, 2022; on those of the Nazi regime in Germany, see Bartels 2019. Interestingly, for Germany some quantitative evidence has been provided which suggests that political connections with members of the Nazi Party led certain firms to outperform others by a large margin (Ferguson and Voth 2008).

62. On the relatively limited political influence of the rich in the United States especially in 1930–60, see Dawley 2005.

63. Some important studies, based on a comparison of growth rates and of patterns of fiscal reform in a range of rich countries, have found that reductions in the progressivity of fiscal systems have not paid off in terms of quicker GDP growth. They did, however, promote economic inequality. On this point, which admittedly remains highly debated due to its political implications, see, e.g., Alvaredo et al. 2013; Piketty, Postel-Vinay and Rosenthal 2014.

64. See, e.g., for the case of the United States, Lind 2005; Volscho and Kelly 2012.

65. On Trump's pro-rich fiscal reforms, see Saez and Zucman 2019; Piketty 2020, 888–9.

66. Arnd 2020, 144, 152–3. A recent study based on a survey of political elections in Western democracies from 1948 to 2020 has argued that those with high incomes tend to vote more for right and centre-right parties, although it could not observe wealth systematically; when this is possible, like for France, the effect of wealth on political preferences is found to be stronger and more stable over time than that of income (Gethin, Martínez-Toledano and Piketty 2022, particularly 21, n. 18).

67. Estimates from Jaher 1980, 253, and Bonica and Rosenthal 2018, 41.

68. On the way in which the rich influence politics in the United States, see Mills 1956; Domhoff 2010; Martin 2013; for a historical perspective, see Fraser and Gerstle 2005. On the tendency of U.S. senators of all political camps to be more responsive to the preferences of their most affluent constituents, see Bartels 2008, 253–4, and on a similar note, Mettler 2015, 252–3. For broader international comparisons, see Piketty 2020; Gethin, Martínez-Toledano and Piketty 2022. For an overview of the literature on how wealth distribution can affect democratic political systems, see Scheve and Stavasage 2017.

69. On the role that ideology might have played in this story, see Piketty 2020. For a brief history of changes in the structure of personal income tax in OECD countries, see Messere, de Kam and Heady 2003; Scheve and Stavasage 2016, 53–92. For a discussion of how 'pro-rich' fiscal reforms came to be pursued by both the political right and the political left in the context of financial globalization, see Lierse 2022.

70. On 'hidden wealth' in Britain, see Cummins 2022; on the related practices, see Collins 2021; on the tendency for tax evasion to concentrate at the top of the wealth distribution, see Alstadsæter, Johannesen and Zucman 2019.

71. 'In Tax We Trust', https://www.intaxwetrust.org/, consulted 19 April 2022.

11. The Rich in Times of Crisis from the Black Death to COVID-19

1. On the inequality-reducing impact of the Black Death, see Alfani 2015 for the Sabaudian State, Alfani and Ammannati 2017 for Tuscany, Alfani, Gierok and Schaff 2022 for Germany, and Alfani 2021, 2022 for a synthesis. On the prevalence of the rich, see the 'How Many Were Rich across Time?' section in chapter 2, as well as Alfani 2017a. On the levelling impact of catastrophes in general, see Scheidel 2017.

2. On the impact of the Black Death on poverty, see Broadberry et al. 2015 and Campbell 2016 for England, and Alfani 2020a, 2022 for a broader European comparison. On the impact of the Black Death on social-economic mobility, see Alfani, Ammannati and Balbo 2022.

3. Dyer 2015, 195.

4. On decrees *contra laboratores* and post-Black Death labour legislation, see Cohn 2007; Epstein 2009, 186–7. On inheritance-driven equalization, see the synthesis in Alfani 2021.

5. For example, Benedictow 2004; Schmid et al. 2015. For a more nuanced view, see Jedwab, Johnson and Koyama 2022.

6. As argued by Hunt (1994, 246), in Florence 'After the 1340s . . . no new enterprises emerged even approaching the stature of the super-companies [of the pre-Black Death decades]'. See also, on the impact of the Black Death on European textile production, Lopez and Miskimin 1962, 419–20; on finance and the grain trade in Florence, see Hunt 1994, 246–50; on the damage done to the Spanish trade network, see Álvarez-Nogal, Prados de la Escosura and Santiago-Caballero 2020.

7. Scheidel 2017, 305.

8. Padgett 2010, 369.

9. On the Anglo-French wine trade, see Blackmore 2020. On post-Black Death changes in the market for textiles, see Lopez and Miskimin 1962; Hunt and Murray 1999, 166–70.

10. Note that the timing of the Black Death was different depending on the area of Europe considered, reflecting its spread across the continent. These differences in timing contributed to prolonging the disruption that it caused to economic activities and particularly to trade.

11. On the original debate on the economic consequences of the Black Death, see Lopez and Miskimin 1962; Cipolla 1964. For recent updated syntheses, see Alfani and Murphy 2017; Jedwab, Johnson and Koyama 2022.

12. On the epidemiology of the seventeenth-century plague, see Alfani 2013b; Alfani and Murphy 2017. For an analysis of the different distributive impacts of the Black Death and of the seventeenth-century plagues, see Alfani 2022.

13. Alfani and Bonetti 2019; Alfani, Bonetti and Fochesato 2023.

14. In the 'A Thorny Issue: Inheritance' section in chapter 7.

15. Under this social system, marriage was restricted to one brother per generation, in order to allow his children to inherit their uncles' shares of the *fraterna* as well as their father's. Interestingly, this system seems to have caused a much higher than normal extinction rate of Venetian family lines (Davis 1962, 62–74). On the spread of the *fideicommissum* in Italy, see Lanaro 2000, 2009; Leverotti 2005, 162–7. On the case of Tuscany, see Cohn 1998; Calonaci 2012. For a European comparison, see Chauvard, Bellavitis and Lanaro 2012. On the *fraterna* system in Venice, see Bellavitis 2013; Alfani and Di Tullio 2019, 84–5. On *in solido* inheritance in Piedmont, see Alfani 2010b.

16. Regarding institutional resilience to plagues and other mortality crises and how it affected distributive dynamics, see Alfani 2022, 19–20.

17. Especially that conducted in the context of the ERC-funded project, *SMITE—Social Mobility and Inequality across Italy and Europe, 1300–1800* (www.dondena.unibocconi.it /SMITE).

18. On this definition and its implications, see Ó Gráda 2009, 2; Alfani and Ó Gráda 2017, 1–4.

19. On private food reserves and the way in which they could be used for profiteering, see Alfani 2013c, 73–8.

20. Straparola 1927 [1556], book II, Night X, Tale IV, my translation.

21. Le Roy Ladurie 1966.

22. Tilly 1984; Alfani 2021, 29. For a chronology of the main European famines, see Alfani and Ó Gráda 2017.

23. Kaplan 1976; Guenzi 1995; Alfani 2013c, 70–8.

24. Fawcett 2016, 159.

25. '*In casu extremae necessitatis omnia sunt communia*'. Thomas Aquinas, *Summa Theologiae*, quoted from Fanfani 1931, 556.

26. Genoa had traditionally relied upon grain imports from the Black Sea area, but this had become impossible due to the hostility of the Ottoman Empire, and no grain was to be found in Sicily and in other grain-producing areas of the Mediterranean, due to the continental scale of the crisis.

27. Alfani 2017b, 156–8.

28. On the 'entitlements approach' to famines, which focuses on distribution, see in particular Sen 1981. For a discussion of different views, see Alfani and Ó Gráda 2017, 1–4. On the root causes of preindustrial European famines, see Alfani and Ó Gráda 2018.

29. For example, Hobsbawm 1989, 307–8.

30. Machiavelli 2018 [1521], book 7, 1111, my translation.

31. On early modern sacks, see Alfani 2013c, 27–9.

32. Daly 2019.

33. Dean 2010, 3.

34. Dean 2010, 4.

35. Pezzolo 1990, 163–8; more generally on the inegalitarian and 'pro-rich' nature of pre-industrial military expenditures, see Alfani and Di Tullio 2019, 169–72.

36. Cattini 1988, 31, my translation

37. On the Italian system of the *condotte*, see Mallett 1974; Alfani 2013c, 114–16.

38. On Albrecht von Wallenstein, see Schilling 1994; Asch 1997; Whaley 2012, 571–2.

39. Parker 1988.

40. On the United States, see Jaher 1980, 195; on Ireland, see Turner 2010, 636–7; Ó Gráda 1994, 602–3.

41. The *École Nationale Supérieure de l'Aéronautique* was the first dedicated aviation engineering school ever established (in 1909).

42. On Potez and Bloch, see Chadeau 1987; Villette and Vuillermot 2009, 121–8.

43. For the figures on Germany, see chapter 2 as well as Alfani, Gierok and Schaff 2022; for the levelling power of the Thirty Years' War see also Scheidel 2017. Note that we should not over-interpret the slight decline reported in the wealth share of the richest 5% in Germany between 1550 and 1600 (before the Thirty Years' War), as during that period the wealth share of the richest 10% remained unchanged and the overall inequality levels even increased (from a Gini index of 0.637 in 1550 to 0.661 in 1600).

44. Piketty 2014; Scheidel 2017.

45. Cummins 2022, S4, 60–1.

46. For France, see Scheidel 2017, 139–40, based on Piketty 2007, 43–81.

47. See also the figures presented in chapter 2.

48. Scott 2021, 646.

49. Piketty 2014, 136.

50. Piketty 2014, 135–8, 181–6; Scheidel 2019, 130ff.

51. See in particular the 'Why Does Wealth Concentration (Almost) Always Grow?' section in chapter 2, and the 'Politics and Taxation' section in chapter 10. On the 'conscription of wealth' during the World Wars, see also Scheve and Stavasage 2016, 135–69.

52. For a detailed discussion of this point, see the 'Red Threads in History' section in chapter 8; on the contributions requested from the rich during the Classical Age, see the 'Maecenatism and Patronage between Public Good and Personal Interest: From Antiquity to Early Modern Times' section in chapter 9. Note that the rich were not the only buyers of twentieth-century war loans: in the United States during World War I, for example, many working- and middle-class individuals purchased liberty bonds in part due to aggressive marketing by the government (even the Boy Scouts of America were enlisted to solicit subscriptions door-to-door; Quinn and Turner 2020, 116).

53. Income Inequality and the Great Recession, Report of the U.S. Congress Joint Economic Committee, September 2010.

54. Saez and Zucman 2016, 521 and online appendix.

55. Albers, Bartels and Schularick 2022.

56. Roine and Waldenström 2015, 520–40.

57. On the causes of the stagnation of middle-class incomes, see, e.g., Milanović 2016. On the connection between inequality, consumption and the onset of the 2007 crisis, see Piketty 2014, 372–4; McCombie and Spreafico 2017, 45–50.

58. Compare with the 'The Consumption Habits of the Rich: From Medieval (Relative) Moderation to Conspicuous Consumption' section in chapter 6.

59. See the examples reported by Geisst 2000, 126–7, and, along similar lines, Piketty 2014, 650.

60. See chapter 5 for details about the 'money trust' and the political reactions against it.

61. On the 1929 Wall Street crash, see White 1990; Quinn and Turner 2020, 115–33.

62. Quoted from Quinn and Turner 2020, 123.

63. On Fisher, see Allen 1993; U.S. wealth shares from Saez and Zucman 2016, online appendix, Table B1.

64. Data about top wealth shares of individuals in 2007–12 are from the *World Inequality Database* (https://wid.world/data/), consulted on 15 April 2022; the alternative estimate for the United States is from Saez and Zucman 2016, online appendix, Table B1. For an example of how a reduction in the wealth share of the richest was expected (but did not take place) in the aftermath of the crisis, see Volscho and Kelly 2012, 694. On the good fortune of the super-rich during the crisis, see also Milanović 2016, 39–45.

65. According to Wolff (2016, 38–40), wealth inequality growth during the Great Recession remains a puzzle. For him, a possible explanation could lie in the different wealth portfolios of the rich (who owned relatively more stock) compared to the middle class (who owned relatively more real estate). An enduring collapse in the prices of real estate and a rebound in stock-market prices might have jointly led to the impoverishment of the middle class relative to the rich. Others point to the 'boom and bust' in the consumption rates of the rich: they tended to save a larger proportion of their incomes after the onset of the Great Recession (due to large 'wealth effects' triggered by the drop in the absolute value of their patrimonies) and consequently also accumulated relatively more wealth than those lower down the wealth pyramid (Bakker and Feldman 2014).

66. See Eichengreen 2015 for a comparison of the policy interventions during the Great Recession and the Great Depression.

67. See the 'The Progressive Financialization of the Modern Economy' section in chapter 5 for further discussion.

68. For this kind of criticism, see, e.g., de Ceukelaire and Bodini 2020; Williams 2020; Baum et al. 2021; Cooper and Szreter 2021.

69. On tax reforms during the COVID-19 pandemic, see OECD 2021 and the related database (accessed on 19 April 2022 from https://www.oecd.org/ctp/tax-policy-reforms-26173433 .htm).

70. Most definitely, COVID-19 was not an 'egalitarian' pandemic like the Black Death was (see the first section of this chapter), as demonstrated by a rapidly expanding body of studies. Instead, it showed a marked social-economic gradient in mortality as well as in the subtler (and more difficult to determine) 'long-COVID' symptoms. COVID-19 did not kill nearly as many as the plague did, which is undoubtedly a good thing, but for this very reason it could not be expected to lead to increases in real wages, nor to reductions in income inequality or easier upward mobility—quite the opposite, exactly as happened at the time of the Spanish Flu of 1918–19, which of all the great pandemics of the past is the one epidemiologically closest to COVID-19. In general, see Alfani 2022 on how mortality rates and social-economic gradients in mortality and infection contribute to determining the overall distributive impact of a pandemic; for more recent pandemics, see also Alsan, Chandra and Simon 2021.

71. Pousaz's case is discussed further in the 'Achieving Great Wealth in the Age of Information: Opportunities for All?' section in chapter 4.

72. With COVID-19, what was really unexpected was not so much the occurrence of a lethal pandemic (an event which many experts had been warning about for decades), but the mass lockdowns which were introduced to contain it. And it was the lockdowns, not the pandemic itself, which made Amazon's business model of selling online and delivering a vast range of goods to the home a winner throughout the crisis period.

73. Berkhout et al. 2021, 23.

74. For an early survey of the activity of foundations during the COVID-19 pandemic, see Finchum-Mason, Husted and Suárez 2020; for some reflections by a foundation president (Ford Foundation), see Walker (2020).

Concluding Remarks

1. 'In Tax We Trust', https://www.intaxwetrust.org/; see chapters 10 and 11 for further discussion.

BIBLIOGRAPHY

Abrahamson, Eric John, Sam Hurst, and Barbara Shubinski. 2013. *Democracy and Philanthropy: The Rockefeller Foundation and the American Experiment*. New York: Rockefeller Foundation.

Acciari, Paolo, and Salvatore Morelli. 2020. "Wealth Transfers and Net Wealth at Death: Evidence from the Italian Inheritance Tax Records 1995–2016." Working Paper no. 27899, National Bureau of Economic Research.

Acemoglu, Daron, and James A. Robinson. 2000. "Why Did the West Extend the Franchise? Democracy, Inequality, and Growth in Historical Perspective." *Quarterly Journal of Economics* 115, no. 4 (November): 1167–99.

Acemoglu, Daron, and James A. Robinson. 2005. "The Rise of Europe: Atlantic Trade, Institutional Change and Economic Growth." *American Economic Review* 95, no. 3 (June): 546–79.

Acheson, Graeme G., Gareth Campbell, Áine Gallagher, and John D. Turner. 2021. "Independent Women: Investing in British Railways, 1870–1922." *Economic History Review* 74, no. 2 (May): 471–95. https://doi.org/10.1111/ehr.12968.

Aftalion, Florin. 1990. *The French Revolution: An Economic Interpretation*. Cambridge: Cambridge University Press.

Albers, Thilo N. H., Charlotte Bartels, and Moritz Schularick. 2022. "Wealth and Its Distribution in Germany, 1895–2018." Discussion Paper no. DP17269, CEPR.

Albers, Thilo N. H., and Charlotte Bartels. 2023. "Inequality and Its Drivers in Germany, 1840–1914." In *An Economic History of the First German Unification: State Formation and Economic Development in a European Perspective*, edited by Ulrich Pfister and Nikolaus Wolf. London: Routledge, forthcoming.

Alesina, Alberto, and Roberto Perotti. 1996. "Income Distribution, Political Instability, and Investment." *European Economic Review* 40, no. 6 (June): 1203–28.

Alfani, Guido. 2010a. "Wealth Inequalities and Population Dynamics in Northern Italy during the Early Modern Period." *Journal of Interdisciplinary History* 40, no. 4 (spring): 513–49.

Alfani, Guido. 2010b. "The Effects of Plague on the Distribution of Property: Ivrea, Northern Italy 1630." *Population Studies* 64, no. 1 (March): 61–75.

Alfani, Guido. 2012. "Reformation, 'Counter-Reformation' and Economic Development from the Point of View of Godparenthood: An Anomaly? (Italy and Europe, 14th–19th Centuries)." In *Religione e istituzioni religiose nell'economia europea. 1000–1800*, edited by Francesco Ammannati, 477–89. Florence: Firenze University Press.

Alfani, Guido. 2013a. "Fiscality and Territory: Ivrea and Piedmont between the Fifteenth and Seventeenth Centuries." In *Sabaudian Studies: Political Culture, Dynasty, & Territory 1400–1700*, edited by Matthew Vester, 213–39. Kirksville, MO: Truman State University Press.

Alfani, Guido. 2013b. "Plague in Seventeenth Century Europe and the Decline of Italy: An Epidemiological Hypothesis." *European Review of Economic History* 17, no. 4 (November): 408–30.

Alfani, Guido. 2013c. *Calamities and the Economy in Renaissance Italy: The Grand Tour of the Horsemen of the Apocalypse*. Basingstoke: Palgrave Macmillan.

Alfani, Guido. 2014. "Back to the Peasants: New Insights into the Economic, Social, and Demographic History of Northern Italian Rural Populations during the Early Modern Period." *History Compass* 12, no. 1: 62–71.

Alfani, Guido. 2015. "Economic Inequality in Northwestern Italy: A Long-Term View (Fourteenth to Eighteenth Centuries)." *Journal of Economic History* 75, no. 4 (December): 1058–96.

Alfani, Guido. 2017a. "The Rich in Historical Perspective: Evidence for Preindustrial Europe (ca. 1300–1800)." *Cliometrica* 11, no. 3 (September): 321–48.

Alfani, Guido. 2017b. "Famines in Late Medieval and Early Modern Italy: A Test for an Advanced Economy." In *Famines during the 'Little Ice Age' (1300–1800)*, edited by Dominik Collet and Maximilian Schuh, 149–69. Cham: Springer.

Alfani, Guido. 2019. "Wealth and Income Inequality in the Long Run of History." In *Handbook of Cliometrics*, 2nd ed., edited by Claude Diebolt and Michael Haupert, 1173–201. Cham: Springer.

Alfani, Guido. 2020a. "The Economic History of Poverty, 1450–1800." In *The Routledge History of Poverty in Europe, c.1450–1800*, edited by Daniel Hitchcock and Julia McClure, 21–38. London: Routledge.

Alfani, Guido. 2020b. "Pandemics and Asymmetric Shocks: Evidence from the History of Plague in Europe and the Mediterranean." *Journal for the History of Environment and Society* 5: 197–209.

Alfani, Guido. 2021. "Economic Inequality in Preindustrial Times: Europe and Beyond." *Journal of Economic Literature* 59, no. 1 (March): 3–44.

Alfani, Guido. 2022. "Epidemics, Inequality and Poverty in Preindustrial and Early Industrial Times." *Journal of Economic Literature* 60, no. 1 (March): 3–40.

Alfani, Guido, and Francesco Ammannati. 2017. "Long-Term Trends in Economic Inequality: The Case of the Florentine State, ca. 1300–1800." *Economic History Review* 70, no. 4 (November): 1072–102.

Alfani, Guido, Francesco Ammannati, and Nicoletta Balbo. 2022. "Pandemics and Social Mobility: The Case of the Black Death." Paper presented at the World Economic History Congress (25–9 July), Paris.

Alfani, Guido, Francesco Ammannati, and Wouter Ryckbosch. 2022. "Poverty in Early Modern Europe: New Approaches to Old Problems." Working Paper no. 222, European Historical Economics Society.

Alfani, Guido, and Marco Bonetti. 2019. "A Survival Analysis of the Last Great European Plagues: The Case of Nonantola (Northern Italy) in 1630." *Population Studies* 73, no. 1: 101–18.

Alfani, Guido, Marco Bonetti, and Mattia Fochesato. 2023. "Pandemics and Socio-Economic Status: Evidence from the Plague of 1630 in Northern Italy." *Population Studies*, forthcoming.

Alfani, Guido, and Andrea Caracausi. 2009. "Struttura della proprietà e concentrazione della ricchezza in ambiente urbano: Ivrea e Padova, secoli XV–XVII." In *Ricchezza, valore, proprietà in Età preindustriale. 1400–1850*, edited by Guido Alfani and Michela Barbot, 185–209. Venezia: Marsilio.

Alfani, Guido, and Matteo Di Tullio. 2019. *The Lion's Share: Inequality and the Rise of the Fiscal State in Preindustrial Europe.* Cambridge: Cambridge University Press.

Alfani, Guido, and Roberta Frigeni. 2016. "Inequality (Un)perceived: The Emergence of a Discourse on Economic Inequality from the Middle Ages to the Age of Revolution." *Journal of European Economic History* 45, no. 1 (November): 21–66.

Alfani, Guido, and Hector García Montero. 2022. "Wealth Inequality in Pre-Industrial England: A Long-Term View (Late Thirteenth to Sixteenth Centuries)." *Economic History Review* 75, no. 4 (November): 1314–48.

Alfani, Guido, Victoria Gierok, and Felix Schaff. 2022. "Economic Inequality in Preindustrial Germany, ca. 1300–1850." *Journal of Economic History* 82, no. 1 (March): 87–125.

Alfani, Guido, Victoria Gierok, and Felix Schaff. 2023. "Poverty, Inequality and Inequality Extraction in the German Area, ca. 1300–1850." Unpublished manuscript, forthcoming.

Alfani, Guido, and Vincent Gourdon. 2009. "Fêtes du baptême et publicité des réseaux sociaux. Grandes tendances de la fin du Moyen-âge au XXe siècle." *Annales de Démographie Historique* 117, no. 1: 153–89.

Alfani, Guido, and Tommy E. Murphy. 2017. "Plague and Lethal Epidemics in the Pre-Industrial World." *Journal of Economic History* 77, no. 1 (March): 314–43.

Alfani, Guido, and Cormac Ó Gráda, eds. 2017. *Famine in European History.* Cambridge: Cambridge University Press.

Alfani, Guido, and Cormac Ó Gráda. 2018. "The Timing and Causes of Famines in Europe." *Nature Sustainability* 1, no. 6 (June): 283–8.

Alfani, Guido, and Marco Percoco. 2019. "Plague and Long-Term Development: The Lasting Effects of the 1629–30 Epidemic on the Italian Cities." *Economic History Review* 72, no. 4 (November): 1175–201.

Alfani Guido, and Riccardo Rao, eds. 2011. *La gestione delle risorse collettive. Italia settentrionale, secoli XII–XVIII.* Milan: Franco Angeli.

Alfani, Guido, and Wouter Ryckbosch. 2016. "Growing Apart in Early Modern Europe? A Comparison of Inequality Trends in Italy and the Low Countries, 1500–1800." *Explorations in Economic History* 62 (October): 143–53.

Alfani, Guido, and Sonia Schifano. 2021. "Wealth Inequality in the Long Run." In *How Was Life? Volume II: New Perspectives on Well-Being and Global Inequality since 1820*, edited by Jan Luiten van Zanden, Marco Mira d'Ercole, Mikolaj Malinowski, and Auke Rijpma, 103–23. Paris: OECD Publishing.

Allen, Robert C. 2009. *The British Industrial Revolution in Global Perspective.* Cambridge: Cambridge University Press.

Allen, Robert L. 1993. *Irving Fisher: A Biography.* Cambridge, MA: Blackwell.

Alsan, Marcella, Amitabh Chandra, and Kosali Simon. 2021. "The Great Unequalizer: Initial Health Effects of COVID-19 in the United States." *Journal of Economic Perspectives* 35, no. 3 (summer): 25–46.

Alstadsæter, Annette, Niels Johannesen, and Gabriel Zucman. 2019. "Tax Evasion and Inequality." *American Economic Review* 109, no. 6 (June): 2073–103.

Alvaredo, Facundo, and Emmanuel Saez. 2010. "Income and Wealth Concentration in Spain in a Historical and Fiscal Perspective." In *Top Incomes: A Global Perspective*, edited by Anthony B. Atkinson and Thomas Piketty, 482–559. Oxford: Oxford University Press.

Alvaredo, Facundo, Anthony B. Atkinson, Thomas Piketty, and Emmanuel Saez. 2013. "The Top 1 Percent in International and Historical Perspective." *Journal of Economic Perspectives* 27, no. 3 (summer): 3–20.

Alvaredo, Facundo, Bertrand Garbinti, and Thomas Piketty. 2017. "On the Share of Inheritance in Aggregate Wealth: Europe and the USA, 1900–2010." *Economica* 84, no. 334 (April): 239–60.

Álvarez-Nogal, Carlos, and Christophe Chamley. 2014. "Debt Policy under Constraints: Philip II, the Cortes, and Genoese Bankers." *Economic History Review* 67, no. 1 (February): 192–213.

Álvarez-Nogal, Carlos, Leandro Prados de la Escosura, and Carlos Santiago-Caballero. 2020. "Economic Effects of the Black Death: Spain in European Perspective." *Investigaciones de Historia Económica—Economic History Research* 16, no. 4 (December): 35–48.

Amatori, Franco. 2011. "Entrepreneurial Typologies in the History of Industrial Italy: Reconsiderations." *Business History Review* 85, no. 1 (spring): 151–80.

Amatori, Franco, and Andrea Colli. 1999. *Impresa e industria in Italia. Dall'unità ad oggi*. Bologna: Il Mulino.

Anderson, Stuart. 2005. "From Pills to Philanthropy: The Thomas Holloway Story." *Pharmaceutical Historian* 35, no. 2 (June): 32–6.

Andreoni, James. 2018. "The Benefits and Costs of Donor-Advised Funds." *Tax Policy & the Economy* 32, no. 1: 1–44.

Andrews, Kenneth R. 1984. *Trade, Plunder and Settlement: Maritime Enterprise and the Genesis of the British Empire, 1480–1630*. Cambridge: Cambridge University Press.

Antunes, Catia, and Filipa Ribeiro da Silva. 2012. "Amsterdam Merchants in the Slave Trade and African Commerce, 1580s–1670s." *Tijdschrift voor Sociale en Economische Geschiedenis* 9, no. 4 (December): 3–30.

Aquinas, Thomas. (1269–1272) 2003. *On Evil*. Translated by Richard J. Regan. Oxford: Oxford University Press.

Arndt, H. Lukas R. 2020. "Varieties of Affluence: How Political Attitudes of the Rich Are Shaped by Income or Wealth." *European Sociological Review* 36, no. 1 (February): 136–58.

Asch, Ronald G. 1997. *The Thirty Years War: The Holy Roman Empire and Europe, 1618–48*. New York: Macmillan.

Atkinson, Anthony B. 1974. *Unequal Shares: Wealth in Britain*, new edition. London: Pelican Books.

Atkinson, Anthony B., ed. 1980. *Wealth, Income, and Inequality*. Oxford: Oxford University Press.

Atkinson, Anthony B. 2004. "Income Tax and Top Incomes over the Twentieth Century." *Hacienda Pública Española / Revista de Economía Pública* 168, no. 1 (March): 123–41.

Atkinson, Anthony B. 2018. "Wealth and Inheritance in Britain from 1896 to the Present." *Journal of Economic Inequality* 16, no. 2 (June): 137–69.

Atkinson, Anthony B., Thomas Piketty, and Emmanuel Saez. 2011. "Top Incomes in the Long Run of History." *Journal of Economic Literature* 49, no. 1 (March): 3–71.

Augustine, Dolores L. 1994. *Patricians & Parvenus: Wealth and High Society in Wilhelmine Germany*. Oxford: Berg.

Babbitt, Susan M. 1985. "Oresme's Livre de Politiques and the France of Charles V." *Transactions of the American Philosophical Society* 75, no. 1: 1–158.

Bagchi, Sutirtha, and Jan Svejnar. 2015. "Does Wealth Inequality Matter for Growth? The Effect of Billionaire Wealth, Income Distribution, and Poverty." *Journal of Comparative Economics* 43, no. 3 (August): 505–30.

Bagchi, Sutirtha, and Jan Svejnar. 2016. "Does Wealth Distribution and the Source of Wealth Matter for Economic Growth? Inherited v. Uninherited Billionaire Wealth and Billionaires' Political Connections." In *Inequality and Growth: Patterns and Policy. Volume II: Regions and Regularities*, edited by Kaushik Basu and Joseph E. Stiglitz, 163–94. London: Palgrave Macmillan.

Bakija, Jon, Adam Cole, and Bradley T. Heim. 2012. "Jobs and Income Growth of Top Earners and the Causes of Changing Income Inequality: Evidence from U.S. Tax Return Data." Working Paper no. 2010–22, Department of Economics, Williams College.

Bakker, Bas B., and Joshua Feldman. 2014. "The Rich and the Great Recession." Working Paper no. 225, IMF.

Barker, John. 2004. "Primogeniture." In *International Encyclopedia of Marriage and Family*, 2nd ed., edited by James J. Ponzetti, 1280–1. New York: Macmillan Reference USA.

Bartels, Charlotte. 2019. "Top Incomes in Germany, 1871–2013." *Journal of Economic History* 79, no. 3 (September): 669–707.

Bartels, Larry M. 2008. *Unequal Democracy: The Political Economy of the New Gilded Age*. Princeton: Princeton University Press.

Barth, James R., R. Dan Brumbaugh, and James A. Wilcox. 2000. "The Repeal of Glass-Steagall and the Advent of Broad Banking." *Journal of Economic Perspectives* 14, no. 2 (spring): 191–204.

Battiston, Stefano, Mattia Guerini, Mauro Napoletano, and Veronika Stolbova. 2018. "Financialization in the EU and Its Consequences." European Policy Brief, http://www.isigrowth.eu/wp-content/uploads/2018/04/PB_Financialization.pdf.

Baum, Fran, Toby Freeman, Connie Musolino, Mimi Abramovitz, Wim De Ceukelaire, Joanne Flavel, Sharon Friel, et al. 2021. "Explaining Covid-19 Performance: What Factors Might Predict National Responses?" *BMJ* 372, no. 91 (January).

Bayard, Françoise. 1988. *Le monde des financiers au XVIIe siècle*. Paris: Flammarion.

Bebchuk, Lucian A., and Jesse Fried. 2004. *Pay without Performance: The Unfulfilled Promise of Executive Compensation*. Cambridge, MA: Harvard University Press.

Becker, Sascha O., and Ludger Woessmann. 2009. "Was Weber Wrong? A Human Capital Theory of Protestant Economic Theory." *Quarterly Journal of Economics* 124, no. 2 (May): 531–96.

Beckett, John V. 1986. *The Aristocracy in England, 1660–1914*. New York: Basil Blackwell.

Beeghley, Leonard. 2016. *The Structure of Social Stratification in the United States*, 5th ed. New York: Routledge.

Behringer, Wolfgang. 1990. *Thurn und Taxis. Die Geschichte ihrer Post und ihrer Unternehmen.* Munich: Piper Verlag.

Bellavitis, Anna. 2013. "Family and Society." In *A Companion to Venetian History, 1400–1797,* edited by Eric Dursteler, 319–51. Leiden: Brill.

Benedict, Burton. 2004. "Sociological Characteristics of Small Territories and Their Implications for Economic Development." In *Social Anthropology of Complex Societies,* edited by Michael Banton, 23–36. London: Routledge.

Benedictow, Ole J. 2004. *The Black Death 1346–1353: The Complete History.* Woodbridge: The Boydell Press.

Bengtsson, Erik, Anna Missiaia, Mats Olsson, and Patrick Svensson. 2018. "Wealth Inequality in Sweden, 1750–1900." *Economic History Review* 71, no. 3 (August): 772–94. https://doi.org /10.1111/ehr.12576.

Bengtsson, Erik, Anna Missiaia, Ilkka Nummela, and Mats Olsson. 2019. "Unequal Poverty and Equal Industrialisation: Finnish Wealth, 1750–1900." *Scandinavian Economic History Review* 67, no. 3: 229–48.

Berkhout, Esmé, Nick Galasso, Max Lawson, Pablo Andrés Rivero Morales, Anjela Taneja, and Diego Alejo Vázquez Pimentel. 2021. *The Inequality Virus,* Oxfam Briefing Paper, January 2021, https://oxfamilibrary.openrepository.com/bitstream/handle/10546/621149/bp -the-inequality-virus-250121-en.pdf.

Beresford, Philip, and William D. Rubinstein. 2007. *The Richest of the Rich: The Wealthiest 250 People in Britain since 1066.* Petersfield: Harriman House.

Berghoff, Hartmut. 1994. "Aristokratisierung des Bürgertums? Zur Sozialgeschichte der Nobilitierung von Unternehmern in Preußen und Großbritannien 1870 bis 1918." *Vierteljahrschrift für Sozial- und Wirtschftsgeschichte* 81: 178–204.

Bertrams, Kenneth, Nicolas Coupain, and Ernst Homburg. 2013. *Solvay: History of a Multinational Family Firm.* Cambridge: Cambridge University Press.

Bertrand, Marianne, Matilde Bombardini, Raymond Fisman, and Francesco Trebbi. 2020. "Tax-Exempt Lobbying: Corporate Philanthropy as a Tool for Political Influence." *American Economic Review* 110, no. 7 (July): 2065–102.

Biagioli, Giuliana. 2000. *Il modello del proprietario imprenditore nella Toscana dell'ottocento: Bettino Ricasoli. Il patrimonio, le fattorie.* Florence: Olschki.

Birnbaum, Marianna D. 2003. *The Long Journey of Gracia Mendes.* Budapest: Central European University Press.

Bivens, John, and Lawrence Mishel. 2013. "The Pay of Corporate Executives and Financial Professionals as Evidence of Rents in Top 1 Percent Incomes." *Journal of Economic Perspectives* 27, no. 3 (summer): 57–78.

Blackmore, Robert. 2020. *Government and Merchant Finance in Anglo-Gascon Trade, 1300–1500.* Cham: Palgrave Macmillan.

Blendinger, Friedrich. "Fugger Family." In *Encyclopædia Britannica Online.* Accessed January 2021. https://www.britannica.com/topic/Fugger-family.

Blair, Gwenda. 2015. *The Trumps: Three Generations of Builders and a President,* reprint edition. New York: Simon & Schuster.

Bogaard, Amy, Mattia Fochesato, and Samuel Bowles. 2019. "The Farming-Inequality Nexus: New Methods and Evidence from Western Eurasia." *Antiquity* 93, no. 371: 1129–43.

Bogart, Dan. 2019. "Investing in Early Public Works: Financial Risks and Returns in English and Welsh Turnpikes, 1820–82." *Economic History Review* 72, no. 3 (August): 848–68.

Bolle, Jacques. 1963. *Solvay : l'invention, l'homme, l'entreprise industrielle. 1863–1963*. Brussels: Weissenbruch.

Bolton, Patrick, Hamid Mehran, and Joel D. Shapiro. 2011. "Executive Compensation and Risk Taking." Report no. 456, Federal Reserve Board of New York Staff.

Bonica, Adam, and Howard Rosenthal. 2018. "The Wealth Elasticity of Political Contributions by the Forbes 400." Working Paper, http://dx.doi.org/10.2139/ssrn.2668780.

Bonney, Richard. 1999. *The Rise of the Fiscal State in Europe, c.1200–1815*. Oxford: Oxford University Press.

Borgerhoff Mulder, Monique, Samuel Bowles, Tom Hertz, Adrian Bell, Jan Beise, Greg Clark, Ila Fazzio et al. 2009. "Intergenerational Wealth Transmission and the Dynamics of Inequality in Small-Scale Societies." *Science* 326, no. 5953 (October): 682–8.

Bottani, Tarcisio, ed. 2012. *I Tasso e le poste d'Europa*. Bergamo: Corponove.

Botticini, Maristella. 1999. "A Loveless Economy? Intergenerational Altruism and the Marriage Market in a Tuscan Town, 1415–1436." *Journal of Economic History* 59, no. 1 (March): 104–21.

Boudjaaba, Fabrice. 2009. "La distribuzione delle fortune fondiarie in Francia alla fine dell'Ancien Régime: un approccio dinamico a partire dall'esempio della Normandia." In *Ricchezza, valore, proprietà in Età preindustriale. 1400–1850*, edited by Guido Alfani and Michela Barbot, 371–90. Venice: Marsilio.

Bowie, Ewen L. 2013. "Herodes Atticus." In *The Encyclopedia of Ancient History*, 1st ed., edited by Roger S. Bagnall, Kai Brodersen, Craige B. Champion, Andrew Erskine, and Sabine R. Huebner. Oxford: Wiley-Blackwell. https://doi.org/10.1002/9781444338386.wbeah18056.

Bowles, Samuel, Eric A. Smith, and Monique Borgerhoff Mulder. 2010. "The Emergence and Persistence of Inequality in Premodern Societies." *Current Anthropology* 51, no. 1 (February): 7–17.

Bracciolini, Poggio. (1428–1429) 1952. "De avaricia." In *Prosatori latini del Quattrocento*, edited by Eugenio Garin, 248–301. Naples: Ricciardi.

Brady, David, and Benjamin Sosnaud. 2010. "The Politics of Economic Inequality." In *Handbook of Politics: State and Civil Society in Global Perspective*, edited by Kevin T. Leicht and J. Craig Jenkins, 521–41. New York: Springer.

Brandolini, Andrea, Luigi Cannari, Giovanni D'Alessio, and Ivan Faiella. 2004. "Household Wealth Distribution in Italy in the 1990s." Working Paper no. 530, Banca d'Italia.

Braudel, Fernand. 1966. *The Mediterranean and the Mediterranean World in the Age of Philip II*. Glasgow: William Colins & Sons.

Braudel, Fernand. 1977. *Afterthoughts on Material Civilization and Capitalism*. Baltimore: Johns Hopkins University Press.

Braudel, Fernand. 1992. *Civilization and Capitalism 15th–18th Century*. Berkeley: University of California Press.

Bringmann, Klaus. 1998. *Storia romana*. Translated by Alessandro Cristofori. Bologna: Il Mulino.

Broadberry, Stephen, Bruce M. S. Campbell, Alexander Klein, Mark Overton, and Bas van Leeuwen. 2015. *British Economic Growth*. Cambridge: Cambridge University Press.

Bruner, Robert F., and Sean D. Carr. 2007. *The Panic of 1907: Lessons Learned from the Market's Perfect Storm*. Hoboken: John Wiley & Sons.

Bullard, Melissa M. 1994. *Lorenzo il Magnifico: Image and Anxiety, Politics and Finance*. Florence: Olschki.

Bulst, Neithard. 2003. "La legislazione suntuaria in Francia (secoli XIII-XVIII)." In *Disciplinare il lusso. La legislazione suntuaria in Italia e in Europa tra Medioevo ed Età Moderna*, edited by Maria G. Muzzarelli and Antonella Campanini, 121–36. Rome: Carocci.

Burgess, Clive. 1987. "'By Quick and By Dead': Wills and Pious Provision in Late Medieval Bristol." *English Historical Review* 102, no. 405 (October): 837–58.

Burnard, Trevor and Giorgio Riello. 2020. "Slavery and the New History of Capitalism." *Journal of Global History* 15, no. 2: 225–44.

Burt, Nathaniel. (1963) 1999. *The Perennial Philadelphians: The Anatomy of an American Aristocracy*. Philadelphia: University of Pennsylvania Press.

Callahan, William J. 1972. *Honor, Commerce and Industry in Eighteenth-Century Spain*. Boston: Baker Library, Harvard Graduate School of Business Administration.

Calonaci, Stefano. 2012. "Promesse da realizzare. I fedecommessi nello «Stato Nuovo» di Siena (secc. XVI–XVIII)." *Mélanges de l'École française de Rome—Italie et Méditerranée modernes et contemporaines* 124, no. 2: 551–77. https://doi.org/10.4000/mefrim.824.

Campbell, Bruce M. S. 2010. "Nature as Historical Protagonist: Environment and Society in Pre-Industrial England." *Economic History Review* 63, no. 2 (May): 281–314.

Campbell, Bruce M. S. 2016. *The Great Transition: Climate, Disease and Society in the Late-Medieval World*. Cambridge: Cambridge University Press.

Cannadine, David. 1999. *The Decline and Fall of the British Aristocracy*. New York: Vintage Books.

Cantoni, Davide. 2015. "The Economic Effects of the Protestant Reformation: Testing the Weber Hypothesis in the German Lands." *Journal of the European Economic Association* 13, no. 4 (August): 561–98.

Capuano, Stella, Tat-kei Lai, and Hans-Jörg Schmerer. 2014. "The US Finance Wage Premium before and after the Financial Crisis: A Decomposition Exercise." *Applied Economics Letters* 21, no. 16: 1144–7.

Carlos, Ann M., and Larry Neal. 2004. "Women Investors in Early Capital Markets 1720–1725." *Financial History Review* 11, no. 4 (October): 197–224.

Carnegie, Andrew. (1889) 1900. "The Gospel of Wealth." In *The Gospel of Wealth and Other Timely Essays*, 1–44. New York: Century Co.

Carnegie, Andrew. (1891) 1900. "The Advantages of Poverty." In *The Gospel of Wealth and Other Timely Essays*, 47–82. New York: Century Co.

Carosso, Vincent P. 1987. *The Morgans: Private International Bankers 1854–1913*. Cambridge, MA: Harvard University Press.

Carroll, Christopher D. 1998. "Why Do the Rich Save So Much?" Working Paper no. 6549, National Bureau of Economic Research, https://www.nber.org/papers/w6549.

Carroll, Christopher D. 2000. "Why Do the Rich Save So Much?" In *Does Atlas Shrug? The Economic Consequences of Taxing the Rich*, edited by Joel B. Slemrod, 465–84. Cambridge, MA: Harvard University Press.

Cashman, Sean D. 1993. *America in the Gilded Age*, 3rd ed. New York: New York University Press.

Casson, Catherine, and Mark Casson. 2019. "'To Dispose of Wealth in Works of Charity': Entrepreneurship and Philanthropy in Medieval England." *Business History Review* 93, no. 3 (autumn): 473–502.

Cattini, Marco. 1988. "Dall'economia della guerra alla guerra 'in economia'. Prime indagini sull'organizzazione militare estense nei secoli XV e XVII." In *Guerra stati e città. Mantova e l'Italia padana dal secolo XIII al XIX*, edited by Carlo M. Belfanti, Francesca Fantini D'Onofrio and Daniela Ferrari, 31–40. Mantua: Gianluigi Arcari Editore.

Cattini, Marco, Enrico Decleva, and Aldo De Maddalena. 1992. *Storia di una Libera Università*, vol. 1. Milan: Egea.

Cattini, Marco, and Marzio A. Romani. 2005. "Per lo studio delle élites municipali di due capitali di Stato: Parma e Modena nei secoli dell'Età Moderna." In *Per una Storia sociale del Politico. Ceti dirigenti urbani italiani e spagnoli nei secoli XVI-XVIII*, edited by Marco Cattini, Marzio A. Romani and José M. de Bernardo Arés, special issue, *Cheiron* 41: 101–33.

Cavalcanti, Giovanni. (1450 ca.) 1838. *Istorie Fiorentine*. Florence: Tipografia All'Insegna di Dante.

Cavarzere, Marco. 2019. "TASSO, Francesco." In *Dizionario Biografico degli Italiani*, vol. 95. Accessed May 2021. https://www.treccani.it/enciclopedia/francesco-tasso_(Dizionario-Biografico).

Cecconi, Giovanni. A. 2017. "L'economia romana tra pubblico e privato: le spese per l'edilizia municipale." In *Atti e Memorie dell'Accademia di Scienze e Lettere La Colombaria: volume LXXXI; nuova serie. Vol. 67, Anno 2016*, 38–48. Florence: Leo S. Olschki.

Chadeau, Emmanuel. 1987. *L'industrie aéronautique en France 1900–1950. De Blériot à Dassault*. Paris: Fayard.

Chancel, Lucas, Thomas Piketty, Emmanuel Saez, and Gabriel Zucman. 2022. *World Inequality Report 2022*, World Inequality Lab, wir2022.wid.world.

Chandler, Alfred D. 1959. "The Beginnings of 'Big Business' in American Industry." *Business History Review* 33, no. 1 (spring): 1–30.

Chandler, Alfred D. 1977. *The Visible Hand: The Managerial Revolution in American Business*. Cambridge, MA: Harvard University Press.

Chaudhuri, Kirti N. (1965) 1999. *The English East India Company: The Study of an Early Joint-Stock Company 1600–1640*. London: Routledge/Thoemmes Press.

Chaudhuri, Kirti N. 1978. *The Trading World of Asia and the English East India Company, 1660–1760*. Cambridge: Cambridge University Press.

Chaunu Pierre. 1977. "Du pluriel au singulier." In *Histoire économique et sociale du monde*, vol. 1, edited by Pierre Léon, 15–38. Paris: A. Colin.

Chauvard, Jean-François, Anna Bellavitis, and Paola Lanaro. 2012. "De l'usage du fidéicommis à l'âge moderne. État des lieux." *Mélanges de l'École française de Rome—Italie et Méditerranée modernes et contemporaines* 124, no. 2: 321–37. https://doi.org/10.4000/mefrim.650.

Chernow, Ron. 1990. *The House of Morgan: An American Banking Dynasty and the Rise of Modern Finance*. New York: Grove Press.

Chesnais, François. 2016. *Finance Capital Today: Corporations and Banks in the Lasting Global Slump*. Leiden: Brill.

Cipolla, Carlo M. 1964. "The Economic Depression of the Renaissance?" *Economic History Review* 16, no. 3 (April): 519–24.

Clark, Gregory, and Neil J. Cummins. 2015a. "Malthus to Modernity: Wealth, Status and Fertility in England, 1500–1879." *Journal of Population Economics* 28, no. 1 (January): 3–29.

Clark, Gregory, and Neil J. Cummins. 2015b. "Is Most Wealth Inherited or Created: England, 1858–2012." *Tax Law Review* 68, no. 3 (spring): 517–44.

Clemens, Elisabeth S. 2020. *Civic Gifts: Voluntarism and the Making of the American Nation-State*. Chicago: University of Chicago Press.

Clift, Imelda. 2008. *The Wedgwood/Darwin Dynasty*. Ely: Melrose Books.

Cohen, Norma. 2019. "How Britain Paid for War: Bond Holders and the Financing of the Great War 1914–32," PhD thesis. Queen Mary University of London.

Cohn, Samuel K. 1988. *Death and Property in Siena 1205–1800: Strategies for the Afterlife*. Baltimore: Johns Hopkins University Press.

Cohn, Samuel K. 2006. *Lust for Liberty: The Politics of Social Revolt in Medieval Europe, 1200–1425*. Cambridge, MA: Harvard University Press.

Cohn, Samuel K. 2007. "After the Black Death: Labour Legislation and Attitudes towards Labour in Late-Medieval Western Europe." *Economic History Review* 60, no. 3 (August): 457–85.

Colli, Andrea. 2003. *The History of Family Business 1850–2000*. Cambridge: Cambridge University Press.

Collins, Chuck. 2021. *The Wealth Hoarders: How Billionaires Pay Millions to Hide Trillions*. Cambridge and Malden: Polity Press.

Collins, Chuck, and William H. Gates. 2002. *Wealth and Our Commonwealth: Why America Should Tax Accumulated Fortunes*. Boston: Beacon Press.

Collins, James B. 1988. *Fiscal Limits of Absolutism: Direct Taxation in Early Seventeenth-Century France*. Berkeley: University of California Press.

Cooper, Hilary, and Simon Szreter. 2021. *After the Virus: Lessons from the Past for a Better Future*. Cambridge: Cambridge University Press.

Corley, Tony A. B. 2004. "Holloway, Thomas." In *Oxford Dictionary of National Biography*. Accessed December 2021. https://doi.org/10.1093/ref:odnb/13577.

Coulton, George G. 1918. *Social Life in Britain from the Conquest to the Reformation*. Cambridge: Cambridge University Press.

Cournède, Boris, Oliver Denk, and Peter Hoeller. 2015. "Finance and Inclusive Growth." Economic Policy Paper no. 14, OECD.

Cozzi, Gaetano. 1995. "Venezia nello scenario europeo (1517–1669)." In *Storia d'Italia. Tomo XII. La Repubblica di Venezia nell'età moderna*, vol. 2, edited by Gaetano Cozzi, Michael Knapton and Giovanni Scarabello, 5–200. Turin: UTET.

Cringely, Robert X. 1996. *Accidental Empires: How the Boys of Silicon Valley Make Their Millions, Battle Foreign Competition and Still Can't Get a Date*, 2nd ed. London: Penguin.

Crippa, Flavio. 1990. "Il torcitoio circolare da seta: evoluzione, macchine superstiti, restauri." *Quaderni Storici* 73, no. 1 (April): 169–211.

Crook, Malcolm. 1996. *Elections in the French Revolution: An Apprenticeship in Democracy, 1789–1799*. Cambridge: Cambridge University Press.

Cummins, Neil. 2022. "The Hidden Wealth of English Dynasties, 1892–2016." *Economic History Review* 75, no. 3 (August): 667–702.

Cunningham, Hugh. 2016. "Layered History of Western Philanthropy." In *The Routledge Companion to Philanthropy*, edited by Tobias Jung, Susan D. Phillips and Jenny Harrow, 42–55. New York: Routledge.

Daly, Gavin. 2019. "'The Sacking of a Town Is an Abomination': Siege, Sack and Violence to Civilians in British Officers' Writings on the Peninsular War—The Case of Badajoz." *Historical Research* 92, no. 255 (February): 160–82.

Damon, Frederick H. 1980. "The Kula and Generalised Exchange: Considering Some Unconsidered Aspects of the Elementary Structures of Kinship." *Man* 15, no. 2 (June): 267–92.

Damon, Frederick H. 2002. "Kula Valuables: The Problem of Value and the Production of Names." *L'Homme—Revue française d'anthropologie* 162 (April–June): 107–36.

Daumard, Adeline. 1973. *Les fortunes française au XIXe siècle: Enquête sur la repartition et la composition des capitaux privés á Paris, Lyon, Lille, Bordeaux et Toulouse d'après l'enregistrement des déclarations de succession*. Paris: Mouton.

Daumard, Adeline. 1980. "Wealth and Affluence in France since the Beginning of the Nineteenth Century." In *Wealth and the Wealthy in the Modern World*, edited by William D. Rubinstein, 90–121. London: Croom Helm.

Daunton, Martin J. 1989. "Gentlemanly Capitalism and British Industry, 1820–1914." *Past and Present* 122 (February): 119–58.

Daunton, Martin J. 1997. "Churchill at the Treasury: Remaking Conservative Taxation Policy, 1924–1929." *Revue belge de philologie et d'histoire* 75, no. 4: 1063–83.

Davies, James B., and Livio Di Matteo. 2018. "Filling the Gap: Long Run Canadian Wealth Inequality in International Context." Research Report no. 2018–1, Department of Economics, University of Western Ontario.

Davies, James B., Rodrigo Lluberas, and Anthony F. Shorrocks. 2010–21. *Credit Suisse Global Wealth Databook*. Zurich: Credit Suisse.

Davies, James B., and Anthony F. Shorrocks. 2000. "The Distribution of Wealth." In *Handbook of Income Distribution*, edited by Anthony B. Atkinson and François Bourguignon, 605–75. London: Elsevier.

Davies, Richard, Peter Richardson, Vaiva Katinaite, and Mark J. Manning. 2010. "Evolution of the UK Banking System." *Bank of England Quarterly Bulletin* 50, no. 4: 321–32.

Davis, James C. 1962. *The Decline of the Venetian Nobility as a Ruling Class*. Baltimore: Johns Hopkins University.

Davis, Lance E., and Robert A. Huttenback. 1987. *Mammon and the Pursuit of Empire: The Political Economy of British Imperialism, 1860–1912*. Cambridge: Cambridge University Press.

Davis, Richard W. 1983. *The English Rothschilds*. London: Collins.

Davis, Ron. 1985–6. "Thomas Holloway, Entrepreneur and Philanthropist." *Surrey History* 3, no. 2: 67–75.

Dawley, Alan. 2005. "The Abortive Rule of Big Money." In *Ruling America: A History of Wealth and Power in a Democracy*, edited by Steve Fraser and Gary Gerstle, 149–80. Cambridge, MA: Harvard University Press.

Dean, Martin. 2010. *Robbing the Jews: The Confiscation of Jewish Property in the Holocaust, 1933–1945*, reprint edition. New York: Cambridge University Press.

De Ceukelaire, Wim, and Chiara Bodini. 2020. "We Need Strong Public Health Care to Contain the Global Corona Pandemic." *International Journal of Health Services* 50, no. 3 (July): 276–7.

Deene, Marloes. 2013. "Seeking for Honour(s)? The Exploitation of Philotimia and Citizen Benefactors in Classical Athens." *Revue belge de philologie et d'histoire* 91, no. 1: 69–87.

Delacroix, Jacques, and François Nielsen. 2001. "The Beloved Myth: Protestantism and the Rise of Industrial Capitalism in Nineteenth-Century Europe." *Social Forces* 80, no. 2 (December): 509–53.

Del Negro, Piero. 1984. "La distribuzione del potere all'interno del patriziato veneto del Settecento." In *I ceti dirigenti in Italia in età moderna e contemporanea*, edited by Amelio Tagliaferri, 311–35. Udine: Del Bianco.

Del Negro, Piero. 1998. "L'ultima fase della serenissima: nota introduttiva." In *L'ultima fase della Serenissima*, vol. 8 of *Storia di Venezia*, edited by Piero Del Negro and Paolo Preto, 1–80. Rome: Istituto della Enciclopedia Italiana.

De Long, J. Bradford. 1991. "Did JP Morgan's Men Add Value?: An Economist's Perspective on Financial Capitalism." In *Inside the Business Enterprise: Historical Perspectives on the Use of Information*, edited by Peter Temin, 205–36. Chicago: University of Chicago Press.

De Luca, Giuseppe. 1996. *Commercio del denaro e crescita economica a Milano tra Cinquecento e Seicento*. Milan: Polifilo.

Denk, Oliver. 2015. "Financial Sector Pay and Labour Income Inequality." Working Paper no. 1225, Economics Department, OECD. https://doi.org/10.1787/5js04v5wjw9p-en.

Dermine, Jean. 2002. "European Banking, Past, Present and Future." Paper presented at the Second Central Banking Conference, Frankfurt. https://papers.ssrn.com/sol3/papers.cfm?abstract_id=357500.

Dermineur, Elise M. 2014. "Single Women and the Rural Credit Market in Eighteenth-Century France." *Journal of Social History* 48, no. 1 (autumn): 175–99.

Dermineur, Elise M. 2018. *Women and Credit in Pre-Industrial Europe*. Turnhout: Brepols.

De Roover, Raymond. 1963. *The Rise and Decline of the Medici Bank, 1397–1494*. Cambridge, MA: Harvard University Press.

Desierto, Desiree and Mark Koyama. 2023. "The Political Economy of Status Competition: Sumptuary Laws in Preindustrial Europe." *Journal of Economic History*, forthcoming.

Despy-Meyer, Andrée, and Didier Devriese. 1997. *Ernest Solvay et son temps*. Brussels: Archives de l'Université de Bruxelles.

Dewald, Jonathan. 1996. *The European Nobility: 1400–1800*. Cambridge: Cambridge University Press.

De Vries, Jan. 1976. *The Economy of Europe in an Age of Crisis, 1600–1750*. Cambridge: Cambridge University Press.

De Vries, Jan, and Ad van der Woude. 1997. *The First Modern Economy: Success, Failure, and Perseverance of the Dutch Economy, 1500–1815*. Cambridge: Cambridge University Press.

De Zwart, Pim, and Jan L. van Zanden. 2018. *The Origins of Globalization: World Trade in the Making of the Global Economy, 1500–1800*. Cambridge: Cambridge University Press.

Diamond, Jared. 1997. *Guns, Germs, and Steel: A Short History of Everybody for the Last 13,000 Years*. London: Vintage.

Di Matteo, Livio. 2018. *The Evolution and Determinants of Wealth Inequality in the North Atlantic Anglo-Sphere, 1668–2013: Push and Pull*. New York: Palgrave Macmillan.

Di Tullio, Matteo. 2014. *The Wealth of Communities: War, Resources and Cooperation in Renaissance Lombardy*. Farnham: Ashgate.

Diodato, Emidio, and Federico Niglia. 2018. *Berlusconi 'The Diplomat': Populism and Foreign Policy in Italy*. Cham: Palgrave Macmillan.

Dittmar, Jeremiah E., and Ralf R. Meisenzahl. 2020. "Public Goods Institutions, Human Capital and Growth: Evidence from German History." *Review of Economic Studies* 87, no. 2 (March): 959–96.

Dolan, Brian. 2004. *Wedgwood: The First Tycoon*. New York: Viking Press.

Domhoff, G. William. 2007. "C. Wright Mills, Floyd Hunter, and 50 Years of Power Structure Research." *Michigan Sociological Review* 21 (autumn): 1–54.

Domhoff, G. William. 2010. *Who Rules America? Power, Politics & Social Change*, 6th ed. New York: McGraw Hill.

Donovan, Mark, and Mark Gilbert. 2015. "Silvio Berlusconi and Romano Prodi." In *The Oxford Handbook of Italian Politics*, edited by Erik Jones and Gianfranco Pasquino, 394–406. Oxford: Oxford University Press.

Doob, Christopher B. 2013. *Social Inequality and Social Stratification in US Society*. London and New York: Routledge.

Dorfman, Joseph. 1940. "The Economic Philosophy of Thomas Jefferson." *Political Science Quarterly* 55, no. 1 (March): 98–121.

Dow, Sheila C. 1996. "Why the Banking System Should Be Regulated." *Economic Journal* 106, no. 436 (May): 698–707.

Drelichman, Mauricio, and Hans-Joachim Voth. 2014. *Lending to the Borrower from Hell: Debt, Taxes, and Default in the Age of Philip II*. Princeton: Princeton University Press.

Duby, Georges. 1973. *Hommes et structures du Moyen Age*. Paris: Mouton.

Duby, Georges. 1978. *Les Trois Ordres ou l'imaginaire du féodalisme*. Paris: Gallimard.

Duffie, Darrell. 2019. "Prone to Fail: The Pre-Crisis Financial System." *Journal of Economic Perspectives* 33, no. 1 (winter): 81–106.

Dumolyn, Jan, and Jelle Haemers. 2015. "Reclaiming the Common Sphere of the City: The Revival of the Bruges Commune in the Late Thirteenth Century." In *La Légitimité implicite*, edited by Jean-Philippe Genet, 161–88. Paris: Éditions de la Sorbonne.

Duquette, Nicolas J. 2018. "Inequality and Philanthropy: High-Income Giving in the United States 1917–2012." *Explorations in Economic History* 70 (October): 25–41.

Duquette, Nicolas J. 2019. "Founders' Fortunes and Philanthropy: A History of the U.S. Charitable-Contribution Deduction." *Business History Review* 93, no. 3 (autumn): 553–84.

Dye, Thomas R. 2002. *Who's Running America? The Bush Restoration*, 7th ed. Upper Saddle River: Prentice-Hall.

Dyer, Christopher. 1996. "Taxation and Communities in Late Medieval England." In *Progress and Problems in Medieval England: Essays in Honour of Edward Miller*, edited by Richard Britnell and John Hatcher, 168–90. Cambridge: Cambridge University Press.

Dyer, Christopher. 2015. "A Golden Age Rediscovered: Labourers' Wages in the Fifteenth Century." In *Money, Prices and Wages*, edited by Martin Allen and D'Maris Coffman, 180–95. Basingstoke: Palgrave Macmillan.

Dynan, Karen E., Jonathan Skinner, and Stephen P. Zeldes. 2004. "Do the Rich Save More?" *Journal of Political Economy* 112, no. 2 (April): 397–444.

Edge, Laura B. 2004. *Andrew Carnegie: Industrial Philanthropist*. Minneapolis: Lerner.

Eichengreen, Barry. 2015. *Hall of Mirrors: The Great Depression, the Great Recession, and the Uses—and Misuses—of History*. New York: Oxford University Press.

Eltis, David, and David Richardson. 2010. *Atlas of the Transatlantic Slave Trade*. New Haven: Yale University Press.

Endres, Rudolf. 1993. *Adel in der Frühen Neuzeit*. München: Oldenbourg.

Epstein, Steven A. 2009. *An Economic and Social History of Later Medieval Europe, 1000–1500*. Cambridge: Cambridge University Press.

Evangelisti, Paolo. 2016. *Il pensiero economico del Medioevo. Ricchezza, povertà, mercato e moneta*. Rome: Carocci.

Evans, Eric J. 1983. *The Forging of the Modern State: Early Industrial Britain, 1783–1870*. New York: Longman.

Evans, Jonathan D. 2005. "'As Rare as They Are Dire': Old Norse Dragons, Beowulf, and the Deutsche Mythologie." In *The Shadow-Walkers: Jacob Grimm's Mythology of the Monstrous*, edited by Thomas A. Shippey, 207–69. Turnhout: Brepols.

Fanfani, Amintore. 1931. "Le soluzioni tomistiche e l'atteggiamento degli uomini dei secoli XIII e XIV di fronte ai problemi della ricchezza." *Rivista Internazionale di Scienze Sociali e Discipline Ausiliarie* 2, no. 5 (September): 553–81.

Fanfani, Amintore. 1935. *Catholicism, Protestantism, and Capitalism*. London: Sheed and Ward.

Fawcett, Peter. 2016. "When I Squeeze You with Eisphorai: Taxes and Tax Policy in Classical Athens." *Hesperia: The Journal of the American School of Classical Studies at Athens* 85, no. 1 (January–March): 153–99.

Feci, Simona. 2004. *Pesci fuor d'acqua: Donne a Roma in età moderna: diritti e patrimoni*. Rome: Viella.

Feci, Simona. 2018. "Exceptional Women: Female Merchants and Working Women in Italy in the Early Modern Period." In *Gender, Law and Economic Well-Being in Europe from the Fifteenth to the Nineteenth Century: North versus South?*, edited by Anna Bellavitis and Beatrice Zucca Micheletto, 62–76. London: Routledge.

Ferrari, Maria Luisa. 2012. *L'onorato sistema: Vicende economiche di una famiglia nobile nel Veneto tra Sette e Ottocento*. Verona: QuiEdit.

Ferguson, Niall. 1999. *The House of Rothschild: Money's Prophets 1798–1848*. New York: Penguin.

Ferguson, Niall. 2000. *The House of Rothschild: The World's Banker 1849–1999*. New York: Penguin.

Ferguson, Thomas, and Hans-Joachim Voth. 2008. "Betting on Hitler: The Value of Political Connections in Nazi Germany." *Quarterly Journal of Economics* 123, no. 1 (February): 101–37.

Fesseau, Maryse, and Maria L. Mattonetti. 2013. "Distributional Measures across Household Groups in a National Accounts Framework." Statistics Working Paper no. 53, OECD. https://doi.org/10.1787/18152031.

Finchum-Mason, Emily, Kelly Husted, and David Suárez. 2020. "Philanthropic Foundation Responses to COVID-19." *Nonprofit and Voluntary Sector Quarterly* 49, no. 6 (December): 1129–41.

Findlay, Ronald, and Kevin H. O'Rourke. 2009. *Power and Plenty: Trade, War, and the World Economy in the Second Millennium*. Princeton: Princeton University Press.

Fisher, Irving. 1919. "Economists in Public Service: Annual Address of the President." *The American Economic Review* 9, no. 1 (March): 5–21.

Fitton, Robert S. 1989. *The Arkwrights: Spinners of Fortune.* Manchester: Manchester University Press.

Fleming, Robin. 1991. *Kings and Lords in Conquest England.* Cambridge: Cambridge University Press.

Fochesato, Mattia. 2018. "Origins of Europe's North-South Divide: Population Changes, Real Wages and the 'Little Divergence' in Early Modern Europe." *Explorations in Economic History* 70: 91–131.

Fouquet, Roger, and Steve Broadberry. 2015. "Seven Centuries of European Economic Growth and Decline." *Journal of Economic Perspectives* 29, no. 4 (autumn): 227–44.

Fourquin, Guy. 1969. *Histoire Économique de L'occident Médiéval.* Paris: Armand Colin.

Fourquin, Guy. 1981. "Tendenze economiche nell'Occidente cristiano (1300–1500)." In *Storia economica e sociale del mondo,* vol. 2, edited by Pierre Léon, 357–459. Bari: Laterza.

Franceschi, Franco. 2020. "Big Business for Firms and States: Silk Manufacturing in Renaissance Italy." *Business History Review* 94, no. 1 (spring): 95–123.

Fraser, Steve, and Gary Gerstle. 2005. *Ruling America: A History of Wealth and Power in a Democracy.* Cambridge, MA: Harvard University Press.

Freund, Caroline. 2016. *Rich People Poor Countries: The Rise of Emerging-Market Tycoons and Their Mega Firms.* Washington: Peterson Institute for International Economics.

Friedman, Alan. 2015. *Berlusconi: The Epic Story of the Billionaire Who Took Over Italy.* New York: Hachette Books.

Friedman, Milton. 1957. *Theory of the Consumption Function.* Princeton: Princeton University Press.

Friedman, Sam, and Daniel Laurison. 2019. *The Class Ceiling: Why It Pays to Be Privileged.* Bristol: Policy Press.

Friedman, Sam, and Aaron Reeves. 2020. "From Aristocratic to Ordinary: Shifting Modes of Elite Distinction." *American Sociological Review* 85, no. 2 (April): 323–50.

Fubini, Riccardo. 1990. *Umanesimo e secolarizzazione da Petrarca a Valla.* Rome: Bulzoni.

Fulford, Roger. 1967. *Samuel Whitbread, 1764–1815: A Study in Opposition.* London: Macmillan.

Furió, Antonio. 2017. "Inequality and Economic Development in Late Medieval Iberia: Catalonia, Majorca and Valencia, 13th–16th Centuries." Paper presented at the Rural History Conference (11–14 September), Leuven.

Fusaro, Maria. 2015. *Political Economies of Empire in the Early Modern Mediterranean: The Decline of Venice and the Rise of England, 1450–1700.* Cambridge: Cambridge University Press.

Gabbuti, Giacomo. 2021. "Il fascismo 'liberista' e la 'quasi abolizione' dell'imposta di successione del 1923." In *Le sirene del corporativismo e l'isolamento dei dissidenti durante il fascismo,* edited by Piero Barucci, Piero Bini and Lucilla Conigliello, 171–96. Florence: Firenze University Press.

Gabbuti, Giacomo. 2022. "Those Who Were Better Off: Capital and Top Incomes in Fascist Italy." LEM Working Paper Series no. 2022/31.

Garbade, Kenneth D. 2012. *Birth of a Market: The U.S. Treasury Securities Market from the Great War to the Great Depression.* Cambridge, MA: MIT Press.

García-Montero, Héctor. 2015. "Long-Term Trends in Wealth Inequality in Catalonia, 1400–1800: Initial Results." Working Paper no. 79, Dondena Centre for Research on Social Dynamics and Public Policy.

Garin, Eugenio. 1994. *L'Umanesimo italiano: Filosofia e vita civile nel Rinascimento*, 7th ed. Rome: Laterza.

Garlati, Loredana. 2011. "La famiglia tra passato e presente." In *Diritto della Famiglia*, edited by Salvatore Patti and Maria G. Cubeddu, 1–48. Milan: Giuffré.

Gazzini, Marini. 2002. *Dare et habere: Il mondo di un mercante milanese del Quattrocento*. Florence: Firenze University Press.

Geisst, Charles R. 2000. *Monopolies in America: Empire Builders and Their Enemies from Jay Gould to Bill Gates*. Oxford: Oxford University Press.

Geisst, Charles R. 2012. *Wall Street: A History*, 3rd ed. Oxford: Oxford University Press.

Geloso, Vincent, and Peter Lindert. 2020. "Relative Costs of Living, for Richer and Poorer, 1688–1914." *Cliometrica* 14, no. 3 (September): 417–42.

Gethin, Amory, Clara Martínez-Toledano, and Thomas Piketty. 2022. "Brahmin Left Versus Merchant Right: Changing Political Cleavages in 21 Western Democracies, 1948–2020." *Quarterly Journal of Economics* 137, no. 1 (February): 1–48.

Giannotti, Donato. (1531) 1722. *Della Repubblica fiorentina*. Venice: Hertz.

Gilbert, Martin. 2000. *Churchill: A Life*. London: Pimlico.

Gobbini, Mauro. 1969. "Bocconi, Ferdinando." In *Dizionario Biografico degli Italiani*, vol. 11. Accessed May 2021. https://www.treccani.it/enciclopedia/ferdinando-bocconi_(Dizionario-Biografico).

Goddard, John, Philip Molyneux, and John O. S. Wilson. 2019. "Banking in the European Union: Deregulation, Crisis, and Renewal." In *The Oxford Handbook of Banking*, 2nd ed., edited by Allen N. Berger, Philip Molyneux and John O. S. Wilson. Accessed June 2021. Oxford: Oxford University Press. https://academic.oup.com/edited-volume/34288/chapter-abstract/290690897?redirectedFrom=fulltext.

Gold, Barbara K. 1982. *Literary and Artistic Patronage in Ancient Rome*. Austin: University of Texas Press.

Golding, B. 2013. *Conquest and Colonisation: The Normans in Britain 1066–1100*, 2nd ed. Basingstoke: Palgrave Macmillan.

Goldthorpe, John H. 2007. *On Sociology*, vol. 2, 2nd ed. Stanford: Stanford University Press.

Goldthwaite, Richard A. 1968. *Private Wealth in Renaissance Florence*. Princeton: Princeton University Press.

Goldthwaite, Richard A. 1987. "The Medici Bank and the World of Florentine Capitalism." *Past and Present* 114 (February): 3–31.

Goody, Jack. 1983. *The Development of the Family and Marriage in Europe*. Cambridge: Cambridge University Press.

Goody, Jack, and Stanley J. Tambiah. 1973. *Bridewealth and Dowry*. Cambridge: Cambridge University Press.

Goody, Jack, Joan Thirsk, and Edward P. Thompson. 1978. *Family and Inheritance: Rural Society in Western Europe, 1200–1800*. Cambridge: Cambridge University Press.

Görner, Regina. 1987. *Raubritter: Untersuchungen zur Lage des spätmittelalterlichen Niederadels, besonders im südlichen Westfalen*. Münster: Aschendorff.

Goy, Joseph. 1988. "Pour une cartographie des modes de transmission successorale deux siècles après le code civil." *Mélanges de l'école française de Rome—Moyen-Age, Temps modernes* 100, no. 1: 431–44. https://doi.org/10.3406/mefr.1988.2982.

Graverini, L. 1997. "Un secolo di studi su Mecenate." *Rivista Storica dell'Antichità* 27: 231–89.

Guenzi, Alberto. 1995. "Le magistrature e le istituzioni alimentari." In *Gli archivi per la storia dell'alimentazione*, 285–301. Rome: Ministero per i Beni Culturali e Ambientali.

Guerzoni, Guido. 2006. *Apollo e Vulcano: I mercati artistici in Italia (1400–1700)*. Venice: Marsilio.

Guicciardini, Francesco. (1508–9) 1998. *Storie fiorentine*. Milan: Rizzoli.

Gullino, Giuseppe. 1984. *I Pisani Dal Banco e Moretta. Storia di due famiglie veneziane in età moderna e delle loro vicende patrimoniali fra 1705 e 1836*. Rome: Istituto Italiano per l'età moderna e contemporanea.

Guriev, Sergei, and Andrei Rachinsky. 2005. "The Role of Oligarchs in Russian Capitalism." *Journal of Economic Perspectives* 19, no. 1 (winter): 131–50.

Häberlein, Mark. 1998. *Brüder, Freunde und Betrüger: Soziale Beziehungen, Normen und Konflikte in der Augsburger Kaufmannschaft um die Mitte des 16. Jahrhunderts*. Berlin: Akademie Verlag.

Häberlein, Mark. 2012. *The Fuggers of Augsburg: Pursuing Wealth and Honor in Renaissance Germany*. Charlottesville: University of Virginia Press.

Hage, Per, Frank Harary, and James Brent. 1986. "Wealth and Hierarchy in the Kula Ring." *American Anthropologist* 88, no. 1 (March): 108–15.

Hamelin, Alonzo M. 1962. *Un traité de morale économique au XIVe siècle: Le Tractatus de usuris de maître Alexandre d'Alexandrie*. Louvain: Éditions Nauwelaerts.

Hardbury, Colin D. 1962. "Inheritance and the Distribution of Personal Wealth in Britain." *The Economic Journal* 72, no. 288 (December): 845–68.

Hardbury, Colin D. 1980. "Inheritance and Characteristics of Top Wealth Leavers in Britain." In *Wealth, Income, and Inequality*, edited by Anthony B. Atkinson, 269–90. Oxford: Oxford University Press.

Harivel, Maud. 2019. *Les Élections politiques dans la République de Venise (XVIe-XVIIIe siècle): entre justice distributive et corruption*. Paris: Les Indes Savantes.

Harvey, Charles, Mairi Maclean, Jillian Gordon, and Eleanor Shaw. 2011. "Andrew Carnegie and the Foundations of Contemporary Entrepreneurial Philanthropy." *Business History* 53, no. 3: 425–50.

Harvey, Charles, Mairi Maclean, and Roy Suddaby. 2019. "Historical Perspectives on Entrepreneurship and Philanthropy." *Business History Review* 93, no. 3 (autumn): 443–71.

Haseler, Stephen. 2000. *The Super-Rich: The Unjust New World of Global Capitalism*. London: Palgrave Macmillan.

Heilbroner, Robert L. 2008. "Wealth." In *The New Palgrave Dictionary of Economics*, 2nd ed., edited by Steven N. Durlauf and Lawrence E. Blume, 711–15. Basingstoke: Palgrave Macmillan.

Hergemöller, Bernd-Ulrich. 2012. *Uplop—Seditio: Innerstädtische Unruhen des 14. und 15. Jahrhunderts im engeren Reichsgebiet. Schematisierte vergleichende Konfliktanalyse*. Hamburg: Verlag Dr. Kovac.

Herlihy, David. 1967. *Medieval and Renaissance Pistoia: The Social History of an Italian Town, 1200–1430*. New Haven: Yale University Press.

Herlihy, David. 1968. "Santa Maria Impruneta: A Rural Commune in the Late Middle Ages." In *Florentine Studies: Politics and Society in Renaissance Florence*, edited by Nicolai Rubinstein, 242–76. London: Faber & Faber.

Herlihy, David. 1977. "Family and Property in Renaissance Florence." In *The Medieval City*, edited by Harry A. Miskimin, David Herlihy and Abraham L. Udovitch, 3–24. New Haven: Yale University Press.

Herlihy, David, and Christiane Klapisch-Zuber. 1985. *Tuscans and Their Families: A Study of the Florentine Catasto of 1427*. New Haven: Yale University Press.

Hobsbawm, Eric. 1968. *Industry and Empire: The Making of Modern English Society, 1750 to the Present Day*. New York: Pantheon Books.

Hobsbawm, Eric J. 1989. *The Age of Empire: 1875–1914*. New York: Vintage Books.

Hoffman, Philip T. 2006. "The Church in Economy and Society." In *The Cambridge History of Christianity*, vol. 7, edited by Stewart J. Brown and Timothy Tackett, 72–88. Cambridge: Cambridge University Press.

Hoffman, Philip T., Gilles Postel-Vinay, and Jean-Laurent Rosenthal. 2000. *Priceless Markets: The Political Economy of Credit in Paris, 1660–1870*. Chicago: University of Chicago Press.

Hoffman, Philip T., Gilles Postel-Vinay, and Jean-Laurent Rosenthal. 2019. *Dark Matter Credit: The Development of Peer to Peer Lending and Banking in France*. Princeton: Princeton University Press.

Holtz-Eakin, Douglas, David Joulfaian, and Harvey S. Rosen. 1993. "The Carnegie Conjecture: Some Empirical Evidence." *Quarterly Journal of Economics* 108, no. 29 (May): 413–35.

Hoyle, Richard W. 1994. *Tudor Taxation Records: A Guide for Users*. London: PRO Publications.

Howard, Peter. 2008. "Preaching Magnificence in Renaissance Florence." *Renaissance Quarterly* 61, no. 2 (summer): 325–69.

Hunt, Edwin S. 1994. *The Medieval Super-Companies: A Study of the Peruzzi Company of Florence*. Cambridge: Cambridge University Press.

Hunt, Edwin S., and James M. Murray. 1999. *A History of Business in Medieval Europe, 1200–1550*. New York: Cambridge University Press.

Huston, James L. 1993. "The American Revolutionaries, the Political Economy of Aristocracy, and the American Concept of the Distribution of Wealth, 1765–1900." *American Historical Review* 98, no. 4 (October): 1079–105.

Huston, James L. 2017. *The American and British Debate Over Equality, 1776–1920*. Baton Rouge: Louisiana State University Press.

Hyde, Allen. 2020. "'Left Behind?' Financialization and Income Inequality between the Affluent, Middle Class, and the Poor." *Sociological Inquiry* 90, no. 4 (November): 891–919.

Irigoin, Alejandra, and Regina Grafe. 2013. "Bounded Leviathan: Fiscal Constraint and Financial Development in the Early Modern Hispanic World." In *Questioning Credible Commitment: Perspectives on the Rise of Financial Capitalism*, edited by D'Maris Coffman, Adrian Leonard and Larry Neal, 199–227. New York: Cambridge University Press.

Irvin, George. 2008. *Super Rich: The Rise of Inequality in Britain and the United States*. Cambridge: Polity Press.

Israel, Jonathan I. 1985. *European Jewry in the Age of Mercantilism, 1550–1750*. Oxford: Oxford University Press.

Jaher, Frederic C. 1972. "Nineteenth-Century Elites in Boston and New York." *Journal of Social History* 6, no. 1 (autumn): 32–77.

Jaher, Frederic C. 1973. "Style and Status: High Society in Late Nineteenth-Century New York." In *The Rich, the Well Born, and the Powerful: Elites and Upper Classes in History*, edited by Frederic C. Jaher, 258–83. Urbana: University of Illinois Press.

Jaher, Frederic C. 1980. "The Gilded Elite: American Multimillionaires, 1865 to the Present." In *Wealth and the Wealthy in the Modern World*, edited by William D. Rubinstein, 189–276. London: Croom Helm.

Jedwab, Remi, Noel D. Johnson, and Mark Koyama. 2022. "The Economic Impact of the Black Death." *Journal of Economic Literature* 60, no. 1 (March): 132–78.

Johnson, Lisa. 2014. "Renegotiating Dissonant Heritage: The Statue of J.P. Coen." *International Journal of Heritage Studies* 20, no. 6: 583–98.

Jones, Alice Hanson. 1980. *Wealth of a Nation to Be: The American Colonies on the Eve of Revolution*. New York: Columbia University Press.

Jones, Eric L. 2010. *Locating the Industrial Revolution: Inducement and Response*. Singapore: World Scientific Publishing.

Jungnickel, Christa, and Russell McCormmach. 2016. *Cavendish: The Experimental Life*, 2nd ed. Berlin: Edition Open Access.

Jütte, Robert. 1994. *Poverty and Deviance in Early Modern Europe*. Cambridge: Cambridge University Press.

Kampfner, John. 2014. *The Rich: From Slaves to Super-Yachts: A 2,000-Year History*. New York: Little, Brown.

Kaplan, Steven L. 1976. *Bread, Politics and Political Economics in the Reign of Louis XV*. The Hague: Martinus Nijoff.

Kelly, Morgan, and Cormac Ó Gráda. 2010. "The Poor Law of Old England: Institutional Innovation and Demographic Regimes." *Journal of Interdisciplinary History* 41, no. 3 (winter 2011): 339–66. https://doi.org/10.1162/JINH_a_00105.

Kent, Dale. 1975. "The Florentine Reggimento in the Fifteenth Century." *Renaissance Quarterly* 28, no. 4 (winter): 575–638.

Kent, Dale. 1978. *The Rise of the Medici: Faction in Florence, 1426–1434*. Oxford: Oxford University Press.

Kersting, Felix, Iris Wohnsiedler, and Nikolaus Wolf. 2020. "Weber Revisited: The Protestant Ethic and the Spirit of Nationalism." *Journal of Economic History* 80, no. 3 (September): 710–45.

Khan, Shamus Rahman. 2011. *Privilege: The Making of an Adolescent Elite at St. Paul's School*. Princeton: Princeton University Press.

Khan, Shamus Rahman. 2012. "The Sociology of Elites." *Annual Review of Sociology* 38, no. 1 (August): 361–77.

Kilbride, Daniel. 2006. *An American Aristocracy: Southern Planters in Antebellum Philadelphia*. Columbia: University of South Carolina Press.

Kindleberger, Charles P. 1984. *A Financial History of Western Europe*. Winchester, MA: Allen & Unwin.

Klein, M. 1978. "In Search of Jay Gould." *Business History Review* 52, no. 2 (summer): 166–99.

Knapton, Michael. 1995. "Tra dominante e dominio (1517–1630)." In *Storia d'Italia. Tomo XII. La Repubblica di Venezia nell'età moderna*, vol. 2, edited by Gaetano Cozzi, Michael Knapton and Giovanni Scarabello, 201–550. Turin: UTET.

Kohler, Timothy A., Michael E. Smith, Amy Bogaard, Gary M. Feinman, Christian E. Peterson, Alleen Betzenhauser, Matthew Pailes et al. 2017. "Greater Post-Neolithic Wealth Disparities in Eurasia than in North America and Mesoamerica." *Nature* 551: 619–22.

Kopczuk, Wojciech, and Emmanuel Saez. 2004. "Top Wealth Shares in the United States, 1916–2000: Evidence from Estate Tax Returns." *National Tax Journal* 57, no. 2.2 (June): 445–87.

Korom, Philipp, Mark Lutter, and Jens Beckert. 2017. "The Enduring Importance of Family Wealth: Evidence from the Forbes 400, 1982 to 2013." *Social Science Research* 65 (July): 75–95.

Kuznets, Simon. 1955. "Economic Growth and Income Inequality." *American Economic Review* 45, no. 1 (March): 1–28.

Lagueux, Maurice. 1998. "Was Keynes a Liberal and an Individualist? Or Keynes Reader of Mandeville." *Cahiers d'économie Politique / Papers in Political Economy* 30/31: 255–63.

Lanaro, Paola. 2000. "'Familia est substantia': la trasmissione dei beni nella famiglia patrizia." In *Edilizia privata nella Verona rinascimentale*, edited by Paola Lanaro, Paola Marini and Gian M. Varanini, 98–117. Milan: Electa.

Lanaro, Paola. 2012. "Fedecommessi, doti, famiglia: la trasmissione della ricchezza nella Repubblica di Venezia (XV–XVIII secolo). Un approccio economico." *Mélanges de l'École française de Rome—Italie et Méditerranée modernes et contemporaines* 124, no. 2: 519–31.

Landes, David S. 1969. *The Unbound Prometheus: Technological Change and Industrial Development in Western Europe from 1750 to the Present.* Cambridge: Cambridge University Press.

Landes, David S. 1998. *The Wealth and Poverty of Nations: Why Some Are So Rich and Some So Poor.* New York: Norton.

Landes, David S. 2006. *Dynasties: Fortunes and Misfortunes of the World's Great Family Businesses.* New York: Viking.

Lane, Frederic C. 1944. *Andrea Barbarigo, Merchant of Venice, 1418–1449.* Baltimore: Johns Hopkins University Press.

Lane, Frederic C. 1973. *Venice: A Maritime Republic.* Baltimore: Johns Hopkins University Press.

Lane, Kris. 2015. "Corsairs." In *The Princeton Companion to Atlantic History*, edited by Joseph C. Miller, 391–395. Princeton: Princeton University Press.

Lansley, Stewart. 2006. *Rich Britain: The Rise and Rise of the New Super-Wealthy.* London: Politico.

Laurence, Anne. 2009. "Women, Banks and the Securities Market in Early Eighteenth-Century England." In *Women and Their Money, 1700–1950: Essays on Women and Finance*, edited by Anne Laurence, Josephine Maltby and Janette Rutterford, 46–58. London: Routledge.

Laurence, Anne, Josephine Maltby, and Janette Rutterford. 2009. *Women and Their Money, 1700–1950: Essays on Women and Finance.* London: Routledge.

Lavan, Miles, and John Weisweiler. 2022. "Capital in the Roman Empire: The Scope for Pikettian Dynamics in an Ancient Agrarian Economy." In *Capital in Classical Antiquity*, edited by Max Koedijk and Neville Morley, 205–42. Cham: Palgrave.

Le Goff, Jacques. 1964. *La civilisation de l'Occident médiéval*. Paris: Arthaud.

Le Goff, Jacques. 1986. *La bourse et la vie: Economie et religion au Moyen Age*. Paris: Hachette.

Lenski, Gerhard E. 1966. *Power and Privilege: A Theory of Social Stratification*. New York: McGraw Hill.

Le Roy Ladurie, Emmanuel. 1966. *Les Paysans de Languedoc*. Paris: S.E.V.P.E.N.

Leverotti, Franca. 2005. *Famiglia e istituzioni nel Medioevo italiano dal tardo antico al rinascimento*. Rome: Carocci.

Levi, Giovanni. 2003. "Aequitas vs Fairness: Reciprocità ed equità fra età moderna ed età contemporanea." *Rivista di storia economica* 19, no. 2 (August): 195–204.

Levy, Jonathan I. 2012. *Freaks of Fortune: The Emerging World of Capitalism and Risk in America*. Cambridge, MA: Harvard University Press.

Levy, Jonathan I. 2021. *Ages of American Capitalism: A History of the United States*. New York: Random House.

Licini, Stefania. 2020. *Ricchi e ricchezza a Milano nell'Ottocento*. Milan: TAB.

Lierse, Hanna. 2022. "Globalization and the Societal Consensus of Wealth Tax Cuts." *Journal of European Public Policy* 29, no. 5: 748–66.

Lind, Michael. 2005. "Conservative Elites and the Counterrevolution against the New Deal." In *Ruling America: A History of Wealth and Power in a Democracy*, edited by Steve Fraser and Gary Gerstle, 250–85. Cambridge, MA: Harvard University Press.

Lindert, Peter H. 1986. "Unequal English Wealth since 1670." *Journal of Political Economy* 94, no. 6 (December): 1127–62.

Lindert, Peter H. 2000. "Three Centuries of Inequality in Britain and America." In *Handbook of Income Distribution*, vol. 1, edited by Anthony B. Atkinson and François Bourguignon, 167–216. Amsterdam: North-Holland.

Lindert, Peter H. 2004. *Growing Public: Social Spending and Economic Growth since the Eighteenth Century*. Cambridge: Cambridge University Press.

Lindert, Peter H. 2021a. *Making Social Spending Work*. Cambridge: Cambridge University Press.

Lindert, Peter H. 2021b. "Social Spending and the Welfare State." In *How Was Life? Volume II: New Perspectives on Well-Being and Global Inequality since 1820*, edited by Jan Luiten van Zanden, Marco Mira d'Ercole, Mikolaj Malinowski, and Auke Rijpma, 72–102. Paris: OECD Publishing.

Lindert, Peter H., and Jeffrey G. Williamson. 2016. *Unequal Gains: American Growth and Inequality since 1700*. Princeton: Princeton University Press.

Lindert, Peter H., and Jeffrey G. Williamson. 2017. "Inequality in the Very Long Run: Malthus, Kuznets, and Ohlin." *Cliometrica* 11, no. 3 (September): 289–95.

Lindholm, Richard T. 2017. *Quantitative Studies of the Renaissance Florentine Economy and Society*. London: Anthem Press.

Livesay, Harold C. 2006. *Andrew Carnegie and the Rise of Big Business*, 3rd ed. New York: Pearson.

Livi-Bacci, Massimo. 2006. "The Depopulation of Hispanic America after the Conquest." *Population and Development Review* 32, no. 2 (June): 199–232.

Lizardo, Omar. 2006. "How Cultural Tastes Shape Personal Networks." *American Sociological Review* 71, no. 5 (October): 778–807.

Lopez, Robert S. 1952. "China Silk in Europe in the Yuan Period." *Journal of the American Oriental Society* 72, no. 2 (April–June): 72–6.

Lopez, Robert S. 1976. *The Commercial Revolution of the Middle Ages: 950–1350*. Cambridge: Cambridge University Press.

Lopez, Robert S., and Harry A. Miskimin. 1962. "The Economic Depression of the Renaissance." *Economic History Review* 14, no. 3 (April): 408–26.

Lorenzini, Marcella. 2021. "The Other Side of Banking: Private Lending and the Role of Women in Early Modern Italy." In *Change and Transformation of Premodern Credit Markets: The Importance of Small-Scale Credits*, edited by Stephan Nicolussi-Köhler, 177–97. Heidelberg: heiBOOKS.

Lucassen, Jan. 2004. "A Multinational and Its Labor Force: The Dutch East India Company, 1595–1795." *International Labor and Working-Class History* 66 (autumn): 12–39.

Lukowski, Jerzy. 2003. *The European Nobility in the Eighteenth Century*. Basingstoke: Palgrave Macmillan.

Lundberg, Ferdinand. 1937. *America's 60 Families*. New York: Vanguard Press.

Lundberg, Ferdinand. 1973. *The Rich and the Super-Rich: A Study in the Power of Money Today*. New York: Bantam Books.

Luzzati, Francesco. 1987. "Datini, Francesco." In *Dizionario Biografico degli Italiani*, vol. 33. Accessed June 2021. https://www.treccani.it/enciclopedia/francesco-datini_(Dizionario-Biografico).

Luzzatto, Gino. 1963. *Il debito pubblico della Repubblica di Venezia dagli ultimi decenni del XII secolo alla fine del XV*. Milan: Istituto Editoriale Cisalpino.

MacCulloch, Robert. 2003. "The Taste for Revolt." *Economics Letters* 79, no. 1 (April): 7–13.

Machiavelli, Niccolò. (1521) 2018. "Dell'arte della guerra." In *Niccolò Machiavelli: Tutte le opere*, edited by Mario Martelli, 923–1128. Florence: Bompiani.

Machiavelli, Niccolò. (1532) 2006. *History of Florence and of the Affairs of Italy*. Gutenberg Project. Accessed July 2021. https://www.gutenberg.org/files/2464/2464-h/2464-h.htm.

MacKenney, Richard. 2019. *Venice as the Polity of Mercy: Guilds, Confraternities and the Social Order, c. 1250–c. 1650*. Buffalo: University of Toronto Press.

Maclaren, Sarah F. 2003. "Magnificenza e mondo classico: Storia di un'idea estetica non politicamente corretta." Monographic issue, *Ágalma: Rivista di studi culturali e di estetica* 5 (May).

Mączak, Antoni. 2001. "Aristocracy/Nobility/Gentry, History of." In *International Encyclopedia of the Social & Behavioral Sciences*, edited by Neil J. Smelser and Paul B. Baltes, 737–42. Oxford: Pergamon.

Maddison Project. 2020. "Maddison Project Database." University of Groningen, Groningen Growth and Development Centre. Accessed June 2022. https://www.rug.nl/ggdc/historicaldevelopment/maddison/releases/maddison-project-database-2020.

Malanima, Paolo. 1977. *I Riccardi di Firenze: Una famiglia e un patrimonio nella Toscana dei Medici*. Florence: Olschki.

Malinowski, Bronislaw. 1922. *Argonauts of the Western Pacific*. London: Routledge & Kegan.

Mallett, Michael E. 1974. *Mercenaries and Their Masters. Warfare in Renaissance Italy*. London: Bodley Head.

Mandeville, Bernard. (1732) 1988. *The Fable of the Bees or Private Vices, Publick Benefits. With a Commentary Critical, Historical, and Explanatory by F.B. Kaye. Volume One*. Indianapolis: Liberty Fund.

Manigat, Matari P. 2020. "Finance Capital and Financialization: A Comparative Reading of Marx and Hilferding." *Œconomia* 10, no. 4 (December): 687–710.

Manning, Patrick. 1992. "The Slave Trade: The Formal Demographics of a Global System." In *The Atlantic Slave Trade: Effects on Economies, Societies and Peoples in Africa, the Americas, and Europe*, edited by Joseph E. Inikori and Stanley L. Engerman, 117–44. Durham, NC: Duke University Press.

Markus, Stanislav, and Volha Charnysh. 2017. "The Flexible Few: Oligarchs and Wealth Defense in Developing Democracies." *Comparative Political Studies* 50, no. 12 (October): 1632–65.

Marongiu, Antonio. 1968. *Medieval Parliaments: A Comparative Study*. London: Eyre and Spottiswoode.

Martin, Isaac W. 2013. *Rich People's Movements: Grassroots Campaigns to Untax the One Percent*. New York: Oxford University Press.

Marx, Karl. (1894) 1993. *Capital: Volume III*. London: Penguin Books.

Mason, J. J. 2004. "Arkwright, Sir Richard (1732–1792)." *Oxford Dictionary of National Biography*. Oxford: Oxford University Press.

Mauss, Marcell. 1967. *The Gift: Forms and Functions of Exchange in Archaic Societies*. Translated by Ian Cunnison. New York: Norton.

Mazzoleni, Gianpietro. 2011. "Berlusconi? A Communication Wizard." *Zeitschrift für Politikberatung (ZPB)/Policy Advice and Political Consulting* 4, no. 1: 36–8.

Mays, Andrew, and Gary S. Shea. 2011. "East India Company and Bank of England Shareholders during the South Sea Bubble: Partitions, Components and Connectivity in a Dynamic Trading Network." Working Paper no. 11/09, Centre for Dynamic Macroeconomic Analysis, University of St Andrews.

McCall, Leslie. 2013. *The Undeserving Rich: American Beliefs about Inequality, Opportunity, and Redistribution*. Cambridge: Cambridge University Press.

McCloskey, Deirdre N. 2006. *The Bourgeois Virtues: Ethics for an Age of Commerce*. Chicago: University of Chicago Press.

McCloskey, Deirdre N. 2016. *Bourgeois Equality: How Ideas, Not Capital or Institutions, Enriched the World*. Chicago: University of Chicago Press.

McCombie, John, and Marta Spreafico. 2017. "On Income Inequality: The 2008 Great Recession and Long-Term Growth." In *The Crisis Conundrum: How to Reconcile Economy and Society*, edited by Mauro Magatti, 41–63. Cham: Palgrave.

McGoey, Linsey. 2015. *No Such Thing as a Free Gift: The Gates Foundation and the Price of Philanthropy*. London: Verso Books.

McKendrick, Neil. 1960. "Josiah Wedgwood: An Eighteenth-Century Entrepreneur in Salesmanship and Marketing Techniques." *Economic History Review* 12, no. 3 (April): 408–33.

Meade, James E. 1964. *Efficiency, Equality, and the Ownership of Property*. London: Allen and Unwin.

Medeiros, Marcelo. 2006. "The Rich and the Poor: The Construction of an Affluence Line from the Poverty Line." *Social Indicators Research* 78, no. 1 (August): 1–18.

Medeiros, Marcelo, and Pedro H. G. Ferreira de Souza. 2014. "The Rich, the Affluent and the Top Incomes: A Literature Review." Working Paper no. 105–14, IRLE. https://irle.berkeley.edu/files/2014/The-Rich-the-Affluent-and-the-Top-Incomes.pdf.

Medeiros, Marcelo, and Pedro H. G. Ferreira de Souza. 2015. "The Rich, the Affluent and the Top Incomes." *Current Sociology* 63, no. 6 (October): 869–95.

Melis, Federigo. 1962. *Aspetti della vita economica medievale* (Studi nell'Archivio Datini di Prato). Florence: Olschki.

Ménard, Pierre. 2017. *Le Français qui possédait l'Amérique: La vie extraordinaire d'Antoine Crozat.* Paris: Le Cherche Midi.

Mension-Rigau, Eric. 2007. *Aristocrates et Grands Bourgeois: Education, Traditions, Valeurs.* Paris: Perrin.

Mension-Rigau, Eric. 2008. *Boni de Castellane.* Paris: Perrin.

Messere, Ken, Flip de Kam, and Christopher Heady. 2003. *Tax Policy: Theory and Practice in OECD Countries.* Oxford: Oxford University Press.

Mettler, Suzanne. 2015. "From Pioneer Egalitarianism to the Reign of the Super-Rich: How the U.S. Political System Has Promoted Equality and Inequality over Time." *Tax Law Review* 68, no. 3 (spring): 563–612.

Milanović, Branko. 2011. *The Haves and the Have-Nots: A Brief and Idiosyncratic History of Global Inequality.* New York: Basic Books.

Milanović, Branko. 2016. *Global Inequality: A New Approach for the Age of Globalization.* Cambridge, MA: Harvard University Press.

Milanović, Branko. 2019. "Income Level and Income Inequality in the Euro-Mediterranean Region, C. 14–700." *Review of Income and Wealth* 65, no. 1 (March): 1–20.

Milanović, Branko. 2020. "Historical Wealth: How to Compare Croesus and Bezos." *Global Policy Journal.* Accessed May 2022. https://www.globalpolicyjournal.com/blog/27/02/2020/historical-wealth-how-compare-croesus-and-bezos.

Milanović, Branko, Peter H. Lindert, and Jeffrey G. Williamson. 2007. "Measuring Ancient Inequality." Policy Research Working Paper no. 4412, World Bank.

Milanović, Branko, Peter H. Lindert, and Jeffrey G. Williamson. 2011. "Pre-Industrial Inequality." *Economic Journal* 121: 255–72.

Miller, Joseph C. 1988. *Way of Death: Merchant Capitalism and the Angolan Slave Trade, 1730–1830.* Madison: University of Wisconsin Press.

Miller, Joseph C. 2015. *The Princeton Companion to Atlantic History.* Princeton: Princeton University Press.

Mills, C. Wright. 1956. *The Power Elite.* Oxford: Oxford University Press.

Mira, Giuseppe. 1940. *Vicende economiche di una famiglia italiana dal XIV al XVII secolo.* Milan: Vita e Pensiero.

Miskimin, Harry A. 1977. *The Economy of Later Renaissance Europe 1460–1600.* Cambridge: Cambridge University Press.

Mitchell, Richard E. 1973. "The Aristocracy of the Roman Republic." In *The Rich, the Well Born, and the Powerful: Elites and Upper Classes in History,* edited by Frederic C. Jaher, 27–63. Urbana: University of Illinois Press.

Mocarelli, Luca. 2009. "The Attitude of Milanese Society to Work and Commercial Activities: The Case of the Porters and the Case of the Elites." In *The Idea of Work in Europe from Antiquity to Modern Times,* edited by Josef Ehmer and Catharina Lis, 101–21. Farnham: Ashgate.

Mokyr, Joel. 2017. *A Culture of Growth: The Origins of the Modern Economy.* Princeton: Princeton University Press.

Mörke, Olaf. 1996. "Social Structure." In *Germany—A New Social and Economic History. Vol. II: 1630–1800,* edited by Sheilagh Ogilvie, 134–63. London: Arnold.

Mousnier, Roland. 1974. *Les institutions de la France sous la monarchie absolue, 1598–1789,* vol. 1. Paris: Presses Universitaires de France.

Mueller, Holger M., Paige P. Ouimet, and Elena Simintzi. 2017. "Within-Firm Pay Inequality." *The Review of Financial Studies* 30, no. 10 (October): 3605–35.

Munro, John. 2010. "Tawney's Century, 1540–1640." In *The Invention of Enterprise: Entrepreneurship from Ancient Mesopotamia to Modern Times*, edited by David S. Landes, Joel Mokyr and William J. Baumol (eds.), 107–55. Princeton: Princeton University Press.

Mutini, Claudio. 1979. "Cavalcanti, Giovanni." In *Dizionario Biografico degli Italiani*, vol. 22. Accessed September 2021. https://www.treccani.it/enciclopedia/giovanni-cavalcanti_(Dizionario -Biografico).

Muzzarelli, Maria G. 1991. "Beatrice de Luna, vedova Mendes, alias donna Gracia Nasi: un'ebrea influente (1510–1569ca)." In *Rinascimento al femminile*, edited by Ottavia Niccoli, 83–116. Rome: Laterza.

Muzzarelli, Maria G. 2002. *La legislazione suntuaria secoli XIII–XVI: Emilia Romagna*. Rome: Ministero per i beni e le attività culturali.

Muzzarelli, Maria G. 2003. "Una società nello specchio della legislazione suntuaria: il caso dell'Emilia-Romagna." In *Disciplinare il lusso: La legislazione suntuaria in Italia e in Europa tra Medioevo ed Età Moderna*, edited by Maria G. Muzzarelli and Antonella Campanini, 17–31. Rome: Carocci.

Muzzarelli, Maria G. 2020. *Le regole del lusso: Apparenza e vita quotidiana dal Medioevo all'età moderna*. Bologna: Il Mulino.

Muzzarelli, Maria G. 2022. "Prolusione." In *Fashion as an Economic Engine: Process and Product Innovation, Commercial Strategies, Consumer Behavior*, edited by G. Nigro, 5–12. Florence: Florence University Press.

Muzzarelli, Maria G., and Antonella Campanini. 2003. *Disciplinare il lusso: La legislazione suntuaria in Italia e in Europa tra Medioevo ed Età Moderna*. Rome: Carocci.

Najemy, John A. 2006. *A History of Florence 1200–1575*. Oxford: Blackwell.

Nanni, Paolo. 2010. *Ragionare tra mercanti. Linguaggio e concezioni nelle relazioni di Francesco di Marco Datini (1335 ca.–1410)*. Pisa: Pacini.

Neal, Larry. 2015. *A Concise History of International Finance: From Babylon to Bernanke*. Cambridge: Cambridge University Press.

Neal, Larry, and Eugene N. White. 2012. "The Glass-Steagall Act in Historical Perspective." *The Quarterly Review of Economics and Finance* 52, no. 2 (May): 104–13.

Nederman, Cary J. 2004. "Body Politics: The Diversification of Organic Metaphors in the Later Middle Ages." *Pensiero Politico Medievale* 2: 59–87.

Nicholas, Tom. 1999. "Wealth Making in Nineteenth- and Early Twentieth-Century Britain: Industry v. Commerce and Finance." *Business History* 41, no. 1: 16–36.

Nigro, Giampiero, ed. 2010. *Francesco di Marco Datini: The Man the Merchant*. Florence: Florence University Press.

North, Douglass C., and Robert P. Thomas. 1973. *The Rise of the Western World: A New Economic History*. Cambridge: Cambridge University Press.

North, Douglass C., and Barry R. Weingast. 1989. "Constitutions and Commitment: The Evolution of Institutions Governing Public Choice in Seventeenth-Century England." *Journal of Economic History* 49, no. 4 (December): 803–32.

Ober, Josiah. 2015. *The Rise and Fall of Classical Greece*. Princeton: Princeton University Press.

O'Brien, Patrick. 1982. "European Economic Development: The Contribution of the Periphery." *Economic History Review* 35, no. 1 (February): 1–18.

O'Callaghan, Joseph F. 1969. "The Beginnings of the Cortes in León-Castile." *American Historical Review* 74, no. 5 (June): 1503–37.

Ó Gráda, Cormac. 1994. *Ireland: A New Economic History 1780–1939*. Oxford: Clarendon Press.

Ó Gráda, Cormac. 2009. *Famine: A Short History*. Princeton: Princeton University Press.

OECD. 2013. *OECD Guidelines for Micro Statistics on Household Wealth*. Paris: OECD Publishing.

OECD. 2015. "OECD Income Inequality Data Update: Sweden." http://www.oecd.org/sweden/OECD-Income-Inequality-Sweden.pdf.

OECD. 2018. *A Broken Social Elevator? How to Promote Social Mobility*. Paris: OECD Publishing.

OECD. 2020. *Taxation and Philanthropy*. Paris: OECD Publishing.

OECD. 2021. *Tax Policy Reforms 2021: Special Edition on Tax Policy during the COVID-19 Pandemic*. Paris: OECD Publishing.

Ogilvie, Sheilagh. 2010. "Consumption, Social Capital, and the 'Industrious Revolution' in Early Modern Germany." *Journal of Economic History* 70, no. 2 (June): 287–325.

Oresme, Nicole. (1370–1374) 1970. In *Maistre Nicole Oresme. Le Livre de Politiques d'Aristote*, edited by Albert D. Menut, *Transactions of the American Philosophical Society* 60, no. 6: 1–392. Philadelphia: American Philosophical Society. https://doi.org/10.2307/1006105.

Origo, Iris. 1957. *The Merchant of Prato: Francesco di Marco Datini, 1335–1410*. New York: Alfred A. Knopf.

Osberg, Lars, and Timothy Smeeding. 2006. "'Fair' Inequality? Attitudes toward Pay Differentials: The United States in Comparative Perspective." *American Sociological Review* 71, no. 3 (June): 450–73.

Ostrower, Francie. 1995. *Why the Wealthy Give: The Culture of Elite Philanthropy*. Princeton: Princeton University Press.

Oulhen, Jacques. 2004. "La société athénienne." In *Le monde grec aux temps classiques, tome 2: Le IVe siècle*, edited by Pierre Brulé and Raymond Descat, 251–351. Paris: Presses Universitaires de France.

Paci, Renzo. 1987. "Vivere 'more nobilium.'" *Proposte e Ricerche* 19: 30–6.

Padgett, John F. 2010. "Open Elite? Social Mobility, Marriage, and Family in Florence, 1282–1494." *Renaissance Quarterly* 63, no. 2 (summer): 357–411.

Padgett, John F., and Christopher K. Ansell. 1993. "Robust Action and the Rise of the Medici, 1400–1434." *American Journal of Sociology* 98, no. 6 (May): 1259–319.

Padgett, John F., and Paul D. McLean. 2006. "Organizational Invention and Elite Transformation: The Birth of Partnership Systems in Renaissance Florence." *American Journal of Sociology* 111, no. 5 (March): 1463–568.

Pakulski, Jan. 2005. "Foundations of a Post-Class Analysis." In *Approaches to Class Analysis*, edited by Erik Olin Wright, 152–79. Cambridge: Cambridge University Press.

Pampaloni, Guido. 1971. "I magnati a Firenze alla fine del Dugento." *Archivio Storico Italiano* 129, no. 4 (472): 387–423.

Pamuk, Şevket. 2007. "The Black Death and the Origins of the 'Great Divergence' across Europe, 1300–1600." *European Review of Economic History* 11, no. 3: 289–317.

Parker, Geoffrey. 1988. *The Military Revolution: Military Innovation and the Rise of the West, 1500–1800*. New York: Cambridge University Press.

Parker, Grant. 1991. "Patronage of Letters in the Early Roman Empire." *Akroterion* 36, no. 4 (January): 140–52.

Partington, James R. 1962. "Cavendish." In *A History of Chemistry*, vol. 3, edited by James R. Partington, 302–62. London: Palgrave.

Pasciuta, Beatrice. 2018. "'Juribus masculorum gaudeat': il lavoro delle donne e i lavori da donna nella dottrina del diritto comune." *Rivista Critica del Diritto Privato* 36, no. 3: 359–81.

Peichl, Andreas, Thilo Schaefer, and Christoph Scheicher. 2010. "Measuring Richness and Poverty: A Micro Data Application to Europe and Germany." *Review of Income and Wealth* 56, no. 3 (September): 597–619.

Pezzolo, Luciano. 1990. *L'oro dello Stato: Società, finanza e fisco nella Repubblica veneta del secondo Cinquecento*. Venice: Il Cardo.

Pezzolo, Luciano. 1995. "Elogio della rendita: Sul debito pubblico degli Stati italiani nel Cinque e Seicento." *Rivista di Storia Economica* 12, no. 3 (October): 283–318.

Pezzolo, Luciano. 1996. "La finanza pubblica: dal prestito all'imposta." In *Storia di Venezia dalle origini alla caduta della Serenissima*, vol. 5, edited by Alberto Tenenti and Ugo Tucci, 703–51. Rome: Treccani.

Pezzolo, Luciano. 1998. "Finanza e fiscalità nel territorio di Bergamo (1450–1630)." In *Storia economica e sociale di Bergamo. Il tempo della Serenissima. Il lungo Cinquecento*, edited by Marco Cattini and Marzio A. Romani, 49–70. Bergamo: Fondazione per la storia economica e sociale di Bergamo.

Pezzolo, Luciano. 2012. "Republics and Principalities in Italy." In *The Rise of Fiscal States: A Global History, 1500–1914*, edited by Bartolomé Yun-Casalilla and Patrick K. O'Brien, 267–84. Cambridge: Cambridge University Press.

Pezzolo, Luciano. 2021. "Essere e diventare ricchi." In *Popolazioni e società delle Venezie*, edited by Irene Barbiera, Gianpiero Dalla Zuanna and Andrea Zannini, 345–64. Vicenza: Viella.

Pfister, Ulrich. 2017. "The Timing and Pattern of Real Wage Divergence in Pre-Industrial Europe: Evidence from Germany, c. 1500–1850." *Economic History Review* 70, no. 3 (August): 701–29.

Philippon, Thomas, and Ariell Reshef. 2012. "Wages and Human Capital in the U.S. Finance Industry: 1909–2006." *Quarterly Journal of Economics* 127, no. 4 (November): 1551–609.

Phillips, Kevin. 2002. *Wealth and Democracy: A Political History of the American Rich*. New York: Broadway Books.

Phillips, Susan D., and Tobias Jung. 2016. "A New 'New' Philanthropy." In *The Routledge Companion to Philanthropy*, edited by Tobias Jung, Susan D. Phillips and Jenny Harrow, 5–34. New York: Routledge.

Piketty, Thomas. 2000. "Theories of Persistent Inequality and Intergenerational Mobility." In *Handbook of Income Distribution*, vol. 1, edited by Anthony B. Atkinson and François. Bourguignon, 429–76. Amsterdam: North-Holland.

Piketty, Thomas. 2007. "Income, Wage, and Wealth Inequality in France, 1901–98." In *Top Incomes over the 20th Century: A Contrast between Continental European and English-Speaking*

Countries, edited by Anthony B. Atkinson and Thomas Piketty, 43–81. Oxford: Oxford University Press.

Piketty, Thomas. 2014. *Capital in the Twenty-First Century.* Cambridge, MA: Harvard University Press.

Piketty, Thomas. 2015a. "Putting Distribution Back at the Center of Economics: Reflections on Capital in the Twenty-First Century." *Journal of Economic Perspectives* 29, no. 1 (winter): 67–88.

Piketty, Thomas. 2015b. "Capital and Wealth Taxation in the 21st Century." *National Tax Journal* 68, no. 2 (June): 449–58.

Piketty, Thomas. 2020. *Capital and Ideology.* Cambridge, MA: Harvard University Press.

Piketty, Thomas, Gilles Postel-Vinay, and Jean-Laurent Rosenthal. 2006. "Wealth Concentration in a Developing Economy: Paris and France, 1807–1994." *American Economic Review* 96, no. 1 (March): 236–56.

Piketty, Thomas, Gilles Postel-Vinay, and Jean-Laurent Rosenthal. 2014. "Inherited vs Self-Made Wealth: Theory and Evidence from a Rentier Society (Paris 1872–1927)." *Explorations in Economic History* 51 (January): 21–40.

Piketty, Thomas, Emmanuel Saez, and Stefanie Stantcheva. 2014. "Optimal Taxation of Top Labor Incomes: A Tale of Three Elasticities." *American Economic Journal: Economic Policy* 6, no. 1 (February): 230–71.

Piketty, Thomas, and Gabriel Zucman. 2014. "Capital is Back: Wealth-Income Ratios in Rich Countries, 1700–2010." *Quarterly Journal of Economics* 129, no. 3 (August): 1255–310.

Pinçon-Charlot, Monique, and Michel Pinçon. 2010. *Le Président des riches: Enquête sur l'oligarchie dans la France de Nicolas Sarkozy.* Paris: La Martinière.

Pinçon-Charlot, Monique, and Michel Pinçon. 2019. *Le président des ultra-riches: Chronique du mépris de classe dans la politique d'Emmanuel Macron.* Paris: Zones.

Pirenne, Henri. 1927. *Les villes du moyen âge, essay d'histoire économique et sociale.* Brussels: Lamertin.

Pomeranz, Kenneth. 2000. *The Great Divergence: China, Europe, and the Making of the Modern World Economy.* Princeton: Princeton University Press.

Prak, Maarten. 2005. *The Dutch Republic in the Seventeenth Century.* Cambridge: Cambridge University Press.

Prak, Maarten, and Jan L. van Zanden. 2022. *Pioneers of Capitalism: The Netherlands 1000–1800.* Princeton: Princeton University Press.

Przeworski, Adam. 2009. "Conquered or Granted? A History of Suffrage Extensions." *British Journal of Political Science* 39, no. 2 (April): 291–321.

Pullan, Brian. 1971. *Rich and Poor in Renaissance Venice.* Oxford: Basil Blackwell.

Quinn, William, and John D. Turner. 2020. *Boom and Bust: A Global History of Financial Bubbles.* Cambridge: Cambridge University Press.

Raines, Dorit. 2007. "Manin, Lodovico Giovanni." In *Dizionario Biografico degli Italiani*, vol. 69. Accessed December 2021. https://www.treccani.it/enciclopedia/lodovico-giovanni-manin _(Dizionario-Biografico).

Rapp, Dean. 1974. "Social Mobility in the Eighteenth Century: The Whitbreads of Bedfordshire, 1720–1815." *Economic History Review* 27, no. 3 (August): 380–94.

Ratner, Sidney. 1953. *New Light on the History of Great American Fortunes: American Millionaires of 1892 and 1902*. New York: Augustus M. Kelley.

Rawls, John. 1971. *A Theory of Justice*. Cambridge, MA: Harvard University Press.

Reeves, Aaron, Sam Friedman, Charles Rahal, and Magne Flemmen. 2017. "The Decline and Persistence of the Old Boy: Private Schools and Elite Recruitment 1897 to 2016." *American Sociological Review* 82, no. 6 (December): 1139–66.

Reich, Rob. 2018. *Just Giving: Why Philanthropy Is Failing Democracy and How It Can Do Better*. Princeton: Princeton University Press.

Resti, Enrico. 1990. *Ferdinando Bocconi: Dai grandi magazzini all'Università*. Milan: Egea.

Richardson, David. 2015. "Slaving, European, from Africa." In *The Princeton Companion to Atlantic History*, edited by Joseph C. Miller, 429–33. Princeton: Princeton University Press.

Robb, George. 2017. *Ladies of the Ticker: Women and Wall Street from the Gilded Age to the Great Depression*. Urbana: University of Illinois Press.

Robeyns, Ingrid, Vincent Buskens, Arnout van de Rijt, Nina Vergeldt, and Tanja van der Lippe. 2021. "How Rich Is Too Rich? Measuring the Riches Line." *Social Indicators Research* 154, no. 1 (February): 115–43.

Rockoff, Hugh. 2012. "The Great Fortunes of the Gilded Age and the Crisis of 1893." *Research in Economic History* 28: 233–62.

Rogers, Clifford J. 1995. *The Military Revolution Debate: Readings on the Military Transformation of Early Modern Europe*. Boulder: Westview Press.

Roine, Jesper, and Daniel Waldenström. 2015. "Long Run Trends in the Distribution of Income and Wealth." In *Handbook of Income Distribution*, vol. 2, edited by Anthony B. Atkinson and François Bourguignon, 469–592. Amsterdam: North-Holland.

Romaniuk, Scott N., and Joshua K. Wasylciw. 2014. "Canada's Evolving Crown: From a British Crown to a 'Crown of Maples.'" *American, British and Canadian Studies* 23, no. 1 (December): 108–25. https://doi.org/10.1515/abcsj-2014-0030.

Roth, Cecil. 1977. *Dona Gracia of the House of Nasi*. Philadelphia: Jewish Publication Society.

Rothkopf, David. 2009. *Superclass: The Global Power Elite and the World They Are Making*. New York: Farrar, Straus & Giroux.

Rousseau, Jean-Jacques. (1754) 2011. *Le discours sur l'origine et les fondements de l'inégalité parmi les hommes*. Les Échos du Maquis. https://philosophie.cegeptr.qc.ca/wp-content/documents/Discours-sur-linégalité-1754.pdf.

Rubinstein, Nicolai. 1997. *The Government of Florence under the Medici (1434 to 1494)*, 2nd ed. Oxford: Clarendon Press.

Rubinstein, William D., ed. 1980. *Wealth and the Wealthy in the Modern World*. London: Croom Helm.

Rubinstein, William D. 1991. "Gentlemanly Capitalism and British Industry, 1820–1914: Comment." *Past and Present* 132 (August): 150–70.

Rubinstein, William D. 2006. *Men of Property: The Very Wealthy in Britain since the Industrial Revolution*, updated edition. Brighton: Edward Everett Root Publishers.

Rubinstein, William D. 2011. "The Wealth Structure of Britain in 1809–39, 1860–1, and 1906." In *Men, Women, and Money: Perspectives on Gender, Wealth, and Investment 1850–1930*, edited by

David R. Green, Alastair Owens, Josephine Maltby and Janette Rutterford, 31–53. Oxford: Oxford University Press.

Rubinstein, William D. 2018. *Who Were the Rich? 1809–1839: A Biographical Directory of British Wealth-Holders*, 2nd ed., vol. 2. Brighton: Edward Everett Root Publishers.

Rubinstein, William D. 2022. *Beyond the Dreams of Avarice: The Very Wealthy in Modern Britain*. Brighton: Edward Everett Root Publishers.

Ryckbosch, Wouter. 2016. "Economic Inequality and Growth before the Industrial Revolution: The Case of the Low Countries (Fourteenth to Nineteenth Centuries)." *European Review of Economic History* 20, no. 1 (February): 1–22.

Sabbadini, Roberto. 1995. *L'acquisto della tradizione. Tradizione aristocratica e nuova nobiltà a Venezia (sec. XVII–XVIII)*. Udine: Istituto Editoriale Veneto Friulano.

Saez, Emmanuel, and Gabriel Zucman. 2016. "Wealth Inequality in the United States since 1913: Evidence from Capitalized Income Tax Data." *Quarterly Journal of Economics* 131, no. 2 (May): 519–78.

Saez, Emmanuel, and Gabriel Zucman. 2019. *The Triumph of Injustice: How the Rich Dodge Taxes and How to Make Them Pay*. New York: Norton.

Sałach, Katarzyna, and Michal Brzezinski. 2020. "Political Connections and the Super-Rich in Poland." Working Paper no. 553, ECINEQ.

Santiago-Caballero, Carlos, and Eva Fernández. 2013. "Income Inequality in Madrid, 1500–1850." Paper presented at the Economic History Society Annual Conference, York.

Sapori, Armando. 1926. *La crisi delle compagnie mercantili dei Bardi e dei Peruzzi*. Florence: Olschki.

Sardone, Sergio. 2019. "Forced Loans in the Spanish Empire: The First Requisition of American Treasures in 1523." *Economic History Review* 72, no. 1 (February): 57–87.

Savage, Mike. 2015. *Social Class in the 21st Century*. London: Pelican Books.

Scarabello, Giovanni. "Il Settecento." In *Storia d'Italia. Tomo XII: La Repubblica di Venezia nell'età moderna*, vol. 2, edited by Gaetano Cozzi, Michael Knapton and Giovanni Scarabello, 553–681. Turin: UTET.

Schaff, Felix. 2022. "The Unequal Spirit of the Protestant Reformation: Particularism and Wealth Distribution in Early Modern Germany." London School of Economics, unpublished manuscript.

Scheidel, Walter. 2015. "The Early Roman Monarchy." In *Fiscal Regimes and the Political Economy of Premodern States*, edited by Andrew Monson and Walter Scheidel, 229–57. Cambridge: Cambridge University Press.

Scheidel, Walter. 2017. *The Great Leveler: Violence and the History of Inequality from the Stone Age to the Twenty-First Century*. Princeton: Princeton University Press.

Scheidel, Walter. 2019. *Escape from Rome: The Failure of Empire and the Road to Prosperity*. Princeton: Princeton University Press.

Scheidel, Walter, and Steven J. Friesen. 2009. "The Size of the Economy and the Distribution of Income in the Roman Empire." *The Journal of Roman Studies* 99 (November): 61–91.

Scherman, Matthieu. 2009. "La distribuzione della ricchezza in una città: Treviso e i suoi estimi (1434–1499)." In *Ricchezza, valore, proprietà in Età preindustriale: 1400–1850*, edited by Guido Alfani and Michela Barbot, 169–84. Venice: Marsilio.

Scheve, Kenneth, and David Stasavage. 2016. *Taxing the Rich: A History of Fiscal Fairness in the United States and Europe*. Princeton: Princeton University Press.

Scheve, Kenneth, and David Stavasage. 2017. "Wealth Inequality and Democracy." *Annual Review of Political Science* 20 (May): 451–68.

Schilling, Heinz. 1994. *Aufbruch und Krise: Deutschland 1517–1648*. Berlin: Siedler.

Schmid, Boris V., Ulf Büntgen, W. Ryan Easterday, Christian Ginzler, Lars Walløe, Barbara Bramanti, and Nils Chr. Stenseth. 2015. "Climate-Driven Introduction of the Black Death and Successive Plague Reintroductions into Europe." *PNAS* 112, no. 10 (March): 3020–5.

Schneider, Britta. 2016. *Fugger contra Fugger: Die Augsburger Handelsgesellschaft zwischen Kontinuität und Konflikt (1560–1597/98)*. Augsburg: Wißner Verlag.

Schofield, Roger. 2004. *Taxation under the Early Tudors, 1485–1547*. Malden: Blackwell.

Schumpeter, Joseph A. 1934. *The Theory of Economic Development*. Cambridge, MA: Harvard University Press.

Schumpeter, Joseph A. 1942. *Capitalism, Socialism and Democracy*. New York: Harper and Brothers.

Scott, Peter. 2021. "The Anatomy of Britain's Interwar Super-Rich: Reconstructing the 1928/9 'Millionaire' Population." *Economic History Review* 74, no. 3 (August): 639–65.

Seager, Robin. 1973. "Elitism and Democracy in Classical Athens." In *The Rich, the Well Born, and the Powerful: Elites and Upper Classes in History*, edited by Frederic C. Jaher, 7–26. Urbana: University of Illinois Press.

Sen, Amartya. 1981. *Poverty and Famine: An Essay on Entitlement and Deprivation*. Oxford: Oxford University Press.

Shammas, Carole. 1993. "A New Look at Long-Term Trends in Wealth Inequality in the United States." *The American Historical Review* 98, no. 2 (April): 412–31.

Smith, Edmond. 2021. *Merchants: A New History of England's Trade and Empire*. New Haven: Yale University Press.

Soltow, Lee. 1975. *Men and Wealth in the United States, 1850–70*. New Haven: Yale University Press.

Soltow, Lee. 1989. *Distribution of Wealth and Income in the United States in 1798*. Pittsburgh: University of Pittsburgh Press.

Soltow, Lee. 1990. "Inequality of Wealth in Land in Scotland in the Eighteenth Century." *Scottish Economic and Social History* 10: 38–60.

Soltow, Lee, and Jan L. van Zanden. 1998. *Income and Wealth Inequality in the Netherlands, 16th–20th centuries*. Amsterdam: Het Spinhuis.

Sorokin, Pitirim. 1925. "American Millionaires and Multi-Millionaires: A Comparative Statistical Study." *Journal of Social Forces* 3, no. 4: 627–40.

Soros, George. 2011. "My Philanthropy." In *The Philanthropy of George Soros: Building Open Societies*, edited by Chuck Sudetic, 1–57. Philadelphia: Public Affairs Books.

Sreenivasan, Govind P. 2013. "Beyond the Village: Recent Approaches to the Social History of the Early Modern German Peasantry." *History Compass* 11, no. 1: 47–64.

Stavasage, David. 2020. *The Decline and Rise of Democracy: A Global History from Antiquity to Today*. Princeton: Princeton University Press.

Steinmetz, Greg. 2015. *The Richest Man Who Ever Lived: The Life and Times of Jacob Fugger*. New York: Simon & Schuster.

Straparola, Gian F. (1556) 1927. *Le piacevoli notti*. Bari: Laterza.

Stumpo, Enrico. 1979. *Finanza e stato moderno nel Piemonte del Seicento*. Rome: Istituto storico italiano per l'età moderna e contemporanea.

Sutch, Richard. 2016. "The Accumulation, Inheritance, and Concentration of Wealth during the Gilded Age: An Exception to Thomas Piketty's Analysis." Paper presented at the UCR Emeriti/ae Association (4 February), Orbach Science Library, University of California, Riverside.

Sutch, Richard. 2017. "The Ultra-Rich of the Gilded Age: The Untold Story of How They Made, Spent, and Gave Away Their Fortunes." Paper presented at the Social Science History Association Conference (2–5 November), Montreal.

Tagliaferri, Amelio. 1966. *L'economia veronese secondo gli estimi dal 1409 al 1635*. Milan: Giuffrè.

Tawney, Richard H. 1926. *Religion and the Rise of Capitalism: A Historical Study*. New York: Harcourt, Brace and Company.

Temin, Peter, and Hans-Joachim Voth. 2013. *Prometheus Shackled: Goldsmith Banks and England's Financial Revolution after 1700*. Oxford: Oxford University Press.

Thomas, William I., and Dorothy S. Thomas. 1928. *The Child in America*. Oxford: Knopf.

Thompson, Francis M. L. 2001. *Gentrification and the Enterprise Culture: Britain 1780–1980*. Oxford: Oxford University Press.

Thorndike, Joseph J. 2013. *Their Fair Share: Taxing the Rich in the Age of FDR*. Washington, DC: Urban Institute Press.

Tietz-Strödel, Marion. 1982. *Die Fuggerei in Augsburg: Studien zur Entwicklung des sozialen Stiftungsbaus im 15. und 16. Jahrhundert*. Tübingen: Mohr Siebeck.

Tilly, Charles. 1984. "Demographic Origins of the European Proletariat." In *Proletarianization and Family History*, edited by David Levine, 1–85. Orlando, FL: Academic Press.

Tilly, Charles. 1992. *Coercion, Capital and European States, AD 990–1992*. Cambridge, MA, and Oxford: Blackwell.

Todeschini, Giacomo. 2002. *I Mercanti e il Tempio: La società cristiana e il circolo virtuoso della ricchezza fra medioevo ed età moderna*. Bologna: Il Mulino.

Todeschini, Giacomo. 2008. "Theological Roots of the Medieval/Modern Merchants' Self-Representation." In *The Self-Perception of Early Modern Capitalists*, edited by Margaret C. Jacob and Catherine Secretan, 17–46. New York: Palgrave Macmillan.

Todeschini, Giacomo. 2009. "Eccezioni e usura nel Duecento: osservazioni sulla cultura economica medievale come realtà non dottrinaria." *Quaderni Storici* 44, no. 131 (2) (August): 443–60.

Todeschini, Giacomo. 2011. *Come Giuda: La gente comune e i giochi dell'economia all'inizio dell'epoca moderna*. Bologna: Il Mulino.

Todeschini, Giacomo. 2019. "Stérilité de la monnaie et productivité du capital à la fin du Moyen Âge: Le signifié scolastique des notions d'utilité de l'argent et d'intérêt (XIIIe-XVe siècle)." In *Le Droit face à l'économie sans travail, Tome I, Sources intellectuelles, acteurs, résolution des conflits*, edited by Luisa Brunori, Serge Dauchy, Olivier Descamps and Xavier Prévost, 43–56. Paris: Garnier.

Tomaskovic-Devey, Donald, and Lin Ken-Hou. 2011. "Income Dynamics, Economic Rents, and the Financialization of the U.S. Economy." *American Sociological Review* 76, no. 4 (August): 538–59.

Tocqueville, Alexis de. (1835–1840) 2017. *Democracy in America*. Mineola: Dover Publications.

Trump, Donald J., and Tony Schwartz. 1987. *The Art of the Deal*. New York: Ballantine Books.

Tsigos, Stamatios, and Kevin Daly. 2020. *The Wealth of the Elite: Towards a New Gilded Age*. Singapore: Palgrave Macmillan.

Tudor, Victoria. 1981. "Reginald of Durham and Saint Godric of Finchale: Learning and Religion on a Personal Level." *Studies in Church History* 17: 37–48.

Tugwell, Rexford G., and Joseph Dorfman. 1937. "Alexander Hamilton: Nation-Maker. Part 1" *Columbia University Quarterly* 29, no. 4 (December): 210–26.

Turner, John D. 2010. "Wealth Concentration in the European Periphery: Ireland, 1858–2001." *Oxford Economic Papers* 62, no. 4 (October): 625–46.

Van Bavel, Bas. 2016. *The Invisible Hand? How Market Economies Have Emerged and Declined since AD 500*. Oxford: Oxford University Press.

Van Bavel, Bas. 2022. "Wealth Inequality in Pre-Industrial Europe: What Role Did Associational Organizations Have?" *Economic History Review* 75, no. 3 (August): 643–66.

Van Bavel, Bas, and Auke Rijpma. 2016. "How Important Were Formalized Charity and Social Spending before the Rise of the Welfare State? A Long-Run Analysis of Selected Western European Cases, 1400–1850." *Economic History Review* 69, no. 1 (February): 159–87.

Van der Linden, James. 2012. "The Thurn and Taxis Postal Administration in the Spanish Netherlands from 1492 to 1713: A Postal Historical Survey." In *I Tasso e le poste d'Europa*, edited by Tarcisio Bottani, 289–306. Bergamo: Corponove.

Van Zanden, Jan L. 1995. "Tracing the Beginning of the Kuznets Curve: Western Europe during the Early Modern Period." *Economic History Review* 48, no. 4 (November): 643–64.

Van Zanden, Jan L., Eltjo Buringh, and Maarten Bosker. 2012. "The Rise and Decline of European Parliaments, 1188–1789." *Economic History Review* 65, no. 3 (August): 835–61.

Van Zanden, Jan L., Tine De Moor, and Sarah Carmichael. 2019. *Capital Women: The European Marriage Pattern, Female Empowerment and Economic Development in Western Europe 1300–1800*. New York: Oxford University Press.

Varón Gabai, Rafael. 1997. *Francisco Pizarro and His Brothers: The Illusion of Power*. Norman: University of Oklahoma Press.

Varón Gabai, Rafael, and Auke P. Jacobs. 1987. "Peruvian Wealth and Spanish Investments: The Pizarro Family during the Sixteenth Century." *Hispanic American Historical Review* 67, no. 4 (November): 657–95.

Veblen, Thorstein. (1899) 2007. *The Theory of the Leisure Class*. Oxford: Oxford University Press.

Veblen, Thorstein. 1904. *Theory of Business Enterprise*. New York: Charles Scribner's Sons.

Ventura, Jaume, and Hans-Joachim Voth. 2019. "Debt into Growth: How Sovereign Debt Accelerated the First Industrial Revolution." Paper presented at the CEPR Workshop (25–26 April), Odense.

Villette, Michel, and Catherine Vuillermot. 2009. *From Predators to Icons: Exposing the Myth of the Business Hero*. Translated by George Holoch. Ithaca, NY: Cornell University Press.

Volscho, Thomas W., and Nathan J. Kelly. 2012. "The Rise of the Super-Rich: Power Resources, Taxes, Financial Markets, and the Dynamics of the Top 1 Percent, 1949 to 2008." *American Sociological Review* 77, no. 5 (October): 679–99.

Wade, Robert H. 2014. "The Strange Neglect of Income Inequality in Economics and Public Policy." In *Toward Human Development: New Approaches to Macroeconomics and Inequality*, edited by Giovanni Andrea Cornia and Frances Steward, 99–121. Oxford: Oxford University Press.

Waldenström, Daniel. 2009. *Lifting All Boats? The Evolution of Income and Wealth Inequality over the Path of Development*, Lund Studies in Economic History, no. 51. Lund: Lund University.

Walker, D. 2020. "The Work of Philanthropy in Responding to COVID-19 and Addressing Inequality." *JAMA* 324, no. 6 (August): 541–2.

Ward, John R. 1974. *The Finance of Canal Building in Eighteenth-Century England*. London: Oxford University Press.

Wealth-X. 2017. *Billionaire Census 2017*. https://www.wealthx.com/report/the-wealth-x -billionaire-census-2017/.

Weber, Max. (1930) 2005. *The Protestant Ethic and the Spirit of Capitalism*. Translated by Talcott Parsons. London: Routledge.

Weber, Max. 1946. *From Max Weber: Essays in Sociology. Translated, Edited, and with an Introduction by H.H. Gerth and C. Wright Mills*. New York: Oxford University Press.

Weber, Max. (1956) 1978. *Economy and Society: An Outline of Interpretative Sociology*. Berkeley: University of California Press.

West, Thomas G. 1997. *Vindicating the Founders: Race, Sex, Class, and Justice in the Origins of America*. Lanham, MD: Rowman & Littlefield.

Whaley, Joachim. 2012. *Germany and the Holy Roman Empire Volume 1: From Maximilian I to the Peace of Westphalia 1493–1648*. Oxford: Oxford University Press.

White, Eugene A. 1990. "The Stock Market Boom and Crash of 1929 Revisited." *Journal of Economic Perspectives* 4, no. 2 (spring): 67–83.

White, Richard. 2011. *Railroaded: The Transcontinentals and the Making of Modern America*. New York: Norton.

Williams, Owain D. 2020. "COVID-19 and Private Health: Market and Governance Failure." *Development* 63, no. 2–4 (December): 181–90.

Winkel, Harald. 1968. *Die Ablösungskapitalien aus der Bauernbefreiung in West- und Süddeutschland*. Stuttgart: Gustav Fischer Verlag.

Wolff, Edward N. 2000. "Who Are the Rich? A Demographic Profile of High-Income and High-Wealth Americans." In *Does Atlas Shrug? The Economic Consequences of Taxing the Rich*, edited by Joel B. Slemrod, 74–113. Cambridge, MA: Harvard University Press.

Wolff, Edward N. 2016. "Household Wealth Trends in the United States, 1962 to 2013: What Happened over the Great Recession?" *The Russell Sage Foundation Journal of the Social Sciences* 2, no. 6: 24–43.

Wolff, Edward N. 2017. *A Century of Wealth in America*. Cambridge, MA: Harvard University Press.

Woolf, Stuart J. 1963. *Studi sulla nobiltà piemontese nell'epoca dell'assolutismo*. Turin: Accademia delle Scienze di Torino.

Wren, Daniel A. 1983. "American Business Philanthropy and Higher Education in the Nineteenth Century." *Business History Review* 57, no. 3 (autumn): 321–46.

Wrigley, Edward A. 2016. *The Path to Sustained Growth: England's Transition from an Organic Economy to an Industrial Revolution*. Cambridge: Cambridge University Press.

Yun-Casalilla, Bartolomé, and Francisco Comín Comín. 2012. "Spain: From Composite Monarchy to Nation-State, 1492–1914. An Exceptional Case?" In *The Rise of Fiscal States: A Global History, 1500–1914*, edited by Bartolomé Yun-Casalilla and Patrick K. O'Brien, 233–66. Cambridge: Cambridge University Press.

Yun-Casalilla, Bartolomé, and Patrick K. O'Brien, eds. 2012. *The Rise of Fiscal States: A Global History. 1500–1914*. Cambridge: Cambridge University Press.

Zelinsky, Edward A. 2014. "Why the Buffett-Gates Giving Pledge Requires Limitation of the Estate Tax Charitable Deduction Estate Tax Charitable Deduction." *Florida Tax Review* 16, no. 7: 393–427.

INDEX

A NOTE ON THE TYPE

This book has been composed in Arno, an Old-style serif typeface in the classic Venetian tradition, designed by Robert Slimbach at Adobe.